John R. Hicks

B

John R. Hicks

THE ECONOMIST'S ECONOMIST

O. F. Hamouda

BLACKWELL
Oxford UK & Cambridge USA

First published 1993

Blackwell Publishers
108 Cowley Road
Oxford OX4 1JF
UK

238 Main Street, Suite 501
Cambridge, Massachusetts 02142
USA

British Library Cataloguing–in–Publication Data

A CIP catalogue record for this book is available from the British Library.

Library of Congress Cataloging-in-Publication Data

Hamouda, O. F.
John R. Hicks: The Economist's Economist/O. F. Hamouda.
p. cm.
"Bibliography of Hicks' works": p.
Includes bibliographical references and index.
ISBN 1-55786-065-3 (h/bk.)
1. Economics. 2. Equilibrium (Economics) 3. Capital. 4. Money.
5. Keynesian economics. 6. Economics–History.
7. Hicks, John Richard, Sir, 1904– I. Title.
HB103.H47H36 1993
330′.092–dc20 92-15426 CIP

Typeset in 10.5 on 12.5 pt Ehrhardt
by Setrite Typesetters Ltd., Hong Kong
Printed in Great Britain by T.J. Press Ltd., Padstow, Cornwall

This book is printed on acid-free paper

'Va, ch'i' son forte e ardito?

I'm ready for the road; let's go.
Dante, *Inferno*, XXIV, 60

Translated by Margaret Bottrall

Contents

Preface

The ideas of Sir John Hicks have provided sparks of stimulus and guidance in almost every aspect of economics for over six decades, and a book devoted to him is truly overdue. Over time Hicks and economics have become almost synonymous. Any attempt to evaluate his work must thus be viewed as an assessment of the evolution of the discipline of economics in the second half of the twentieth century.

Trying to summarize in a single volume six decades of the work of such a prolific writer as Sir John Hicks is indeed a formidable task. My purpose in the present volume is not to expose every detail of his thought, nor is it to provide just a simple narration of his *oeuvre*. Instead it is to present Hicks's work in such a way as to show that his early thought was by no means his only significant contribution and to analyse the coherence of the whole of his work over time. Although Hicks was seen to change his mind from time to time, it will be argued that there was an underlying constancy in the evolution of his ideas which to a large extent strengthened his initial intuitions.

Hicks was a modest man who did not consider it appropriate to write his own biography; he thought that was a task best left to others. He felt he had provided sufficient autobiographical information about his professional contributions scattered throughout his works. His one concession to posterity was his writing of a very brief, unpublished account of his childhood and youth which he read and glossed for me on one of my visits to Hicks's home at Blockley. For the biographical chapter in this volume, both the published information and unpublished details Hicks himself provided have been complemented by the reminiscences about Hicks as recounted by his sister Mary Elliot, by Paul Samuelson, Robin Matthews, Robert Clower, Michio Morishima and in the informal reflections of Geoff Harcourt, Bob Wallace, Axel Leijonhufvud, Robin Rowley, Warren Young, John Smithin and many others. I am well aware that Hicks had many friends, professional acquaintances, devoted pupils and admirers who would certainly have more to say about him. Just as Keynes launched an era, Hicks will no doubt be followed by his own. With it much of what remains to be written about him and his economics will emerge.

In the last few years, just before Hicks died, many conferences, volumes of essays and papers devoted to Hicksian economics had already begun to come out. Hicks himself made the life of his future analysts much easier with the recent publication of his collected essays in three volumes (1981, 1982, 1983), so making forgotten or not easily accessible papers readily available. Further, Cunningham Wood and Ronald Woods have gathered in four volumes a considerable number of articles and reviews on Hicks (1989). Also, with the collaboration of Professor Harald Hagemann, I have thought it appropriate to record the contributions of Sir John Hicks through the eyes of his contemporary economists, colleagues and friends with a forthcoming volume of their essays, *The Legacy of Hicks*. These materials already have made it, and will continue to make it, much easier to draw a comprehensive picture of Hicks and Hicksian economics. One could expect there to be a future critical study devoted exclusively to Hicks's work in relation to that of others, to which this volume might serve as a preamble.

For this book many friends and colleagues provide useful comments either on the actual drafts of chapters or through conversational exchanges. Thanks are due to Geoff Harcourt, Sayed Ahmed, and Robin Rowley. My colleague, the historian Betsey Price has not only read and commented on the entire manuscript, but also provided me with so many of the arguments for chapter 10, 'Theory of History' that it would only be fair to say the chapter has been jointly written. Financial support was provided by the Social Sciences and Humanities Research Council of Canada, the Glendon College Research Committee, and the York University Ad Hoc Research Funds Committee.

O. F. Hamouda

Introduction

The title of this book might seem to reflect an ambitious undertaking, which indeed it is. Perhaps it is over-optimistic to try to encompass in one volume sixty years of the uninterrupted work of anyone, let alone that of one of the most prolific and influential economists of the twentieth century, who helped shape the very foundations of modern economics. This is certainly a challenge. The work of Sir John Hicks was abundant not only in quantity but in quality. It is certainly no exaggeration to say that for both these characteristics Hicks's work has been a source of tremendous inspiration.

No book has yet been written on Hicks or Hicksian economics, even though he was among that small group of economists whose work is constantly mentioned in the literature. One of the reasons might be that, as is often said, Hicks wrote so simply and eloquently that there has simply not been seen to be any need to explain what is already clearly set out and accessible to the understanding. Another reason might be that Hicks, so demanding of himself, so often cautious and critical of his own work, has apparently left his critics with little to do. Having acknowledged these reasons, it must none the less be said that Hicks's writing style, though simple and eloquent, was far from self-evident in its meaning. An overall assessment of his work, given its importance and abundance, might thus help to put his achievements in perspective and to shed more light on how complete a scholar he was.

Looking at the reception of Hicks's numerous works one finds that he was often praised or sometimes criticized by different people for specific ideas. In considering his entire achievement, however, it is noticeable that there has been much confusion in tying the overall thought of Hicks to particular economic schools. Many anti-orthodox economists have catalogued him as a neo-classical economist and have blindly refused to consider him otherwise. Some economists of the dominant school have considered Hicks's early work to be his most brilliant achievement in that it channelled economic theory into what has become mainstream economics; they therefore interpret Hicks's own questioning of that early work as ill-advised. Still other economists, for example, H. Johnson, accused Hicks of 'sailing against the wind' in his latest work. As a result of this assessment, Hicks's latest work has been given less than its deserved attention. Clearly his approach generated much dissension and some misunderstanding and dissatisfaction.

In reviewing *Economic Perspectives*, Leijonhufvud (1979), rightly in his context, identified two Hicks: 'Hicks the Younger' and 'the elder Hicks'. This analytic distinction is reinforced by the fact that Hicks himself attempted to demarcate his early work, which he jokingly said was the work of J. R. Hicks, from his later work, which he consequently signed as the product of John Hicks. Unfortunately this division, into young and old (or 'mature' as Solow put it, 1984, p. 13), which should have been understood as subtle, has been taken literally by the profession to represent a strict dichotomy. It is, instead, no exaggeration, as it will be shown in the book, to say that Hicks was mature from the start. He was remarkably astute and aware of the difficulties involved in theorizing behaviours and processes, from the moment he began to contribute to economics. He already knew in 1939, for example, that pure economics had 'a remarkable way of producing rabbits out of a hat' (1939a, p. 23) and indeed produced some himself. Earlier still, he had made the choice of concentrating on the technical aspect of economics, leaving out or avoiding deliberately all possible complications. Those very omissions so pursued and preoccupied him later that eventually he came round to facing them. A great deal of Hicks's later work was thus devoted to filling those gaps. In his rethinking, Hicks repudiated his own theories with regard to certain elements; by questioning their foundation he attempted to improve on what he thought were their deficiencies (or rather his unfinished business); most of these he had been aware of at the time that he first proposed the theories. Although for the most part his ideas evolved slowly and evidence of his shifts appear gradually, there are some examples of apparently rapid and radical changes.

Hicks was an extremely careful economist, but above all, a humble thinker who believed that economics is about people and must be a reflection of its time. He constantly reflected that ideas 'came into being by a sort of social process' (1939a, p. vi) and thus acknowledged the contribution of others and their impact on him. Hicks in fact paid such tremendous attention to the work of his predecessors and some of his contemporaries that most of his ideas, almost as soon as they were produced, were conventionally fused into the mainstream of economics. Hicks provided useful links between existing theories and his own, which were always at the cutting edge, correcting, extending, generalizing, improving and offering original suggestions for further research. With his eclectic style he had a powerful way of simplifying what was complex and used simple language almost in a conversational manner to explain it. Often, Hicks stepped back from economics in order to have a wider perspective on his subject matter, reflecting in so doing his powerful command over a considerable breadth of general knowledge.

In an almost Marshallian way Hicks's style was clear while at the same time cryptic and full of nuances. This style was an asset that often permitted him, throughout his career, to respond to critics or to reconsider many of his ideas, recognizing when he was wrong, without having to contradict himself. Hicks acknowledged his critics and took them seriously. Through thorough reflection on their comments his work ended up benefiting from the reconsideration of his ideas. To engage his reader was the reason why Hicks wrote his books and articles, and it seems that his critics provided him with the positive stimulus to help him continue advancing.

Within the economics profession many, especially the adherants of general equilibrium theory, consider Hicks's *Value and Capital* (1939a) to be the jewel of his entire work and focus too much attention on that book and pieces related to it. Indeed, for Hicks also the book was important. However, in elevating it these particular followers relegate Hicks's other contributions to a unmerited secondary place. Similarly, the admirers of the young Hicks choose to value the earlier part of his work at the expense of the later and in so doing concentrate on only half of his career.

The aim of this book is to provide a comprehensive picture of Hicks's writings and to show that he had a coherrent methodology and a complex but complete vision of what economics is. As will be seen from the exposition in each chapter, all aspects of Hicks's vision cannot be deduced or appreciated just from a single work. This assessment of Hicks's extensive *oeuvre* is therefore made in relation to specific themes, within which an analysis will be provided to show when and how his ideas were proposed, how and why they were transformed over time and how, through time, the pieces fit together.

From a general point of view, three main periods can be identified in Hicks's six-decade career, in each of which his approach to economics was somehow different from the other periods. The transition points from one period to another are not, however, clear cut; their delineation is only meant to help to place Hicks's work in chronological perspective. The first of his three periods runs from the late 1920s up to the publication of *A Contribution to the Theory of the Trade Cycle* (1950a). In this early stage, Hicks promoted in particular the work of Walras, Pareto and other continental marginalists. In addition to making independent contributions, he generalized the work of many of his predecessors as well as those of his contemporaries. Hicks's theories (alongside the contributions of a small group of contemporary economists) gave birth to both post-war micro- and macro-economics.

Hicks's second period extends from the mid-1950s up to his suggestion of a neo-Austrian theory in early 1970s. During this period he reflected on the premisses of his early theories and continued to develop his theories both of money and of capital, with which he was dissatisfied. Although increasingly suspicious of mechanical models, he none the less continued to rely on them. Hicks's final period extended from the publication of *Capital and Time* (1973d). From the 1970s on, he stopped building mathematical models and became more interested in methodological and philosophical questions. This shift in interests did not, however, stop him from writing about inflation, unemployment and policy issues right through to his very last work.

Another point worth mentioning here concerning the presentation of Hicks's contribution to economics, which will be explained in chapter 7, is his deliberately imposed dichotomy between the real economic sector emphasized in his pure economic theory and his almost separate study of monetary theory. Only in his very last book, *A Market Theory of Money* (1989a), did Hicks attempt to bring the two sides together. In the development of his pure economic theory, he began by analysing, in *The Theory of Wages* (1932b), price formation in one market. He then proceeded, in *Value and Capital* (1939a), to study price determination in a multi-market system. In his *Contribution to the Theory of the Trade Cycle* (1950a), Hicks shifted his attention to the issue of quantity adjustment while prices are kept constant. Subsequently he provided many versions of growth models (1965a, 1973a, 1973d) in which he attempted to integrate both fix- and flexprice methods.

The organization of this book will follow neither the chronological course of Hicks's works nor the development of the dichotomy. Instead a division along the following lines will be pursued:

Chapter 1 is a short biography which traces Hicks's childhood, his education and aspects of his professional life.

Chapter 2 deals with the concept of equilibrium. A concept of equilibrium is fundamental to most of Hicks's theories, but he often made the concept take on different meanings depending on the circumstances in which he used it. Its importance is discussed. The different variants of the concept which appeared in various writings are identified, and illustrations of its applicability are provided.

Since in a great deal of his writing Hicks treated the issues of how markets are organized, how they work, who fixes the prices, and when and why firms hold inventory stocks, chapter 3 is devoted entirely to the theory of market and the fix- and flexprice methods.

The main business of economics, Hicks believed, is to understand the dynamics of economic activity. In attempting to grasp its variety of dynamic aspects he provided many models. His various dynamic economic models including those of growth are described and discussed in chapter 4.

Employment and the distribution of a nation's income are at the heart of the study of human economic activity. Chapter 5 deals with Hicks's theory of labour, production and distribution. An explanation of the functioning of the labour market and of wage determination is provided. It is followed by a discussion of the evolution of Hicks's approach to the production function through to his ultimate abandonment of it.

Capital is the other crucial component in the study of economic activity. In chapter 6, Hicks's many attempts at grasping and elucidating the concept of capital, at making the distinction between fixed and circulating capital, at clarifying the related problem of capital measurement and at explaining capital accumulation are discussed.

Hicks's monetary theory is set out in chapter 7. The transition period between his two major contributions, his earlier portfolio approach to demand for money, and his later liquidity theory and concept of the credit economy is addressed. It will be argued that Hicks's later rejection of certain elements of his portfolio approach should not be exaggerated. In contrast to Keynes, Hicks was a very mild interventionist in the monetary sphere.

In chapter 8 it is argued that, despite the many overlapping themes in the work of Hicks and Keynes, Hicks as an independent thinker dissociated himself from his overshadowing contemporary. The general relationship of the two as distinct thinkers will be discussed in the context of four themes: money wages, real wages and the labour market; liquidity theory and the interest rate; the multiplier and the saving–investment equilibrium; and the IS–LM device.

Explanation and prediction in economics figured, prominently among his favourite topics in the later part of Hicks's life. It is argued in chapter 9 that his pursuit of the philosophical questions of economics in the end made his vision of economics and thus his theories much stronger.

Even though a great deal of history of economic thought is evident in all of Hicks's writing, his concern with general history, economic history, and theories of history is less known. In chapter 10, some of these aspects of Hicks's work are discussed.

Finally in the conclusion, some comments are added about Hicks's well-known contribution to welfare economics, which scholars have already extensively discussed and debated.

1

Hicks the Man

No doubt when most economists of the twentieth century have long been forgotten, the name of Sir John Hicks will still be remembered. His work has already become as much a part of the history of economic thought as that of such great economists as Ricardo, Mill, Marshall, Walras, Keynes, Hayek and Sraffa. Given the present manner in which the discipline of economics is becoming partitioned into overly specialized sub-fields, the mechanical way in which research in economics is conducted individually and in teams, and the increase in the number of working economists, it is unlikely, should the trend continue, that the profession of economics will witness future scholars of Hicks's breath. John Hicks, whose work has touched and left its mark on almost every aspect of economic theory, was perhaps among the last giant, electric economists.

The reputation of John Hicks has become universally established. He was from the start a gifted child. As a young boy and adolescent, he was ahead of his schoolmates. As a student, his teachers could not keep up with him. As a young economist, he quickly led the way and became one of the most valuable sources of inspiration in the profession. Hicks travelled extensively around the world, lecturing at almost all the major universities in both the developed and developing economies. His books were translated into many languages and continue to be used as the main texts for teaching economics to many generations of students. Although he has come to be known mainly as an economic theoretician, he was consistently interested in the practical aspect of economics. He always considered himself a problem-solver, believing that theory must be the servant of the economist, and not the other way around.

Despite his early remarkable potential and an ensuing international reputation, Hicks was a very private, simple and shy man whose only ambition was to advance knowledge. Although uncomfortable with big, public gatherings, among those with whom he had developed a real friendship Hicks was open and occasionally even mischievous. He was relaxed and delightfully witty in private, for his knowledge and curiosity was by no means limited to economics. Throughout his life Hicks's keen interest in history, literature, languages, music, poetry and philosophy spiced his conversation, as it enhanced his economics.

John Richard Hicks was born on 8 April 1904 in Warwick. In 1886, well before John Hicks's birth, his father Edward Hicks articled in journalism with the *Warwick Advertiser*. As a young journalist, Edward Hicks was sent to Birmingham for part of his training, to get some reporting experience on the much larger newspaper, the *Birmingham Post*. During his time in Birmingham Edward met Dorothy Stephens. They married in 1903 when Edward returned to his job in Warwick with enough of a promotion to allow him to consider supporting a family. Mrs Catherine Stephens, Edward's mother-in-law, also moved to Warwick to live within her daughter's family until her death in 1929. John Richard was the first of three children of Edward and Dorothy Hicks and was brought up along with Phyllis D. (20 months younger), and Mary C. (ten years his junior) in Warwickshire.

John Richard was not personally acquainted with the direct male antecedents of either parent. Both of his grandfathers had died before he was born. His paternal grandfather, Richard Hicks, stemmed from a farming family who worked land near St Colomb in northern Cornwall, which John Richard's greatuncles were still farming during his childhood. Shortly after his youngest son, Edward Hicks, was born in the 1870s, Richard Hicks moved his large family and livestock from Cornwall to take up farming in Gloucestershire in the Cotswolds. He settled on a site between Burford and Northleach named Woeful Lake. His eldest sons took up farming, and Woeful Lake remained within the family until the 1940s. Edward Hicks, like several of his brothers, left the farm which could not, in any case, be the future support of so many male heirs. Among all his siblings, Edward alone showed such intellectual promise as a child that he was sent first to school in Northleach and then away to boarding school, to Llandovery College in south Wales. There he acquired some Latin, an appreciation for education and a budding interest in history. Inspired by the work of the Harvard historian Kittridge, in 1928 Edward Hicks had a monograph published by Harvard University Press on Sir Thomas Malory (author of *Morte d'Arthur*): *Sir Thomas Malory: His Turbulent Career*. In it, as a result of his research in the Public Record Office, Edward Hicks reinforced Kittredge's identification of Thomas Malory with a Malory of the same name from the village of Newbold Revell near Leamington.

John Richard's maternal grandfather was John Mortimer Stephens, a Baptist minister, son of a Baptist minister. From near Bath, John Stephens had trained in London at Regent's Park College and after his start at the chapel of Naunton, between Cheltenham and Stow-on-the-Wold, he had charge of two major churches during his ministry, first in Sheffield and then in Newcastle-on-Tyne from 1875 to 1890; here his five children, two sons and three daughters, were born. He had been to the Continent as a young man, and with his health failing, sometime between 1890 and 1895, John Mortimer took his family to Wiesbaden in Germany to follow a cure for a few months. After his death in 1895 at the age of 51, his wife, Catherine, originally of Cirencester in the Cotswolds, moved with the second of her three daughters, Dorothy, to Birmingham to be close to adequate schooling for a younger son who was to study to be a chemist. It was in Birmingham that the families of the Hicks and the Stephens were joined. The ties of the Stephens to the Baptist faith continued to be strongly maintained. Edward Hicks joined the Baptists at the time of his marriage, and the Hicks family became associated with the little Open Baptist Church in Warwick where they lived. Of his religious connections, John Richard Hicks would write much later, 'When I began to grow up, I read a book in which it was said that the poet John Milton had been reported to be an "irregular and defective" Baptist; that, I thought, was just the kind of Baptist for me' (1983a, p. 114).

From low beginnings in the newspaper world Edward Hicks gradually climbed to the top. In 1906 he became the secretary of the organizing committee of a historical pageant in Warwick, a position which brought him to the attention of the *Leamington Spa Courier*, a more important newspaper than the *Warwick Advertiser*. Having already advanced to chief reporter and sub-editor of the *Warwick Advertiser*, Edward Hicks joined the *Leamington Spa Courier* in 1909 as its editor. As the newspaper grew over time, he became an important shareholder and the newspaper's chairman. Edward Hicks worked for the newspaper as its editor until 1944, more than thirty years, and retained his position of director until his death in 1952.

John Richard Hicks received his first education from his parents at home. His mother had taken an interest in higher education for herself and while in Birmingham had attended the extension lectures on Dante at Wicksteed College. While John Richard was very young, she devoted herself to teaching him reading and writing. From the age of 6 to 9 his mother's lessons were complemented by his training at the Leamington High School for Girls (now the Kingsley School), a school which took boys in the lower forms and in which John Richard's father took a special interest, serving for many years on its school council. Edward Hicks himself started John Richard on Latin at the age of 7.

In 1911 John Richard entered Warwick School, a traditional grammar school. There, from the age of 9 to 11 Hicks had his first lessons in Greek, algebra and geometry. When he discovered the local public library, he began to develop an independent passion for history. His father, who was constantly fostering his own interest in history, encouraged John Richard to read as much as he could. Already in his early years at school John Richard was doing much better than his classmates, and still his teachers noticed that he was under-functioning. While his classmates were wading through the middle of a book given to them, John Richard would have already finished reading it.

In 1915, just before his eleventh birthday, John Richard was transferred from Warwick School, at the encouragement, if not insistence, of his aunt Winifred, to a preparatory school in Leamington, the Greyfriars School under the headmastership of Mr Beaven, a parson. It was an expensive private grammar school which prepared boys up to the age of 13 to enter public school. Although they were not financially well off, John Richard's parents were concerned that he should receive the best education possible. Since his parents could not afford the tuition and expenses, the school accepted John Richard on favourable terms, and Edward Hicks borrowed the money necessary to pay the fees. At the Grey Friars School, John Richard was taught Greek, Latin, history, elementary mathematics and literature in the pre-Reform Bill English tradition. (Master Beaven has little use for science or modern languages.) John Richard was also made to remember vast quantities of hitorical facts, from reams of authors and titles of books to the names and dates of the kings and prime ministers, not just of England but also of other countries.

John Richard liked Master Beaven's school very much, and even as a boy had great admiration for the teacher who made him work so hard. During his two years spent there he did extremely well, and his teacher made sure that he would be passed on into good hands with all the financial help required. Thus, at the end of his school days in Leamington John Richard was nominated for a scholarship competition, which he easily won. It had not taken long for John Richard to become one of Beaven's favorite 'billiards', as the master used to call his pupils, and years after John Richard had left, Beaven asked Edward Hicks to bring his son to see him. On that occasion Beaven gave his former prize pupil a book in which he had inserted a Latin inscription. It was only then, from that inscription, that John Richard learned how special he had been to Beaven. Hicks treasured the book, but even more so the inscription, for it expressed the deep feelings of a man who could say in Latin what he never would have said in English.

In 1917 Hicks went to Clifton Public School, where one of Beaven's sons, Harold Beaven, was the mathematics master. The generous scholarship Hicks had won, in mathematics, paid for most of his expenses there, which greatly eased the strain of his parents' finances. At Clifton Hicks received a great deal of special attention; he, along with a few other boys, comprised a form created especially for them. It was from Harold Beaven that Hicks felt he received his good training as a mathematician. He maintained much later that he had learned at Clifton all the mathematics he subsequently needed when he began to develop his mathematical work in economics. Hicks also continued at Clifton the study of Greek and Latin, and enjoyed reading parts of Homer, Plato and Virgil in their original languages. In his last year at Clifton, English literature was his chosen subject.

There were two aspects of his Clifton days which, however, Hicks found, less than pleasant. A mathematics course requirement obliged him to study experimental physics which, for want of manual dexterity, he did not really enjoy and which, along with mathematics, consumed most of his study hours. Also, his initial year at Clifton was the last year of the First World War. As a young man, he, like his schoolmates, had the duty of training for war. The schoolboys' military preparation had begun in 1918–19 to be taken quite seriously, and Hicks saw much of his valuable study time spent on military exercises which he did not like. In fact, he did not particularly enjoy any form of organized physical exercise or sport. He even disliked cricket and football, since he couldn't seem to keep his mind on the action. He once said of his playing that his reactions 'were not just slow, they were almost non-existent'. He much preferred to read history and literature or to listen to good music.

At the end of his public school studies, at the age of 17, Hicks stood and easily qualified for the Sebag Montifiore closed scholarship from Clifton to Balliol College, Oxford. Oxford seemed to Hicks a good location for study; it was conveniently close to his parents' home in Warwick. Of far more importance, however, was that the scholarship would allow him to continue his study with expenses paid and thus escape imposing financial worries on his parents. Hicks accepted the award and set out for Oxford.

Hicks entered Balliol College in 1922 to study mathematics. He did not feel very comfortable right away within the new intellectual environment of the college. Further, since he had been so well taught at Clifton, his university course work was a mere repetition of the same material, and his interest in mathematics understandably began to wane. Except for the course given by G. H. Hardy, Hicks found the first-year mathematics offering boring and of little value. Owing to the generous mathematical exhibition scholarship he had been offered at Balliol, however, he felt, obliged to continue to concentrate on mathematics.

It did not, however, take much time for him to be noticed by his professors as a student of promise. It was the practice at the time for all first-year students at Balliol to write a series of essays on general topics, which were assessed by fellows of the college whose own field was different from each student's. A prize was then presented by the fellows for the best set of essays in the college. Hicks won the prize with a set of essays having nothing to do with mathematics. In one essay Hicks took the unorthodox view that Shakespeare's *Henry IV, Part II* was not intended as a history, but rather as a response to popular demand for more plays with Falstaff, like *The Merry Wives of Windsor*. As a result of his winning the essay prize, some of Hicks's professors wondered whether mathematics was the best subject for him, and at the end of his first year Hicks was told that he did not have to continue in the subject if he did not wish to. Of course, history appealed to him (as was especially manifest in a remarkable epic-length poetic panegyric he wrote while an undergraduate), and so did the academic career a history degree might offer. Having been advised that mathematics, in which course he was placed first, would be useful, Hicks was, however, channelled into a new programme in philosophy, politics and economics (PPE), which the college had just devised especially to train politicians.

The programme of PPE was very extensive. The philosophy course started with Descartes; the economics began with the history of economic thought and extended from Adam Smith to Marx. The programme also included much study of the constitutional and economic history of Britain and the Commonwealth. Hicks was impressed neither by his instructors nor by the programme, which was in its extreme infancy. His philosophy tutors, McMurray and Morris, saw little of value in Russell and Whitehead, and the economics tutor, the military historian Rodger, had no interest in economics and could not handle the ideas of Edgeworth, who had only recently become professor emeritus of Oxford. Hicks was tutored in politics by Sumner. While he found he was learning a lot, it was not from his teachers. It was his fellow students, some of whom were in history and some in PPE, who were more stimulating. Hicks was especially close to Robert Birley, who later became a headmaster of Eton, and Denis Brogan in history and in PPE Darsie Gillie, Godfrey Samuel and especially Norman Robertson, with whom he discussed philosophy.

While in PPE Hicks had to do a compulsory translation paper in French and hence was pressured to acquire French quickly. He often consulted his maternal aunt Winifred Stephens, who had studied in France and become a school teacher, and a political and arts journalist. She was editor of *The Book of France* and *The Soul of Russia*, translator of several books by Anatole France and the author of two popular histories, one, the life of the second Marguerite de Valois and another on the Trémouille family. In 1923 Winifred married George Whale, a successful, wealthy solicitor in London. On vacations Hicks visited them in their home in York Terrace where they had a literary salon. On one occasion he met James George Frazer, author of *The Golden Bough*, and his wife and the political scientist Graham Wallace for the first time.

Hicks was uninspired by course homework in French, but delighted by the riches of French literature. He worked his way through Baudelaire, Stendhal and Voltaire, always discussing their writings with his aunt. After the death of her husband in 1925 and that of Hicks's own mother and grandmother in 1929, Mrs Whale became his second mother, and Blockley in the Cotswolds, her new residence and site of her fabulous general library collection, his second home. In his reading he discovered he liked the rationalist Voltaire, although he continued to prefer Milton and Dante. Since Hicks, while still a boy at home, had taught himself to read Italian by comparing, with the help of his Latin, the Italian to the face-to-face English translation in his mother's copy of Dante, he was able to read all three masters in the original.

For numerous reasons, because he had so much reading to do for his PPE courses and because he was distracted with the study of things not strictly related to PPE, and with the illness and death of his mother that year, Hicks scored only an overall second in his final examination, despite a first in philosophy and politics. The results were a blow to Hicks, but it seems they also made others think twice. The then master of Balliol, A. D. Lindsay, felt he had misdirected Hicks into the two-year PPE course, and he arranged for the college to award him a War Memorial Student scholarship for one year so that he could do a year of postgraduate research, in 1925–6. Graham Wallace, then Professor of Political Science at the London School of Economics (LSE), to whom Hicks had been introduced by his aunt Winifred in her home in London, urged Hicks to read economics that year. Hicks decided to follow Wallace's advice, meanwhile taking on the tutoring of many Oxford students, including the Crown Prince, later King Olaf, of Norway.

Economics, Wallace had told Hicks, was a field in which he could make use of his mathematical skill. Wallace had also assured him that there was a great employment demand for economists, an argument which had carried some weight with Hicks, since he was only one year away from entering the job market. On the advice of Wallace, Hicks had further consulted Edwin Cannan, Wallace's colleague at the LSE. Cannan had suggested that he write a graduate thesis on wage differences in the skilled and unskilled labour markets. Hicks proposed this idea to A. D. Lindsay, who sent him to be supervised by the labour economist G. D. H. Cole of Magdelen College. At the time, 'economics, at Oxford, was very "social"' (1983a, p. 356) and although Cole did not provide him with much training in economics in general, Hicks did acquire good guidance in labour economics. Under Cole's supervision he wrote the thesis, 'Skilled and unskilled wages in the building and engineering trades' and had finished most of his work for the B.Lit. by the end of 1925.

The extra year at Oxford had not, however, given him quite enough time to be sure what he would like to do next. Not knowing exactly what to choose, Hicks consulted his aunt Winifred for advice. With his B.Lit. degree virtually in hand, he was directed toward journalism with the idea that it might well be in his blood from his paternal side. He thus spent six months, starting early in 1926, as a junior reporter at the *Manchester Guardian*. During that time he realized that journalism was not for him.

By mid-1926 Hicks had thus already applied for a teaching job at the LSE. He modestly thought at the time that his qualifications in economics were deficient, and was aware that he had acquired a very good general, but very unspecialized, education at Oxford. He none the less received a one-year appointment as an assistant lecturer. It was his suspicion that Wallace, who had seen clearly the state of the market for economists, was instrumental in the decision to hire him. The appointment was renewed year after year, and in the end Hicks, who was in turn appointed lecturer, taught at the LSE until 1935. He made good use of his time there, using it to catch up in economics generally. He liked to repeat later that while he was thankful for the general education he had received from Oxford, it was the LSE that made him an economist. Hicks's time at the LSE can be divided into two periods: the early years during which he worked on his own, and the later years when Robbins took charge of the economics department and began his graduate seminar, in which Hicks participated actively.

When Hicks came to interview for a job at the LSE, the appointing committee was under the impression that he was applying to the money and commerce department. Hicks insisted, however, that he was only interested in an appointment in economics and was given a temporary one as assistant. At the same time Barrett Whale was hired into the more senior position open in the money and commerce department. Although the two departments were in relatively little contact with one another, Whale and Hicks were to become very good friends. Discussions were also to develop between Hicks and Whale's colleagues Gregory and Sayers.

In 1926 the economics department at the LSE was very small, consisting of Edward Hugh Dalton as reader and Lionel Robbins as lecturer. Dalton was at the time of Hick's appointment temporarily in charge of the department. He was, however, already deeply involved in the politics of the Labour Party, aiming at becoming Foreign Secretary, and was giving the LSE only part of his time. While working as Dalton's assistant in 1926, Hicks attended his academic lectures, which he found rather like political speeches. Hicks did later feel, however, that he had learnt some important things from Dalton. Dalton had been a pupil of Pigou in Cambridge and had Hicks read Pigou. He also told Hicks that since he could read Italian, he ought to read Pareto. Dalton had himself come across Pareto's work in 1918, when he had spent several months in an Italian hospital recovering from a wound received during the First World War, while in a detachment of the British army in Italy. He learned Italian there and also enquired about Italian economics. Thus Hicks came to read (and reread) Pareto's *Manuale* and to discover Walras through Pareto. Of course, Hicks also read Dalton's own books, taking especial interest in his *Inequality of Incomes in Modern Communities* (1920). In it there was a geometric diagram which attracted his attention; Hicks had a strong initial suspicion that there was something wrong with it and went on thinking about it. His pondering led him, a few years later, in his lectures on general equilibrium, to develop the concept of the 'elasticity of substitution', which is found in his *Theory of Wages*.

Like Dalton, Robbins was scarcely seen during Hicks's first period at the LSE. Robbins spent a good part of his time following the progress of Edwin Cannan, whose disciple he had become. Cannan's ideas on the free market had already been dominant at the LSE for long time. After two years at the LSE, Robbins, with Cannan's retirement, left at the end of 1926 to return to New College, Oxford.

In the autumn of 1927 Allyn Young arrived at the LSE as Professor to fill the gap created by Cannan's retirement. He had come from Harvard, where he had been the supervisor of the famous thesis by Chamberlin, 'Monopolistic competition'. Hicks was at the time unaware of current economics at Harvard and did not benefit much from Young's presence in London (certainly not as much as did Kaldor, who had just arrived at the LSE as a student from Hungary). In fact Hicks did not have much time to get to know Young. Young was at the LSE only from October 1927 to February 1929, when he died suddenly, and Hicks himself was away from London for half of that period.

In early 1928 the LSE received a call for help from the University of the Witwatersrand in Johannesburg, South Africa. Could someone be sent to teach economics in the term to begin that March? A replacement was desperately needed for the distinguished Professor Layfelt, who had just died. The job was eventually offered to Hicks, then only 24 years old; he immediately accepted, tempted by the excitement and the challenge of the experience. Hicks left the LSE in the middle of the autumn term of 1928 to return in time for the start of the LSE autumn term in 1929.

Like the LSE, the University of the Witwatersrand had a very small economics department of two appointees. To replace the late professor, Hicks was therefore expected to give lectures on all sorts of subjects varying from medieval economic history to statistics, with most of which he was quite unfamiliar at the time. He worked hard to prepare his courses, buoyed up by his conversations with W. H. Hutt during his travel there by ship and once on location. All in all he found the demands of teaching good training. Hicks also had an important professional encounter in South Africa. In 1929 he attended the meeting of the British Association in Cape Town where he heard the President of the Economics Section, Section F, Henry Clay. Later, in 1955, he wrote of Clay's paper, 'The public regulation of wages in Great Britain', 'I remember from that time, how great a stimulus that paper was to my own thinking, and I have not changed my opinion of it' ([1955b] 1959a, p. 85).

At the end of his teaching commitment in June 1929 Hicks made several excursions within South Africa, one into Zululand and another, a very revealing one, to the Transkei, the Homelands. He was invited by a professor of history at Johannesburg, a very liberal-minded man with whom he had become quite friendly, to travel with him and his wife through the Transkei. During the week with them Hicks was able to observe the economic conditions under which blacks in the Homelands were living. In addition, Dalton had given Hicks an introduction to the leader of the South African Labour Party, Dalton's 'fellow-socialist', and Hicks also conversed extensively with Arnold Plant, then Professor of Economics at Cape Town. Through conversation and observation Hicks learned still more about the conditions for South African blacks: trade unions were exclusively for white workers; their job was to protect their minority white members from competition from blacks. This realization gave Hicks a view of trade unions quite different from the ones he had been taught by Cole and Dalton. 'Up to then, I had been looking at them through the pink-coloured spectacles that I had acquired from my Oxford teachers' (1982, p. 5). With scales fallen from his Labour-economist eyes Hicks saw that the labour unions in South Africa were primarily functioning as monopolies, not at all as associations interested in promoting the welfare of all labour. He wrote of the impact of his realizations later in 'The formation of an economist':

> The reservation of skilled jobs to White labour, and the confinement of the best land in the country to White ownership, were the economic obstacles in the way of progress for the Black majority. In a free market system these would wither away, so I became a free market man, even before I left South Africa ([1979b] 1983a, p. 357)

The only thing Hicks published directly about South Africa was a review of *A Modern Economic History of South Africa* by Goodfellow. It was Hicks's first review in the *Economic Journal* (1932c). The South African experience, however, undoubtedly reinforced his ideas on the ideal labour market mechanism, which was to coalesce in the opening theoretical part of his first book, *The Theory of Wages*. The *Theory's* chapters on the working of competition in the labour market and the growth of trade union power, essentially descriptive chapters closely related to Hicks's thesis on wages in the building and engineering sectors, had already been written before Hicks went to South Africa. *The Theory of Wages*, Hicks would write later, 'had nothing to do with the state of the world at the time when I was writing. I had diagnosed a disease, but it was not the right disease. The unemployment of 1932 was of quite a different character from what I had supposed' ([1973c] 1977a, p. 5).

Hicks returned to England, and before the end of 1930 completed the first chapter of *The Theory of Wages*, his attempt to deal with marginal productivity in Walras and Pareto terms; the last chapters of the book were written heavily under the influence of Wicksell. Hicks was becoming increasingly more Wicksellian than Walrasian, especially on money, and as he did, Walras as a person seemed to interest him almost as much as the ideas themselves. By 1934 Hicks had met the great biographer of Walras, W. Jaffé, who helped him out with some biographical points for his article 'Leon Walras' ([1934d] 1983a, pp. 85–95). Jaffé showed Hicks 'the beginnings of his great collection of letters', and Hicks remained Jaffé's admirer and friend throughout his life, even visiting Jaffé's widow in Canada in 1987. Hicks wrote in the 1980s that the work of Patinkin on Walras had also influenced him greatly. 'I could not have dismissed the money theory so lightly [in the 1930s] if I had known what Patinkin was to make of it' (1983a, p. 85).

After his first three years of teaching and extensive reading of economics, Hicks felt that he was beginning to master the discipline. With the LSE library at his disposal and Robbins, Dalton and his friend Whale periodically available for assistance, he had read and questioned very hard. Hicks had, however, also made time to keep in good contact with his friends, especially Godfrey Samuel, and former students he had tutored in Balliol, many of whom had moved to London. He travelled abroad occasionally with them, using one particular trip to Switzerland to teach himself German and others to visit the family of Elie Halevy, author of *L'Histoire du peuple anglais*, in France.

In 1929 Allyn Young died. Robbins was appointed back at the LSE as his successor, and as Hicks put it, 'then things began to hum' ([1973c] 1977a, p. 134). Just before Robbins's return Hicks visited him in New College, Oxford, to discuss with him his progress in economics. He was able to show Robbins that he was abreast of Walras and Pareto. Robbins himself was more familiar with and felt closer to the economics of Knight and Viner of Chicago and the Austrians than to that of Walras or the British schools of that time. As a result of their discussion he gave Hicks a personalized bibliography, moving him 'from Cassel to Walras and Pareto, to Edgeworth [*Mathematical Psychics*] and Taussig, to Wicksell [*Lectures*] and the Austrians' ([1932b] 1963b, p. 306) and asked Hicks to lecture on general equilibrium. Once professor, Robbins encouraged young members of his department to teach the advanced courses in whose subject area they could do research at the same time. Thus Hicks was relieved of the labour course and began to lecture on general equilibrium (Walras and Pareto) as well as to prepare a course on risk theory. At the same time he also taught one of the elementary courses, Applied Economics. Entitled 'On the state of the British

Economy', it was based largely on an official government report on key industries.

In the autumn of 1929 Robbins started a seminar. From about the same point Hicks's Oxford friends were noticeably drifting away, but through the seminar Hicks began to meet postgraduate students at the LSE and to make new friends in London. Hicks found the intense discussions of the papers which he circulated at Robbins's seminar a very stimulating 'sort of social process' (1939a, p. vi). Especially important to him were the reactions of a group of young economists (R. G. D. Allen, N. Kaldor, A. Lerner, R. Sayers, P. N. Rosenstein-Rodan, Dr Edelberg, M. Bowley and U. Webbs, F. von Hayek in 1931–5, and G. L. S. Shackle) with a common interest and common faith in the free market mechanism. With his return, Robbins had set himself the task of restoring Cannanism to the LSE. The school's collective faith in the free market 'price mechanism' was reinforced by Robbins's new appointments of A. Plant, Frederic Benham, and of Hayek in 1931. It was, however, not long sustained, since especially for the individuals of the seminar Hayek's view of the neutrality of money 'was to cause us quite a lot of trouble' (1982a, p. 3). The LSE later became known for views quite different from those of Cannan and Hayek. As Hicks reflected in 'The formation of an economist', during those years the LSE in fact already had influential thinkers from other schools of thought:

> It was surprising, to outside observers, that these very Right-ish doctrines could have had such a vogue at the London School, which was popularly considered to be a hotbed of socialists. We did indeed have our eminent socialists, such as Laski and Tawney (Dalton, by now, had gone off into politics); but it was significant of the tolerant atmosphere of the school that personal relations with them were friendly. There was indeed a substratum of 'liberal' political principles which our socialists and our free market men had in common. ([1979b] 1983a, pp. 357–8)

The combination of Robbins's own interests, his seminar and the accompanying emphasis on the study of non-British economists such as Wicksell, G. Myrdal, and E. Lindahl, those of the Austrian school, French and Italian theorists, as well as the arrival of Hayek at the LSE, opened up the school to international scholars and attracted many visitors passing through London. 'We were such "good Europeans" at that stage', Hicks wrote later, 'that it was Cambridge that seemed "foreign"' ([1932b] 1963b, p. 306). During those active years, Hicks was able to meet Taussig, Viner, Mises, Schumpeter, Haberler, Ohlin, and Lindahl, as well as other European scholars, many of whom were fleeing Nazism and were in transit on their way to America.

In early 1929 Robbins had directed Hicks toward thinking about risk. It was in the summer of 1930 that Hicks began to lecture on it for the first time. His initial understanding derived from Knight's *Risk and Uncertainty* (1921) and Hardy's *Risk and Risk Bearing* (1923) which he thought were very good books. Hardy's *Risk* contained a useful summary of what had been done in risk theory until the early 1930s, and included some helpful material on hedging and speculative markets, while Knight's book expressed the author's particular approach. Before the end of 1930 Hicks quickly synthesized the lectures he had written on risk for an article published in 1931 in *Economica* as 'The theory of uncertainty and profit' (1931c). (Incidentally, since Hicks lectured predominantly from fragmentary notes and memory, such publications are the only real form in which Hicks's lectures can be said to survive. For some much later examples, see 1983a, pp. xv, 17–31, 60–70.) The article was a discussion about a choice among prospects, each with an occurrence probability attached, treated 'in terms of the current flow account, not in terms of the balance sheet' ([1973c] 1977a, p. 135). Hicks's concept of probability was not at all well developed, which is probably why his article was rejected, with the comment that it was 'rather half-baked' (p. 135), when he first submitted it to the *Economic Journal* of which Keynes was the editor. Even though Keynes's *Treatise on Probability* was circulating, Hicks's article was a reflection of the still inadequate level of discussion on probability in the discipline in general. Like many others at the time, Hicks had looked at Keynes's work but he had found it a formidable book.

In June 1930, Hicks's first theoretical article. 'Edgeworth, Marshall and the indeterminateness of wages', a by-product of his work on the theory of wages, was published in the *Economic Journal* (1930b). For the article to be accepted Hicks had had to please Keynes, the editor, by including a section on M. H. Dobb, 'whose "Sceptical view" had appeared in a recent number' of the journal. Although in later republication of the article Hicks suppressed that addition (1983a, p. 71ff), he none the less reaffirmed that it was that article which 'set him up as an economic theorist' ([1973c] 1977a, p. 135). Although he had been known to dismiss the *Economic Journal* as the children's magazine (most of the people connected with it were barely in their thirties), Dennis Robertson at Trinity College, Cambridge was, among others, attracted to the issue in which Hicks's article appeared. Both in his 'Wage grumbles' article and in a lecture, based on that article, given at the

LSE later in the summer of 1930, Robertson referred to Hicks's paper and showed some knowledge of the work that Hicks was doing. Hicks was extremely flattered, especially as their mutual appreciation turned into friendship.

The following September Hicks was visiting Vienna with a Balliol friend, essentially as a tourist and found himself staying in the same pension as Robertson. Robertson was pleased to see Hicks. They went to a production of the *Meistersinger* together and Robertson showed Hicks around the city. He also introduced him to Morganstern and Tintner at the University of Vienna.

Shortly thereafter Robertson was to referee Hicks's *Theory of Wages* for Macmillan all in all quite favourably. However, in forwarding his report to Macmillan on to Hicks, he noted that he felt '"a good deal out of sympathy with the extravagant dogmatism of the stable from which it comes'" ([1973c] 1977a, p. 136). Hicks, remembering his own state of mind at the time wrote, 'I was too much out of tune with Cambridge to derive much benefit, at that stage, from the cirticisms which I got from Dennis Robertson' ([1932b] 1963b, p. 307). During his remaining years at the LSE, however, Hicks's correspondence with Robertson was incessant. Although in the early part of his career the exchange may have been somewhat one-sided, with only Hicks really testing out his ideas, later on they discussed as equals. Until his death in 1963, Robertson was Hicks's invaluable commentator and critic, with whom, Hicks wrote, he 'kept up a running argument, sometimes on paper, sometimes (whenever we met) by word of mouth. He kindly referred to me, in one of his papers, as his 'mentor'; the word would be more appropriately used by me of him' (1967, p. x).

Very often over the years Hicks would let his reader know what Robertson thought of his ideas. Hicks remarked in 1950, 'it is now a good many years since I have enjoyed the privilege of submitting everything I have written ... whether it proved in the end to be publishable or not – for his kind but searching criticism'. As a touching finale to an introductory note to a reprint of his 1955 article, 'Economic foundations of wage policy', Hicks added, 'this was the last of my papers which I discussed with Robertson' ([1955b] 1982a, p. 194). In the early years, Robertson's invaluable help to Hicks began with his guiding him toward some understanding of the Cambridge (Marshallian) positions as well as of his own perspective on liquidity theory.

Before the arrival of Hayek at the LSE in 1931, Hicks's work was mainly non-monetary. Even though he had Keynes's *Treatise on Money* at his disposal, he paid little attention to monetary theory; 'its method as a whole was to me uncongenial' (1982a, p. 8). His *Theory of Wages* (1932b) was tuned to the old classical dichotomy between real and monetary economics. Hicks spoke of the personal side of its being written thus:

> When I wrote the *Theory of Wages* I was very young, young in years, young as an economist, and as an economic theorist younger still. I only took up economics at all seriously after I graduated in 1925, and at first I regarded myself as a labour economist, not a theoretical economist at all . . . It was only in 1929 when Lionel Robbins came back to London as professor, that my interest in theoretical economics was really aroused. It is not much of an exaggeration to say that I had just three years in which to learn my economic theory, to apply it to what I knew of labour problems, and to write it up. ([1932b] 1963b, pp. 305–6)

It was Hayek's discussion of money in his intertemporal equilibrium article, 'Das intertemporale Gleichgewichtssystem' (1928) and his *Prices and Production* (1931) as well as Shove's review (1933) of his *Theory of Wages* that made Hicks think about the issue of money. As Hicks would himself write in 1965, 'soon after its birth, *The Theory of Wages* began to look like the last gasp of an *ancien régime*' ([1932b] 1963b, p. 305). Hayek's theory of money was initially quite puzzling to Hicks, for when Robbins asked him to turn Hayek's model into mathematics, he realized that it could not be done. Hicks came thus to the same conclusion as had Knight (1921): the concept of money and the idea of equilibrium are simply incompatible. Hicks realized that to analyse money one needed to consider expectations and uncertainty.

Hicks explained in his paper, 'Gleichgewicht und Konjunktur', written in German no doubt as part of the German language discussion surrounding Hayek's 1928 article (1933b; translated into English, 1980b), how money does not belong to equilibrium, although he was clearly not yet able to incorporate expectations. Soon after the article's publication, however, Hicks reviewed Myrdal's original German version of 1933 of *Monetary Equilibrium* (1934f) from which he derived some specific ideas on how to introduce expectations as data into a short-period analysis. In 1933 Hicks made his first personal 'contact with Italian economists', visiting, in Turin, Einaudi and Cabiati, del Vecchio at Bologna and Marco Fanno at Padua' ([1979b] 1983a, p. 356). In the summer of 1934 and during 1935 Hicks had the opportunity to discuss the Swedish method of incorporating expectations with E. Lindahl, on whose work much of Myrdal's book was based. Hicks's contact with Lindahl in London was quite personal, for Hicks had found Ursula Webb to help Lindahl translate his essays into English ([1979b] 1983a, p. 360, n. 14).

In his 'A suggestion for simplifying the theory of money' (1935b), Hicks subsequently produced what he thought of as his third version of his ideas on money, a more elaborate theory entailing expectations. Before it appeared in *Economica*, it was first read at the Economic Club of the LSE, a quite small and rather informal club whose meetings drew together working economists in London, the few in the Civil Service as well as those from finance houses or the newspapers. Hawtrey attended very regularly and most likely heard Hicks in February 1935, for 'it had got about, on this occasion, that I had something to say, so there was an unusually large attendance' (1982a, p. 46). Hicks felt his seminar colleagues must have realized that, in responding to an atmosphere dominated by the Depression, he was separating himself from their faith in the free market. To readers thereafter there seemed to be some strong similarities between Hicks's simplification ideas and Keynes's liquidity theory in his *Treatise on Money* (1930).

Upon reading the first draft in English of Hicks's 'Gleichgewicht' article (now lost), Whale found what he thought were signs of Keynes's influence on Hicks. Whale's remarks brought Hicks to look at Keynes's *Treatise* and to make direct, though superficial, reference to it in his German version. When Hicks submitted to Keynes himself a polished English version of the article for publication, Keynes replied in August 1933

> as you suppose, there is a good deal with which I do not agree, but it is now clear that our minds are no longer moving in opposite directions. In the last few weeks I think I have put my finger on the fundamental point which, quite apart from saving and investment decisions, separates me not only from you and Pigou but from everyone since Ricardo. But it is more than can be discussed in a letter. (Hicks [1973c] 1977a, p. 141)

It was in fact never discussed between them, and Hicks claimed that he was at the time virtually unaware of what was developing in Cambridge. He staunchly maintained that his ideas on money in particular had developed independently, and there are many incidents to support his case. Hicks received a postcard from Keynes in December 1934 in reply to his having sent Keynes a proof copy of the 'Simplifying' article. 'Many thanks', Keynes wrote, 'for the proof of your article. I like it very much. I agree with you that what I now call 'Liquidity Preference' is the essential concept for Monetary Theory.' In response to Keynes's comments on his 'Simplifying' article, he reflected later, 'that was the first time I had heard of Liquidity Preference', and 'what I was saying there is by no means the same as Keynes's Liquidity Preference, as Keynes ... thought at first that it was' ([1973c] 1977a, pp. 142, 148).

Also, Keynes was himself aware that Hicks was not getting a clear version of his ideas. In fact, when Keynes realized later the form his ideas were taking outside Cambridge, based largely, it seems, on lecture notes by R. Bryce, he was appalled. Expressing this to Hicks in June 1935, Keynes wrote, 'The channels through which my ideas are reaching you sound rather alarming! Probably you will gather the tendency, but do not take the details too seriously' ([1973c] 1977a, p. 142). Lastly, there is no denying that the issue of money was a hot topic well beyond the limits of Cambridge.

Parallel to his new work on money Hicks produced, during the second half of his time at the LSE, several theoretical articles on the theory of value, including 'A reconsideration of the theory of value' with R. Allen (1934a) and 'Wages and interest: the dynamic problem' (1935f). Hicks traced the steps which led to his article with Allen, beginning with his lectures on general equilibrium at the LSE, as follows:

> *Theory of Wages* elasticity of substitution; Joan Robinson's elasticity of substitution (*Imperfect Competition*) 1933; proof of equilivalence on two-factor case; Lerner's proof that the Robinson elasticity is a property of an isoquant: my own realization that the same geometrical property would hold for an indifference curve. ([1973c] 1977a, p. 135)

He also noted elsewhere that his general interest in econometrics and the work of Schultz were important factors. The paper on wages and interest (the 'Bread' paper) was, for its part, produced under some influence of Keynes, since by 1935 Hicks had learned that Keynes was trying to determine the interest rate in the money market. 'It looks back to the *Theory of Wages* (1932b) and forward to *Value and Capital* (1939a). And it is looking sideways at Keynes . . . Wicksell and Keynes come together. My "Bread" paper is the link between them' ([1935f] 1982a, pp. 64, 66). 'I was curious to test out this doctrine [of money and the interest rate] on the model with which I was working, an early version of that which was to be elaborated in *VC* [*Value and Capital*]' (1982a, p. 10). His influence was apparently favourably acknowledged by Keynes as well, since the article was published in the *Economic Journal*.

Along with Hicks's earlier publications these articles testify to the fact that even before leaving the LSE, Hicks was puzzling through almost all the theoretical elements he was to develop in his second book, *Value and Capital*. He had reached the stage where his ideas began to drift away from their roots in the faith of the free market to converge with those advocated by Keynes in Cambridge. In 1974 Hicks recollected, 'by the end of 1934, when my ideas were more formed, I was publishing things which were recognized by Keynes (in correspondence) as being more on his side than on the other' (1974b, p. 6).

Also before leaving the LSE Hicks was to meet his future wife. In 1932 Hicks became friendly with Ursula Kathleen Webbs, whom he had first met in Robbins's seminar. They both went to an econometrics conference in Leiden in 1933. Hicks ended his period at the LSE with a decision to move to Cambridge in the summer of 1935. Webb, also a graduate of Oxford, in history, had been occupied during her years of graduate work at the LSE primarily with founding and editing *The Review of Economics* as she had named it. (She was to continue to be an editor of the journal for twenty-seven years). Although Webb was to have been appointed to the lectureship Hicks was vacating, his change of place coincided with their decision in September 1935 to be married that following December in London.

Their romance could not have been completely secret. During the early 1930s Hicks had become quite close to his sister Mary who was training in nursing at Barts and also living at the time in London. They used to go for long walks together, and she was no doubt one of the first to know his plans. In 1935, Webb told Lindahl, to whom she had been introduced by Hicks and for whom she had been engaged to help with translating, that she and Hicks had decided to be married; Lindahl indicated no surprise. Presuming, it seems, that the move to Cambridge would settle them there for some time, Hicks and Webb set about purchasing a house as early as September. For £1800 they found a brand-new one on Tropington Road which backed up against farmland. Their marriage coincided with the move of Hicks's aunt Winifred out of Blockley, and she presented the couple with as much of her library as they cared to have, a present Hicks gratefully accepted and treasured.

By this time Hicks was probably curious about Keynes and his impact in Cambridge, in part since competition between the LSE and Cambridge had been growing during Hicks's time at the LSE. It was also because Hicks, living in Bloomsbury on a modest salary of £240 annually, knew something of the extravagant and eccentric cultural life of both John Maynard and Geoffrey Keynes and the Bloomsbury Group. It was, however, his friendship with Robertson which attracted him to Cambridge. Hicks's invitation to a university lectureship at Cambridge came from Pigou, the examination commissioner for whom Hicks had served as an external examiner in 1934. It had, however, most certainly been backed, if not proposed, by Robertson. Thus, when it came, Hicks unhesitatingly accepted the appointment and the election to a fellowship at Gonville and Caius College, and moved to Cambridge in the summer of 1935. He was, however, very surprised to find Robertson distant and uncommunicative and was immediately to miss the physical closeness and collaboration of other economists he had had within the LSE seminar group.

It seems that through his acceptance of the position Hicks had been caught in an internal power struggle to determine the appointment to the post. Keynes and his partisans had favoured Joan Robinson as a candidate, and looking back Hicks came to think in his last years that Pigou and Robertson had probably invited him in an effort to keep Joan Robinson out. As a consequence, unbeknown to Hicks when he arrived in Cambridge, Robertson, and to lesser extent Pigou, did not want to associate with him much, for fear that it might appear that they had indeed recruited him for their purposes. By the time *The General Theory* came out in early 1936, during Hicks's second term in Cambridge, the sides had, begun to draw their dividing lines very sharply. Clearly ill at ease with the situation, Robertson kept a very low profile throughout. When he learned in 1938 that Hicks was considering leaving Cambridge, he deliberately went to see him to let him know that he too was deciding to leave, for London. Once aware of their respective imminent departures from Cambridge, their friendly relationship resumed.

The disharmonious atmosphere reigning at Cambridge for Hicks was fortunately no obstacle to Webb's finding a fair number of teaching opportunities. She was busy writing *The Finance of British Government, 1920–1936*. Hicks prized immensely her intellectual companionship and stimulation, as he would throughout her life. With the exception of Ursula and his friend Claude Guillebaud, Marshall's nephew and editor, Hicks found himself in Cambridge basically on his own. His first year there was the year of *The General Theory*.

Hicks wrote two review papers of Keynes's book in 1936, neither of which increased his popularity at Cambridge. The first was solicited by the *Economic Journal* upon the book's publication in January. The journal had sought him out as a young, non-partisan economist who would really read Keynes's book thoroughly before passing judgement, but Hicks felt very pressed in having to complete it by the April deadline. 'It is, therefore, in many ways, no more than a first impression' ([1973c] 1977a, p. 142), he wrote. The second review Hicks initially presented at the meeting of the Econometric Society in Oxford in September 1936. 'It was seeking to explain the Keynes theory to econometrists (and mathematical economists)' (1982a, p. 100). Although Keynes responded to the second review in a private letter to Hicks with 'I found it very interesting and really have next to nothing to say by way of criticism' ([1973c] 1977a, p. 144), the two reviews were portrayed in Cambridge as anti-Keynesian, and as a result, Hicks's interpretation received there very little discussion.

Amid the flurry over Keynes's *General Theory*, Hicks was busy preparing his *Value and Capital*, which he submitted for publication by the middle of 1938. Hicks had worked out the outline of *Value and Capital* between 1930 and 1935 while 'in constant collaboration' with many members of Robbins's seminar at the LSE (1939a, p. vi). 'La théorie mathematique de la valeur', the French translation of the first draft of the book's mathematical appendix, had already appeared in 1936. In it all the equations appeared in the form of the elasticity of substitution (a formulation which with all its essential determinants was not used in *Value and Capital* itself). The only part of the book that had remained to be sorted out in Cambridge was part IV, the wage theorem. Hicks had already decided on what he intended to say and had the detailed framework of both sections in his mind. the impact of *The General Theory* did alter the shape of his original plan, though not markedly.

In *Value and Capital* Hicks asserted, 'I am almost entirely concerned with novelties. I shall confine myself to those aspects of each subject I treat on which I have something new to say; or at least I shall deal with familiar aspects quite cursorily' (1939a, p. 1). In so saying Hicks proceeded along two routes, a static and a dynamic one. His interest in following the first path was a matter of wanting to integrate income substitution effects into the theory of value of Pareto, the inspiration for his static route. On the dynamic side, Hicks's initial idea was to try to produce a workable dynamic theory of economic activity, one which would enable economists to say something about processes which are not in a stationary condition. Hicks made progress along both routes, but most notably along the dynamic one.

None the less, the content of *Value and Capital* was to be a casualty of the poor timing of the book's publication in 1939. '*Value and Capital* had been published at the beginning of 1939; so it got distributed throughout the world before the War broke out' ([1979b] 1983a, p. 361). First, interest in the economic situations the book contemplated was not what it might have been. During the war and for a good many years thereafter, many economies, including that of Britain, were so highly controlled that many of the problems which could have presented themselves in less economically restricted circumstances, the subject of *Value and Capital*, just did not occur. Second, in this same period, the already quite well-known Keynes was making his own serious effort to produce a dynamic theory and, as Hicks put it, 'got in first' (1939a,

p. 4). The models of Keynes immediately had much greater success than did those of Hicks. Unlike the case of *The Theory of Wages*, where Hicks did attribute its reception to poor timing, '1932 was not a lucky date for the appearance of a book like this. It was the blackest year of the Great Depression; there has been no date in this century to which the theory I was putting out could have been more inappropriate' ([1932b] 1963b, p. 305). In the case of *Value and Capital*, Hicks reflected later that, to his mind, the superseding appreciation of Keynes was primarily due to Keynes's skill in making powerful simplifications.

In fact, *Value and Capital* had more in common with the economics of the LSE than with that of Cambridge. Hicks had tried to bridge static and dynamic economics in a model of a free market economy. In a sense the approach was a regress, even in terms of his own work. Many of Hicks's thoughts on monetary theory which he had already developed could have made their way into *Value and Capital* but did not. The stumbling block was the temporary equilibrium model which, Hicks became well aware, could not be compatibly fitted with his more novel theory of money.

The fact that Hicks's way of thinking persisted from his LSE days well into his time in Cambridge is not surprising, since he remained very much on his own. All in all Hicks had minimal contact with Keynes or his most devoted followers, Joan Robinson and Richard Kahn. When Hicks first arrived in Cambridge, he had called on Joan Robinson. She was so hostile, however, that Hicks was not encouraged to do so again. Although during his LSE period Hicks had corresponded with Keynes, he did not actually meet him until May 1935 when he was interviewed in Cambridge, over lunch, by Keynes and Pigou for the position of university lecturer. Hicks was subsequently invited several times by Keynes to lunch, but Keynes's work and his weak health during most of the time that Hicks was in Cambridge seemed to preclude much more serious intellectual contact. 'I only just knew him personally; we had very little conversation on theoretical matters' (1967, p. ix). Hicks went on occasion to Keynes's famous Political Economy Club, but said very little during the meetings. He never considered himself part of the club's group, although some of its participants, to his recollection, were economists who came from London, as well as Keynes's Cambridge followers.

Ironically, if Keynes and especially his 'Circus' had been more receptive and attentive to Hicks, Keynesian economics would have probably gained a very powerful ally. While at the LSE Hicks had given the impression in his work that his ideas were converging with those of the Cambridge school. Once in Cambridge, however, he was neither trusted nor given the chance to develop his thoughts along lines that would have been favourably received there. A window was perhaps beginning to open just as he had decided there was no point in staying among the Cambridge economists. Despite the apparent lack of support from his colleagues, Hicks was eventually elected to the faculty board. By that time, however, he was set on leaving Cambridge, especially after he heard that Robertson was also departing.

Robbins in London had all along wanted Hicks to remain at the LSE. He knew that Hicks had left because he was not offered a readership. Robbins tried to persuade W. H. Beveridge, then director of the LSE, to appoint Hicks as reader, but Beveridge was particularly keen on attracting distinguished scholars from elsewhere, and Robbins had no success. Thus, with nothing forthcoming at the LSE, Robbins, most probably, when consulted about candidates for an appointment in economic theory at the University of the Manchester, suggested Hicks. In 1938 Hicks was invited to interview for the position before a large committee of professors from a variety of disciplines, the Council of Manchester University. Hicks was indeed pleased by the invitation and gladly travelled there for the interview.

Two months after the interview, at the age of 34, Hicks was offered the post of Stanley Jevons Professor of Political Economy at the University of Manchester, which he accepted and held until 1946. The Hicks sold their Cambridge home to Hartley Withers, author of *The Meaning of Money* (1928), and moved to Manchester. The years in Manchester were unexciting for Hicks. While he did mostly elementary teaching, he none the less did not remain idle. Inspired initially by Kaldor's 1939 paper, 'Welfare propositions and interpersonal comparisons of utility' and its geometrical apparatus, which subsequently gave rise to much controversy, Hicks wrote a series of articles on the 'new welfare economics' (1939f, 1941b, 1942d, 1944a, 1946a, 1949c, 1950b, 1951a). 'In the course of writing these papers', Hicks noted later, 'a consistent theory was gradually worked out; one point after another became clear to the author' (1981, p. 114). He also still laboured on the ideas of *Value and Capital*, 'working out the consequences of a most fruitful suggestion' by Alexander Henderson, which led ultimately to his theory of consumer surplus published in 1956 as chapters 10 and 18 of his *A Revision of Demand Theory*. In his work on demand, Hicks pursued the theoretical rather than the econometric path. Econometrics had begun with the demand studies of the 1930s, but for Hicks, whose formal mathematical training had ended in 1923, the techniques seemed uninteresting and laborious.

When the war broke out in 1939, Hicks was virtually cut off from direct professional contacts beyond his university. The British universities remained open throughout the war (ironically the LSE moved to Cambridge), but their activity was limited. Manchester was very quiet, well outside the intellectual circle for economics which was confined to Cambridge, London and Oxford. Only once, on holiday in the Lake District in 1942, did Hicks find himself close to a number of the Cambridge economists, among them P. Sraffa, D. Champernowne, and N. Kaldor accompanied by his wife. They had all retreated to the inns of Langdale, the Lake District being about the closest place to go for holidays during the war. While in Manchester Hicks also saw Keynes once and remembered their meeting as being, for him, the best of all their encounters. It was at the formal occasion of Keynes's receiving an honorary degree from the University of Manchester.

During the time Hicks was in Manchester he produced *The Social Framework*, which was designed to be an elementary text in the teaching of economics. It was one of the first texts of basic social accounting. 'It should have been called *The Social Accounts*, for its novelty consisted in the systematic use of social accounting material for elementary teaching; but the idea of social accounting was then unfamiliar, so I was persuaded to fall back on that unsatisfactory title' ([1979b] 1983a, p. 360).

The idea behind it was to use the published British national accounts as the means of illustrating economic concepts in an elementary fashion. It was a well-received idea, which Hicks, of course, welcomed. Its success also meant, however, that Hicks was committed approximately every ten years to spending quite lot of time revising the earlier edition, to bring its data up to date for republication.

The first edition of *The Social Framework* (1942a) was based on pre-war national accounts figures for 1938, which had been published in sketchy form in wartime White Papers. Hicks then prepared a new edition (1952) with 1949 data, intended as a look at the post-war economy. Although the average figures for 1949 were not seriously affected by the monetary crisis at the end of that year, they were none the less, given the wartime shortages still in effect, for all intents and purposes still wartime figures. Using 1957 figures, Hicks tackled a truly post-war edition, representative of a 'normal' economy. He undertook the fourth and last edition in 1969; despite the addition of appendices with brief descriptions of the main aspects of economic concepts (for example, depreciation) and the relegation of some of the more complex uses of data to a separated final section, the abundance of data alone had rendered the text too heavy for elementary teaching, especially at the secondary school level.

Hicks was not drawn as an economic expert into any political role during the war. He did, however, correspond with Keynes on at least one occasion, on 4 October 1939, about the first war budget of Sir John Simon and did a great deal of work for the National Institute of Economic and Social Research, including sitting on their advisory committee. In the latter part of the war he and Webb both worked extensively on local finance. This was really Ursula's domain but Hicks devoted much energy to her projects. During those war years Hicks also managed to write several important articles on national accounting (1941a, 1941c, 1943a, 1944b, 1945a).

While in Manchester Hicks was a member of the Manchester Statistical Society, but he found his closest colleague and friend in the economic historian, T. S. Ashton. They extensively discussed monetary history. When in 1944 Ashton decided to leave Manchester for Oxford, it struck Hicks definitively that he was in an intellectual desert. Webb had thought all along that the move to Manchester had been a mistake because she had not been offered teaching possibilities there as she had in Cambridge. Even on location it had been impossible for Hicks to help Ursula to find a job, given the way the university was organized. After the evacuation of Liverpool, she was, however, invited to the University of Liverpool to be in charge of maintaining the economics department there. The Hicks lived near Manchester in Prestbury, and Ursula was faced with commuting by car to Manchester, then from Manchester to Liverpool by train at least two days a week, which was not easy at the time. None the less, she ran the department at Liverpool from about 1941 to 1945, an experience which she enjoyed very much. When the war came to an end, those with regular university appointments returned, thanking Ursula for her services and sending her on her way. At that point, both the Hicks felt that there was not much left for them in Manchester and its environs, and decided to return to Oxford.

Hicks began looking for advertisements for openings in the Oxford colleges. The first one he spotted was for a teaching fellowship at Balliol College. Although Hicks held a professional chair in Manchester, he knew that it was unheard of for a provincial professor to step straight into a position of similar rank at Oxford. Since he was thus willing to give up his rank, he thought that it would be easy for him to get the job at Balliol. Actually the master of Balliol was so impressed that Hicks, a Fellow of the Swedish Academy of Science (a distinction rarely offered to a foreigner) and of the British Academy of Economists (elected in 1942), was applying to Balliol that he told him that he could have a very good position if he wanted. At the time the British Academy was a much more exclusive and therefore distinguished association than it became five decades later, when much expanded. In the year of Hicks's election, the same year in which Robbins was also chosen, its members were only Keynes, Pigou and Robertson from Cambridge, Bowley and Beveridge from London, and Hawtrey from the British Treasury.

There was, however, another advertisement for a position at Nuffield College, Oxford's graduate institution for research and advanced study in the social sciences, to which Hicks also responded. Henry Clay was then Warden of Nuffield, and he and Hicks were both members of the Council of the Royal Economic Society. (Hicks was also on the Council of the Econometric Society.) In December 1945, the Royal Economic Society gave a farewell party in a luxurious London hotel to honour Keynes, who had decided to give up (not very long before he died) the editorship of the *Economic Journal*, the periodical of the RES. Clay and Hicks were both at that December gathering which, because of the war, was a rather unattractive party with little to drink or eat. By this time Clay had received Hicks's letter stating his interest in the position at Nuffield. Clay told Hicks after the party that if he really wanted the job he could have it.

In accepting the appointment as an Official Fellow of Nuffield College in 1946, Hicks felt that he had somehow forced the hand of the college, since many fellows had actually had another candidate in mind. Clay was a Manchester man. He had left the city some time before Hicks arrived, but having been largely responsible for founding the Manchester economics department he felt that the people there were still 'his' people. Clay had left in order to go to the Bank of England, and it is now clear that he was very influential there in the 1930s. When Clay was elected Warden of Nuffield College, the idea was that he would use his Bank of England connections for future appointments to the college. Instead he used the Manchester connection far more. There were two other people appointed to Nuffield at same time as Hicks: Alec Loveday, who had been the head of the economic section at the League of Nations, first in Geneva and then during the war in Princeton, New Jersey, and Norman Chester, both of whom subsequently became Wardens of the College.

The Hickses moved themselves and their by now immense library to Blockley near Oxford, the earlier home of his aunt Winifred Stephens Whale who died in 1944 (and the earlier home of much of their library). Even when living in Oxford, Ursula Hicks did not get a job immediately. She had, however, already published her book, *The Finance of British Government 1920–1936* (1938) and by the mid-1940s was becoming quite well known. In 1946 Cole, Hicks's thesis supervisor of twenty years earlier, now influential in the social studies faculty, offered her a senior lectureship in public finance. She thus acquired the position of University Lecturer in Public Finance at Oxford. Although the position did not carry any affiliation to a college, Ursula was able to have an office in Queen Elizabeth House. In 1952 her book, *British Public Finance, 1888–1952* was published and when Linacre College was founded Ursula was chosen to be one of its senior members, which she remained for more than a decade after official retirement age.

In 1946 Hicks visited the United States for the first time, to serve as visiting professor at Columbia University in New York City. He was surprised to find out how well known he had become in the United States; both his *Theory of Wages* and *Value and Capital* were being used as standard texts in the major universities. During the war Hicks had found himself cut off from reactions to his books; 'it was only after the War that I found out what had been happening' ([1979b] 1983a, p. 361), he wrote. Hicks was not totally happy to learn that he was regarded as the founder of the 'neo-classical synthesis' and that North American economists had chosen to concentrate primarily on the content of his *Theory of Wages* and on the static general equilibrium half of *Value and Capital.*

> There was one occasion which I particularly remember. I was entertained to dinner by a small group of very eminent economists (I will not name the others, but one of them was Josef Schumpeter); we spent the evening, I trying to persuade them that my *Theory of Wages* was a thoroughly bad book, they trying to persuade me that it was a good one. They did not persuade me of that, but they certainly did persuade me that it was still alive. ([1932] 1963b, p. 311)

In 1963 Hicks reasoned that the support of his work was motivated by conservative anti-Keynesian American politics. More important perhaps, he no longer denied that *The Theory of Wages* was an integral part of his corpus and was considered to be the basis of what was becoming a 'new American economics', which was mathematically very complex. By 1963 Hicks reflected on this trend: 'my Walrasian–Wicksellian approach (more fully developed in *Value and Capital*, but already represented in *The Theory of Wages*) was not foreign to it; it was on this kind of thing that the Americans themselves were building' ([1932] 1963b, p. 312). He was, however, sceptical about this mathematical direction of economics and felt uneasy about his role as initiation of that movement.

On the occasion of his stay in the United States Hicks was, however, pleased not only to speak with Schumpeter and Viner whom he had met in the 1930s in London, but also to meet K. Arrow, M. Friedman, D. Patinkin, P. Samuelson and many other of the young economists in North America. 'I did not know them,' he wrote later almost ominously, 'but they knew me . . . I am afraid I disappointed them; and have continued to disappoint them. Their achievements have been great; but they are not in my line' ([1979b] 1983a, p. 361). Partly under the influence of and partly as a result of exchanges with such prominent economists in America, Hicks continued to rethink his ideas on demand and welfare. This rethinking culminated in *A Revision of Demand Theory* (1956a) at which point he recalled the catalysts of his work:

> Perhaps I may be allowed to recall an occasion in the autumn of 1946, at Harvard, when I was called upon to expound my work on consumer's surplus to a most select audience of five or six (which included Samuelson [and Lange, Mosak and Roy]) . . . In that discussion the seed of this book was already sown. But as it has grown in my mind it has been subjected to other influences: first of all that of Samuelson's book (which did not appear until 1947), then of those who may be called his followers, among whom Arrow, Little and Houthakker must be especially mentioned. (1956a, pp. v–vi)

A sketch, yet to become the core, of the *Revision* was presented as part of a series of public lectures at the LSE in 1951. Although Hicks indicated that 'much of the book was written soon after that date', 'other occupations' (1956a, p. vi) caused its completion and publication to be delayed until 1956.

Between 1947 and 1955 Hicks wrote a series of essays prompted by problems of post-war reconstruction (1982a, pp. 147–216). In one, '"Full Employment" in a Period of Reconstruction', published in 1947, Hicks set out to analyse specific qualifications to Keynes's doctrine of 'Full Employment', but reflected later that he had formulated 'the regular objections which have been raised by the economic establishment in England against such things as the budgetary policy of Sir Geoffrey Howe, since 1979' (1982a, p. 162).

In the 1930s and 1940s there was much written about business or trade cycles. Hicks had himself contemplated the issue for some time. The 'seed-bed', as Hicks called it, had been prepared by his close friend, D. Robertson. To his salutary encouragement Hicks also credited his later success in 'getting any way beyond the formal model-building' (1950a, p. xiii). In his *Theory of Wages* Hicks had already announced that he would eventually produce a theory of the business cycle. In

1949 Hicks reviewed Harrod's *Toward a Dynamic Economics*. He later wrote that 'anyone who was [*sic*] worked through the paper [Hicks's review] (it does need a bit of working through) will have got, with one exception, nearly everything that is of importance in the book' (1982a, p. 173). The exception was his section on induced investment, occupying chapter 4 of his book (1950a), which came out after the review. None the less, Hicks did take note, after writing his review, of the work of many others, for example, of R. Goodwin, W. Leontief and F. Modigliani, who had also taken an interest in the issue of economic fluctuations. He was, in fact, so impressed with R. Goodwin, former student of Schumpeter and Harrod, that he tried around 1950, to no avail, to find a position for him at Oxford.

During 1948–9 Hicks extended his Harrod review article into *A Contribution to the Theory of the Trade Cycle* (1950a). The achievement of the book was to have combined Keynes's saving–investment mechanism first with the 'multiplier', then with the Clark–Samuelson–Hansen accelerator principle and with Harrod's notion of instability to produce what Hicks called a general theory of the trade cycle. Hicks considered what he had devised to be a Keynesian theory, of fluctuations, even though he recognized that the early post-war boom in which he was writing the book 'would not be prematurely cut off by monetary restriction' (1950a, p. ix).

The book generated many controversial reviews, some of which led Hicks to rethink his concept of dynamics. Some of his revisions, perhaps the most important, are found in his 'Methods of dynamic analysis' (1956c). In it Hicks felt he had found a way of fitting his 'dynamic' theory of *Value and Capital* and that of *A Contribution to the Theory of the Trade Cycle* together. Hicks later attributed much of the lack of impression *Capital and Growth* made on the economic audience to the fact that he did not choose to reproduce within the book the contents of his 'Methods of dynamic analysis'. In a sense, Hicks's book on the trade cycle marked the end of one era of contributions by him to economic theory. From its publication onward he no longer held the conviction that he was producing general theories.

In the meantime at Oxford, Balogh, Burchardt and Worswick from the Oxford Institute of Economics and Statistics dominated the faculty board and Hicks was advised to keep a low profile. He found Balogh and Worswick rather difficult colleagues, but managed to develop a working relationship with Burchardt. Hicks felt later that he had probably made a mistake in distancing himself from the institute and in not seeking a room there. At the same time he was developing a good rapport with Harrod with whom he liked to have discussions. Although Hicks was receiving visitors from as far away as Japan, his closest colleague at the time was close to home in Oxford, George Richardson, who later gave up economics to become the head of Oxford University Press, after which position he became master of Keble College. Within four years Hicks was himself elected to the economics faculty board and later on to the general university board. In the early 1950s Hicks was suggested for the Drummond chair in political economy; Harrod, who had badly wanted the chair at the time of Henderson's election in 1944, had by 1952 acquired a readership at Christ Church College, and chose not to compete. In 1952, at the age of 47, Hicks was appointed Drummond Professor of Political Economy, the chair he held until 1965.

Along with Hicks's good fortune in 1952 came the deaths, only four months apart, of his sister Phyllis from diabetes and his father from a heart attack. Like her father, Phyllis had been an avid amateur historian and had completed a local history book. Hers would be privately printed posthumously as *A Quest of Ladies: the Story of a Warwickshire School*. Hicks felt an especial loss in the passing of these family members, with whom he had travelled and whose common interest in history had made them particularly kindred spirits throughout his life.

For Hicks, the 1950s can be said to have been his years of reflection on economic theory, which is not to say that he was inactive. While busy with academic and official duties at Nuffield College, some of which included his unwelcomed strong lobbying for a bipartite or single course devoted to economics rather than PPE, he did enjoy the Nuffield economics seminars and collaborated extensively with Ursula on her work on public finance, taking strong account of the devaluation of the pound sterling in 1949, and economic development. He was a member of the Economic Committee of the Royal Commission on Population, and between 1950 and 1953 of the British Royal Commission on the Taxation of Profits and Income; on this he served with N. Kaldor. As the British empire was slowly folding, and many countries were becoming independent, there was a great demand for non-government affiliated British economists to advise the emerging nations. Thus until the early 1960s the Hickses travelled extensively to all parts of the world: to Nigeria in 1950–1 as part of the Revenue Allocation Commission; to Jamaica in 1954 as advisers to that government on finance and taxation; to East, Central and South Africa and South America and to the developing countries of Ceylon, Pakistan and India where he was visiting professor at the University of Delhi, and many others as advisers (occasionally on subjects as fundamentally political as a country's constitution and often under the auspices of the British government) or as guest lecturers.

Selections of Hicks's work from this period on economic development and international economics were collected from their original form as lectures at Harvard, Yale and University College, Dublin or as publications in bank reviews and economic journals, into *Essays in World Economics* (1959a). With an eye to an audience not exclusively British, Hicks had tried 'to see the British problem in its world setting' (1959a, p. v). Of concern, he felt, was the political context of 'the emergence of former colonies into political independence, and the competition of power blocs for influence in what seems to them to be a power vacuum' (p. 161). The experience Hicks acquired from offering concrete proposals in the developing nations and from seeing the practical application there of his earlier economic principles reinforced his views on the purpose of economics. It was not, he thought, for the economist to be primarily prescriptive.

To Hicks's mind, the economist's concern ought essentially to be one of undertanding, not of recommending or advising. Hicks was not thereby advocating that the economist shy away from forming opinions about contemporary issues. 'One should have some idea', he wrote, 'at the bottom of one's mind, about the things, the conditions or the arrangements, which one thinks to be good or to be bad. (How far such judgements are necessarily implied in formal theory', he added however, 'is quite another matter') (1959a, p. viii). None the less, one has, Hicks felt, 'no right to pronounce on practical problems unless one has been through the labour, so often the formidable labour, of mastering the relevant facts' ([1979b] 1983a, p. 362). Indeed he began to have a new perspective on how to approach economic theory.

Hicks's role as economic adviser outside Britain predominantly involved viewing the economic and political situation of an area or country and holding extensive interviews with local officials. This period of travel was not surprisingly also extremely interesting to him for its cultural encounters. During his travels he became profoundly disturbed by what happened when a country's borders had been determined by diplomacy rather than geography. He was as fascinated by local native costumes as by the religious and artistic expressions and flora and fauna which exceeded an immediate locale. Hicks remembered numerous harrowing stories about close encounters with lions, hippopotamuses, giraffes, elephants, and even barracuda. He was an astute observer of regional technologies and was taken to see some technological wonders, such as the radio telescope of southern India. Of special enjoyment to him were, however, the remains of ancient architecture which he viewed with great enthusiasm and historical understanding. He never tired of seeing new sites and recorded his travels with many photographs.

The early 1960s can be characterized as the economists' period of confidence in economic theory and econometrics. Much was written during this period on production functions, capital, and growth as well as on measurement, aggregation, and large models (Hamouda and Rowley, 1988). At the time, Hicks felt the need to update himself on what others were doing and to come back to the forefront in economic theory. First he set out to assimilate the most recent developments in mathematics and growth theory, particularly those of Dorfman, Samuelson and Solow. This led him to write his survey article, 'Linear theory' (1960b), with the help of H. W. Kuhn of Princeton who spent the academic year 1958/9 in London, as well as of K. Arrow and G. Dantzig, and M. Morishima, when Hicks himself travelled to California and Osaka. Distinguishing himself from other writers on linear theory, Hicks said later, 'I was not trying to teach a technique; I was trying to write up its story, as an episode in the history of economics' (1983a, p. 246).

In 1964 Hicks was knighted by the Queen. In 1965, finding no enjoyment in the political and administrative responsibilities in the organization of postgraduate studies he felt he had assumed with the Drummond Chair, Hicks chose to retire early and to become Professor Emeritus of Nuffield College. His formal retirement did not, however, deter him from continuing to work on many fronts. Hicks started to confront his own more recent views with those he had held in the 1930s as well as to reconsider the contributions of Keynes. In monetary economics in particular he readdressed issues left incomplete, in a sense, since 1935, and produced a paper, 'Liquidity' (1962a), which marked the beginning of his new monetary theory.

Outside Oxford, Hicks gave many guest lectures, including a return to the LSE in 1966 for a series on the foundations of monetary theory (whose content he also discussed with R. Sayers, his former colleague at the LSE, and his seminar group), to the University of Manchester in 1970 for a series on capital measurement, and to the United States in 1978. In Oxford, Hicks still maintained a teaching and writing schedule with an even closer college affiliation, now at All Souls College, which fellowship had been part of his appointment as Drummond Professor. Hicks made a number of friends within the college and was very pleased to have been elected first Distinguished and subsequently

Honorary Fellow. In 1985 Hicks was asked to have his portrait painted by Mark Wickham for the college; he considered this honour to have been one of the greatest ever bestowed upon him.

At All Souls Hicks continued to supervise some students, especially those whose subject he found interesting enough for him to hand-pick them from among the undergraduates for whom he had to find suitable supervisors. Hicks felt grateful to the college for the 'privilege' of doing a little teaching and of continuing to work with students. He derived great stimulus from his circle of young economists, whom he acknowledged by name in several of his last books. It was, no doubt, with these last students in mind that Hicks presented his very last book to today's 'teachers of economics' and 'their critically minded students, some of whom will be the teachers of the next generations' (1989a, p. 4). His scholarly work also continued as he provided ingenious alternatives to controversial issues in the areas of monetary, growth, market, and capital theory, as well as history and methodology. In fact, he produced as much after 1965 as he had during his entire professional career to that point.

Capital and Growth (1965a) was the product of Hicks's continued reflection on alternative approaches to economic dynamics. At the very least it was, as he himself described it, a survey of the current ideas in growth theory, 'critical and expository, rather than constructive ... [reflecting] no desire to champion any one to the exclusion of others' (1973d, p. v.). In fact, however, the book was much more than an assessment of others, since Hicks tried in it to set up his own new version of growth analysis using the traverse. He attempted to integrate both fix- and flexprice theories into the analysis as well as to provide a theory of capital. He felt the book owed a great deal to Morishima, who had spent a full year with him at All Souls College, from the summer of 1963 to 1964, 'a period during which a large part of this book was written' (1965a, p. vii). Hicks asserted that he could not have written chapters 18 and 19 without Morishima's help; while 'the central diagram (Fig. 9, p. 229) was my idea, it is only through his buttressing that it has been made to stand up' (1965a, p. vii). Although it was a highly ambitious attempt at being comprehensive, *Capital and Growth* was not Hicks's greatest success. In the years following its publication he persevered in dealing with the difficulties its analysis entailed.

In 1973 Hicks completed *Capital and Time: a Neo-Austrian Theory*, a work in which he proposed a different approach, one which he felt he had overlooked in *Capital and Growth*. In its preface, using the simile of a building, he wrote of the book, 'As I now realize it, I have been walking round my subject [of capital], taking different views of it. Though that which is presented here is just another view, it turns out to be quite useful in fitting the others together' (1973d, p. v).

Stimulated by the work of Charles Kennedy, *Capital and Time* demonstrated again Hicks's remarkable skill in modelling the complexity of the impact of capital and technological change with simple and imaginative devices. The book's subtitle was retained from its first draft, an article which was published as 'A neo-Austrian growth theory' in 1970. That article and subsequently the use of neo-Austrian theory in the book aroused much interest among the group of followers of L. von Mises at New York University, 'who like to think of themselves as the true heirs of the old' "Austrian School"' (1983a, p. 113). In January 1978 Hicks was invited to the United States to explain the place of his ideas in neo-Austrian theory. In New York he gave the paper, 'Is interest the price of a factor of production?' (1979c), which acquaintances and friends from all over the United States, such as John Hughes from Chicago, came to hear. It began,

> I find myself addressing a congregation of rather particular Austrians, while I myself am no more than an 'irregular and defective' Austrian. I have ventured to give the description 'neo-Austrian' to the theory which has been developed in one of my books, and it has been stamped on for heresy. So I know that I have got to defend myself. ([1979c] 1983a, p. 114)

Although the paper Hicks offered 'in defense' did 'not have much to do with *Capital and Time*' ([1973a] 1983a, p. 111), he recalled that he had great fun 'calling in all candidates' for status as capital. While Hicks, by this time, had truly revived the interest of economists from all sides in the capital controversy, he was himself already moving on to his next concern, the difficulty of explaining a historical process.

In *A Theory of Economic History* (1969a) Hicks discussed from a historical perspective his premises in dynamic economics for the hypothesis of the growth theory traverse model. He seemed to have taken up the task he recommended to economic historians in his preface to *A Contribution to the Theory of the Trade Cycle* in 1950: 'the next stage will be the concern of statisticians, econometrists, and (most of all) economic historians, who will have to see whether it does prove possible to make sense of the facts in the light of these hypotheses'. In the book Hicks clearly revealed his eclectic knowledge, which had always stretched beyond economic boundaries. *A Theory of Economic History* had all the trademarks of an economist as author. None the less, it harked back to

Hicks's youth when history was his favorite subject and displayed the intensity of his interest in history ever since.

The book was inspired in 1967 by an invitation to Hicks to give the Gregynog lectures at the University of Wales, and its ideas were honed at lectures and seminars in Canberra, Oxford and Vienna. For those occasions Hicks tried to collect some of his ideas on the rise of the merchant and the Industrial Revolution. He also remarked that he had looked back to the numerous holidays he had spent as a boy on his grandfather's farm; it was useful to him to have experienced first-hand farming life during the time that it was becoming transformed by modern inventions. The historical issues of economic and technological change had been in his mind ever since he had lectured in medieval economic history at the University of the Witswatersrand in 1928. At that time he had received much guidance from the notes of the medieval historian, Eileen Power.

For his new venture into history Hicks also drew on his discussions, past, with M. M. Postan in the 1930s when they were both lecturers in London, and current, with many of the academics with whom he talked daily at Oxford; he benefited from both lawyers and economic historians, especially T. S. Ashton, with whom he had remained close friends since their time together in Manchester. Hicks was also an avid reader of the *Economic History Review*. It was, none the less, to his mind and to that of some of his critics an unfinished project: 'it was remarked by some readers of that book, that its "story" went as far as the Industrial Revolution (in the conventional sense) but was very sketchy on what has happened afterwards' (1977a, p. xvii). Hicks admitted later that in fact he had not yet devised a theoretical structure with which to write about the later period. That would not come to pass for almost another ten years, until his work on time in economics.

Already in the early 1960s, Hicks had begun laying the new foundation of his monetary theory, rethinking his own initial contributions and exploiting what he considered the unfinished aspects of Keynes's treatment of money and liquidity. In 1967 he compiled his *Critical Essays in Monetary Theory* as a 'record of a process, extending over many years, by which I have at last formed my present conception of monetary theory' (1967, p. v). In it Hicks was intent on showing that pre-Keynesian monetary theory was not as monolithic as Keynes had seemed to imply. He also clarified his own position which, he thought, owed 'as much to Hawtrey as to Keynes' (1977a, p. xiii) and fell somewhere between those of Keynes and Robertson. Hicks further developed his ideas on inflation and economic cycles, among other topics, in several of his later papers and books, *The Crisis in Keynesian Economics* (1974b), *Economic Perspectives* (1977a) and *Causality in Economics* (1979g). Having been convinced recently by A. Leijonhufvud that what he had written was not yet everything he could say, Hicks wrote a last synthesis of his ideas on money, his *A Market Theory of Money*, which was published posthumously in 1989.

Money was really a side issue in *Causality in Economics*. Its primary subject, causation, was one Hicks maintained he had come upon 'rather suddenly' (1979g, p. vii). After an intellectually disappointing conference in Spain in 1974, he realized that he could not develop his ideas on the relationship between micro- and macro-economics without taking a stand on the place of economics in the study of causation. In this work Hicks was indeed taking a stand, new for him, on the question of the scientific nature of economics. He had more than once asserted his position that economics was a science.

In 1972 the disciplinary ranks of economists (and specifically the Nobel Prize committee of which Professors Bertil Ohlin and Ragnar Bentzel, its chairman, were members) recognized the achievement of Sir John Richard Hicks with its choice of him as a recipient of the Alfred Nobel Memorial Prize in Economic Science (a prize instituted in 1968). While Hicks, aged 68, was the first Briton to be awarded the prize, it was unfortunate that he had to share it that same year with American Kenneth Arrow, another giant economist who equally deserved the prize on his own. The academy had chosen to recognize Hicks's early contributions to general equilibrium and welfare economics, especially those encapsulated in *Value and Capital* and in his numerous works on welfare economics, such as 'his analysis of criteria for comparisons between different economic situations and his revision of the concept of consumer surplus' (Nobel Prize citation speech). Indeed, *Value and Capital* was for Hicks an important work which had long since become a foundational classic in the discipline. By 1972, however, it represented only a small part of his *oeuvre* that was worthy of honour. As for welfare economics, as Hicks had said as recently as 1962, upon being elected to the presidency of the Royal Economic Society,

> I fancy that I would attach less importance to the economic aspects of society – to 'economic welfare' as a 'constituent of general welfare' – than would most of my fellow economists. I am, for instance, by no means convinced that we do our best for the community in which we live by trying to maximise its growth rate. ([1962a] 1982a, p. 238)

Hicks was extremely flattered and pleased with the Nobel Prize. He gave the £20,500 in prize money to the library of the LSE as a gesture of gratitude. He had none the less mixed feelings about what the prize meant. Although he never expressed it publicly, he would have liked to have been the sole recipient for the year, especially since in the preceding years scholars had been honoured singly. The fact that the prize was shared, he felt, accentuated its purpose in praising his contribution of general equilibrium, not the whole scope of his achievements as a scholar. Hicks found that he was being honoured for work which he himself had outgrown and that his later, more electric work was being benignly neglected. Hicks made this point very subtly in his Nobel lecture itself: 'What I mainly want to talk about is a side of my work which has gradually developed over the years, and which, I now feel, is more promising.' Later in a footnote to the reprinted lecture, 'Though the prize was given to me for work on "general equilibrium" I preferred to trace the evolution of my thinking on capital, wages, and invention . . .' ([1973b] 1977a, p. 4, p. 1n.).

Several years later, sensing that his message had not yet sunk in, Hicks was much less subtle, if more playful, in a reply to a journal article surveying his books:

> Clearly I needed to change my pen name. [*Hicks had indeed done so.*] Let it be understood that *Value and Capital* (1939) was the work of J. R. Hicks, a 'neoclassical' economist now deceased; while *Capital and Time* (1973) – and *A Theory of Economic History* (1969) – are the work of John Hicks, a non-neoclassic who is quite disrespectful towards his 'uncle'. The latter works are meant to be read independently, and not be interpreted, as Harcourt interprets them, in the light of their predecessor. (1975f, p. 365)

In addition to the Nobel Prize, Hicks received many other prizes and honours, including honorary degrees, beginning in the 1960s, from the Universities of Manchester, Leicester, Warwick, Kent, Bristol, and Stirling among others. The list of guest lectures and honorary speeches he gave both at home and abroad is too long to include. Invited year upon year, he travelled on average half a dozen times annually to official and unofficial gatherings the world over. Italy, he loved to say, was his second home. It is remarkable how his enthusiasm for writing and travel never waned, despite his retirement, and the death of his closest travelling companion, his wife Ursula, in July 1985. As the introductions to his later books reveal, Hicks realistically recognized and worked within the limits of his strength and stamina as he aged, rather than railing against them. He remained independent and alert even throughout his last years. Missing his 'fellow-worker for fifty years' was perhaps his only complaint; of the process of writing his last book, *A Market Theory of Money*, he wrote, speaking of his wife's absence, 'it has been written in monastic seclusion, without the benefit of continual discussion' (1989a, p. 3). In one of his last personal letters in 1989 he expressed delight at having received proofs of the book and was looking forward as always to starting a new project, a collection of his latest material. Unfortunately he died before he could complete this last project himself.

It is remarkable that in a discipline where there is great animosity among economists at the cutting edge, whose extreme sensitivity and political views render them perpetrators as well as targets of academic nastiness, Hicks seems to have avoided falling deep into this mould. He made very few lasting enemies. Perhaps unique was his ability to maintain an amicable relationship with, for example, Keynes, Sraffa, Hayek and Robertson at a time when they were not all on speaking terms with each other. It may have been his generally open approach to the ideas of others that helped him manœuver where some could not. Concerning Keynes, for example, Hicks wrote, 'I know that he did read the things which I wrote, in his lifetime, about his work; I have taken account of what he wrote to me about them.' Hicks stayed in friendly contact with Austin Robinson and Kaldor as well as with most economists beyond the London–Cambridge–Oxford triangle.

Despite his high standards for himself, Hicks even in private never had a harsh word for acquaintances or friends; he never returned the animosity of those who considered him an enemy. In fact, he always turned the criticism of his ideas (even as he acknowledged it a 'blasting'), from whatever source, into positive and constructive recommendations. He said to himself that he 'realized that truth is many-sided' (1967, p. v) and ascribed to a personal motto, 'one must always be prepared to state the truth as one sees it, but one must never refuse to see further than that truth and to state it, just because one has committed onself in the past to a statement which now seems imperfect'. Far more modest, however, than to quote his own aphorisms in his writing, Hicks turned to Blake for apologetics: '"The man who never alters his opinions", said Blake in one of his *Prophetic Writings*, "is like standing water, and breeds reptiles of the mind"' (Helm, 1984a, p. 145).

Although at the end of his life Hicks had already outlived by some years most of his contemporaries, he did in his eighties try to resolve with the still-living early economists of Cambridge any personal grudges or misunderstandings which might have built up over the years. Before he died, he made an effort to contact Joan Robinson, George Shackle and Richard Kahn. He was warmly received by Joan Robinson in

Cambridge in the early 1980s. George Shackle was also very pleased to meet Hicks at Malvern in August 1987. Unfortunately during his last visit to Cambridge illness prevented him from keeping an invitation to see Richard Kahn.

In his later years Hicks remained professionally close to Pat Rathbone Utechin, originally his secretary at Nuffield College. Although his eyesight remained very good and his hand firm, secretarial help was invaluable to him. Mail poured into his home from around the world. Economists who had become friends corresponded with warmth. Professionals young and old sought his opinion on their own work. Hicks continued to respond selectively and with verve. One of his last vigorous exchanges was with Alan Walters, monetarist and commentator for *The Times*.

Throughout his life Hicks displayed a strong feeling for family. As a boy and young man, he was particularly close to his sister Phyllis, with whom he shared a love of literature and history. With her blindness and premature death as a diabetic he felt a great loss. Although he and Ursula had no children, they remained close to their respective extended families, visiting her cousins in Dublin and staying in touch with their many relatives outside the British Isles. On both sides of Hicks's own family an uncle had emigrated from England. His mother's eldest brother had left for Canada when quite young, and Hicks had many relatives in Winnipeg. Of all his relatives he remained particularly close to his sister, Mary, who lived near Leicester and her family of four children, who had eventually spread as far afield as South Africa and Australia. In his eighties he gave the garden house on his residential property of Blockley to one of his nieces in London and took great delight in the weekend visits of his little grandniece.

Hicks never came to feel particularly close to any part of England for the role it had played in his youth. In his native Warwickshire, he explained, his parents were 'immigrants'. The land of his Cornish ancestors was also not home to him. Even the Cotswolds, which came to mean a good deal to him later on, he remembered from his youth as merely a place to visit. In fact, rather than becoming especially attached to any particular part of England, Hicks identified more with the country as a whole. On a theoretical level, he wrote of his feelings, 'The attachment to one's own people, and to the dwelling-place of own's own people, has far too much that is good and lovely about it for one to wish it to disappear' (1969a, p. 160). In the course of his life of travel and work Hicks came to revere greatly the distinctiveness and rich variety of the world's cultures. 'The groups that have formed nations, and some of the groups within nations, are social units that have value'

(1969, p. 160). While Hicks was aware when he travelled outside of England, that he was not 'at home', he would not have wanted it otherwise. Great would be the loss, he felt, if all were put into a 'melting pot'; one's social identity is a preserving force.

The finale to his career was a succession of conferences where he was the guest of honour or where his works were being commemorated, many of which had long since been translated into numerous foreign languages including Japanese. The International Economic Society, helped by the remarkable organizational skill of Stefano Zamagni, a former student of Hicks, hosted a memorable conference in Bologna in 1989 in honour of the fiftieth anniversary of the publication of *Value and Capital*. As with the awarding of the Nobel Prize, however, Hicks saw in the event that again too much emphasis was still being placed on aspects of his thought in *Value and Capital* that he felt he had outgrown. Hicks was, none the less, very pleased, moved and honoured by the presence there of many distinguished participants and especially of Arrow, Hahn, Malinvaud and Sen for whom he had always had great respect. When asked some months later by his sister Mary what he might like by way of a memorial when he died, Hicks said with great joy that he felt the conference in Bologna had been his memorial.

Still in very good health at the age of 83, in the spring of 1988 Hicks visited Glendon College, York University in Toronto, Canada for a month. He was extremely pleased to meet L. Tarshis, for whom he had been the external thesis examiner in the 1930s, and to find himself once again surrounded by undergraduate students. During this time J. Tobin, D. Laidler, and R. McKinnon came to Toronto to share in informal open discussions with him on international monetary issues. While in Toronto, Hicks also arranged to visit the widow of William Jaffé, biographer of L. Walras. During the glorious May weather of his visit, Glendon's economics faculty and students quickly got used to the 'Hicksian' lunches taken outside under the willows on the beautiful Glendon College campus. Hicks created a vibrant and exciting atmosphere, with his extraordinary way of moving at ease from economics to other topics. He continued to impress and earn the affection of all who met him.

In the following year, on the evening of 20 May, Hicks, aged 85, died peacefully in his cottage 'The Porch House', at Blockley. He was just crossing the room to change a tape of classical music. His death caught many by surprise, including myself. We had intended in our next meeting in June that I would consult him further about my draft of this volume. Unfortunately he did not live to see its publication.

On 28 October 1989, at a memorial service at the University Church of St Mary the Virgin, Oxford, friends and acquaintances from around the world joined in mourning the loss of a great economist and world citizen.

Hicks's metaphor for intellectual change was growth. Throughout his life Hicks repeatedly referred to himself as having outgrown ideas, statements or whole books which he had developed at an earlier stage. If he sensed any frustration in his own career, it was that others could not always follow his growth pattern; once he had outgrown his ideas, he wanted most for them to be forgotten. Fortunately for posterity, Hicks's wish has not been fulfilled. Instead, most of the corpus of his writings has survived, from his juvenile work of the LSE days to his last thoughts on monetary theory. It is a fortunate thing, for with all his work extant Hicks's own insistence upon his growth is not the only evidence. A life's work stands as his testimony.

2

Expectations, Equilibrium and Disequilibrium

Hicks, like Marshall, had a remarkable understanding of the working of the market economy. This was to be seen as early as the late 1920s, in his ideas on the labour market, which he subsequently developed in *The Theory of Wages* (1932b). In this work Hicks meticulously described the characteristics of labour, the detailed relationship between various factors of production, and the dynamic forces in the bargaining process between employees and employers. Although he emphasized the working of competitive forces in the free market, he was well aware that the world was actually the result of much more complex interactions.

Hicks had an ingenious way of reducing the economic environment under study to a basic, manageable framework. To make the dynamics of the world understandable he would, as the first stage of his investigations, simplify its complexities so as to expose its essentials. He always found a way to build simple models that were still powerful enough to capture the economic picture. Hicks considered simplification an essentially pedagogical instrument. It was to be complemented with common sense and general knowledge appropriate to the particular issues and circumstances.

As will be illustrated throughout this volume, Hicks's originality and skill in conceiving technical models was remarkable. His contribution, however, did not stop there. He always hinted at the limitations and weaknesses of his theories and also gave guidance as how to expand them. In the hands of other economists, especially mathematical economists, almost all his work led to a proliferation of sophisticated models in which, with no difficulty, Hicks could have participated. However he resisted any temptation personally to complicate his simple models.

To build simple models Hicks had to rely heavily on the concept of equilibrium. Unlike Young (1928) and Kaldor (1972, 1984) who underemphasized the relevance of a concept of equilibrium in economic analysis, Hicks maintained that it was essential, but asked,

What is the meaning which we are to give to the concept of 'equilibrium'? In statics, equilibrium is fundamental; in dynamics, as we shall find, we cannot do without it; but even in statics it is treacherous, and in dynamics, unless we are very careful, it will trip us up completely. It is inevitable that we should build our conception of dynamic equilibrium on the more familiar conception of equilibrium in statics. It will be wise to begin by getting the static foundation as firm as we can. (1965a, p. 15)

It is thus appropriate to devote the opening chapter of a study of Hicks's economic thought to the concept of equilibrium. Equilibrium is a notion arousing equivocality; see, for example, Machlup's survey of economists' different understandings (1967). Hicks on his own certainly used different definitions of it in different circumstances. For him equilibrium was not restricted to static economics; it was also to be used in dynamic economics. To set the stage for the following chapters, it is thus essential to explain the different meanings of the notion of equilibrium that appear frequently in his writings and to illustrate them in the models in which they have been used.

The concept of equilibrium

Hicks's economic theory was initially influenced by the *Manuel d'économie politique* of Pareto ([1906] 1927) and the *Eléments d'économie politique pure* of Walras ([1874] 1952). He read these two books well before he wrote his first theoretical article to be published, 'Edgeworth, Marshall and the indeterminateness of wages' (1929). In that article, and in *The Theory of Wages* (1932b) in which he applied marginal analysis to the labour market, Hicks already had a sophisticated concept of equilibrium. Basing his work primarily on that of Pareto and Walras he developed his own early notion of equilibrium. Hicks's discussion of Pareto's and Walras' concepts of equilibrium is found in his 'Gleichgewicht und Konjunktur' (1933b), 'A reconsideration of the theory of value' (1934a) and 'Leon Walras' (1934d).

Hicks began his own work with the following notion of equilibrium. Equilibrium he defined, in 'Marginal productivity and the principle of variation', as a state in which 'no one has any incentive to change' (1932a, p. 84) and which 'would be maintained indefinitely if there were no change in the conditions in which it is observed' ([1933b] 1980b, pp. 523–34). Such an equilibrium would occur in an economic system in which individuals (consumers and producers, labourers and entrepreneurs) are exchanging goods and services according to preferences and in which given initial conditions (such as population, tastes, knowledge, technology and stocks of capital, goods, and land) fix the set of prices.

This definition of equilibrium, which Hicks found in both Pareto and Walras, was in his opinion ambiguous. He thought two different states were described by it. Either equilibrium is the state 'reached at which no further voluntary exchange is possible between any two parties' and this can be maintained indefinitely. Or it is the state reached when exchange 'under unchanging conditions of demand and supply, can be maintained indefinitely so that no one needs to sell tomorrow at prices different from those attained today' (1933b, p. 524). (See also 1934d, p. 342.)

It was the second understanding of equilibrium that Hicks retained as the basis for his own concept. In his interpretation of a first state of equilibrium, exchanges would take place at varying prices and equilibrium would be reached only when all exchanges cease. He rejected this understanding, considering it to be non-functional. He favoured instead the second state of equilibrium, in which each exchange takes place at a determined fixed price, and this situation remains forever. He was, none the less, not totally satisfied with the second state as derived, for he understood the 'equations' of Walras and Pareto to describe a stationary state situation. For him the idea of stationarity was not satisfactory.

To the notion of equilibrium he retained from Walras and Pareto, Hicks added the concept of the 'week' and a succession of 'weeks'. The concept of the 'week' period is a descriptive device that Hicks used very extensively in his models to relax any assumption of a stationary equilibrium. Hicks made expectations the dominant determining factor of equilibrium. The 'week' period he thus defined as a lapse of time 'so short that the movement of prices *within* it can be neglected'. During a single 'week' period, expectations are taken to be constant, given and unchanging. Recognizing that expectations can change, Hicks divided the span of time during which 'wants and resources change in a manner that is foreseen' (1933b, p. 525) into his 'week' periods of arbitrary length. When expectations are revised, a new equilibrium is conceived and a new 'week' period begins. Though he himself was at the time interested only in a single 'week' period, he gave directions as to how a sequence of equilibria could be handled.

Hicks called his equilibrium one of perfect foresight, and defined disequilibrium as 'the Disappointment of Expectations' (1933b, p. 526). He assumed that in any one 'week' period, prices and production are determined by future expectations as well as by past expectations. For Hicks, future expectations imply that individuals have plans for the future and act as if these will be realized. By planning in a current period what future demand and supply will be in each subsequent period, the corresponding current supply and demand can be determined 'without expectations ever being mistaken' (1933b, p. 526). Hicks used 'this assumption, not to determine the details of the purchases which may (or may not) be planned to be made in the future, but to determine the details of current expenditure alone' (1939a, p. 229).

Hicks referred to his equilibrium as 'dynamic equilibrium': time, and thus plans made according to expectations and parameters in succeeding periods are all involved in determining it. (By contrast he defined static equilibrium as equilibrium determined solely by the parameters of a single current period.)

> a 'dynamic equilibrium' is obviously still far from being a description of reality. It does nevertheless serve as a model of a *perfectly working* economic system . . . such perfect Equilibrium is never attainable. A real economy is always in disequilibrium. The actual disequilibrium may be compared with the idealized state of dynamic equilibrium to give us a way of assessing the extent or degree of disequilibrium. (1933b, p. 526)

Hicks revealed in this passage that his equilibrium describes one which in a perfectly working economy prevails during a single 'week'. He referred to it none the less as a 'dynamic' equilibrium because at any time that mistaken expectations are revised, a new equilibrium and a new 'week' period begins. It seems also that he distinguished between the idealized equilibrium, in which expectations would be fulfilled, and the actual state of the real economy, a disequilibrium in which expectations are disappointed. In this comparison the dynamic aspect was irrelevant to Hicks. He was actually undertaking comparative statics of two states, the ideal and the actual.

This is not the whole story, and more will be said about the broader distinctions between static and dynamic economics in chapter 5. Already, however, at this stage some further clarification of Hicks's concepts of statics and dynamics as they pertain to equilibrium would be helpful. In *Capital and Growth*, Hicks wrote,

> There are cases in which static analysis of equilibrium in the single period can suffice; dynamics intervenes in the linkage of various single periods. There are cases in which more dynamics is required within the single period and between periods. Also the meaning of dynamics differs sharply whether one is dealing with Welfare Economics, Pure Positive Economics or Applied Positive Economics. (1965a, p. 9)

The complication he noted was that an equilibrium can not only be static or dynamic, it can also have different functions according to the area of economics in which it plays a role. Hicks's notion of perfect-foresight equilibrium is viewed as the idealized standard of reference; but depending on the type of analysis to which it is applied, it serves either as a state to which an actual or an alternative (hypothetical) outcome can be compared (welfare economics), or as a state to which an economic system can be seen to be tending (Hicks's positive economics), or as a path around which the values of the actual economy gravitate (Hicks's applied positive economics).

Different functions of equilibrium

Hicks believed that much of economics 'is pure theory, not tied down to a particular time and place' (1965a, p. 9). So in the light of the kind of economic enquiry (pure or applied) and the notion of time involved in the theoretical analysis (parametric or historical), three functions of equilibrium are discussed.

The ideal equilibrium and the degree of disequilibrium

In one area of pure economics, welfare economics, equilibrium is a state describing a first-best solution or an ideal. Equilibrium implies conditions of optimization which, 'according to some conception of "best"', satisfy 'wants in the "best" way' (1965a, p. 7). Time is not a factor. Hicks asserted that a static economy in which wants and resources are given is in a state of ideal equilibrium when 'all the "individuals" in it are choosing those quantities, which, out of the alternatives available to them, they prefer to produce and to consume' (p. 15). Disequilibrium is measured in degrees of discrepancy between the ideal (unattainable or unattained) first-best solution and any other second-best alternative.

Although welfare economics is primarily static, Hicks allowed it to be dynamic by varying the initial givens, resources or behaviour. The descriptive 'week' device is still applicable. Since the length of Hicks's 'week' period is arbitrary, it can be so short as to coincide with one point in time. In Hicks's dynamic welfare economics, a series of such 'week' periods becomes a series of discrete cases of optimization, yielding in fact comparative static welfare economics. The degree of disequilibrium in one case is simply compared to that in another whose initial conditions are different.

The equilibrium of expectations and the realized outcome

Hicks also defined equilibrium as a state of fulfilled expectations. In his discussion of it he focused on the existence and stability of that equilibrium. His analysis consisted in comparing the state of equilibrium, or one's expected position in an economy perfectly organized according to some given structure, and the position which might 'actually' be realized in that economy. It cannot be assumed that the equilibrium of fulfilled expectations exists for any type of economic organization, hence its existence must first be established for the organization under consideration (monopoly, duopoly, oligopoly, competition, etc.). Even in a single market there is no guarantee that the equilibrium of supply and demand, for example, will occur. (In economies in which the approach to an equilibrium is extremely slow, the existence of an equilibrium might also be doubted). If equilibrium can be shown to exist, then analysis can turn to the question of its stability: what is the reaction to disequilibrium in a particular economic system? Pure theoretical analysis of industrial structure for the equilibrium of expectations, referred to by Hicks as pure positive economics, might employ, for example, principles such as profit maximization, growth maximization, cost pricing, price discrimination, etc.

In pure positive economics, disequilibrium arises when what is expected is not 'actually' realized, theoretically. Hicks's 'week' period device is also applicable in this area of economics, but differently. Unlike the case in welfare economics where 'weeks' are isolated, in pure positive economics the periods are related. Their length, equally arbitrary, is determined by the stipulated length over which expectations should hold. Disequilibrium, or the disappointment of expectations, brings about the instantaneous revision of expectations at the end of a period and announces the beginning of another. Despite adjustments between periods due to disequilibrium, an economic system in each period is always in equilibrium. Hicks's method in pure positive economics is thus one of proposing equilibria for dynamic theory.

The equilibrium path as a standard of reference

Equilibrium, in Hicks's applied positive economics (that is, his applied counterpart to pure positive economics), is determined in relation to a process in the course of time. In applied positive economics, actual economic facts of the past and parameters of the future pertinent to a particular historical period are relevant. Information about both the past and the future determine the equilibrium. Past parameters are introduced as givens through the current resources in which they are embodied. The future, which, however, 'has no such *current* representative' (1965a, p. 24), must be expressed by expectations.

Since theories of applied positive economics are concerned with particular lapses of time, Hicks felt it necessary to distinguish between an equilibrium at one point in time and an equilibrium over a lapse of time. The applied counterparts of Hicks's pure equilibria are his stock equilibrium and flow equilibrium. With the help of these further notions of equilibrium, he could conceive the concepts of a growth equilibrium and a path equilibrium as standards of reference in a dynamic economics.

Hicks assumed specific definitions for his pure equilibria in continuous time: equilibrium at a point in time as the state at that point at which individuals have reached 'a preferred position, with respect to their expectations' (1965a, p. 24), and equilibrium over a given lapse of time as one in which at every point of time there is equilibrium based upon expectations for every point of time within the lapse. In the case of continuous time, as soon as expectations are expressed, there is an immediate drive to fulfill them, that is, a tendency to move toward that state. It is, however, only the equilibrium at a point in time which should be conceived as a goal to which there can be a tendency. Equilibrium over lapse of time serves as a standard of reference for continuity in dynamic theory.

Hicks defined the applied equilibrium counterparts to his pure equilibria, stock equilibrium and flow equilibrium, as an equilibrium of the 'balance sheet' (or 'stock') whereby all assets and debts form a combination that is the alternative best in line with plans and expectations, and an equilibrium over the lapse (or 'flow') of time during which stock equilibrium is maintained. Stock and flow equilibria determine an equilibrium path or a path that the economy would follow from a starting point of stock equilibrium if everything were going exactly according to expectations. Only the remote future is still considered arbitrary. This path is Hicks's 'long-period equilibrium' (1965a, p. 93). The path serves as a standard of reference around which an economy's stock disequilibria gravitate.

Hicks referred frequently to a special-case equilibrium path, that of growth equilibrium, whose concept of equilibrium is somewhat peculiar. Growth equilibrium is an economy's equilibrium correctly foreseen over a lapse of time during which fundamental data (such as tastes and technology) are unchanging and 'the only change that is admitted is uniform expansion' at a constant rate (1965a, p. 132). During the course of growth equilibrium economic activity is changing, and current conduct is adjusted to those anticipated changes.

An absence of stock equilibrium defined disequilibrium for Hicks. While along an economy's equilibrium path what is expected is realized, along its actual path, this is not necessarily the case. It is the divergence between these two paths which measures the extent of its disequilibrium. At every point in time the actual state of an economy (its 'balance sheet') is compared to its expected state of stock equilibrium for the same point in time which serves as a reference. Since any disequilibrium is carried forward, an equilibrium path serves as a convenient standard of reference.

The discussion above has referred to continuous time with no mention of Hicks's period device. In fact, he incorporated it only in a scheme of discrete time, by equating a point in time to a period and a lapse of time to a series of periods. 'Equilibrium at a point in time' became 'equilibrium of the single period' and 'equilibrium over a lapse of time' became 'equilibrium over a sequence of periods'. The same relationship between equilibrium at a point in time and equilibrium over a lapse of time holds between a single period and a sequence of periods. The equilibrium path for a sequence of periods in growth equilibrium, for example, would exhibit a regular and uniform step function; the analysis still consists in a comparison of states.

In sum, Hicks used the concept of equilibrium in three different manners. His first two equilibria are states to be referred to in the remainder of this chapter as the optimal equilibrium state and the expectation equilibrium state. His third, the flow equilibrium path, a series of states, is about process. These three concepts of equilibrium, though distinct, are related and often, as will be illustrated below, were employed by Hicks either in pairs or all together.

With Hicks's three meanings and possible applications of equilibrium clarified, it will now be explained how they were fitted into the many models that he built over his six decades of writing.

Illustrations of equilibrium models

The variety of models chosen here to illustrate Hicks's use of equilibrium show also his broad interest in many aspects of economic theory: labour, general equilibrium, fixprice, flexprice, trade cycle and growth. They are presented here in their simplest versions. The detailed elements of each model will be discussed as they become pertinent in the rest of the volume.

The equilibrium of the labour model

Hicks's model of the labour market was the first in which he made extensive use of a concept of equilibrium. He first discussed the concept in the context of the labour market in 'Edgeworth, Marshall and the indeterminateness of wages' (1930b), and then applied it in his classic book *The Theory of Wages* (1932b). In his model of the labour market Hicks was concerned with questions of both welfare and positive economics; thus both his optimal and expectation equilibrium states were operative.

Hicks's theory of the labour market was initiated in his contrast of Edgeworth's and Marshall's discussions of indeterminateness or arbitrariness in fixing wages under various market conditions: monopoly, oligopoly and perfect competition. From the contrast was derived his own description of circumstances under which an equilibrium in the labour market is determinate. Like Edgeworth, Hicks accepted that contracts determined solely by market forces in a system of perfect competition yield a determinate equilibrium.

The market condition of perfect competition is characterized by free communication, total mobility of labour and an infinitely large number of buyers and sellers. Acting on his own, each individual must be free to contract with any number of others; there must be no agreement among groups to enter open contracts simultaneously. The market should be fluid, with individuals free to move from one employment into another. The labour market must function, like any other commodity market, according to the supply and demand for labour. There is to be no government, union nor any rule obstructing the market's functioning.

In perfect competition Hicks believed there would be full determinateness for at least two important reasons. 'Determinateness' meant, for him, in part perfect foresight, that is, expectations fulfilled. First, employers and workers alike foresee fluctuations in their demands ([1932b] 1963b, p. 50). For example, in the case in which a worker demands a higher wage than that arrived at by other workers and employers, the worker knows that the employer will offer only the going wage and threaten dismissal if the worker insists. In another instance, if an employer offers a lower wage than the going market wage, then he knows that the worker, threatening to leave, would demand a higher wage. Each knows that workers without jobs will lower their wage demands and employers wanting additional workers will raise their wage offers.

Second, once employers and workers act independently in large numbers the bargaining power of any one individual is severely limited. 'As the number of buyers and sellers is increased, the minimum rises and the maximum falls. Thus, in the limit, the range of indeterminateness will tend to disappear, and we have a state of perfect competition with determinate equilibrium' (1930b, pp. 220–1). Any range of indeterminateness due to bargaining power is thus highly reduced; according to Hicks, indeterminateness would be 'far more likely to be due to the characteristics of the trade cycle than to any "bargaining advantage"' (p. 231).

So Hicks described the equilibrium of an ideal labour market in pure positive economics. Although his description gives the impression that the labour market undergoes a process of actual adjustment, in fact it merely records a scenario by which market forces in perfect competition work themselves out. The resulting equilibrium is the expected equilibrium state.

Hicks was also interested in welfare economics questions related to the labour market. He described the conditions under which a market arrives at an optimal equilibrium state. The level of wages is fixed such that demand and supply balance, and there is no tendency for wages to rise or to fall. The balancing of demand and supply is brought about by a stationary demand in each firm's labour force; no employer has any incentive to vary the size of the firm's labour force. The supply of labourers is thus given. Their efficiencies are given and equal such that every labourer receives the same wage. That wage is equal to the value of the marginal product of the labourers. 'In equilibrium, both the scale of production and the method of production must be chosen in such a way that no opportunity remains open for employers [or workers] to benefit themselves by a change' ([1932b] 1963b, p. 11).

Hicks's two labour market equilibria, expected and optimal, have different functions. In welfare economics, any economic system, with given technology and factors of production, will generate various optimum states which together form a frontier of maximum output. In the context of the labour market, every point on the frontier represents a state of equilibrium. Realization of conditions of perfect competition is so unlikely, however, that the position an economy attains (under imperfect competition) will lie within the frontier. In an actual economy, welfare disequilibrium, meaning departure from the optimum, inevitably occurs, but a comparison of the optimal ideal states and the actual state is still of concern.

As for the expected equilibrium of positive economics, on the other hand, a frontier as optimal is 'irrelevant'. What is relevant now is the difference between actual and expected outcomes. Of ultimate interest is 'the way in which the *actual* position [of an economy] will change in response to changes in data' ([1932b] 1963b, p. 333). The most accessible means of determining an economy's response is to compare the degree of disequilibrium between one actual (and expected) position and other actual (and expected) positions which may arise in different circumstances. For example, 'a change in demand for the finished product will be met by employers in a different way according as they expect it to be temporary or permanent; this expectation will affect their demand for labour and so will affect wages' (1930b, p. 230).

If, by comparison, the degree of disequilibrium is deemed to be least when the increased demand is expected to be brief, Hicks posited that change in demand would not lead to any extension of a firm; it would be met instead by extending workers' hours and 'only to a slight extent by taking on more labour' (1930b, p. 230).

Hicks used the concept of equilibrium in two senses in the context of the labour market, in the sense of the optimal and the expectation equilibrium. In each case he achieved a model of the market in equilibrium by adapting his 'abstract and rigorous' conceptions of equilibrium. In each case he effectively ruled out truly dynamic problems.

Temporary equilibrium model and the 'bread' model equilibrium

Hicks's labour market theory was influenced by the capital theory and marginal theory of J. B. Clark and Bohm Bawerk which he believed were both inherently stationary state theories. In his article 'Wages and interest: the dynamic problem' (1935f) and in *Value and Capital* (1939a) Hicks introduced an equilibrium method compatible with economic dynamics which he said was inspired by the works of Lindahl and Myrdal. In so doing he introduced a method of equilibrium which was different from the one used in his *Theory of Wages*.

Hicks's temporary equilibrium model was the dynamic analysis of price determination in the multi-market model fully elaborated in *Value and Capital*. He began by presenting the micro-foundation of a value theory, then he generalized it into a macro-theory. He started by working out the static aspects of the market mechanism. Then he attempted to integrate the concepts of money, capital, expectations and the 'week' period to provide what he called the foundation of the macro-dynamic theory.

The inherent feature of this method is that equilibrium is quickly obtained on Monday morning and prevails during the week. The temporary equilibrium of the following week can be different if market conditions are different. The temporary equilibrium during the current week depends on what is inherited from the past and 'the economic problem consists in the allotment of these resources, inherited from the past, among the satisfaction of present wants and future wants' (1939a, p. 130).

Hicks considered first a highly abstract and simplified 'bread' economy model with the following assumptions. In a perfect competition model, he assumed a production of a single homogenous good: bread. Bread is produced by homogenous labour and heterogeneous capital. Capital includes land, machinery, buildings, raw materials and half-finished output, all of which Hicks called equipment. He considered one period in which past information is taken as datum at the beginning of the period. At the beginning, there exists a certain amount of equipment and finished goods owned by entrepreneurs. Against these assets, entrepreneurs have debts to labour and rentiers. All prices including the rate of interest are expressed in terms of bread. On Monday, loans are made for one week, and this implies that all loans are short.

In the 'bread' model Hicks considered three markets: product, labour and loans, where respectively price, wages and interest are determined by supply and demand of three social groups of entrepreneurs, labourers and rentiers. The price of bread is used as numeraire, which leaves only wages and the rate of interest to be determined. Since Hicks distinguished current prices from expected prices, four variables – current wages, current interest, expected wages and expected interest – have to be determined.

Given this very simple model Hicks tried to determine a plan 'which maximises the present value of the entrepreneur's net assets'. He then analysed the substitution effect between inputs and outputs in various hypothetical situations (for example, changing one price while keeping everything else constant). The prices are determined by supply and demand.

> These demands and supplies are simply the resultants of the actions of individual entrepreneurs, labourers and rentiers; so that in order to discover the principles governing them, we have to examine the position

> of the representative entrepreneur, a representative labourer, and a representative rentier respectively. (1935f, p. 459)

Decisions to consume depend on present and future preferences of entrepreneurs; labourers and rentiers and also on relative present and future prices. Production on the other hand depends on profitability. The value of net assets depends partly on current prices and partly on expected prices. (Expected prices are pure estimates.)

> the marginal productivity conditions are therefore enough to determine the production plan . . . like the marginal productivity conditions of static theory, our present marginal productivity conditions are only a means to an end. What we want to discover from them is the way in which the firm's production plan will be affected by changes in the prices and price anticipations which govern it . . . changes with which we are concerned are purely hypothetical changes. We are still on our first Monday; we are examining the differences between the production plan actually adopted and that which would have been adopted if price-anticipations had been different. (1935f, pp. 461–2)

Thus Hicks's 'bread' model is a simple application of his expectation equilibrium state (the second definition of equilibrium above). The exercise consists in analysing notional changes and comparing them to the production plan actually adopted. If discrepancy arises between the expected and the actual, then the degree of disequilibrium is that described under the expectation equilibrium state.

Hicks extended his 'bread' model into a general equilibrium model referred to as the temporary equilibrium model. His technique was to use equilibrium analysis for one period when more than one period of time is involved. He assumed that the same good in two different periods is considered as two different goods and therefore that every good is dated only once. If there are n goods which can be found in m periods, then the model will contain $n \times m$ goods (or markets) and subsequently $n \times m$ prices are to be determined. The question of price determination becomes a matter of counting and solving equations of demands and supplies. Notice the similarity of this model and that of Walras described in Hicks's 'Leon Walras' (1934d).

The model consists of $n - 1$ equations of supply and demand for commodities, one equation of supply and demand for loan, and one equation of supply and demand for money, making a system of $n + 1$ equations all together. If the price of one good is taken as numeraire, there remain $n - 1$ prices and one interest rate to be determined. The system has therefore one equation too many. Assuming a state of equilibrium, Hicks used Walras's law to discard one equation, leaving the system with *n* equations to determine *n* unknowns.

In the temporary equilibrium model Hicks did not restrict himself simply to counting and discussing equations. He also attempted to take into account the Marshallian bargaining process in the determining of prices. He supposed, like Marshall, that during the bargaining process people come to the market on Monday morning not knowing exactly what the market conditions are. They begin by fixing prices through trial and error, trade takes place and 'in the course of trading the price will move up and down' (1939a, p. 128). While exchanges are going on, buyers and sellers are adjusting their plans and decisions.

The bargaining process takes place because people do not have precise knowledge about the market. Some arbitrary price is fixed at the opening of the market, then exchange takes place. This is the first information of the market reaction. Buyers and sellers will then realize that too much or too little has been sold at that price. Some information is now available to them and the prices are revised accordingly. In the second round, buyers and sellers will exchange commodities at the revised prices. The resulting exchange will provide further information about market reactions and the process continues. When information is imperfect, the process can go on forever without converging to any equilibrium, and over the course of one period like goods are sold at varying prices. Hicks's so-called bargaining process does not resemble Marshall's, since Hicks ruled out exchange at varying prices. Hicks tells us that when the market opens on a Monday morning, it 'proceeds quickly and smoothly to a position of temporary equilibrium' (1939a, p. 123). In fact Hicks does not pay much attention at all to the process of equilibration and assumes the system 'to be always in equilibrium' (1939a, p. 131).

Furthermore, even if, as already noted, the length of Hicks's 'week' period is fairly arbitrary and defined in terms of expectation, in this model he added some confusion by saying that 'it may often be legitimate to spin it out into something like a Marshallian "short-period" – the time during which existing equipment (in a broader or narrow sense) can be taken as given' (1939a, p. 247).

Hicks, however, did not further refer to the complexities of considering the life of capital equipments in defining his period. Instead he implicitly retained capital constant during the whole of any week period. For the economy as a whole there are simply too many different kinds of capital and contracts with different lengths. His week period is instead consistently artificially imposed, and it is assumed that all changes can only take place at the beginning on Monday: 'No new contracts can be made until Monday week' (1939a, p. 122). The length of the week period is the same for all individuals and all firms. The model cannot incorporate the overlapping of various periods which would result if periods corresponded to specific markets and their capital. An opportunity arising in the middle of the 'week' which might make some individuals or firms better off (even without making others worse off), cannot be seized on the spot, but will have to wait until the beginning of the next Monday. It is thus clear that while Hicks referred to Marshall's bargaining process and his definition of short period, Hicks' own concepts are unMarshallian.

To reconcile the attractive idea of a process of bargaining with the concept of equilibrium Hicks supposed 'perfect contemporaneous knowledge' (1939a, p. 123). It permits that instantaneously at the opening of the market on Monday morning, equilibrium will be reached, since people are assumed to have precise knowledge about the equilibrium prices. It does not mean that this precise knowledge holds into the indefinite future; it is limited to the period. Hicks treated 'a process of change as consisting of a series of temporary equilibria; this enables us still to use equilibrium analysis in the dynamic field' (p. 127). During the 'week' period, equilibrium over time is defined as the situation which occurs not only 'when demands equal supplies at the currently established prices, but also when the same prices continue to rule at all dates' (p. 132). Hicks explicitly admitted that 'our method seems to imply that we conceive of the economic system as being always in equilibrium' (p. 131).

In the temporary equilibrium model Hicks seemed to use the concept of equilibrium both in the sense of an optimal equilibrium state and an expectation equilibrium state. Since, on the one hand, he defined equilibrium as 'the most preferred position' (1939a, p. 58) and disequilibrium as 'a mark of waste' (p. 133), clearly this is compatible with the definition of optimal equilibrium state above. On the other hand, the introduction of plans in the analysis allowed him to relate 'those actions devoted to the present ends and those actions which are directed to the future' (pp. 123–4). He assumed that plans adopted in one week period depend both on current prices and on the expectations of future prices. Indeed, he interpreted expectations 'in a strict and rigid way', and assumed that 'every individual has a definite idea of what he expects any price which concerns him to be in any future week' (p. 124). With, however, his accompanying definition of disequilibrium as 'the extent to which expectations are cheated, and plans go astray' (p. 132), and his insistence that the discrepancy between anticipated and realized prices was of extreme theoretical importance, Hicks was thus also using the notion of equilibrium in the sense of expectation equilibrium state.

In the temporary equilibrium model, Hicks was dealing with an artificial device: a world of perfect competition, definite expectations, synchronizations of decisions and plans within the week. He excluded uncertainty altogether from the analysis; he said of it, 'I can do very little about it' (1939a, p. 126). There is no difference between the analysis at one point in time or during the period of time. Even though there is constant reference to a period of time, nothing is said about flow and stock equilibrium. Hicks's model was about states of equilibrium and not about a process.

Hicks on Keynes's equilibrium model

Another interesting Hicksian illustration of the concept of equilibrium along the lines of the temporary equilibrium model is found in his interpretation of Keynes. Hicks reviewed Keynes's *General Theory of Employment, Interest and Money* when it was first published in 1936. In his review, 'Mr Keynes' Theory of Employment' (1936b), Hicks discussed his interpretation of Keynes's method of equilibrium, the very interpretation Hicks had himself adopted for his well-known IS–LM framework. More will be said about Hicks on Keynes in a subsequent chapter, 'Keynes and Keynesian Economics'. The discussion in this section is limited to Hicks's interpretation of Keynes's concept of equilibrium.

Hicks's first reaction to the *General Theory* was to refute its generality; he simply referred to it as a theory of employment. None the less, he accepted that it was a new theory of employment in terms of the practical problems of unemployment. (Thus it falls within Hicks's classification of applied economics.) Hicks saw Keynes's theory as employing a shifting equilibrium method. He understood the theory to be not about a static world but about a changing economy. He wrote, with 'Mr Keynes' method – even in a changing economy, supplies and demands are equal'; stocks exist and are carried over into the future. In Keynes, 'current supply is then largely determined by people's willingness to hold goods over the future, and that depends on their expectations for the future' (1936b, p. 239). According to Hicks, in Keynes's theory it is possible to use equilibrium analysis in a world of actual disequilibrium.

Presenting Keynes's *General Theory* in the context of equilibrium allowed Hicks to say that Keynes's method was not new; indeed some

Swedish economists and he himself had already looked at the use of this type of equilibrium method in a disequilibrium situation. Despite Hicks's expressed admiration for Keynes's equilibrium method as one of a stock and flow process, his own pragmatic interpretation of Keynes's method was much closer to his static expectational equilibria. Since Hicks's interest was in determinateness, he analysed Keynes's method as effectively confined to a short period. Hicks's account of the details of Keynes's equilibrium method reduced it to his own expectation equilibrium state.

It is thus evident why Hicks insisted that 'the point of the [Keynes's] method is that it reintroduces determinateness into a process of change'. How did Hicks perceive this determinateness to have been introduced by Keynes? In the short period, with expectations and the stock of goods, including capital, given, output and employment of labour can be determined. Hicks then proceeded to extend Keynes's theory to comparative statics:

> we can deduce, by ordinary economic reasoning, what the outputs, employment and prices would be if expectations were different, capital equipment different, tastes different, and so on. But all that this reasoning gives us is hypothetical results ... The method is thus an admirable one for analysing the impact effect of disturbing causes. (1936b, p. 241)

It is thus clear that because Hicks first perceived Keynes's theory as being one of applied economics; and since Keynes, in the *General Theory*, was concerned with expectations and the realization of plans (not with optimality in the welfare sense), reference to Keynes's equilibrium as optimal equilibrium state is ruled out.

In Keynes, Hicks saw a notion of 'period' based on expectations like his own week period, of short enough length to permit ignoring changes in expectations. While emphasizing the period's being based on expectations, he also was aware that Keynes's short period was Marshallian. Keynes's division of expectations into two types, short and long term, enabled him, according to Hicks, to divide the economy into two industries (capital or investment goods, and consumer goods) and to make the capital industry depend on long-term expectations and the consumer goods industry depend on short-term expectations. Hicks took inspiration from the fact that Keynes had applied Marshallian partial equilibrium analysis to the consumer goods industry, while keeping the capital goods industry constant (1936b, p. 243). From this perspective Hicks believed that Keynes's method was, like his temporary equilibrium method, confined to short-period analysis.

Hicks recognized in Keynes a notion of 'degree of disequilibrium', related to changes in stocks. The degree of disequilibrium is determined by the carrying over of unsold stocks. The integration of this notion into Hicks's concept of equilibrium was tricky. Hicks's confining of Keynes' method to short-period analysis in which changes in expectations are ignored meant that within each period all stocks were considered to be in equilibrium, and disequilibrium was only to be recognized in the resetting of expectations 'between' periods. A further tricky aspect derived from the fact the expectations under discussion in Keynes are those of entrepreneurs. So with equivocation, it was possible both for Hicks and for Keynes to posit during any given short period the fulfilment of entrepreneurs' expectations and an economy in temporary equilibrium. For Keynes, the expectations of entrepreneurs are fulfilled and their operation is in equilibrium, although the economy as a whole is in a state of persisting disequilibrium due to underemployment. Firms will continue to produce that level of output that they expect they can sell, even though it is not necessarily at the full employment output level, a situation which may persist for some time. For Hicks, stocks are always in equilibrium in the short period, which also means fulfilment of expectations. His exclusive interest in theory allowed him to consider long-term expectations as exogenous in terms of short-term equilibrium. This meant that to his mind Keynes's method resembled that of the expectation equilibrium state of his temporary equilibrium model.

Trade cycle equilibrium model

In Hicks's model of the trade cycle is another illustration of his equilibrium concept, in fact the first example of his flow equilibrium path. Of Keynesian influence, it surfaced when Hicks reviewed Harrod's *Toward a Dynamic Economics* of 1948 in 'Mr Harrod's Dynamic Theory' (1949d), and later when he wrote *A Contribution to the Theory of the Trade Cycle* (1950a).

Hicks's theory of the trade cycle describes the interaction between consumption, investment and income. By introducing lags for these three variables and by keeping other variables (prices, expectation, interest rate and money) constant, Hicks showed that it was possible to build a trade cycle model in which the lagged interaction of his three variables generates a cyclical fluctuation. Hicks's objective was to model the movement of the trade cycle that was tied, as it were, to a long-term equilibrium trend of economic progression and contained within the binding limits of two other long-term parallel equilibria (an employment ceiling and an investment floor). Hicks's theory of the trade cycle movement had as its foundation the impact of the multiplier and accelerator processes (successive effects of the change of income on changing investment and vice versa), cumulative from the start and thus causing the movement to turn away from the equilibrium trend. Ceiling or floor barriers were thus considered necessary devices to stop the movement from continuing to diverge further and to reverse its course.

To design a model for his trade cycle theory Hicks asked, 'is there any possibility of steady "equilibrium" with reference to which fluctuations might subsequently be defined?' (1950a, p. 56). He proposed using the concept of 'regular progressive' equilibrium, according to which output increases at a constant rate and induced investment and saving are constant proportions of output. In Hicks's model, for the economy to be in regular progressive equilibrium, 'it is not sufficient that capital stock should be adjusted to current output; it is also necessary that it should fall due for replacement at the right dates. The induced investment . . . must be such as to be consistent with steady development' (1950a, p. 64).

Just as he isolated induced investment, Hicks also gave an important role to autonomous investment. It does not occur in response to current changes in output, but is assumed to be given exogenously. In progressive equilibrium, saving and investment are thus related such that 'autonomous investment + induced investment = saving' (1950a, p. 59). In Hicks's model, if *ex ante* investment was always equal to *ex ante* saving, the economy would consistently be in a (Keynesian) equilibrium state. The regular progressive equilibrium path is thus the one which the economy would follow 'if the system remained continually in this sort of equilibrium' (1949d, p. 107), where the growth rates of saving, induced investment and output were all the same.

It is, of course, not the case that the economy is consistently either in an equilibrium state or on an equilibrium path; disequilibrium must be considered. In the trade cycle model, disequilibria of supply and demand, that is, the accumulating or divesting of stocks, were taken care of by the 'period' device. But Hicks noted one type of stock disequilibrium which the period device alone could not handle: 'this is the case in which demands are persistently ahead of supplies at ruling prices, the disequilibrium being met by postponement of delivery' (1950a, p. ix).

The trade cycle model was thus especially designed to deal with the divergence from the equilibrium which occurs when steady development, and the preconditioned changes in output and induced investment which it implies, cannot keep up with demand. Hicks observed that any system which has not been in approximate equilibrium for a long time will in fact be particularly vulnerable to divergence from progressive equilibrium with its upsetting infusions and witholdings of equilibrating investment. In fact the theoretical multiplier and accelerator processes of investment underlying Hicks's model meant that the real challenge for the model was to describe any constancy in a situation of perpetual divergence. Hicks introduced devices which contained any deviation within an upper and lower limit. These took the form of two more equilibria: a ceiling equilibrium and a slump equilibrium.

Hicks supposed the existence of an exogenous direct restraint upon upward expansionary deviation in the form of a scarcity of employable resources (1950a, p. 95). This was his 'full employment' ceiling equilibrium. If an economy is making use of all of its available resources and capacity and sustains its activity at that highest limit of its potential, then it is following the full employment path. This path is, according to Hicks, a long-term equilibrium trend which grows at the natural rate of growth of the population. It defines the limits of trade expansion; no economy will grow any faster than this rate for any length of time.

Hicks also supposed an exogenous limit in depressionary deviation. His floor or slump equilibrium is the point at which investment is at its lowest level possible for the economy still to function. He maintained that when an economy is in a depression, depreciation of capital does slow disinvestment considerably but it does so without bringing it to zero. For Hicks, an economy might conceivably remain for a while in its lowest slump, during which time it would follow its slump equilibrium path.

Hicks stipulated that all three equilibrium paths follow the same growth rate as autonomous investment, which is assumed to grow at a constant rate. Thus given one equilibrium path to which consumption, investment and income are related, two equilibrium paths which establish exogenously the extreme limits of that relationship and the multiplier and accelerator processes mechanism as its dynamic catalysis, Hicks created a model which showed that an economy 'would have a tendency to oscillate ... [and] that a cycle can be generated' (1950a, p. 64).

The new equilibrium of Hicks's trade cycle model, the regular progressive equilibrium, is a flow equilibrium path. Hicks said nothing in his trade cycle type of equilibrium about optimality or expectations. While the silence, and other evidence, would rule out this equilibrium's being of the optimal equilibrium type, Hicks's regular progress equilibrium is, none the less, compatible with the expectation equilibrium state. At each point on the flow path what is expected is realized;

expectations are assumed constant and the long-term change allowed is foreseen. Also, since the economy on that path is in flow equilibrium, stock equilibrium, a form of expectation equilibrium state, is implied.

Imperfect competition equilibrium model

Another example of Hicks's use of equilibrium is found in his lesser-known article, 'The process of imperfect competition' (1954a), in which he combined his 'week' period device, expectations and Marshall's short- and long-period distinctions.

Hicks analysed the fate of a firm which sets up a new plant for a new product in an oligopolistic market. He supposed that the course of events is divided into three periods: the construction period during which the new plant's new product output is zero; a closed period in which the new plant is operational and the firm is the only one producing the new type of output because the competition has not yet completed similar plants; finally, an open period in which the market is openly competitive among many firms producing the same product. The closed period is of limited length, while the open period is of an indefinite length. Hicks supposed that the output per week during the closed period corresponds to the Marshallian short-period output (fixed capacity of production), and that of open period corresponds to the Marshallian long-period output (variable capacity).

Hicks distinguished between the static short-period expectations and the dynamic long-period expectations of the firm. Short-period expectations are the firm's expectations of market demand for output in the closed period. These expectations are effective in both the construction period and the closed period, in dictating the plant's capacity, as well as in that portion of the open period while the firm is realizing that competition is swallowing up a share of its market demand and the replacement of plant capital has not yet occurred. Long-term expectations bring about changes in the firm's initial production strategy for readjusting its capacity at the time when its original equipment has worn out. Thus it is attached to a later phase of the open period.

Static and dynamic are adjectives used by Hicks in reference to capacity. During the closed period, the firm produces at static capacity, that is, it produces all it has planned to produce, which includes a static excess capacity (in reserve). But soon the market is open to competition; if there is any profit to be made, more firms are attracted to the market which should now be considered an industry. Their entry diminishes the initial firm's share of the market (provided that demand has not increased), hence the sales of the initial firm in the open period are less than those in its closed period. The firm, left with dynamic excess capacity (higher than desired reserves), finds itself in stock disequilibrium, while newly established firms produce just enough, with an additional static excess capacity. In a process of the consecutive entry of newer firms into the market, older firms find themselves having to 'continue with their dynamic excess capacity until their plant wears out; when it does so, they replace it with a new plant, more appropriate to their now reduced circumstances'. Ultimately 'the industry is supposed to settle into a *long-period equilibrium*' (1954a, p. 44).

Equilibrium in this model means the realization of plans for market demand, fulfilment of expectations of sales. Disequilibrium 'arises from discrepancy between actual demand conditions and those which were planned for' (1954a, p. 44). The existence of static excess capacity means that the equilibrium of a period is a stock equilibrium. Dynamic excess capacity is a stock disequilibrium, the carry over of an unplanned-for excess of stocks of goods (including capital). In the closed period, for a given demand for its product the firm is all the time in equilibrium since what is expected is realized. In the open period the firm will reach an equilibrium state only when its capacity adjusts to competition. For the industry as a whole, there is a tendency toward an equilibrium state even though some firms might exit from the market.

The equilibrium of Hicks's closed period is an expectation equilibrium state. In the open period, when a firm reaches its equilibrium it finds itself again in an expectation equilibrium state. Now because Hicks takes into consideration stocks and stock equilibrium these period equilibria can also be interpreted as a flow equilibrium path.

The equilibrium of the traverse model

Hicks's use of the three meanings of equilibrium culminated in his traverse model. It is a growth theory model first introduced in his *Capital and Growth* (1965a), then modified and elaborated in his 'The Austrian theory of capital and its rebirth in modern economics' (1973a) and in *Capital and Time* (1973d). Growth theory, Hicks said, 'is no more than a particular Dynamic Economics' (1965a, p. 14).

Hicks began in 1965 with a simple classical model. It is a steady state growth equilibrium of discrete processes of production in which commodities are produced by means of commodities. He assumed a two-sector model of one consumption good and one capital good. Hicks adopted the linear system of Sraffa in which coefficients of production are fixed, but he preferred to call it 'the classical system'. In this system three relationships are established: profit is related to the wage rate in the price equation; the rate of growth is linked to output and consumption in the quantity equation; and finally, in a saving equation, the rate of profit (of the price equation) is related to the rate of growth (of the quantity equation). In this complete system, 'the equilibrium of the economy, at its given rate of real wages, is completely determined' (1965a, p. 142).

The growth equilibrium of the model, an equilibrium already defined earlier, was that of an economy expanding at a constant growth rate, while tastes and technology are unchanging and the economy is experiencing both stock equilibrium and flow equilibrium. It is the progressive equilibrium path or the flow equilibrium path.

With this model and its form of equilibrium Hicks addressed two types of question. One dealt with the comparison of the growth equilibrium paths of two distinct economies. The other was the enquiry into how an economy might move from one equilibrium to another.

The first question is a simple comparison of two equilibrium paths. Equilibrium in its context is that of the flow equilibrium path without reference to optimality or expectations. Hicks did not elaborate on the significance of comparing the equilibria of two different economies, but rather turned to a second question the first one had raised: the complexity of modelling a single economy's non-steady state growth rate.

Hicks started to answer the second question with the instance of an economy, growing along an equilibrium path, in which the rate of growth of one factor of production is suddenly different from the rate of growth of another factor. He questioned whether it would be possible to maintain full employment of both factors and to reach thereby a new equilibrium path. Hicks showed that when the coefficients of production are fixed – depending on which factor is growing faster or slower than the other and whether the sector in question (consumer goods or investment goods) is capital or labour intensive – in certain cases there can be an easy convergence to a new, full, equilibrium, in other cases no smooth adjustment (to full equilibrium) occurs. In the case where convergence is possible, Hicks suggested making the transition easier by allowing for some flexibility in the utilization of factors, that is, to use surplus goods at more than their normal capacity and to under-utilize the scarce goods. For example, if labour is growing faster than capital, he asked, how can capital be increased to incorporate the increased supply of labour, while keeping all factors employed?

Hicks started his analysis with an economy in a steady state equilibrium.

He then asked how another steady state equilibrium might be reached if the initial one were disturbed. Since in a steady state equilibrium there is both stock and flow equilibrium, the equilibrium of Hicks's traverse model must be that of a flow equilibrium path. Should the economy experience the full employment of its resources, its flow equilibrium path also represents a sequence of optimal equilibrium states. Since the traverse model also focused on disruptions in the equilibrated use of resources, Hicks also recognized disequilibrium. To describe disequilibrium, he had to distinguish between stock and flow equilibrium in this model. Disequilibrium could mean either a complete departure from any form of equilibrium path (the traverse period disequilibrium) or it could be used to describe the degree of difference of the economy's realizing stock and flow equilibrium path from its full or optimal stock and flow equilibrium path. In the latter, stock and flow equilibrium exists and yet some resources are unemployed. For such an equilibrium to be sustained there must be fulfilment of the entrepreneurs' expectations, although those of the economy as a whole will not be realized. Thus this equilibrium, the Keynesian underemployment equilibrium, is compatible with a series of expectation equilibrium states.

Hicks was dissatisfied both with his model's excessive emphasis on steady state equilibria and with its rigid one capital and one consumption good traverse model. In 1973 he proposed a modified version of his earlier traverse model.

It was a very simple model in which a production process converts a flow of input into a flow of output. Hicks assumed a fixed coefficient production function and constant return to scale. He supposed one type of input (homogeneous labour) and one type of output (consumer good) in a completely integrated process; there is no reference in his equations to intermediary transformations. The machines and equipment required for production are produced and absorbed within the process. In the model there is only one interest rate, one given price, and one input–output ratio. Input and output are expressed in terms of their value. Wages are expressed in terms of output. All processes have the same time-span, and all are carried through as planned.

The model functions with two distinct periods: a construction period during which machines are built and the utilization period in which these machines are operational. During any period of time, new machines are being produced, while machines previously produced are in operation. At any period there are many processes operating at the same time. While some have just started, some are at their half-life operation and others are near to their retirement. The number of processes which exist at a particular point in time depends on the number of processes started in the past. For convenience Hicks took the year as his unit of time. He supposed all unit-processes identical. All are carried through as planned, that is, all processes are terminating processes. All processes have the same life-span and the same time profile. The rate at which machines are produced is constant.

As in his first traverse model, Traverse I, Hicks derived three relationships for his Traverse II model: the wage–interest relationship, the productivity–growth relation and a saving function. He established the system as complete and then asked what would happen if a technological change were to disturb the equilibrium path of an economy by bearing the impact of saving labour, either in the construction or in the utilization phase.

As in his earlier model of 1965, Hicks supposed the economy as having been in a steady-state equilibrium under an old technique, when an invention or 'impulse' makes a new technique available which is more profitable than the old one. If this change occurs, how will it affect the activity of this economy? Hicks investigated how under the assumptions of maintaining full employment and allowing underemployment the convergence to a new equilibrium is possible. In the case of full employment, the equilibrium in question is that of the flow equilibrium path compatible with a series of optimal equilibrium states. In the case of underemployment, it is a description of a flow equilibrium path consistent with a series of expectation equilibrium states. As will be discussed in a later chapter on dynamics, in Hicks's modified traverse model he was more concerned with the dynamics of traverse analysis than with the concept of equilibrium or the issue of convergence.

These various illustrations of models show that Hicks was consistent in his use of equilibrium though the concept of equilibrium took on different meanings. Over time Hicks became increasingly conscious both of the importance of use of equilibrium as a standard of reference as well as of the constraints its use entails. He became more and more persuaded that in fact the real focus of economic analysis should be dynamics. Before turning to his dynamics, however, clarification of how Hicks understood market functions is necessary.

3

Fixprice, Flexprice and a Theory of Markets

The relationships between quantities and the determination of prices is the most important feature in economic theory, whether at the micro- or macro-economic level. In a great deal of his writing Hicks treated the very questions related to this issue: How are markets organized? How do they work? Who fixes the prices? When and why do firms hold inventory stocks? Since the issue of prices and quantities is central to practically all of Hicks's theoretical work, it is appropriate to devote a chapter to it here.

Hicks used the term 'flexprice' to describe models in which prices are flexible and determined endogenously, and the term 'fixprice' for those in which prices are relatively stable and given exogenously. Although the terms 'fixprice' and 'flexprice' surfaced rather late in Hicks's vocabulary (in the 1960s), the concepts were familiar throughout his time and used in his own work and in that of others. All of Hicks's models are easily identifiable in terms of the two concepts. His early models were designed for particular markets, that is, ones which accommodate only flexprice or fixprice theory. For example, his temporary equilibrium model of *Value and Capital* (1939a) was a pure flexprice model, while his *A Contribution to the Theory of the Trade Cycle* (1950a) was a pure fixprice model. Hicks recognized later that neither a fixprice nor a flexprice theory was realistic; 'What we need', he wrote, 'is a theory which will take account of both sorts of markets, a theory in which both fixprice and flexprice markets have a place' (1974b, p. 24). His new theory was already sketched in 'Methods of dynamic analysis' (1956c), to be developed subsequently in *Capital and Growth* (1965a) and applied in *Capital and Time* (1973d), in *The Crisis in Keynesian Economics* (1974b), in 'Some questions of time in economics' (1976f) and in *A Market Theory of Money* (1989a).

How markets work

In order to explain how prices and quantities are related in Hicks's flexprice or fixprice theory, it is useful to begin by explaining how he considered markets are organized and how they work. Hicks distinguished three types of market organization: '(1) dealings between merchants, (2) dealings between merchants and non-merchants, and (3) direct dealings between non-merchants' (1976f, p. 148). The third type is the least conventional, best exemplified by 'the market in private dwelling-houses' where an agent brings a buyer and a seller together and advises them of a suggested price. The agent receives a commission for his services. Hicks called this an imperfect market and expanded very little on it. It is the other two types which he discussed at length.

Examples of the first type of market he called 'the most perfectly organized'. In these, 'specialist traders trade with one another'. This is closer to the type of market Walras treated. Traders 'develop needs for assurance about the carrying-through of their dealings – needs for legal assurances about property and contract, and other related matters' (1976f, p. 148).

In the second type of market, there are wholesalers and independent shopkeepers. The shopkeepers buy in order to sell, therefore they 'must buy before they sell, so they must hold stocks. The holding of unsold stocks is expensive, so their appearance is again an indication that information is imperfect' (1976f, p. 148). Both kinds of merchants play a role in fixing prices. Changes in stocks are an indication as to how prices change. The market is competitive in a simple sense, but there is also need to take into account uncertainty and the cost of information. Hicks considered this second type of market no longer the typical market, since, as he observed, it is becoming more and more the case that the shopkeeper and wholesaler are one; manufacturers market their products directly.

A variety of historians and economists of various periods have written extensively about market organization and mechanism. None the less, when it comes to modern economic theory, Walras's and Marshall's treatments of the market seem to be the ones which retain economists' attention. Like many others, Hicks too used Walras and Marshall as the foundation upon which he built his own theory of market organization. He explicitly referred to them when explaining price determination. In Walras's theory Hicks explained that the actual transactors do not make the prices; they merely accept them. The prices are made by someone else 'of undetermined providence'. Rejecting the notion of that someone as an auctioneer, Hicks referred to him as 'some independent functionary' (1977a, p. ix). Hicks thought of Walras's approach as descriptive of a very special market, not representative of most markets of his time.

Hicks said that his own approach was founded more on Marshall's ideas of market organization. For Marshall, the merchant (wholesaler or retail shopkeeper) was the key figure. He functioned 'atomistically' as an intermediary, and fixed prices. Buying in order to sell again, he determined both a buying as well as a selling price. Competition in the marketplace, in Marshall's sense, required a large number of merchants whose margin between buying and selling prices was fairly small. According to Hicks, the degree of 'narrowness of the margin would be the sign of a *highly* competitive [Marshallian] market (1977a, p. ix).

Hicks believed that in Marshall's day merchant-determined markets were the most common type. He referred to Marshallian markets as unorganized, in contrast to the special organized markets of Walras. He described the mechanism of the organized markets as working under given rules, 'of a club', as it were. Access to the organized market is 'restricted, to those who promise to keep the rules, and who are willing to pay the costs of administering them' (1977a, p. x). A system of unorganized markets, with prices determined by merchant intermediaries, might dominate, but for Hicks, its presence would not necessarily preclude the existence within the system of special Walrasian organized markets.

The Marshallian unorganized markets in which the merchant played a key role though attractive according to Hicks, seemed to fit best Marshall's time and eras still more remote. Hicks felt that in his own time their appropriateness was in notable decline. They had, to his mind, largely been replaced by markets where producers (or 'some authority'), instead of merchants, set the price. In those markets, where prices are not determined by supply and demand, demand conditions can none the less indirectly affect them, as will be explained below.

While Hicks felt that Walras's organized markets remained 'in existence in some particular fields', he assessed Marshall's type of unorganized market to be 'on the way out' (1977a, p. xi). He observed changes in the scale of industrial organization within economies from numerous small firms to firms of increasing size as well as changes in the standardization of goods as to brand and packaging. The consequences of these changes he identified as two-fold. First, both changes diminished the intermediary merchant, making 'the atomistic type of market harder to operate' (p. xi). The role of the merchant has been transferred to producers who to a large extent have thereby become more important in dictating market terms. Second, as many prices in the market-place have become 'administered' by producers, the impact of producers is not limited to economics, but has become social as well, because the changes they cause in market terms have direct implications, for example, on aggregate output and employment.

Even though Hicks observed that the role of the merchant in Marshall's type of unorganized market was changing over time, he none the less still believed that a proper theory of markets must be based on an updated form of the Marshallian type market and 'include the Walras-type market as a particular case'. (1976f, p. 147). Hicks preferred to refer to these two markets as the speculative market (Walrasian) and the manufacturer-dominated market (Marshallian).

Speculative market and manufacturers' market

Hicks set out a fundamental distinction between the speculative market of the primary merchant (wholesaler or retailer) whose markets are in raw materials and primary products except for non-storable goods, and the manufacturers' market of the secondary merchant (wholesaler or retailer), whose markets are stocks of produced materials and finished products.

Speculative market

In the speculative market, the objective of the merchant, the primary merchant, is to make a profit in one of two ways. If a speculator expects the price of a product to fall, then he would try to sell it in the current market with the promise to deliver it later, when he has bought it at the lower anticipated price. If, on the other hand, a merchant expects the price of the product he holds to rise, then he will choose to withhold all or part of the stocks in possesion from the current market and to sell them later at the higher price. Should the expectations of higher prices indeed be realized, a sustained withholding of stocks will further create a shortage of supply and cause prices to rise still higher.

For a speculative market to exist there must always be two classes of merchants: Hicks's 'optimists' who believe that the price will change in their favour and who act on the basis of those expectations, and his 'pessimists, who take it [the price] to be permanent or more permanent'. Hicks saw the speculative market as 'an "inside" market between the two classes, pessimists selling to optimists, in which (by arbitrage) a regular market is established' (1989a, pp. 15–16).

He noted further that three conditions had to be met for the speculative market to flourish:

> (1) that the article traded should be fairly standardizable, so that supply from one 'outside' supplier should be ... a good substitute for that from at least some others; (2) that dealings should be on a sufficient scale for the costs of some organization to be easily covered; and (3) that arbitrage should be possible, so that most of the participants must be merchants who may either buy or sell. (1989a, p. 19)

The three conditions are most easily satisfied in the market for raw materials and primary products, such as, for example, wheat, coffee, cocoa, therefore the speculative market restricts itself to these types of products.

Hicks believed that regardless of their practical importance, organized speculative markets should play a central role in any theory of markets, for specific reasons. They reflect the highest market sensitivity. Further, they illustrate the fact that prices are not solely determined by supplies and demands, but also 'by the way they are interpreted, thus by the state of mind of those who trade' (1989a, p. 17). In speculative transactions the role of expectations is thus crucial.

Manufacturers' market

The objective of manufacturers, secondary merchants, is also to make a profit. As do speculators, manufacturers hold stocks. They do so, however, not in order to speculate but rather to provide stability in the flow of goods or services. It was in the area of manufacturers' markets that Hicks noted a major practical change. While Marshall's analysis was based on a situation where the manufacturer sold to retailers, 'professionals, who would be able to assess just what it was they were buying', Hicks saw that the situation had changed: 'it is now the producer himself who has to take responsibility for the quality, and usefulness, of what he is selling; for he is selling, at least at the end of the chain, to a consumer who is not an expert' (1989a, pp. 24–5).

In Hicks's theory, the suppliers in the manufacturers' market are, none the less, wholesalers who sell either directly to the consumer or through retailers who have bought the product from them. In order to maintain a constant supply of goods, if the need arises, wholesalers may buy from other wholesalers, just as retailers buy from wholesalers.

The manufacturers' market is one of fairly non-homogeneous products where each supplier's product has its own individuality. Market activity will flourish only if the costs of both the manufacturer and the retailer can be covered. Further, retailer and consumer confidence must exist in the availability, quality and stability of the price of the goods supplied. The price of a good 'must not be changed arbitrarily, at a moment's notice. Arbitrary changes "unsettle" the consumer' (1989a, p. 25). As his connection to the consumer becomes more and more direct, the manufacturer uses advertising to convey information and to try to gain or to reassure the consumer's trust.

The manufacturers' market deals especially with finished products, stocks of machinery and equipment, and perishable goods. Unlike the goods of the speculative market, the goods of this market do not lend themselves to speculative transactions. Either stocks cannot be carried over because the product is perishable or they cannot be accumulated because their stockpiling would jeopardize the production. It might also be the case in some industries that the cost of holding stocks is greater than the gain from speculation, or that the uncertainty constantly exists that the value of the product held as stock might be undercut by an unexpected, new, cheaper product introduced into the market.

In both markets, since stocks play an important role, Hicks felt an interpretation had to be given to the power of supply and demand different from those found in perfectly competitive models. For Hicks, both markets functioned as a 'practical counterpart to the "perfect competition" models of the textbooks' (1989a, pp. 17, 20). Prices in the speculative market have to be seen as determined by stocks and expectations as well as by supply and demand. Hicks was to call his pricing theory of the speculative market a flexprice theory. In the manufacturers' market most prices are set by the wholesalers. Hicks referred to his pricing theory of the manufacturers' market as a fixprice theory.

So far the discussion has centred on the organization of the market. Now attention will be turned to the holding of stocks and price determination within the two distinct markets.

The leverage of stocks

Hicks observed that stocks of all possibly storable products play an important role in both the speculative market and the manufacturers' market. In both markets, their existence offers undeniable leverage in the determination of prices. He noted, however, that the role of stocks in determining prices is different, depending on the type of market. Theirs may be either a manipulative effect on the balance of supply and demand, causing great flexibility in prices, or an accommodation of supply to demand, where they have the potential to keep prices relatively fixed.

As mentioned above, every seller in the market-place expects to make a profit from his transactions, which implies that he will attempt to sell his commodities at a price higher than he himself had to pay for them. In the case of the speculative market, stocks, held in the limbo of the 'uncertainty of price-expectations' (1974b, p. 26) in the hope that prices will rise, can be highly determinating of price. Since speculative market stocks are held voluntarily out of a profit motive, that is, as each merchant deems it financially advantageous to do so, in order for a theory of the speculative market to account plausibly for its functioning, it must take factors other than supply and demand into account. Equilibrium analysis of the market reveals, in fact, that at any point in time, total demand equals total supplies of the product 'including what are added to stocks or taken from stocks'. Thus, even though 'flow demands and flow supplies are unequal', the market must be considered to be in equilibrium, that is, in temporary equilibrium, all the time (1982a, p. 232). In seeing the speculative market as a temporary equilibrium model of stock equilibrium (with lag in flow), Hicks emphasized further still the factor of stocks as the primary determinant of price in the speculative market.

Hicks was also to conclude that in the manufacturers' market, prices, whether they reflect the wholesaler's or retailer's need for profit, cannot be determined by any equation of supply and demand. The frequent inequality of supply and demand should, however, direct attention to the leverage of stocks. First, Hicks observed that in the manufacturers' market stocks are held in a less voluntary fashion than in the speculative market. To maintain their businesses at all, merchants must hold a minimum of stock, which Hicks labelled the 'normal stock' of the manufacturers' market (1974b, p. 24). Further, if demand for a product should be less than its supply, stock in excess must be held, without choice.

On the other hand, with their supply of stock, manufacturers can exercise some control over prices within their market. Although in some areas of the market, such as in perishable or non-storable commodities, there is less possibility of maintaining price stability through stock infusions than in other areas of the manufacturers' market, in general, if demand should exceed output, stocks can be brought into the market to ease the shortage. The use of stocks can thus prevent the price of the product from rising and maintain price stability. While describing the manufacturers' market in terms of a stock and flow equilibrium, Hicks emphasized that stock equilibrium was the basis of its activity. 'Flexprice theory can manage with flow equilibrium alone; but fixprice theory needs both [flow and stock] and it is stock equilibrium which is fundamental' (1982a, p. 233).

Fixprice and flexprice

Hicks gave the methods of fixprice and flexprice analysis a great deal of importance. They figured prominently among his four types of period analysis, which were divided into two groups: one comprised of (1) *ex ante* and *ex post* (expected-realized) and (2) stock–flow and another comprised of (A) *P*-models (flexprice, as it will be subsequently called) and (B) *Q*-models (fixprice, as it will be subsequently called). Hicks envisaged that one from each group of these four types of methods can be paired with one from the other: (1A, 1B, 2A, 2B). (1A) is a naïve flexprice method; an example of it was Hicks's temporary equilibrium model in which analysis is based on price adjustment, while quantities are given and both desired and realized values are taken into consideration. (2B) is a naïve fixprice method; it corresponds to Hicks's trade cycle model where quantities instead of prices are under adjustment and stocks and flows are considered. (1B) would be reflected in a model about quantity adjustment where expected and realized states are analysed, without bringing stocks or flows into account. (2A) is an awkward combined method; it is difficult to conceive of a stock-flow model in which prices are flexible with given expectations-realizations or quantities, or both.

Hicks wanted to develop two new methods: (1A2), a sophisticated flexprice method and (1B2), a sophisticated fixprice method. Both these methods of price or quantity adjustment take into consideration expected and realized values as well as stocks and flows. Hicks felt that a complete dynamic model ought to be conceived as a hybrid model from the combined method, (1AB2), a model which would take into consideration expectations and realizations, and stocks and flows, in an economy where some markets react according to flexprice, and others according to fixprice. Hicks spotted combined methods in the work of others. Part of his admiration for Keynes's *General Theory* stemmed from his having seen in it 'the most distinguished of the hybrids' (1982a, p. 218).

Although Hicks observed that 'the Fixprice method has an inherent tendency to "go macro"' (1965a, p. 78), (and one might, by the same token, associate flexprice with micro-economics) he warned against such restricted use. In fact, Hicks saw in each of the combinations of methods above (1A, 1B, 2A, 2B, 1A2, 1B2) an application either in the single market (micro) or in the aggregate (macro). Only the ultimate hybrid (1AB2) would have to be applied to more than one market simultaneously. In this latter case, one combination of methods would apply to one kind of 'market (or part of the system considered) and another to another [kind of market]' (1982a, p. 218).

Much has been said about the role of stocks in Hicks's speculative and manufacturers' market. His own early models were naïve fixprice or flexprice models in which stocks were not, to his own mind, given adequate attention. For illustrative purposes, none the less, it is useful to present an example of each type of Hicks's models which did not, he felt, give adequate attention to stocks, then to discuss their weaknesses and to explain why the traditional view of determining prices solely by equations of demand and supply must be abandoned.

Illustration of the naïve flexprice and fixprice models

This chapter's discussion begins with a brief explanation of Hicks's simplest price method, the fixprice method of his trade cycle theory. The method is straightforward, and therefore it is relatively easy to point out its weaknesses. Hicks's flexprice method, which follows, is slightly less direct, although its weaknesses can also be detected. Hicks himself recognized the failings of the price theory of each method to such an extent that he undertook their reconsideration, which is also presented below.

Early fixprice method in the trade cycle theory: Hicks's first attempts to employ a fixprice method were within his trade cycle theory. There he presented a general non-monetary macro-model based on a one product market. He devised a model in which real magnitudes could be aggregated and in which quantity, not price, variations were analysed. The variables such variation entails – output, employment, saving, investment and consumption – were introduced in a macro-economic model excluding the components of money and expectations. Hicks assumed that prices were given exogenously. This did not mean, however, that prices were not allowed to change, but that in the case of the trade cycle, they do not necessarily change when current demand and supply are not equal. Any of their variations are ignored within the model.

Hicks's analysis of the trade cycle model was entirely in real terms.

Investment and saving were aggregated in their value terms and then deflated by some general given price index. Hicks believed that 'so long as we are deflating both Investment and Saving by the same price-index, we can correctly express the Investment-Saving Equation in the form Real Investment = Real Saving' (1950a, p. 12). Hicks also assumed that 'the ratio between the price-level of consumption goods and the price-level of investment goods should be approximately constant' (p. 11). Consumption and income were likewise expressed in real terms. Since any changes in prices were supposed to be approximately proportional, their impact in the trade cycle process was ignored.

Hicks had ignored the difficulty associated with price changes, money and expectations, and only a few variables remained in his model. He was thus free to introduce an artificial period device by which he described, in a mechanical way, a cumulative process in which an increase (or decrease) in induced investment leads to an increase (or decrease) in output and income which in turn induces more (or less) investment, hence more (or less) output and income and so on. In the process stocks are lagging by one period and are being adjusted automatically over the course of the cycle. Suppose in period 0 there is an increase in demand; this increase is met by a decrease in stocks which, according to Hicks, induces some investment. In period 1 then, there will be an increase in output and in income. The additional output will be used to restore the stocks to their appropriate level. The additional income will in the subsequent period create an increase in demand which in turn will be met by a decrease in stocks, which induces further investment and so on. In Hicks's description of the trade cycle process, he also emphasized adjustments in capital. 'This has to include (1) investment in stocks, to make up for the raiding of stocks in the first phase; (2) investment in fixed capital, needed to adjust equipment to the production of the larger output' (1950a, p. 51).

In his description of the trade cycle process, Hicks was not interested in asking whether planned investments are realized or whether expectations are fulfilled. He simply assumed that there is a continuous positive adjustment in demand, output, capital and stocks, so long as there are resources available which can permit the increase, and a negative adjustment otherwise. Further, he assumed that each period was 'arbitrary in length' and that 'all induced investment corresponding to a particular change in output is concentrated in a single period' (1950a, p. 67). He avoided all complication of an overlapping and complex lag structure, since changes in the level of stocks, either as they run down or build up, mechanically generate a positive or negative cumulative process. Once the process begins, it does not stop, nor does the direction of the movement fluctuate. Hicks incorporates his notion of a ceiling and a floor barrier as the only fixtures which halt the cumulative process and cause it to reverse direction.

The weaknesses of Hicks's trade cycle fixprice method are endemic to its very ingenuity. Although the model set out to treat adjustment in quantities, it was not adequately descriptive. The working of its mechanism was very simple – in fact, all too simple. The periods of each expansionary or contractionary portion of the cycle predictably reproduced themselves, with unenlightening repetition, however. Expectations were taken for granted; in fact they were not present at all. All the macro-variables in the model were divided by the same deflator; all prices changed proportionally. But what information did this offer? Hicks well recognized that the model, as it stood, would never have been compatible with his own changing ideas on the market structure of an economy composed of a speculative and a manufacturers' market, as described above.

Early flexprice method in Value and Capital: Hicks's temporary equilibrium model described in *Value and Capital* (1939a) employs a flexprice method to create its macro-model based on an aggregate micro-analysis of many consumers' demands and producers' supply. Price determination by equations of supply and demand was the main concern in the temporary equilibrium model.

In *Value and Capital* Hicks's objectives were twofold: to discover the laws of the workings of the price system and to study the effect of differing sets of plans on the variation of prices. The dynamics of Hicks's laws will be discussed in the next chapter. Here attention is turned to the crucial role he gave to supply and demand in price determination.

In the first part of *Value and Capital*, the static part, Hicks discussed how the price system regulates exchange and production, independently and together, in an economy consisting of private individuals and private firms. In this system, the general equilibrium consists of the balance of all demands and supplies of the goods and services that private individuals and entrepreneurs exchange for consumption or for use as factors of production. In the second part of *Value and Capital*, concerned with the dynamic working of the price system, Hicks used the static apparatus he had just developed, but also introduced the variables of capital, interest, saving, investment, and money as well as expectations. He concentrated his attention on one particular week period with a given inherited endowment and horizon plan. He analysed the demand and supply of commodities, securities and money within that week period for a private individual, for a private firm, and then, once generalized by simple aggregation, for the economy as a whole.

Whether from the viewpoint of an individual, a firm or the economy as a whole, he considered a case of price determination by supply and demand for a particular week in the perspective of both, given current and given future demands and supplies. For Hicks, both current and future prices are determined for the week using the method of maximizing the Present Value of the communities' stream of commodities and income (which includes the Present aggregate Value of firms' production plans into the future, and Present aggregate Value of individuals' projected stream of revenue). To calculate the Present Values Hicks used a given discount factor.

To set up his week period model of supply and demand Hicks distinguished three types of transactions in the market-place: spot, forward and loan transactions. For Hicks, spot transactions were those which were arranged and fulfilled in the current period. Forward transactions were those which were arranged now and carried out in a future period. Hicks also introduced the third type of transaction, a loan transaction; 'the essential characteristic of a loan transaction is that its execution is divided in time' (1939a, p. 141). His introduction of the loan type of transaction made it possible for him to include the exchange of current goods for future goods and to incorporate interest as another good available at a definite rate established by supply and demand.

Hicks considered the interest rate entailed in loan transactions to be the price of money, which, like all other prices, 'must be determined with them as part of a mutually interdependent system' (1939a, p. 154), not in isolation. Specifically, however, what would determine the interest rate? According to Hicks, there were different approaches to the determination of the rate of interest. Some, such as Böhm Bawerk, proposed that the interest rate is determined in the real sector; others favoured its determination in the money sector. Among the latter advocates, Hicks identified those who believed it was the demand and supply for loanable funds and those who thought it was the supply and demand for money which determined the interest rate (p. 153).

Hicks was, in this flexprice method, focusing on the money rate of interest rather than on its real rate, and even though, as he maintained, both the loanable funds and the monetary approach lead to the same results, he opted for the determination of the interest rate in a general equilibrium by the equations of demand and supply of money. The general equilibrium money rate depended, according to Hicks, on three factors: expectations, 'the length of time for which the loans are to run' (1939a, p. 142), and the risk of a venture. For Hicks, in principle expectations play a determining role in the price of money, just as they could in the price of any product over time. The money rate of interest is *ex ante*, thus the result both of the market rate of interest and of 'the rate at which people can expect to borrow or lend for short periods', a rate which 'will depend upon their anticipations of the future course of the market rates' (p. 149).

Concerning the various interest rates for different lengths of time for which loans are made, Hicks thought they could all 'be reduced to a standard type of short rate combined with a series of forward short rates' (1939a, p. 145). Thus the only rates Hicks considered in this flexprice method were a single short rate corresponding to one week loans and a single long rate corresponding to the loans for any number of future weeks. He established the relation between the two rates as follows: 'if short rates are not expected to change, the long rate will exceed the short rate by a normal risk-premium' (p. 147). His reference to a 'normal risk-premium' appears to confuse matters, since from the outset of the method he had wished to exclude risk with all its uncertainty. His normal risk premium was the compensation needed to attract the marginal speculator in money to accept the risk of loaning. The premium itself was implicitly taken as given. At the time, Hicks considered the risk factor simply too complex to handle and supposed that if default risk were ignored, it would be possible to homogenize the complex world, to reduce 'the complex system of interest rates for various maturities, which exists in practice, to a single rate' (p. 148). This last step allowed his method to proceed according to the rate of interest, possible, he added, only given 'an economic system where there is *only one* rate of interest' (emphasis added; p. 154).

Having established all these qualifiers leading to the unique rate of interest and being concerned only with the current period, Hicks assumed 'the working of an economic system in which there is still no forward trading in goods and services, and in which there is still only one type of lending' and effectively 'only one rate of interest' (1939a, pp. 149, 150). He succeeded in bringing into a general equilibrium both present and future supply and demand which determine all the prices and the unique rate of interest.

It must be recognized that Hicks was working under the assumption of perfect competition and perfect contemporaneous knowledge. He did not question whether goods are perishable or storable or whether stocks are carried forward. He did not mention the distinction between stocks and flows. Goods and services are sold in the market according to supply and demand, and prices are determined accordingly. Owing to the absence of uncertainty risk, there is no speculation. There is no hoarding, in the sense of money kept idle. No monetary policies, government interference, or banking institutions are allowed. Hicks's general equilibrium did not allow for any distinction to be made between those who organize production (entrepreneurs) and those who lend their capital (rentiers). Profit and the interest rate mean the same thing. As a matter of fact, the rate of profit, the rate of return, the natural rate of interest, the real rate of interest, and the monetary rate of interest are effectively all the same concept. They are represented collectively by the unique rate of interest determined in the interdependent system of supply and demand equations.

Hicks's flexprice method of the temporary equilibrium model is mainly concerned with current decisions and a current plan. While based on a projected future horizon, there is no emphasis on the realization of the projections in future periods. Individuals and firms evaluate the present value of their income for a given length of time according to the unique rate of interest. The fact that in Hicks's general equilibrium model there is only one rate of interest means that all future prices at different dates are discounted by the same rate. The further the period is into the future the higher is the discount factor. Any change in the interest rate will affect both the consumption and the production of all the periods. If individuals or firms expect that future prices or future interest rates will change, then a model can be equated according to their re-estimation of the present value of their income according to that assumed expected price or interest rate. This re-evaluation will generally yield a substitution effect between inputs, outputs and consumption depending on the cases, as well as an income effect and therefore a change in the supply and demand for current and future commodities.

Although, as many scholars have consistently maintained, *Value and Capital* is very rich in substance, its general equilibrium embedded in the temporary equilibrium model is very restrictive. Hicks recognized that

> the fundamental weakness of the Temporary Equilibrium method is the assumption, which it is obliged to make, that the market is in equilibrium – actual demand equals desired demand, actual supply equals desired supply – even in the *very* short period, which is what its single period must be taken to be. This assumption comes down from Marshall, but

> even in a very competitive economy, such very short-run equilibrium is very hard to swallow. (1965a, p. 76)

Considering most of the limitations of the method inherent in his technique of general equilibrium, such as that prices remain unchanged throughout the single period, Hicks none the less acknowledged that some of its difficulties could be modified. To surmount the obstacles of its requirement for perfect competition and its neglect of uncertainty, for example, would, Hicks felt, 'require considerable amendment' (1965a, p. 71). It was not, however, amendments to the temporary equilibrium model which subsequently interested him. Instead, from the mid-1950s on, he reconsidered both the fixprice and the flexprice methods, in light of his analysis of the market economy composed of a speculative and a manufacturers' market.

The sophisticated flexprice and fixprice theory

In his sophisticated flexprice and fixprice theory Hicks laid tremendous emphasis on both the *ex ante* and *ex post* and stock–flow relations. This emphasis was to go hand in hand with his new concern with disequilibrium. In Hicks's applied economics, the existence of disequilibrium was analysed in terms of a distinction between what is expected and what is realized and the potential for adjustments in both prices, quantities or both. He now argued that to account for changes in prices and quantities,

> the traditional view that market price is, at least in some way, determined by an equation of demand and supply had now to be given up. If demand and supply are [no longer to be] interpreted, as had formerly seemed to be sufficient, as flow demand and supplies coming from outsiders, it is no longer true that there is any tendency, over any particular period, for them to be equalized; a difference between them, if it were not too large, could be matched by a change in stocks. It is of course true that if no distinction is made between demand from stockholders and demand from outside the market; demand and supply in that inclusive sense must always be equal. But that equation is vacuous. It cannot be used to determine price, in Walras's or Marshall's manner. (1989a, p. 11)

Whether one is dealing with storable or non-storable goods, disequilibrium manifests itself openly. In the case of non-storable commodities, there is a given stock at one point in time, as in the case of electricity or telephone or labour services, and in some instances for a relatively short length of time, as with fish for sale before refrigeration, for example. If demand exceeds output and cannot be fulfilled with 'available surpluses of substitute commodities either from stocks or current output' (1965a, p. 81), the demand will go unsatisfied and unspent money will be carried forward. If, on the contrary, an unplanned excess of stocks of goods exists owing to low demand, the excess will go to waste, the funds invested in those goods will be lost, and a debt will be acquired by producers. In either of these situations a signal will be given, in the form of unspent money or incurred debt, that future output or demand can decrease or increase. Signals of a demand–supply inequality, Hicks observed, can always be detected 'in someone's stock (or balance sheet) disequilibrium' (p. 82) for the period in which the inequality occurs.

In the case of the markets for storable goods, markets which comprise the bulk of an economy, stocks are routinely held, ideally at the desired level of static excess. In a fixprice market, 'actual stocks may be greater, or may be less, than desired stocks'. On the other hand, in a flexprice market, 'actual stocks are always equal to desired stocks – when the stocks of the traders are taken into account' (1974b, p. 25).

When stocks of commodities can be carried forward, stock equilibrium becomes a key element of price analysis. In the flexprice method of the temporary equilibrium model, Hicks had already maintained that he had included the notion of stocks carried over into the current and future periods, or stock and flow, in his consideration of expectation and interest rate. He had, however, simply affirmed that 'there is one "stock–flow" equilibrium of the single period', and that, seen retrospectively, was not sufficient (1965a, p. 85). While the concept of stock equilibrium was critical also to Hicks's earlier fixprice method, he considered its constancy less crucial. The presence of the concept in fixprice theory, he seemed to say, is rendered obvious by its working absence; it is actually stock disequilibrium, not equilibrium, which is carried forward (p. 86).

For Hicks, the existence of stock equilibrium, as defined in chapter 2, in both the flexprice and fixprice methods, was a matter of the balance sheet. In the flexprice method of the temporary equilibrium model, he noted that the most appropriate monitor of stock equilibrium was to be found at 'the more liquid end of the balance-sheet' (1965a, p. 88). Prices will fluctuate accordingly as expectations of interest rates, yield, etc. are realized or not. In Hicks's fixprice method, however, the accounting of all marketable assets, of all stock, even the least liquid, reflects the state of stock equilibrium or disequilibrium. Particularly as the effort to maintain price stability is strained, all aspects of stock are affected in the fixprice method if its type of expectations, the 'amount that will be demanded' (p. 88), is or is not fully satisfied.

What Hicks had come to realize was that the state of equilibrium in the stocks alone, not the actual ups and downs of supply and demand, could bring prices to change. If this was to be the case, he concluded, 'prices can no longer be given from outside [based on demand and supply], but must be determined, in some manner, as part of the system' (1965, p. 131). Prices must instead be seen to reflect expectations of demand, the degree of internal disequilibrium in stock and flow, and price expectations in an *ex ante* and *ex post* relationship. If, Hicks announced, stocks and expectations, which were dominated in both the flex- and fixprice methods by supply and demand, were to become part of the price equation, a new method would emerge (p. 131).

New method

In an effort to remedy the recognized flaws and to improve generally on his earlier flex- and fixprice methods, Hicks suggested bringing together price disequilibrium and quantity disequilibrium in one model that was based on both the *ex ante* and *ex post* distinction and stock–flow relations. What made his method truly new was his desire to incorporate within one economic system both certain markets which work in one way, according to the vagaries of price disequilibrium, and other markets which respond to quantity disequilibrium. He now thought it made imminently good sense to recognize that

> there are markets where prices are set by producers; and for those markets, which include a large part of the markets for industrial products, the fixprice assumption makes good sense. But there are other markets, 'flexprice' or speculative markets, in which prices are still determined by supply and demand. It is tempting, when one is constructing an economic model, to simplify by assuming just one sort of market. (1974b, p. 23)

Hicks posited that one possible way of avoiding the temptation of simplification and of taking both type of markets into account was to construct a model based on plans and realizations. In it there would be no necessity to have equilibrium between *ex ante* demand and supply; adjustment in terms of unintended accumulation or decumulation would be made *ex post*. As early as 1956, the descriptive roots of this model can be found in his work. He considered 'two types of *ex ante* and *ex post* analysis which may be called the '*Q*', or quantity-disequilibrium, and '*P*', or price disequilibrium, type respectively' (1956c, p. 145). At the time he thought no one had yet devised or undertaken this task.

Hicks believed a comprehensive model could be constructed to accompany his complete stock–flow theory which would 'proceed on *P*-lines when dealing with markets for which a *P*-approach was appropriate, and on *Q*-lines when dealing with markets for which a *Q*-approach was appropriate (1956c, pp. 148–9). More engaging was his enthusiasm about what the model would reveal:

> It would show prices in the *P*-market being *directly* determined by stock equations, with the flow relations affecting price-expectations which would react back on current prices. It would show quantities in the *Q*-markets primarily determined by the flow equations, but with stock relations reacting back on the flow equations by the generation of induced investment (or disinvestment). Thus in both sorts of markets both stock and flow relations would come into the picture, but their role would be different in the two cases. (1956c, pp. 148–9)

To describe the intricacies of price determination was, of course, still the ultimate goal of Hicks's new method. He thought he had captured within it all the elements which would interrelate in a feedback fashion to produce sufficient signals to effect price changes. In markets which behave in a flexprice manner, an increase in production costs above revenue will signal a need for an increase in production in the future period or for an increase in price. Since equality between flow supply and flow demand are relatively constant in that market, with increased production costs, price changes are a more likely response to the signal than quantity or production adjustments. In the case of fixprice markets, there is no necessary equality between current demand and current output. If current demand is higher than current supply, the withdrawal of excess stock signals the need for an increase in output in the future period; or vice versa. Since every effort is made within this market to maintain price stability, if at all possible, production will adjust to stock changes. If, however, stock changes are too dramatic, considerable production delays or stockpiles increasing rapidly, prices may respond to the signals and change.

In neither the flexprice nor the fixprice method were prices dependent upon maintaining equilibrium. Contrary to the temporary equilibrium method, there was no concept of static equilibria operative, either as a succession of single period equilibria or as an expectation equilibrium at each point in time. This is not to say that Hicks did not posit equilibrium pricing. In fact, he assumed a dynamic equilibrium path whose very existence would depend in part on equilibrium pricing. 'We do concern ourselves with the prices which will permit the establishment of equilibrium over time' (1965a, p. 132). Hicks felt in turn, none the less, that such concern was possible only because prices are flexible; the existence itself of the equilibrium would have virtually no effect on the behaviour of prices within a market particularly 'when the system is out of equilibrium'. Once an economy is in disequilibrium, pricing behaviour could be affected by any number of its factors.

Thus Hicks's new method was his attempt to construct a dynamic stock–flow adjustment model which took into account both stock equilibrium and flow equilibrium considerations in a changing economy. Although Hicks thought it worthwhile to go through the algebra of such models, he did say that 'we can invent rules for their working, and calculate the behaviour of the resulting models; but such calculations are of illustrative value only' (1965a, p. 83). He warned of the limitations of such approaches: 'we are unable to "simulate" the behaviour of intelligent business management by any simple rule . . . mechanical principles of adjustment do not offer a good representation' (pp. 102–3).

Hicks made use of his new flexprice-fixprice theory to develop a model in *Capital and Time* (1973d). His creation was not, however, a system in which there are several markets where simultaneously some behave in a flexprice manner and others in a fixprice manner. It was rather the same model as devised earlier which simply operates according to one or other of the two price types. In *Capital and Time* Hicks conducted his analysis of wages and employment in a Marshallian way: either wages were allowed to change while the supply of labour is assumed given, or the wage rate was given exogenously and there is an unlimited supply of labour, *ceteris paribus*. Hicks's supply curve of labour had a reversed L-shape, and the two portions of the curve were analysed independently. This model, like those before it, could not handle the case in which a flex- and a fixprice market were intertwined, that is, where both employment and wages were variable.

As will be explained in chapter 7, Hicks's IS–LM model was the closest he was to come to devising a 1AB2 model, his ultimate goal in price determination modelling. The IS–LM model, however, also had its drawbacks. Although in the model certain markets are flexprice while others are fixprice, at the same time, components 1 (*ex ante* and *ex post*) and 2 (stock–flow) are represented barely if at all. There is no place for expectation-realization. Also, while elements of the model refer to stocks and flow, the model itself is not designed to be analysed according to period intervals.

Apart from his attempt in *Capital and Time*, Hicks did not devise a mechanical model for 1AB2. Indeed, he had set for himself a tremendous task, a task which lies really in the domain of dynamics. The evolution of his dynamics will be illustrated in the next chapter, and some of the difficulties in dealing with integrated flexprice-fixprice determination will be highlighted in several chapters throughout the rest of the volume.

4

Dynamics: Change, Fluctuation and Growth

From the time of his earliest writings Hicks was aware that in the real world economic changes are taking place all the time and often in a non-uniform manner. Some of these changes can be foreseen but most are unforeseen. The business of economics, he believed, is to understand the dynamics of economic activity. He attempted to grasp its various aspects by providing many simple dynamic models. Among other things these models showed Hicks's enthusiasm for the creation of a dynamic economics. The terminology in this chapter is devised in order to maintain a clear distinction between the dynamics of economic activity and the dynamic economic theory that describes it. Although Hicks himself confusingly called his economics 'dynamics' or 'economic dynamics', it is the dynamics of economic activity that will be referred to here as 'economic dynamics', and the models and theory as 'dynamic economics'.

At first Hicks was optimistic about the possibility of capturing economic dynamics in mechanical models, for example, in the temporary equilibrium model of *Value and Capital* (1939a) and in the trade cycle model of *A Contribution to the Theory of the Trade Cycle* (1950a). Even though he recognized these models were oversimplified, he claimed they represented general dynamic economics. Over time, he had mixed feelings about whether a mechanical approach could in fact describe the dynamics of a changing economy. In *Capital and Growth* he raised serious doubts about the possibility of building a comprehensive dynamic theory: 'I do not think that there is such a theory; I much doubt if there can be' (1965a, p. v). Despite his scepticism, Hicks continued to build dynamic models, especially ones tailored to growth theory, such as his Traverse I and II, although without claiming much for them. He came to feel that there must be many different ways of analysing economic dynamics; there was no one theory which could explain everything, but instead partial theories capture certain dynamic aspects at certain times.

The word Hicks used to evoke economic change, 'dynamics', appeared in almost every one of his writings. The significance and scope he attached to 'dynamics' played a crucial role in the methods he tried to develop. Indeed, in different works, he gave 'dynamic economics' different definitions and also produced different methods of analysing change. For instance, in *The Theory of Wages* (1932b), although there is no explicit definition of dynamic economics, there is dynamic analysis. In 'Wages and interest: the dynamic problem' Hicks transformed static economic magnitudes, supposed to be constant and continuous 'flows' through time, into dynamic economic magnitudes which change discontinuously at intervals (1935f, p. 270). He was more explicit about the general differences between static and dynamic economics in his temporary equilibrium model of *Value and Capital*, where static economics encompassed 'those parts of economic theory where we do not trouble about dating' and where dynamic economics was defined as 'those parts of economic theory in which variables must be dated' (1939a, p. 115). In *A Contribution to the Theory of the Trade Cycle*, Hicks extended his definition of dynamic economics to include the definitions of Frisch and Harrod (1950a, p. 10) and constructed a new method of analysis. Soon after, in 'The process of imperfect competition' (1954a) he came up with yet another method of analysing economic dynamics. To analyse a firm which tries to set up a new plant in an oligopolistic market, he defined static and dynamic economics in terms of adjustment in excess capacity.

Having used different definitions of static and dynamic economics and various methods of analysis, Hicks sensed that he had created confusion among his readers. Some critics, such as Harrod, Kaldor and Samuelson, had rejected all his notions of dynamics. Thus, partly in response to his critics and partly as a personal challenge, Hicks felt, in his 'Methods of dynamic analysis', the need to clarify further the matter of dynamics and to 'build a bridge between my own approaches' (1956c, p. 139n). The outcome of his 1956 paper was the beginning of a change in attitude for him towards economic modelling in general. This change crystallized in *Capital and Growth* (1965a): Hicks expressed his acceptance that there had to be different definitions of dynamic economics; he clearly distinguished the scope of economic dynamics from dynamic economic methods; and he acknowledged his recognition that sequential analysis is bound to be mechanical. In dynamic analysis, he reckoned that one must consider several time dimensions, and that models should be conceived in such a way as to accommodate both flexprice and fixprice markets. He thus loosened his notion of dynamic economics, leaving room for the flexible interpretation of his models.

Economic dynamics and dynamic methods

The scope

In his earlier work, Hicks did not always make clear the difference between the scope of economic dynamics and the method of dynamic economics, the method or technique used to analyse economic dynamics. As is the case with many economists, and indeed often in Hicks's early writings, the scope of economic dynamics was simply implied in that of the method of analysis. In 1956 Hicks made clear the difference between his economic dynamics and his dynamic economic method. He argued that different writers, usually depending on their interest, either had concentrated on certain parts of general economic dynamics and had thus defined dynamic economics in a restrictive manner, or had announced a method which implied in itself a particular definition of economic dynamics. Looking at the field from this perspective, he argued, one could see how many definitions could indeed subsist together even if they were not consistent with one another. Hicks himself attempted to define the scope of economic dynamics in the broadest sense as 'the *process of economic change*. So defined, the subject includes the study of fluctuations as well as that of growth; it includes the study of change in particular markets as well as in the whole economic' (1956c, p. 140). As he later phrased it, 'it should deal with specialization and diversification as well as with "growth"' (1965a, p. 6).

In these terms, general economic dynamics encompasses within itself all the changes that may occur in economic activity. To consider all these changes simultaneously is an enormously complex task and that is why 'no commitment is made in advance about the method by which the subject is to be examined'. The question of method is left open and 'remains a separate question' (1956c, p. 140). Defining the scope of economic dynamics in this manner leaves much room for discussion about methods of dynamic economics.

The method

By method, Hicks meant the manner chosen to describe and explain the process of economic change. Hicks asserted that since different kinds of changes can be studied separately, there are different methods of analysis for different processes of change. On the other hand, since one change can be treated with different techniques of abstraction, there are also different methods which can analyse the same phenomena. Owing to the complexity of economic changes, he accepted the fact that an economist can only deal with some aspects and must neglect others. By the same token, for Hicks, every method of dynamic economics could cast 'some light upon some aspect of the phenomena' (1965a, p. v).

Retrospective considerations of dynamic economics: From his 1956 perspective on the scope and method of dynamic economics, Hicks saw his early models no longer as all-encompassing as when he had first presented them, neither with respect to other theories of dynamic economics nor with respect to all the elements comprising the phenomena under its study. About the phenomena under study, Hicks wrote

> the analysis of a number of contemporary interacting processes soon proves to be beyond our powers. It is no accident that dynamic theory tends so largely to run in terms of simple aggregative models. However much we simplify the processes which are to be studied, . . . they are bound to result in depriving the behaviour under study of its purposive character, so that the economic system is reduced to a mere mechanism. (1956c, p. 141)

The year 1956 witnessed a remarkable change in Hicks, who not long before had advanced theories which he believed to be general, as for example, his theory of dynamic economics which he claimed was 'dynamic in *all* of the senses' and hence *the* method of dynamic economics (1950a, p. 10). The above statement served Hicks no doubt both as a concession to the many critics who rejected his dynamic economic analysis and as an announcement of his consideration of his own work. Allowing himself to be dissociated from certain aspects of his early conception of dynamic economics, Hicks was now free to say that his models were not as general as he had claimed. He also revealed that he wanted to follow a different approach to dynamic economics, consistent with his statements on the limitations of mechanical economics in dealing with historical time.

Reconsiderations of economic dynamics: To give more clarification to the methodology of dynamic economics which gave him some trouble with his critics, Hicks focused, in 1956, on two alternative methods of analysis. One was provided by Lindahl (*Studies in the Theory of Money and Capital*, 1939), stressing the comparison of *ex ante* and *ex post* situations; the other was suggested by Keynes (*General Theory*, 1936) and based on the stock–flow relationship. Both of these methods, as explained in previous chapters, were, explicitly or implicitly, conceived in terms of plans, realizations and expectations. In the analysis of economic processes with either of these two methods, Hicks appreciated that it was possible to envisage different courses of change superimposed over time.

Hicks initially saw greater value in Lindahl's *ex ante* and *ex post* model than in the stock–flow model of Keynes. Keynes's method, he wrote, 'works much less explicitly [than Lindahl's] in terms of plans and expectations' (1956c, p. 145). None the less, Hicks still had some reservations about Lindahl's method of analysis, retaining primarily that

> the comparison of what does happen with what is expected to happen becomes a key-point of dynamic analysis . . . Dynamic analysis is not solely concerned with the comparison of what happens in successive periods, so as to build up a story in terms of these *actual* changes; there is also a form, or a phase, of dynamic analysis which concentrates attention upon a *single period* (or *accounting period*), being concerned with the difference between what happens in that period and what is planned . . . to happen in it. (1956c, p. 142)

From both methods, Hicks retained the notions of period and succession of periods and the importance of comparing. In dynamic economics he referred to an analysis of what happens in a single period as single period theory and to an analysis which is concerned with the link between the effect of the events of one period upon succeeding periods as 'continuation theory'. For Hicks, in dynamic economics time was thus present both in the form of a single period and as a succession of periods.

The device of the single period was at home in the *ex ante* and *ex post* analysis. (Hicks had already tried a version in *Value and Capital* (1939a).) *Ex ante* and *ex post* analysis emphasizes the comparison of what does happen with what is expected to happen. Plans and expectations are made at the beginning of one period, and actual facts become available at the end of the period. There might also be the comparison of realizations and planned results within one period of time. The device of a succession of periods seemed, on the other hand, appropriate in stock–flow analysis. This analysis studies how disequilibrium in stocks is carried from one period into another.

Hicks attempted to assess both the *ex ante* and *ex post* and the stock–flow situations according to a '*Q*' or quantity-disequilibrium and a '*P*' or price-disequilibrium analysis. (These theories have been elaborated in chapter 3.) Since Hicks recognized that markets appropriate for stock–flow analysis and markets appropriate for *ex ante* and *ex post* analysis were determined by quantities and prices respectively, he felt a combination of '*Q*' analysis and '*P*' analysis would be applicable in the dynamic economics of interrelated markets. For Hicks, the theories of Lindahl and Keynes both in their own way present special cases. Hicks found Lindahl's *ex ante* and *ex post* theory restrictive in its considering solely a *P*-disequilibrium within the period. Keynes's stock–flow theory, on the other hand, gave overwhelming scope to the *Q*-disequilibrium, maintaining its effect in all markets where the flow side alone was emphasized, and it restricted the *P*-disequilibrium to the bond market, concentrating there exclusively on the stock equation. Hicks's complete stock–flow and *ex ante* and *ex post* theory of economic dynamics would be a theory in which stock and flow of both *P*-equations of the speculative market (not limited to the bond market) and *Q*-equations of the manufacturers' market feed back into each other.

Even after his reconsideration of dynamics in the 1950s, Hicks still believed static economics to be useful and to have an important role to play in the discipline. He asserted that both static and dynamic economics would have a use, dependent on whether the economic question raised was one of comparing states or analysing processes. He stressed that there are cases in which static analysis of the single period can suffice; analysis will, however, become dynamic with the linkage of various single periods. There can also be cases in which dynamic analysis is used within the single period as well as between periods.

In Hicks's reconsidered treatment of the process of economic change, static and dynamic economics are defined in terms of one another. With static economics defined as the study which deals with the situation in which certain key variables are unchanging, a 'dynamic condition is then, by inevitable opposition, one in which they are changing; and dynamic theory is the analysis of the processes by which they change' (1965a, p. 6). The meanings of dynamics economics differed in his writings depending on whether he was dealing with welfare economics or positive economics. Hicks believed that although traditionally welfare economics was static economics, it was possible to render it dynamic by considering its situation one of changing resources: optima under varied endowments. In positive economics, however, dynamic economics is the analysis of processes, as, for instance, how expected and realized variables are interdependent from period to period.

Hicks was cautious when it came to linking certain methods of analysis specifically to any branch of economics, welfare or positive. He even doubted whether a most important part of positive economics – Growth Theory – was significantly dynamic; 'there are too many ways', he wrote, 'in which it remains "semi-static"'. Thus, as will be explained below, he considered Growth Theory 'no more than a particular method of Dynamic Economics' (1965a, p. 14).

In his reconsideration of dynamic economics in 1956, Hicks came to think that his earlier temporary equilibrium model and trade cycle model were not as general as he had first deemed them. He had come to believe that some parts of their dynamics had to be reconsidered and rejected, since they ignored relations over time. Nowhere, however, did he totally renounce his models as a whole; even in *Capital and Growth* he wrote, 'I still want to stand by them all' (1965a, p. v). Changes in Hicks's attitude toward dynamic economics must be seen as a smooth evolution in general. His reconsidered views led to the incorporation in a new light of elements of which he had earlier been aware: the *ex ante* and *ex post* relation he borrowed from Lindahl and Keynes's stock–flow analysis.

The next section is devoted to a discussion of how Hicks saw the development of dynamic economics in which he played a part. He believed that classical economics had not devised a dynamic economics and attributed its fruitful development to his contemporaries and himself. An important aspect of that development was the role played by economic models. Hicks defined a model as a construction for correlating certain selected elements of the state or process under study, to allow their further deduction by reasoning and a general understanding of the state or process from which they derive. A discussion of four of Hicks's models will follow: two models which stem from before 1956 and his reconsideration, the temporary equilibrium model and the trade cycle model, and two later models of his growth theory, Traverse I and II. They have been grouped together to highlight in particular the dynamic character of each and to illustrate a classification of models according to the way in which they handle time and change' (1965a, p. 29).

Throughout this section, it will become clear that Hicks was becoming more and more careful in his use of mechanical approaches in dynamic economics. His new attitude was not strictly speaking a rejection of his own early work or of mathematical models in general. He simply came to think that he could not rely on mechanical models alone to arrive at a reasonable understanding of economic changes. Models, he continued to believe, could however, be of illustrative value; they could be used as indicators, and together with personal judgement they would allow conclusions to be drawn about dynamic problems. Hicks thus continued to rely on and construct models in dynamic economics for most of his career.

Macro-dynamic models

At the opening of his discussion of the development of a notion of dynamic models, Hicks distinguished classical static models of growth from modern dynamic models (such as those of Keynes, Harrod, Lindahl and other Swedish economists). The very first growth models, he asserted, were to be found in the classical economics of Smith and Ricardo. Hicks referred to these as primitive growth models, because of their static characteristics. 'Smith's model, though it looks like a growth model, is not a growth model in the modern sense. It does not exhibit a sequence' (1965a, p. 39, n. 1). Smith had devised a model with two simplifications: the single capital good and the confinement of fixed capital to circulating capital (in terms of labour content).

Hicks felt that the classical models of both Smith and Ricardo were static because of the insufficient attention given by them to an explicit distinction between fixed and circulating capital. As a result of capital simplifications, Smith's model embraced only a single agricultural period, the year, and was thereby self-contained, or static, in time. The model took no account of plans or expectations. In Smith's model there was no mechanism providing links between periods. According to Hicks, this resulted in some tension as to the purpose of the model, for with its neglect of uncertainty and liquidity changes, it could not function as the 'bridge' it was designed to be between economic dynamics and a dynamic monetary economics, 'the possibility of which Hume had some inkling' (1965a, p. 42). Although, as Hicks saw it, Ricardo was much more of a model builder than Smith, for him the character of Ricardo's model was much the same. He noted the same confinement to circulating capital, the same self-confined single period and the same capital homogeneity. He thought that Ricardo, like Smith, confined himself 'to the comparison of static equilibria, even of stationary states'. For all these reasons, their models 'cannot extend to the analysis of dynamic process' (p. 47).

Hicks traced the next step in the development of dynamic models to the writing of Marshall. Marshall, he felt, was aware of the limitations of static and stationary state analysis. Some of Marshall's techniques revealed to Hicks attempts to find a way around the limitations inherited from Smith and Ricardo. Hicks also found them, however, to be quite restrictive. Marshall limited his model to a particular sector and a particular industry. He pursued the enquiry of conditions of partial equilibrium with technology and factors of production unchanging and the demand of the product of that industry fixed. To do so, he incorporated the special device *ceteris paribus*. Also he distinguished between the devices of short period and long period which enabled him to introduce fixed and circulating capital into his analysis. Hicks wrote, 'Marshall, we may say, was treating his *short period* as a single period, in the manner of Smith or Ricardo, and invoking the constancy (or approximate constancy) of the fixed capital stock of the industry, as a justification for treating the single period as self-contained' (1965a, p. 51). In so doing, however, Marshall left out user costs, the rate of usage of fixed capital and stock inventories. For Hicks, therefore, Marshall's use of the 'period' had 'nothing to do with the sense of "period" as it appears in truly dynamic economics' (p. 50). Hicks felt, none the less, that Marshall's method could be regarded 'as a last stage in the evolution of static method, it gets very near to dynamics' (p. 57).

According to Hicks, it was Wicksell who truly 'saw the need for a more dynamic method', to explain capital accumulation. Wicksell, however, 'did not go on to develop it himself. His successors did' (1965a, p. 48). Of his successors, Hicks placed the greatest emphasis on the Swedish economists, especially Lindahl, as the realizers of a truly dynamic method. Although Harrod felt that the exposition of dynamic principles could be found as far back as Smith and Ricardo (Harrod, 1973, p. vii), Hicks asserted that dynamic economics had begun only with his own contemporaries, such as Lindahl. In Lindahl's method of cumulative process, change was represented as a sequence of single periods in which expectations were explicitly introduced. Hicks himself followed Lindahl's route in much greater detail. While he found Lindahl's method the most appealing, he recognized that other contemporaries, such as Keynes, Harrod, Robertson, and other Swedish economists, were also devising dynamic methods.

Illustrations of Hicks's dynamic models

The temporary equilibrium model

The temporary equilibrium model of *Value and Capital* was Hicks's first explicit, detailed and comprehensive model of dynamic economics. He consciously developed the dynamics of that model as an extension of his static principles. The dynamics of the book is entirely centred on the notion of conditions of stability. In parts I and II of *Value and Capital*, which are devoted to static economics, Hicks had not yet introduced money, capital, savings, investment or interest. He left the use of these concepts, of direct concern to dynamic economics, to parts III and IV of the book. In his chapters on static economics he specifically discussed the various equilibria of exchange (consumer), firm and production (general equilibrium) and their corresponding stability conditions.

Hicks presented first the equilibrium of exchange. He enquired what determined the demand for commodities and when preferences and supplies of goods are given. Using income and substitution effects he analysed the impact of changes in prices on consumer's decisions, and thence deduced his Law of Consumer Demand.

In a parallel manner, Hicks set out the equilibrium of the firm. He conceived firms as producing technically new commodities by technical transformation. Introducing the notions of technical complementarity and substitution he investigated the effect of price variations on the firm's production and deduced his Law of Supply. Finally, he brought his equilibria of consumer exchange and firm production together to form what he called a general equilibrium of production. The setting for his general equilibrium consisted of all demands and supplies of all goods and services that private individuals and private entrepreneurs are willing to exchange for consumption or for factors of production. Hicks used Walras's law to determine prices from the equation of all supplies and demands. He established laws of supply and demand for all commodities and then derived the 'laws for the workings of the whole price-system' (1939a, p. 191). Next, he analysed price changes and price stability. In statics, when the current price varies, the stability of its equilibrium depends on the income effect, on the substitution effect and on the notion of complementarity and substitution, whereas in dynamics, the stability of equilibrium depends only on the value of the elasticity of expectations.

What is of greatest concern here is the attention Hicks paid, in his presentation of static economics in *Value and Capital*, to the discussion of stability conditions for the equilibrium of multiple exchange. He defined 'perfect stability' as that state in which, when prices of one market rise and supplies increase above demand (or vice versa), the excess (or limit) in supplies of that one market will react exclusively and independently on price to cause its drop (or rise). If such conditions of stability are not satisfied, however, it might none the less be possible, Hicks noted, to speak of 'imperfect stability'. Conditions which result in imperfect stability are such that notionally, if when the prices in one market rise and supplies increase above demand (or vice versa), a drop (or rise) in prices will occur only through the referred impact of other markets. 'Thus even an imperfect stable system is stable in the end: but its stability is only maintained by indirect repercussions' (1939a, p. 67).

The concept of stability differs, of course, depending on whether the context of the discussion is static or dynamic economics. In his static treatment, Hicks merely defined 'instability', the state of systems 'which could never rest at any determinate system of prices'. Even though he considered their static state 'hardly interesting' and that 'the establishment' of their laws of change would be a nonsense problem' (1939a, p. 67), in his ensuing discussion of dynamic economics he attempted to formulate hypotheses on instability. He also reapplied his notion of imperfect stability, for example, in his later discussion of the instability of credit.

Hicks's discussion of stability conditions seemed to be that which attracted the especial attention of most of his reviewers (see, for example, Machlup 1940, Morgenstern 1941, Samuelson 1941). Although not all his readers accepted his definitions of stability, it was evident that he had for them shed new light on its conditions.

To investigate the price system in a dynamic economics, in parts III and IV of *Value and Capital*, Hicks used all the static apparatus he had developed previously and introduced the elements of time, capital, income and money. His dynamic economics depended heavily on the concepts of the week period, plans and expectations, which have already been discussed in chapters 2 and 3. He concentrated his analysis on one week period (of many), yielding a temporal equilibrium in an intertemporal framework. A major feature of his method was his assumption that a single type of good is at different dates different goods. He made a distinction between current prices and future (or expected) prices which may affect current decisions. In addition to goods and services of the commodity market, he also introduced a market for securities and a market for money.

Taking into consideration both the current and future demands and supplies of commodities, securities and money, Hicks investigated first for the individual consumer or firm and then for groups of individuals or firms 'the laws of the workings of the price-system' (1939a, p. 191). He assumed the aggregate behaviour of a group of individuals and firms to be no different from that of a single individual or single firm, and thus proceeded to generalize his approach to the whole economy. Hicks called his analysis of the aggregate during a particular week the general equilibrium of the whole system. The general conditions for the equilibrium of the aggregate, he insisted, consist of nothing more than a system of equations of supply and demand for commodities, securities and money.

Whether one is examining Hicks's general equilibrium from the perspective of one unit or the economy as a whole, it must be clear, as he himself emphasized, that 'the only laws we can expect to find, in the first place, are the laws of the working of the price-system in any particular "week"' (1939a, p. 191). Furthermore, he admitted that knowledge of the determinants of price changes, which the temporary equilibrium system had established, did not yet place him 'in a position to give an account of the process of price-change, nor to examine the ulterior consequences of changes in data'. Hicks concluded that, however disappointing it might be, 'there is not much which can be said about them in general' (1939a, p. 246). It must be remembered that the changes in prices that Hicks considered in the so-called dynamics of his temporary equilibrium model do not take place within the single week period. Instead he was advocating the comparison of two equilibrium situations during one week period when the situations are different:

> it must be emphasized that the changes in data we have to consider are purely hypothetical changes. We seek to compare the system of prices actually established in a particular week with that system which would have been established in the same week if the data (tastes, resources or expectations) had been rather different. (1939a, p. 246)

Hicks's realization concerning the yield of information from use of the one week period, that it 'is only the beginning of what we should like a dynamic theory to tell us' (1939a, p. 191), was not restricted to the limitations of the single period. In fact he was not content with comparative statics and attempted to give a dynamic dimension to price change analysis. This desire led him to try to integrate some truly dynamic aspects into his dynamic economics. Elasticity of expectation and the bargaining process, independently, appeared to hold the key.

Discussion of dynamics in terms of the concept of the elasticity of expectation of price (an individual's) allowed Hicks to use 'the ratio of the proportional rise in expected future prices of X to the proportional rise in its current price' (1939a, p. 205). He discussed stability conditions as dependent upon the value of that elasticity. Stability would result if elasticity were 0 (expected future prices are equal to current prices, that is, unchanging expectations and unchanging prices) or if elasticity were 1 (the proportional rise in expected future prices is equal to the proportional rise in current prices, that is, unchanging expectations and changing prices at a constant rate). It would also result if elasticity were between 0 and 1 (or between 0 and -1) (the proportional changes in expected future prices are less than the proportional changes in current price). Instability, the heart of Hicks's dynamics, would occur either if elasticity were greater than 1 (the proportional rise (or fall) in expected future prices is greater than the proportional rise (or fall) in current prices) or less than -1 (the proportional change in future prices is expected to be opposite to the proportion change of current prices, that is, each change is interpreted 'as the culminating point of a fluctuation' (p. 205)).

To give a sense of a dynamics of price instability Hicks concentrated on a series of elasticities of expectations greater than 1. When elasticities are greater than 1, Hicks asserted, 'people interpret a change in prices, not merely as an indication that the new prices will go on, but as an indication that they will go on changing in the same direction' in an accelerated fashion. Instability arises from the expected rises in prices and the accompanying response of individuals to those expectations whereby demand will become much greater than supply, and prices will continue to rise. 'A system with elasticities of expectations greater than unity . . . is definitely unstable.' For Hicks, this was 'the most important proposition' in the dynamic economics of *Value and Capital* (1939a, p. 255).

In yet another way, Hicks tried to give the impression that he had incorporated dynamics into the price determination analysis by acknowledging a bargaining process: 'our own approach to the dynamic problem . . . will have more in common with the method of Marshall' (1939a, p. 119). The bargaining process has already been described in the previous chapter on markets. Its dynamics consists of a trial-and-error interaction between buyers and sellers. The most important factors of the interaction to dynamic economics are that time elapses between exchanges and that knowledge about the state of both the expected and the realized demand and supply in the market is imperfect. In the actual economy, from the point when the market 'opens' and exchanges begin, prices fluctuate. According to Marshall, as time goes on, more information about the state of the market becomes available and the bargaining process eventually converges, at the end of the day, *ceteris paribus* to an equilibrium of prices and quantities.

Hicks adopted the Marshallian process of price formation for the temporary equilibrium model. The market, he said, 'proceeds quickly and smoothly to a position of temporary equilibrium – in Marshall's sense' (1939a, p. 123). His interpretation of that bargaining process was tricky. It is not the case in his model that prices are determined through a process of price formation, but simultaneously, it is as though they were so determined. Technically there is no expression of such a process in the temporary equilibrium model. In fact, Hicks discounted its difficulties to his theory by ignoring the process of bargaining altogether. He assumed that bargaining would not affect the equilibrium prices, and thus decided, 'we shall not pay much attention to the process of equilibration which must precede the formation of the equilibrium prices . . . we assume the economic system to always be in equilibrium' (1939a, p. 131). The way he justified his dismissal of the bargaining process was that in his theoretical model he assumed 'perfect contemporaneous knowledge' (p. 123). The bargaining process and perfect contemporaneous knowledge, that is, precise foreknowledge about prices and quantities, are simply mutually exclusive.

The problem with the dynamics of the temporary equilibrium method is due to two features. Hicks's interesting discussion of the elasticity of expectation was not integrated into the model and was unfortunately left suspended. This is not surprising; however, since his theory was embedded in a static framework, to such an extent that even his second hope for dynamics, the bargaining process, also had to be swept under the carpet. It seems that while on the one hand, Hicks believed that in dynamic economics the economic system must be conceived as a process in time, on the other hand, the method he used was not any different from that which he had devised for his static analysis; 'the results of static theory can be used after all; though almost all of them need drastic reinterpretation' (1939a, p. 116).

In *Value and Capital* Hicks did not distance his method of analysing economic dynamics in parts III and IV enough from his initial static methodology. Four features of his static method, perfect competition, definite expectations, synchronization of decisions and plans, and the self-contained week period whose activity at any point is constant and the same, were a prominent part of his dynamic method as well. The problems in realizing a dynamic model that ensued from their presence alone were multiple. Pinpointing some of the culprits, Hicks himself recognized later that the way his dynamic method was constructed in the temporary equilibrium model was not satisfactory.

In his dynamic method for the temporary equilibrium model Hicks supposed perfect competition, persuaded that no 'results of this work are much damaged by this [imperfect competition] omission' (1939a, p. 7). With perfect competition came its companion, contemporaneous perfect knowledge, by which in turn uncertainty was avoided. Hicks simply considered uncertainty to be beyond his dynamic analysis, which again would not be phased by the omission. Without uncertainty, however, the concept of expectations was greatly restricted.

The dynamics of Hicks's temporary equilibrium model was ostensibly governed by expectations. Ultimately, however, he would see that his model had moved in 'a "quasi-static" direction' (1965a, p. 66), because he had assumed that current expectations were completely determined by a given inherited past experience: 'the expectations that rule in the current period are based upon past experience; they are uninfluenced by what happens in the market during the current period itself' (1939a, p. 191). Although this connection to the past gave the impression that periods were dynamically connected to one another, Hicks offered no technical means for the 'linking-on' of periods through expectation. As Hicks himself well realized, lag adjustments for expectations would have been one appropriate device to permit linking. Later, in comparing his temporary equilibrium model to that of Lindahl's, Hicks recognized that while in Lindahl's model the single periods 'linked on', in his own, they did not (1965a, p. 65).

Hicks had concentrated on the self-contained single period with his method of comparing ultra-short period equilibria in a model in which there is no linkage structure. Each period is independent, and comparisons between them are based on 'purely hypothetical changes' (1939a, p. 246). He spoke of the elasticity of expectation, but did not integrate its implied process. Likewise, his equations of supply and demand, which also could have integrated expectations, did not integrate them. Since he provided no mechanism to link periods together, his method had many limitations and could not explain, among other things, capital accumulation, price formation or change. His method depended upon a combination of the self-contained period in expectation equilibrium that takes into account only current prices and of the prices reflecting those static expectations. This double requirement 'ruined the "dynamic" theory of *Value and Capital*' (1977a, p. vii).

Many things went awry in Hicks's setting for the dynamics of the temporary equilibrium model, and in the end the model, with its dominant features of given expectations and no risk, the self-contained period, illiquidity, and an absence of stock and flow analysis, seems to have come full circle to resembling strongly the classical model that Hicks roundly criticized (as noted earlier). Its resemblance should not, however, be mistaken for identity: Hicks's model was not a classical model. It contained the ingredients needed to build a dynamic economic model, but these ingredients were part of a method which was too much embroiled in static analysis. Hicks was well aware of this and tried piecemeal on different occasions to modify various aspects of his method.

In *Value and Capital* Hicks's interest in stability enabled him to identify the ingredients for a theory of instability. In its last few chapters, he turned to a discussion of an economy's internal stabilizers, which provide checks on its instability. He also outlined in general terms his views on the accumulation of capital and the fluctuations of the economy in the trade cycle. His combined interest in the idea of instability and the trade cycle surfaced again in 1949. Then Hicks began work on a formal and complete theory of the trade cycle while reviewing Harrod's *Toward a Dynamic Economics*. He proposed changes to what he thought were the deficiencies of Harrod's theory and outlined a more complete macro-dynamic theory of the trade cycle. He developed those ideas much further in his *A Contribution to the Theory of the Trade Cycle* in 1950.

The trade cycle model

The idea of building a theory of the trade cycle was already in Hicks's mind in the early 1930s. In his first paper that touched on the subject, Hicks suggested that 'the Trade Cycle is a "purely monetary phenomenon"' (1933b, p. 529). He appears to have been suggesting that fluctuations are inherent in a market economy: any monetary economy would be subject to cyclical fluctuations which 'have nothing necessarily to do with monopolistic or political interference' (p. 529). Without providing a complete model in the paper, Hicks outlined the dynamics entailed in correlated monetary factors. For him, any change in economic data which affect the risk factor will in turn have an impact on the velocity of money, and that impact will be cause for a succession of changes. For example, the individual holds different financial assets with different risk and return attached to each. The holding of one or another type of asset depends on individual preferences and expectations. Changes in an individual's expectations may lead to shifts in assets, which will affect capital funds, hence investment, then in turn prices, relative wages and profits, which again will have an impact on expectations, and so on. Economic fluctuations could be, Hicks felt, sufficiently explained by imperfect foresight and the use of means of payment (p. 529).

Once *Value and Capital* was published, Hicks, no doubt under the influence of Keynes and Harrod, reconsidered his views on the primary causes of economic fluctuations. Even though he still thought of the market economy as inherently cyclical, by 1949 he had modified his belief that monetary changes were the primary causes of cyclical fluctuations and saw them rather as secondary causes. He had come to conceive of economic fluctuations theoretically as the interaction between real macro-economic components, such as income, consumption, investment and saving. So he designed a model in which 'the relations between income and consumption, on the one hand, and between investment and changes in income, on the other, should be such as to impart a rather strong tendency to instability in the level of output' (1949d, p. 119). Hicks sought to explain the cause of economic fluctuations as the combined effect of any discrepancy between income and consumption and the lag between investment and output.

He described the dynamics of the typical cycle in light of its most important elements, one of which was output. An increase in output which induces investment in turn generates extra ouput and more income and so on. The ensuing impact of positive output changes will drive the economy into expansion and toward its upward limit of employable resources. Once that limit is reached, Hicks asserted, economic activity will hold at the peak expansionary level until the effect of no further increase in output activates a decrease in investment. A reduction in investment will in turn reduce output and generate continuing smaller investment, and so on. The economy will be driven to contract until the disinvestment is arrested at its lowest limit by the presence of fixed capital in the production sector. Since existing capital and production capacity do not just vanish, Hicks felt that they represent the minimum investment from which the dynamics to expand output from its lowest level will again take off.

From the point of view of investment, changes in investment were also seen as crucial, since an increase (or decrease) in induced investment will lead to an increase (or decrease) in output and income which in turn induces more (or less) investment, more (or less) output, income and so on. Changes in demand and thus in levels of stocks were also an integral part of this dynamics and the one in which the effect of lags is most evident. An increase in demand is met by a decrease in stocks which, according to Hicks, will induce new investment. An increase in output and in income will ensue with the additional output being used to restore the stocks to their normal level and the added income creating an increase in demand, which in turn is met by a new decrease in stocks, which induces further investment and so on. Demand and supply stocks lags are critical to the dynamics, since first with increased demand, there is 'a tendency to dis-investment; the additional output is not yet forthcoming, and the additional demand is satisfied out of stocks' and only later does 'the induced investment take place. This has to include (1) investment in stocks, to make up for the raiding of stocks in the first phase; (2) investment in fixed capital, needed to adjust equipment to the production of the larger output' (1950a, p. 51).

When it came to rendering his description of the trade cycle in the form of a model, Hicks initially resisted strongly any mathematical complications in terms of difference equations. His non-mathematical first forays into dynamic economics and his explanation of the trade cycle in *Value and Capital* immediately drew upon him the criticism of Paul Samuelson for that very reason. Responding to Samuelson, Hicks wrote in 1946,

> one of the greatest economic questions which remains to be settled is whether the trade cycle is more easily to be explained in terms of mechanical periodicities which can be expressed by difference equations, or whether a temporary equilibrium theory of the Keynesian type is ultimately the more potent. The answer to that question will not doubt incidentally settle the question – of approach and method, rather than of detail – which remains at issue between Professor Samuelson and myself. (1946b, p. 337)

The differing views of Samuelson and Hicks reflected some interesting confusion at the time about what was to be considered an appropriate method for dynamic economics and what dynamic economics would entail. Hicks's initial negative reaction to Samuelson's mechanical mathematical approach was temporary; by 1949 he had adopted difference equations similar to Samuelson's to develop his own model of the trade cycle.

Another type of criticism came from Harrod who thought that the discussion about statics and dynamics going on at the time had distorted the very definition of dynamic economics. Harrod noted specifically about *Value and Capital*, 'I have to record that parts III and IV, which allegedly deal with dynamic economics, do not fall within my definition of dynamics' (Harrod, 1948, p. 9). In 1950, Hicks reminded his readers that in *Value and Capital* he had defined dynamic economics as 'that part of the economic theory in which all quantities must be dated' (1950a, p. 10; see also 1939a, p. 115). He also noted that Harrod had defined dynamic economics as 'the study of an "economy in which rates of output are changing"' (1950a, p. 10; see also Harrod, 1948, p. 4). Hicks recorded that dynamic economics had yet another meaning for Frisch. It encompassed that part of economic theory 'in which "we consider the magnitudes of certain variables in different points of time, and we introduce certain equations which embrace at the same time several of these magnitudes belonging to different instances"' (1950a, p. 10; see also Frisch, 1933, p. 171).

Although Harrod clearly felt that such a variety of definitions had 'led to much confusion and fallacy in recent work, particularly in regard to the trade cycle' (Harrod, 1948, p. 9), Hicks was open to all comers. To begin his *A Contribution to the Theory of the Trade Cycle*, he declared that 'the theory advanced in this book is dynamic in all of the senses which have been proposed' (1950a, p. 10). He had challenged himself to model an economy whose rates of output are changing (as in Harrod's conception) and in which all quantities are dated (according to his own earlier definition), via a system of simultaneous equations (as Frisch had proceeded). Hicks himself added yet another element which he felt that Harrod had neglected and that dynamic economics ought to include: lags. 'It is very awkward to analyse a dynamic process (in his sense) without paying more regard than he does to the question of dating; and once one begins to date, it is hardly possible to slide over the question of lags' (1949d, p. 106).

Not only did Hicks come to adopt Samuelson's mathematical formulation, however, by 1950 he also assumed a much less critical stance on the oversights of Harrod's model. Harrod's theory was centred on an equation which related the rate of growth of output and capital coefficient to saving expressed as a proportion of income. Hicks accepted Harrod's fundamental equation and its instability principle, but maintained that 'mathematical instability does not in itself elucidate fluctuation' (1949d, p. 108). None the less, he transformed Harrod's fundamental equation into a difference equation to allow for lags, making 'investment depend upon the increment of income in the preceding period, and *consumption* upon the income of the preceding period' (p. 110). Without denying his own originality, Hicks noted that this way of setting the problem could also be found in the work of Samuelson and Hansen.

Hicks did add his own new devices for checking instability, the lower and the upper limit within which his cycle would fluctuate. 'Something', Hicks wrote, 'has to be introduced to stop the slump' (1949d, p. 111). To arrest the downward movement, he employed Harrod's long-range investments. The model's check in the upward movement was the ultimate exhaustibility of employable resources, making them dependent 'upon the trend value of output ... upon the natural growth of the economy' (p. 112). Both limits would exist, Hicks asserted, provided that four conditions held in the model:

1 that the relations between income and consumption, on the one hand, and between investment and changes in income, on the other hand, should be such as to impart a rather strong tendency to instability in the level of output [a descriptive condition already noted above];
2 that the system should have an upward trend, and that some investment should be geared to that upward trend;
3 that supply of resources, at any given time, should not be inexhaustible;
4 that falls in output should not induce disinvestment in the way that rises

> in output induce investment [expansionary phase and contractionary phase are asymmetrical]. (1949d, p. 119)

Hicks believed that these hypothetical prerequisites were not only necessary, but very reasonable to assume. He was also persuaded that his model, with these prerequisites, explained with 'a minimum number of hypotheses' what the economy experiences; 'it is hardly possible for a *theory* of the Cycle to do more than that' (1949d, p. 119).

The number of additional conditions or simplifications which Hicks introduced 'by choice' would, however, render his model able to do much less than anticipated. In his description of the continuing trade cycle process, Hicks was clearly not wanting to be concerned with determining whether planned investments were realized or demand expectations fulfilled. He simply assumed 'unmotivated' continuous adjustment in demand, output and stocks, as long as resources are available to sustain a process or to permit an increase. Further, he incorporated the device of a period 'arbitrary in length' and assumed that 'all induced investment corresponding to a particular change in output is concentrated in a single period' (1950a, p. 67). In so doing, he avoided complications (and possibilities) of overlapping and a complex lag structure. Under these restrictions, Hicks's dynamic process, described above, was easily put into a mechanistic model. Changes in the level of stocks, as they run down (or build up) generate a positive (or a negative) cumulative process. Once the process begins, it continues in one direction until a ceiling or floor barrier is reached, which alone can halt the process and reverse its course.

The fact that there was no equality between current supply and demand in Hicks's trade cycle model could have been significant, since it raised questions about how the model dealt with prices. The difficulty of handling price changes while analysing quantity changes led him, however, to assume a fixprice model, that is, one in which prices are given exogenously under the one condition that they at least cover costs. In a trade cycle model of the fixprice approach (see chapter 3), the distinction between stock and flow becomes very important. Hicks indeed believed that troubles with his model had arisen 'from inadequate attention to stock conditions' (1965a, p. 109). He felt he had spent too much time on calculating algebraically the period of the cycle, an exercise he labelled 'a pure waste of time' (p. 112), and too much energy on the construction of a model ultimately applicable to a special, particular theoretical case of simple specification with very few macro-variables and a naïve lag structure.

Hicks's claim at the outset of his *A Contribution to the Theory of the Trade Cycle*, that his model was designed to explain economic dynamics, was challenged both theoretically and empirically. (For more of these discussions, see Alexander, 1951; Burns, 1952; Duesenberry, 1950; Goodwin, 1951; Kaldor, 1951). Although Hicks recognized soon after that he had not been completely successful, he was sanguine about the challenge of devising an accurate model of the trade cycle and felt that it ought not be surprising that simple formulae 'rarely provide a good fit to the time-shape of actual cycles . . . things which determine the time-shape of the cycles which they produce are of a more complex character' (1965a, p. 113).

The issue here, however, is not whether Hicks's model explained the actual world, but whether his model succeeded in presenting a dynamic economics. Hicks had attempted to find the simplest interactive process which could explain cyclical movement without introducing the complications of money, prices, or government policies. According to the criteria he himself used to judge the classical models for their dynamics, his was indeed a model which could describe a process in which change is sequential. Hicks had included stock and flow analysis, although he was unhappy about his treatment of stocks. His periods, however self-contained in terms of the definition of each variable (all changes in any variable take place within the single period), were none the less linked, since, for example, the income of one period was connected to the consumption of the next period. Liquidity, medium of exchange and expectations, although not integrated, were in the background. As in his temporary equilibrium model of *Value and Capital*, Hicks had enough ingredients in his trade cycle model to make it dynamic. This time, however, he succeeded in rendering the analysis sequential. None the less, the model's dynamics remained straightforwardly mechanical.

Hicks's trade cycle model was not perceived as dynamic by Kaldor, for example, who was astute in pointing out that Hicks's 'cyclical model works in exactly the same way under static assumptions with no trend as under dynamic assumptions with a trend introduced from the outside' (Kaldor, 1951, pp. 846–7). Goodwin also pointed to Hicks's artificial separation of the trend from the cycle (Goodwin, 1951, pp. 319–20). Later, responding to his critics, Hicks proposed various ways of improving the model descriptively or mathematically. He was, however, very sceptical as to whether complicating the model mathematically could accomplish the goal of incorporating more significant descriptive dynamics.

Growth models

After being critical of the attempts of his two major earlier methods to render economics dynamic, Hicks proceeded with another version of growth theory, to give more consideration to the stock and flow element as well to combine his fix- and flexprice methods. He tried to construct 'a formal theory of an economy which is not in a steady state . . . an economy which has a history, so that things actually happen' (1976f, p. 144). To achieve such a theory with a very simple model he endeavoured to give an account of dynamics through what he called traverse analysis. While not very successful in his first version of the traverse in *Capital and Growth* (Traverse I), Hicks none the less produced a second version in *Capital and Time* (Traverse II) which yielded an interesting way of conceiving dynamic economics.

The definition of the traverse first appeared in 1965 in the context of Hicks's discussion of charting the passage of an economy from one equilibrium to another. For Hicks, the traverse was the course the economy takes while in disequilibrium as it undergoes its transformation from being in a state of equilibrium based on one set of conditions to being in another equilibrium state based on another set. In *Capital and Growth*, while focused on equilibrium theory, Hicks saw the traverse as the disequilibrium passage from one equilibrium state to another. Although he stated that, 'we do not greatly diminish the generality of our study of disequilibrium if we regard it in this way, as a Traverse from one path to another' (1965a, p. 184), Hicks recognized later that his theory was dominated by steady-state path analysis. By 1973 and the writing of *Capital and Time*, however, his concern was no longer with an economy's reaching equilibrium but with the dynamics of the traverse itself.

In both *Capital and Growth* (1965a) and *Capital and Time* (1973d) Hicks tried to integrate his fixprice and flexprice methods in a model which assumed a fixed coefficient production function. Each simple and complete traverse model consisted of three relations: price, quantity, and saving equations. In Traverse I, the three relations were the rate of profit to the wage rate, the rate of growth to output and consumption, and the rate of profit to the rate of growth. These same ingredients were found again as the basic elements of the traverse, presented slightly differently, in *Capital and Time*. In Traverse II, Hicks devised the three relations as the rate of wages to the rate of interest, the rate of productivity to the rate of growth and a bi-level relation of the level of wages to the rate of productivity and the rate of profit to the rate of growth.

Traverse I was rooted in steady-state analysis and was, Hicks realized, not terribly enlightening for dynamic economics. Hicks was in fact unhappy about the way he had conducted his analysis of the traverse in *Capital and Growth* and in various of his works noted its failings. In *Capital and Growth* Hicks had proceeded in Marshallian manner to examine changes in rate of growth in light of a steady-state growth equilibrium with a given technology. He spent a great deal of effort discussing the conditions of equilibrium in which prices are determined in a fixprice manner. As for prices during the traverse when the economic system is out of equilibrium and determination of its prices would be of great theoretical concern, Hicks could include only that the sytem 'may behave as the FIXPRICE model behaved; or it may behave in other ways' (1965a, p. 132). In fact Traverse I could say very little about prices. Hicks posited that the problem might lie with aggregation, saying that 'if we are to deal with the price changes properly, we have to disaggregate; and it is the disaggregate growth equilibrium which is hard to stomach' (p. 183). In fact, problems had arisen because his analysis was a simple, standard growth model confined to steady-state theory in which, as he came to realize, periods 'are linked together; but the price of the linkage is that the periods are made similar; each of them in essential respects, is just like the rest. Such a long-period equilibrium, or growth equilibrium, is indeed a relapse into statics – a much worse relapse' (1977a, p. xv).

Since the features of Traverse I and II were almost alike and the concern here is dynamic economics, concentration will be given to Traverse II. The originality of the dynamic analysis of Traverse II ensued from the introduction of technological changes or 'impulses', as Hicks called them. It could also be characterized by his predominant concern with what happens during the traverse, even though the model begins from a state of equilibrium.

In *Capital and Time* Hicks was interested in applying his traverse analysis to the historical question of the impact of technological change on employment and the distribution of income in both the short and long run. He emphasized the process of factor substitution in an expanding economy in his reworked theory of dynamics, which considered both capital and cause-and-effect relations. Capital and causality are treated in this volume in separate chapters as independently strong interests of Hicks.

In the Traverse II model Hicks suggested beginning from a particular situation at a given date, assuming everything that happened before that date as given, and then comparing two alternative paths which extend into future, of which one is affected by a disturbance while the other is not. The difference between the paths, he wrote, 'extends over time, so that there are "short-run" and "long-run" effects. But merely to distinguish between short-run and long-run is not sufficient'. He considered 'the *whole* of the difference between the paths' significant (1973a, p. 203). Hicks was not so much interested in comparing the initial and terminal paths' positions, though these were his reference equilibria, but rather in observing the traverse at every point in time.

As has already been briefly described in chapter 3, in his Traverse II model, Hicks, like the classical economists, focused his attention on the production side of the economy. He called the production process a process which converts a flow of inputs into a flow of outputs. In a completely integrated process one homogenous input (labour) produces one output (a consumer good). Hicks made no reference to intermediate goods. He assumed constant returns to scale. The model consisted of one price, one interest rate and one input–output ratio. Input and output were expressed in value terms; wages, in terms of the consumer good.

The simple profile model is set out in Table 4.1 as the standard case. Hicks supposed that in year 0 (which he called the construction period) it takes a_0 of labour to produce one machine (with no output yet possible), at a cost of wa_0. In subsequent years, say from period 1 to n (Hicks called this the utilization period), the newly constructed machine operated by a_t labourers will produce b_t output per year at a cost of wa_t. Net output q_t is the difference between the product and its cost $(b_t - wa_t)$. At any moment there will be many machines of different ages in operation. While some will have just started to function, some will be at their half-life of operation and others will be nearly finished. The number of machines and their phases, or the number of 'processes' to Hicks, at any particular point in time depends on the number of processes started in the past. For convenience, a year is taken as the unit of period length. All unit-processes are identical; all have the same time profile. All machines have the same life-span, from construction to termination of function. All plans carry through; once a machine begins its utilization phase, its output in the succession of periods is constant. The growth of the rate of 'process' starts, x_T, is constant; the death rate of processes begun $n + 1$ years ago is compensated for by the current birth-rate. Since every technique has a simple profile, Hicks believed re-switching was excluded. He assumed static expectations, for example, 'when the decision to adopt a particular technique for *new* processes is taken, the current wage is expected to remain unchanged' (1973d, p. 56).

Hicks's Traverse II model consisted of few equations. Net output at any specific time was simply the difference between the value of what is produced and its production cost (Equation 1). The initial capital of process k_0 at time 0 was equal to the present value of the future stream of net output (Equation 2). At any given time, total current input A_T (which was also, in this model, the total current employment) was the sum of all inputs used in every process operating at that time (Equation 3). The total current output was the sum of all current outputs produced by various processes in operation also at a specific time (Equation 4). Given the total current output value and the total current input value at time *T*, Hicks could determine the total current value of net output (Equation 5). Given Equation 5, Hicks derived two types of analysis: one was his Fixwage Theory (fixprice method) in which wages are given exogenously and in which the level of employment remains to be determined; the other was his Full Employment Theory (flexprice method) in which instead the supply of labour is given while the level of wage is yet to be determined. In the Full Employment Theory, the supply of labour was independent of the wage rate. Both theories were used by Hicks to analyse the case of an economy expanding at a constant rate. Technology was taken as unchanging, and the initial choice of it was determined by the coefficients of production ($a_0 a_1$), the quantities of labour used in the construction and in the utilization sectors respectively.

As mentioned above, Traverse II is based on three relations. For a given technique of production, Hicks needed the following:

The wage–interest relation: The portion of the net output reinvested by the entrepreneur will depend on the profitability of each process. For a process to be viable, it must yield at least the market rate of interest. Given this condition, Equation 2 can be written as Equation 7 and easily re-written as Equation 8 (see Table 4.1). It is the relation of Equation 8 which Hicks referred to as the wage-interest curve or the 'Efficient Curve'.

The productivity–growth relation: When the rate of growth is given exogenously and when the rate of starts x_t follows the same expansion (Equation 10), then by combining Equations 3 and 4. Hicks obtained the 'Restricted Efficiency Curve', relating the output per worker, *B/A* (or productivity), to the rate of growth *g*. '*B/A* is the same function of *G* as *w* is of *R*. The same efficiency curve will, so it appears, express either relation' (1973a, p. 65).

Table 4.1 The simple profile

1 *Model*:

(1) Net output at time t: $q_t = b_t - wa_t$

(2) Initial capital: $k_0 = \sum_0^n (b_t - wa_t)R^{-t}$

(3) Total current input: $A_T = \sum_0^n a_T x_{T-t}$

(4) Total current output: $B_T = \sum_0^n b_T x_{T-t}$

(5) Total current net output: $\boxed{Q_T = B_T - w\, A_T}$

w and r relation, $w = w(r)$:

(6) Let $R = I + r$

The margin of viability requires that a given process should yield at least:

(7) $k_0 = 0 = \sum_0^n (b_t - wa_t)R^{-t}$

$$(8)\quad \boxed{w = \frac{\sum_0^n b_t\, R^{-t}}{\sum_0^n a_t\, R^{-t}}}$$

$\frac{B}{A}$ *and g relation*, $\frac{B}{A} = \frac{B}{A}(g)$:

(9) $G = I + g$

(10) $x_T = x_0\, G^T$

$A_T = \sum_0^n a_t\, x_0\, G^{T-t}$

$B_T = \sum_0^n b_t\, x_0\, G^{T-t}$

$$(11)\quad \boxed{\frac{B_T}{A_T} = \frac{\sum_0^n b_t\, G^{-t}}{\sum_0^n a_t\, G^{-t}}}$$

saving relation, $g = sr$

2 *The standard case*:

	construction period	utilization period
years	0	1 to n
Inputs	a_o	a_1
Outputs	0	b
Net output	$-wa_o$	$b - wa_1$

Table 4.1 *Continued*

3 *Indexes*: Let (a_0; a_1) and (a_0^*; a_1^*) be two techniques; then the following are

$$I(r) = \frac{w(r)}{w^*(r)} \quad \text{Index of improvement } w(r) \text{ where:} \quad I(r) = \frac{w(r)}{w^*(r)} = \frac{\dfrac{\sum_0^n b_t R^{-t}}{\sum_0^n a_t R^{-t}}}{\dfrac{\sum_0^n b_t^* R^{-t}}{\sum_0^n a_t^* R^{-t}}}$$

$$h = \frac{a_0^*}{a_0} \quad \text{Index of saving in construction cost}$$

$$H = \frac{a_1^*}{a_1} \quad \text{Index of saving in utilization cost}$$

If $h = H = I$: no bias and no improvement.
If $h = H > I$: no bias but improvement in both cost and utilization.
If $h \neq$ H; if $I(r)$ is near H: the switch is forward bias.
if $I(r)$ is near h: the switch is backward bias.
if $h > I$ and $H > I$: we have a weaker bias.
if h or $H > I$ and h or $H < I$: we have a strong bias.

All that Hicks still needed to complete the model was to introduce a *saving relation*, 'one further condition, to establish a relation between the two "levels" – between r and g, or between w and (B/A)' (1973a, p. 69). The purpose of the additional condition was to link wages and production and hence to join his two initial relations. Hicks assumed that saving was a fixed proportion of profit and that net investment equalled saving, that is $gK = srK$ or $g = sr$, where s is the propensity to save.

Hicks used several indexes which would permit the comparison of two different technologies. The index of improvement *I(r)* measured gain or loss in overall efficiency. Use of a new technology might bring about an improvement in the construction sector (Hicks called this a backward bias), or in the utilization sector (a forward bias), or it might improve both sectors in the same proportion, or in favouring one over the other (see Table 4.1 for the different cases of bias, strong and weak, forward and backward). Technological improvements were viewed as cost saving, and since, in Traverse II labour was the only cost, Hicks referred to technological changes as labour-saving improvements.

Now that a sketch of the model has been set out, the dynamics of Traverse II may be examined. The analysis of the impact of a change in technology differed for Hicks depending on whether it was applied to the Fixwage or Full Employment Theory. For both theories, however, a complete chain of causation could be derived. For instance, in the Fixwage assumption (the fixprice case), given w, Hicks could determine r, which through the saving relation determined g, which in turn determined B/A. When the Full Employment Theory was assumed (the flexprice case), given g, Hicks could determine r which in turn determined w.

In the fixwage assumption (Fixprice Theory), the wage rate is given and the new technology provides a higher rate of return. By keeping the consumption-out-of-profits level constant Hicks assumed that all gains from the change in technology are reinvested. (This is called the Q assumption.) With the increase in the rate of return, profits would increase too. Increased profits means that gross investment would go up, and additional machines would be built and utilized. The increase in processes would in turn increase profits and so on.

Hicks observed that the course of employment and that of output both depend on the type of technological improvement. In the Fixwage Theory, every time there is a technological impulse there will initially be a decreased need for labour and an ensuing ejection of workers from employment. If a new technology were to effect a backward bias to improvement in construction, at first there would be a reduction of employment, but when the reinvested profits increase the rate of starts, both employment and output would increase as the additional machines become operational. If, however, the new technology were to cause a forward bias improving the utilization sector, with new labour-saving machines albeit each of less output capacity than the old, then at first employment and output would be reduced. None the less, profits made in the utilization sector would be reinvested for the construction of additional machinery. This would initially create the need for additional employment in the construction sector, and with the eventual increase in production capacity, it would also create an additional employment need in the utilization sector. This is what Hicks believed the Ricardo case to be: 'The introduction of "machinery" has an adverse effect on employment *in the short run* . . . the harmful effect might persist, for quite a time. But not indefinitely' (1973d, p. 98).

In the full employment assumption (Flexprice Theory), the analysis is more difficult. While no change in employment results from a change in technology, a change in profit does. This in turn causes changes in the wage rate which effect further changes in techniques and technology. To deal with one problem at a time, Hicks first took a single new technology and analysed the introduction of one new technique after another with no substitution involved. He then considered the case of technology substitution.

In the Full Employment Theory, although a new improved technology is available, full employment of labour is maintained. Technological improvement can have different impacts depending on the nature of the improvement it brings about. In the case where a technological improvement entails the introduction of new machines with a larger output, but no labour-saving capacity in either the construction or the utilization sector, the improvement will affect both sectors in the same way. There will be no transfer of labour from one sector to another, but on the whole there will be an increase in production and capacity. If, however, the new technology causes a forward bias, an improvement in utilization, labour will be shifted to the construction period, and an additional number of new machines will be constructed. As these machines become operational, there will be a secondary effect, that is, some labour will gradually be shifted back to the utilization sector. According to Hicks, if the primary effect is greater than the secondary effect, there will be pseudo-convergence to a labour equilibrium. Actually, labour will keep being shifted from one sector to another until all old machines disappear from the production process. In the case of a backward bias, an improvement in construction, there is an opposite effect: labour shifts from construction to the utilization sector.

Hicks concluded from the dynamics of the theory and the model that technological improvement is of benefit to workers, for it will eventually inevitably lead to higher wages. While the consumption of the entrepreneur is not affected by the change in technology and increased profits, if the assumption about saving-out-of-profit is maintained, 'the course of wages will be the same as that of productivity, for the whole of the excess product goes to wages' (1973d, p. 109). All gains from technological improvement are reinvested to become circulating capital in the form of wages.

These conclusions led Hicks to formulate in the context of his Traverse II model and theory what he called his 'substitution function'. From his assertions that technological change in the short term causes an increase in profit either with a decrease in employment (Fixwage Theory) or at no cost to employment (Full Employment Theory) and that wages will inevitably rise from technical improvement, Hicks derived his principal proposition of dynamic economics in *Capital and Time*. It dealt with the schedule for introducing technological impulses:

> The function of substitution, in an expanding economy, is to slow up the rises in wages that come from technical improvement; but the effect of the retardation is to stretch out the rise, making it a longer rise, so that a larger rise, than would otherwise have occurred, is ultimately achieved. That is the Principal Proposition I am advancing in this chapter. It is surely an important proposition, perhaps the most important in all this book. (1973d, p. 115)

The substitution effect is played out between a change in wage and a change in profit. Hicks reminded his readers that new technologies are introduced with the aim of increasing profits. So ever newer machines may well be added to older, but not amortized processes, and wage rate changes will occur as a result of each new impulse. To explain his substitution effect under conditions of full employment, Hicks used both a description and diagram (see 1973a, p. 112). The technical aspects of his discussion will be fully explored in the following chapters on labour and on capital.

Many critics have pointed out weaknesses in Hicks's Traverse II model. It was aggregated, highly integrated and too simple, with many unrealistic assumptions. The very crucial and vital element of the model, capital, was not even treated explicitly. The mechanics of the model was constrained by steady state analysis. Hicks was, however, not only aware of these weaknesses, but admitted that he had deliberately chosen such conditions in order to show that even with a simple profile model it is possible to begin from equilibrium analysis and very quickly, once the basic ingredients are understood, 'to kick down the ladder' (to free oneself from equilibrium theory) and to concentrate finally on the dynamics of the traverse. Unfortunately the kind of dynamics Hicks wished to represent was simply beyond what the model could do. Since technological invention and innovation are unpredictable, it is very difficult to make the traverse model of Hicks, no matter how complex, operational; the same is true of any other model dealing with technological change. None the less, the model can, when based on identifiable past technological shifts, help to give an idea of how historical changes have occurred.

From Hicks's new perspective on dynamic economics, the interesting thing about his Traverse II model is not really its mechanics, but its evocations. Hicks was able to extract from that model of simple profile a powerful dynamic projection. By its extension, which allows for a more flexible and realistic assumption in which both fix- and flexprice theories are operative simultaneously, one can see how, in an economy which is frequently being bombarded by technological impulses, disturbances are constantly shifting labour both from one sector into another as well as in and out of the employment force. From this perspective, convergence of labour to an equilibrium is unimportant. What is crucial is an understanding of the forces which cause labour shifts.

5

Labour, Production and Substitution

The 1929 crisis had a devastating impact on economic activity and on employment, and it preoccupied the minds of leading economists. Indeed, Hicks's early writings, during the period from 1929 to 1932, were on the labour market. At the time, he was, however, still feeling his way into economics, and as he admitted, up until 1930 he was not yet thinking in terms of theory. He did have some knowledge of wage fixing in the British building industry, which was the topic of his M.Litt. paper (1928); however, his interaction with Dalton at the LSE aside, it took the papers of Clay ('The public regulation of wages in Great Britain', 1929) and Dobb ('A sceptical view of the Theory of Wages', 1929) to whet his interest in both the political and theoretical aspects of the labour market. His attempts to work out a response to each started him off as a theoretical economist.

Throughout his long career, Hicks did not devote any whole study to labour theory, after *The Theory of Wages* (1932b). Early on, criticism of the book caused him to reject parts of it and initially to distance himself from the issues of labour theory. Over time, his own interest shifted to general theory, where the labour market formed simply a part of the whole; he did, however, write some tangential articles devoted to clarifying aspects of labour and wages or the implications of policy (1935f, 1936c, 1947b and 1955b). It was not until 1963, in the second edition of *The Theory of Wages*, that Hicks expressed recognition of the bad timing of the book's initial publication and how hasty he had been to consider criticisms of it valid. The experience of high inflation in the 1970s made him see that a great deal of his theory of real wages in the book had actually become pertinent. His new enthusiasm for discussing inflation and wage and employment policies is found in many subsequent articles (1970g, 1972b, 1975a, 1976d, 1977a, chapters 3, 4, 1982a, chapters 20, 24, 1989a, chapter 15).

In this chapter the discussion of labour and production will begin with an explanation of Hicks's conception of the functioning of the labour market both from a theoretical and an applied point of view and with his assessment of the way wages are determined in the competitive free market and in the market dominated by trade unions. Because of the importance of his initial adherence to the production function, especially in *The Theory of Wages*, and the ingenuity of the changes he later made to that function, the evolution of his approach to the production function will be traced through to his ultimate abandonment of it in favour of the production process. Related to labour and production, the question of the distribution of income will also be presented, in conjunction with the issue of the substitution of factors. Finally, Hicks's views on wages in the actual world will be discussed.

How the labour market functions

Hicks's early belief was that wages and employment are primarily determined by supply and demand in the labour market independently of other markets. According to this early conception, the working of the ideal labour market was ruled by economic forces alone. Hicks was to acknowledge that the factors of customs and ethics, for which, he maintained, there 'had always been room' in his theory ([1955] 1982a, p. 195), were so entrenched in society's attitude to work that they were as important as economic forces in determining wages and employment. 'Economic forces do affect wages, but only when they are strong enough to overcome these *social* forces.' Acceptance of a wage by both employee and employer was a crucial part of the efficient operation of the labour market. That notion of an acceptable wage was, Hicks realized, not the product solely of economic forces, but was highly influenced 'by custom ... or by any other principle which affects what the parties to the wage-bargain think to be *just* or *right*' (p. 195).

Also, while in the early 1930s, Hicks had seen the trade union movement as an obstacle to the maintenance of the equilibrated wage level of supply and demand, by the 1950s he began to envisage a justifiable social and economic role even for collective bargaining. 'There are important social and (expectational) elements', he wrote' 'even in the "free market" part of wage-determination' (1963b, p. 319). At first, Hicks seems to have considered labour market regulation responsible for the strong role for such social forces as trade unions in wage rate determination. Near the end of his life, however, he had fully integrated the existence of trade unions into his conception of the competitive labour market. In the language of the 1980s, he wrote, they provide the single worker with the guarantee (and protection) of information about the labour market.

In *The Theory of Wages* Hicks began his contemplation of a theory of labour by enquiring about the ideal economic conditions under which 'just' and 'right' wages are determined by economic forces alone. He assumed that, in the absence of control, wages (the price of labour) were 'determined, like all prices, by supply and demand' ([1932b] 1963b, p. 1). He believed that in the free market system driven by competition and the price mechanism 'free of all "interference", by government or by monopolistic combination', labour would find its equilibrium easily (1982a, p. 3). By a free market system Hicks meant one in which workers and employers are not organized in such a way as to influence the determination of wages. Also, in a free market system there are no government controls or other externalities to obstruct the functioning of the market. Without restriction, workers can sell their labour services and entrepreneurs can buy those services in order to produce goods and services. Allowing for 'certain peculiar properties' of labour ([1932b] 1963b, p. 1), in *The Theory of Wages* Hicks considered the labour market able to function like any other commodity market according to the laws of demand and supply.

For Hicks, labour market interactions were based on the fairness and goodwill of those who sell their services and those who buy these services. Any worker who is unhappy with the going wage would be free to leave his or her employer. Any employer, who is unhappy with a worker's demands for wages he or she thinks are too high, is free not to employ that worker. Such freedom of movement, Hicks thought in 1932, should insure that wage policy would be fair to both parties. In such a system there would be no need for a trade union or any other organization to help in wage settlement.

Hicks believed that even in bad times the behaviour of employers and employees would mesh together in such a way as to overcome difficulties. Employers would not take the opportunity to release all their temporarily excess labour because the selection of good workers entails luck, not likely to reoccur when needed. Employers thus tend to keep their good workers, even if they are not needed for an interim spell. In his opinion, employers also would not take advantage of the bad economic situation to cut wages. Some employers, he observed, might in the very short run take the opportunity to lower wages in order to make more profit. Since, however, they would do so at the risk of losing good workmen, maintaining good relations with the workers and safeguarding their own future, most employers would sacrifice a temporary loss in profit and sustain the level of wages offered ([1932b] 1963b, p. 57). In return, the workers who were still employed would appreciate the difference between their own 'good' employer and other 'bad' ones and weather some of the less pleasant conditions of being in his or her employ during difficult economic times. Hicks relied on the harmony between employer and employee, based on good will, optimism and temporary foreseen fluctuations, to justify long-range stability in the labour market. In a free market, in the absence of the trade union or any other organization affecting work relations, improvement in the economic situation alone could rectify the hardship of temporarily low employment.

In addition to fairness and goodwill in labour relations, competition was an equally important feature of the labour market Hicks envisaged in *The Theory of Wages*. He discussed two conditions as essential for the existence of competition in the labour market place. The first has already been noted, the freedom of the employer and employee to chose their partners and to change those partners. For Hicks, free competition in the labour market was characterized by free communication in a fluid market of an infinitely large number of buyers and sellers. Each individual must be free to contract with a number of others. Every employee must be free to go away from one employer in search of 'a better offer' from another; every employer must be free to dismiss one worker if he or she desires and to engage another.

Hicks also observed the necessity of another condition for the competitive labour market, some continuance of the relation of employer and employed. 'The employer expects the employee to stay with him, at least long enough to make a wage-bargain on that assumption, and the employee the same. It is here that there can most obviously be a market on which a wage is competitively determined' (1989a, p. 29).

Although every individual acts on his or her own in this market, in striking a wage bargain the two parties must come to the agreement to settle and work together for their mutual benefit, in the midst of the environment of free competitive mobility. It is the kind of bargain that, should it be renounced by either, both will be losers. The employee loses a job and is forced to find another. The employer is, at the least, obliged to find a new employee and maybe even to cut back on his production operations. The purpose of the bargain is to forestall the loss. 'In all cases of premature ending there is at least some loss for each, a loss which is better avoided. So it pays to take some trouble, and even to incur some expense to avoid it.' To ensure that the wage bargain is not renounced by the other party, the employee can try always to 'give of his best' and the employer 'can see that he pays a wage which is at least as good as what is being paid by his competitors'. An employer who is happy with his employee's services is unlikely to dismiss him or her, and 'an employee who has become established' at a reasonable wage rate 'is unlikely to be tempted away'. Hicks concluded that competition 'in the *established* sector' works none the less on the possibility that dissatisfaction might arise, 'not by actual change of partners, but by potential change' (1989a, p. 30).

Hicks noted that the type of competition in the established labour market, activated by the potential change of partners, was different from the competition in the goods market. 'Competition on the market for goods works for the most part . . . in terms of actual transactions.' It might be seen that in the case of goods, it is the actual transactions which, in a sense, 'make the market', according to the quantity sold and the price given (1989a). On the other hand, competition in the labour market is not activated through actual transactions: 'It works through the influence of ideas about transactions which might be made, but are not' (1989a, p. 30).

The element of potential change was for Hicks a decisive one in determining the composition of the labour market. He saw it as compelling all parties in the labour market to acquire the most information possible about their potential choices or alternatives. This need, Hicks felt, had effected the most significant change in the composition of the labour market: the presence of trade unions. Trade unions were, for him, the response of employees to their need for as much information as employers have. Workers who could get together could jointly employ a professional to collect and make use of information. That, Hicks called collective bargaining. In the absence of trade unions, the employer, he believed, had a bargaining advantage. 'It is simply that he can afford to be better informed, better informed about the alternatives which for this sort of labour are open' (1989a, p. 30). When the employee can also find the means to keep himself or herself equally well informed, that bargaining advantage is reduced. As Hicks saw it, 'the provision of professional advice to the non-professional party [of employees] is needed to make the competitive market work' (p. 30). Trade unions and their collective bargaining from an informed position, as he pondered late in life, could exist simply to make 'the competitive market work more smoothly' (p. 31).

The kind of trade union Hicks had in mind seems to be not that of a monopoly which tries to dictate wage contracts. He consistently maintained that the agreement among groups to negotiate contracts simultaneously would undermine the competitive market. His trade union was simply an institution which facilitated the gathering of information for employees. Thus, even in his most mature views of 1989, while recognizing a role for trade unions, Hicks was still thinking in theoretical terms about the labour market in an ideal competitive framework. His interest in the mechanism of competition led him to focus on wage determination even more than on employment. To begin to understand Hicks's theory of wages, it is necessary to know something about where he stood initially on wage determination as compared with the many positions held by his contemporaries.

Antecedents to *The Theory of Wages*

During Hicks's time at the LSE, which was under the influence first of Robbins, then of Hayek, the economics of Walras, Edgeworth and Pareto were dominant. Their target of attack had initially been the economics of Marshall at Cambridge. Quite on its own, Marshall's dominance was crumbling. Although Pigou attempted to pick up the pieces, Keynes was exercising an independent, growing and equally challenging influence. Marshall's issue of increasing returns animated many debates, but the harshest criticisms, which reverberated after being initiated by Sraffa (1926), were turned toward Marshall's theory of value. In 1929, Dobb's short article 'A sceptical view of the Theory of Wages' attacked the marginal theory of value as applied to the labour market. This article prompted Hicks to enter the fray, initially with 'Edgeworth, Marshall and the indeterminateness of wages' (1930b), his very first theoretical article, and then with *The Theory of Wages* (1932b).

The substance of the debate between Hicks and Dobb focused on the possibility of different analyses of the 'indeterminateness of wages'. According to Hicks, Marshall advocated that, in a competitive economy, equilibrium in the labour market is obtained when wages are equal to the marginal net product of labour. On the other hand, Marshall explicitly accepted that there is no guarantee that the worker will get a wage corresponding to his marginal net product. The fact that a worker can be offered a lower wage and yet still agree to sell his or her labour is a sign that indeterminateness exists in wage determination. Edgeworth, according to Hicks, was more concerned with showing that a freely competitive labour market is better than a non-competitive one. According to Edgeworth, the indeterminateness of wages is due to the presence of externalities which prevent competitive forces from reaching the optimal equilibrium position. The indeterminateness will disappear when competitive conditions prevail.

Dobb criticized Edgeworth and Marshall's theory of wages. He rejected the application of marginal theory to the labour market, especially as it treated labour as a commodity like any other, and assumed that the demand for and supply of labour were independent. Dobb argued that the assumptions of their independence and of constancy in the marginal utility of income were illegitimate. It was inconsistent, he thought, to treat 'the marginal utility of income to the worker as a "constant" when the income of the worker was implied in the definition of what the marginal utility of that income was' (1929, p. 515). Dobb thought that the determination of wages depended exclusively on the mobility of labour, on bargaining power and subjective factors such as the 'will to work' and the 'will to save'. All these elements contribute to the existence of a range within which wages are indeterminate, that is, wages can be a bit higher or lower without affecting the number of employees hired.

Hicks, thinking that wages ought to be determined by marginal productivity, not by marginal net product, was mildly opposed to Marshall's interpretation of the functioning of the labour market and his reasons for indeterminateness. As for Dobb, Hicks was annoyed by his full rejection of marginal productivity. He found in Edgeworth the most persuasive arguments for competition as the key to the determinateness of wages in the labour market. Not only would competition allow for wage determination, it would also establish wages that would be fair for both employers and employees. In the context of the competitive market, the arguments that workers sell their labour for a wage less that the fair wage (Marshall) or that employers take advantage of their workers (Dobb) would not hold. Hicks believed fundamentally that competition, even if it is slow to have its beneficial effect, 'does tend to abolish the exploitation of labour' (1931a, p. 146), in both the Pigovian and Marxian sense.

The Theory of Wages

In *The Theory of Wages*, Hicks was primarily concerned with price determination in the labour market. He was only indirectly interested in employment. His object was the 'restatement of the theory of wages' in the marginal productivity theory tradition ([1932b] 1963b, p. ix). The principle of marginal productivity was by that time well established and according to Hicks in his preface, there was no need to question 'the validity and the importance of this principle' (p. x). A number of features of the labour market, which he considered to be problematic components of the 'real world', were excluded from analysis:

> we are concerned solely with the internal coherence of the conditions of economic equilibrium. Our problem is purely one of the conditions of equilibrium, and therefore it is extremely unwise to complicate our discussions with the consideration of phenomena which only arise in the real world because the economic system is not in equilibrium, ([1932b] 1963b, p. 234)

In *The Theory of Wages*, Hicks's method, as he described it himself, followed the conventional classical route:

> I assumed: (1) only two factors, and (2) perfect competition in all markets. (3) I neglected complications due to increasing returns, and (4) I neglected complications about the maintenance of capital ... [I considered] (5) complications due to the existence of different sorts of products, and (6) complications due to international trade. ([1932b] 1963b, p. 287)

In neglecting 'complications due to increasing returns', he relied 'for strict validity upon the assumption of "constant returns" in the Wicksteed–Wicksell sense; and thus upon the identity of "private" and "social" marginal products' to give him his 'exact conclusions' ([1932b] 1963b, p. 241).

Hicks developed a model for the determination of wages according to marginal productivity. The wage so determined was both an equilibrium wage, the unique wage which corresponds to the employment in a particular skill, and an optimum wage, the best (fairest) wage for both employer and employee. In order to obtain equilibrium and optimality in the labour market, Hicks found it necessary to assume a production function with all its factors, variable including labour, and to allow for substitution to get that combination of factors which leads to the highest output. From the perspective of the employer, the ultimate goal of a firm is to produce goods and services profitably. Under conditions of optimal equilibrium 'both the scale of production and the method of production must be chosen in such a way that no opportunity remains open for employers to benefit themselves by a change' ([1932b] 1963b, p. 11). The employer pays his workers according to their marginal productivity, which is the market wage. Hicks assumed that any divergence from the market wage would result in a waste of resources. From the perspective of the employee, the service of labour is an individual one. Different individuals have different skills, abilities and efficiencies. Hicks emphasized that 'it is the actual service performed by the labourer which is bought and sold not the sacrifice he endures in order to perform that service, or the effort he expends in doing it' (p. 90). By being paid according to their marginal productivity, workers are fairly remunerated for their service.

In *The Theory of Wages*, under these assumptions, Hicks examined 'the condition of full equilibrium in the labour market' in order to 'isolate the pure problem of [labour] demand'. He did not set up his model in this fashion without recognizing that 'we only achieve this isolation at the expense of a series of highly artificial assumptions'; none the less, he did seem to want to squeeze some aspects of the labour market into its formulation in his model. Among his artificial assumptions were two that 'the supply of labourers [is] given, and their efficiencies [are] given and equal' ([1932b] 1963b, p. 7). For the purposes of his model, the demand for labour was fixed and its composition homogeneous. These assumptions affected Hicks's perspective on both 'real' changes in the demand for labour and 'real' differences in wage determination.

Apart from his assumption in the model that the demand for labour is very inelastic, he thought that when time and adjustment in production are taken into consideration the demand for labour becomes elastic. Also, despite his rigorous assumption for wage determination, Hicks acknowledged that some degree of wage indeterminateness would exist in the labour market. His indeterminateness referred to the range within which the wage rate of a worker might change without his or her being replaced; that is, there would be an upper limit to the increase of the worker's wage at which it would be advantageous to the employer to replace him or her by a more efficient worker, and there would be a lower limit to the decrease of the wage at which the worker could not accept the employment and the employer would have no other choice but to replace him or her with another less efficient worker. There are, Hicks noted, a number of reasons why a range of indeterminateness exists inside which wages can indeed change without affecting the individual and the general demand for labour. Among those reasons are the indivisibility of labour and its heterogeneity in terms of efficiency, ability, and a willingness to work as well as the imperfection of the market itself. In 1932 Hicks was already alluding to the social element of custom as a factor in wage determinateness: since the amount of work supplied by each individual depends on 'what he gets for it', 'his ability to work may be affected by the wage he has been in the habit of receiving in the past' ([1932b] 1963b, p. 89).

Further, despite Hicks's assumptions of full employment in his model, he recognized the existence of two types of unemployment: normal and temporary unemployment. For him, the causes of unemployment range from imperfect knowledge to disability to weather disruptions. There exist some individuals who simply cannot fit into the work-force because of their disability or low efficiency; they are 'normally' unemployed, for with their employment '*net* product falls below the level of subsistence' ([1932b] 1963b, p. 44). Temporary unemployment is due to the fluctuations in economic activities, that is, to the business cycle. Since the demand for labour increases during the expansionary periods and decreases during contractions, these changes cause temporary unemployment. Within his theoretical framework, Hicks argued that temporary unemployment for reasons of the economic cycle would rapidly rectify itself, since 'under competition conditions, this unemployment must lead to a fall in wages' (p. 56), which would in turn lead to a decreased burden on employers and the potential for an upturn in the economy. While his cyclical unemployment might be interpreted as Keynes's involuntary unemployment, in fact, it ought not. Because of Hicks's assumption of competition in the labour market, he distanced himself from Keynes. In 1963, he still believed that his 1932 analysis of unemployment was 'right, both as a matter of history and as a matter of theory. It gives a better picture of the working of the labour market than is given by the corresponding model used by Keynes — his awkward distinction between "voluntary" and "involuntary" unemployment' (p. 318).

Although Hicks supposed in his model that labour is homogeneous and that 'the amount of work offered by each man is something fixed', he recognized that 'the amount of work a man does is partly a matter of choice, and the amount he chooses to do depends on what he gets for it'. An individual's willingness to supply work, according to Hicks, might well depend on his or her conditions of employment: working hours, wage settlement, working conditions, etc. Hicks gave the examples of a supervised worker whose conditions of supervision 'affect the amount he does' and a seasoned worker whose past wages affect 'his ability to work' ([1932b] 1963b, p. 89).

Although Hicks, recognizing many of the issues raised by Marshall and Dobb, was well aware that the characteristic of the labour market were difficult to disentangle and to express as homogeneous entities, he chose to concentrate on those aspects of it that he thought to be its basic uniform characteristics. For him, the determination of wages in a marginal productivity theory demanded that the conditions of equilibrium and stability be satisfied. Stability would be assured through perfect competition in the labour market. Perfect competition and perfect foresight mean instantaneous adjustment. Hicks was in *The Theory of Wages* not dealing with the dynamics of the labour market, but with its static conditions. Instead of beginning with a simplified model and expanding to include the peculiarities of the labour market, Hicks locked himself within the dictates of the simplified version of his competitive equilibrium model and attempted to play down all the special characteristics that he had observed. He instead turned all his attention to the static substitution first within labour, then between labour and capital. His substitution and marginal productivity analysis depended on his concept of the neo-classical production function which posed its own set of difficulties. Hicks tried to address these difficulties on many occasions.

Production function

The neo-classical production function was a technical relationship which associated with each combination of capital and labour a level of production. Capital (input) and production (output) were assumed to be homogeneous and divisible. The production function itself was assumed to be continuous and differentiable. Hicks phrased the production function thus: 'If production (in some sense) is X, labour (in some sense) is L, capital (in some sense) is K, is there any relation $X = F(L,K)$ which can be expected to hold, even very approximately, in a closed system, under a given technology?' Further, he raised the issue of the application of the theory of marginal productivity to the production function. 'Can the share of labour and capital, in the distribution of the product, be determined (even approximately) by marginal productivity?' (1965a, p. 293). In this section, the technical aspects of the various production functions that Hicks suggested will be discussed, while the issue of distribution will be treated separately in the followng section.

Hicks catalogued a list of criticisms against the use of both the theory of marginal productivity and the production function. Those against the production function had to be addressed first, for if the function was to be understood to apply in a macro-sense, he announced, its existence 'must be established before the question of distribution by marginal productivity can arise' (1965a, p. 294). Anyway, weighing the difficulties of supporting each, Hicks maintained that the criticism against the use of marginal productivity could 'be rebutted, or partially rebutted' (1977a, p. 3). As for the production function, he acknowledged that it presented some stumbling blocks. For the factors of the production function to be manipulatable, they each, 'product', 'labour', and 'capital', have to be treatable as uniform quantities. While he noted the necessity of 'reducing their obvious heterogeneity to some kind of uniformity', he also observed that 'for none of the three is the reduction a simple matter' (1977a, p. 3).

While the essential issue of Hicks's theory of wages was labour and employment, because of his reliance on the production function for its analysis of distribution and substitution, Hicks found himself distracted by 'the crucial problem' of capital. The difficulties posed by the uniform quantification of labour were, thus, overshadowed by those of capital. The characteristics of capital which are at odds with uniform quantification will be discussed in the next chapter as issues of measurement. The implication of those very characteristics led Hicks on many occasions to reconsider his concept of the production function. At four distinct intervals, owing to revisions of his definition of the capital component, Hicks changed his production function, as follows.

$$X = F(L,K) \quad (1932)$$
$$P = F(L,C) \quad (1961)$$
$$X = F(L,pK/\pi) \quad (1965)$$
$$P = F(L,E_o,E_n) \quad (1973)$$

Initial production function

In Hicks's initial production function, $X = F(L,K)$, found in *The Theory of Wages*, capital K meant both physical and free (fluid) capital. K was used by Hicks in static comparisons, that is when he was 'merely comparing the states of two economies' (1965a, p. 294). At any one point in time, he said, capital was 'largely incorporated in goods of a certain degree of durability' and 'only a small portion of the total supply of capital is "free" – available for investment in new forms' ([1932b] 1963b, p. 19). Labour was paid from circulating capital, whose amount dedicated to employment was 'equal to the wage paid' (p. 17n.). Hicks thus used both physical and divisible capital in an attempt to satisfy two conditions for the production function and for marginal productivity analysis: physical expression for the determination of capital contribution to total production, and necessary divisibility for substitution.

On the one hand, for purposes of uniformity in the production function, capital had to be manipulatable in the form of physical goods, or rather 'an aggregate of physical goods'. The conditions for this being possible are that 'all components change proportionately' and that 'the price-ratios between the goods, or their marginal rates of substitution, remain constant' (1977a, p. 3). In both of these respects, however, any, measurement of capital is vulnerable for in the case of the first, the property of proportionality is unusable and in the case of the second, 'the constant-price' condition cannot be maintained; it involves a contradiction' (p. 4). On the other hand, Hicks's concept of free capital was consistent with his use of equilibrium analysis. At the same time, if it were to have been considered alone it would have prevented him from using the production function and so jeopardized his application of marginal productivity analysis.

Reduced production function

When Hicks reconsidered his production function theory in 1961, he was most interested in capturing 'the production process *in time*'. He thus attempted to reduce the process into a production function corresponding to its dynamics. His reduced production function took its form with four items and a given technique, conceived for a production process in time. To an initial capital stock 'is applied a Flow Input of labour, and from it there emerges a Flow Output called Consumption; then there is a Closing Stock of Capital left over at the end' ([1961c] 1981, p. 194). Given these four components Hicks thought he could construct a production function of the form $P = F(L,C)$, where P is output and closing stock of capital and C is the initial capital stock (201). In this reduced form, since 'capital appears both as input and as output' stock, and labour and consumption are input and output flows respectively, Hicks observed that in this reduced function 'both input and output have stock and flow components' (p. 194). He saw the production relation in the reduced production function as having virtually the same properties' as that of a static theory production function (p. 195).

As might be expected, the measurement of capital continued to be an issue in the reduced production function. The novelty of the measurement of capital in this function was Hicks's introduction of the concepts of forward and backward measures. He thought he had devised a useful concept of capital by bringing in the notions of volume and value and of stock and flow. He opted for the backward-looking volume measure of capital, that is capital volume measured in units of physical goods, to yield a marginal product of capital. Whereas the idea of capital as both input and output in the production process was developed in *Capital and Time*, Hicks seems to have quickly and silently abandoned his reduced production function. Very shortly thereafter, by 1965, he had come up with another version of the production function.

Sophisticated production function

Although Hicks had developed his notions of forward and backward measure of capital by 1961, he rejected the use of the forward measure as a tautology and seemed uncomfortable using the backward measure in his reduced production function. In this next revision of the production function, he thus turned to a value measure; formulated in terms, of 'pK/π' yielding $X = F(L,pK/\pi)$ (1965a, p. 298).

Hicks's sophisticated production function incorporated a shift in emphasis, which translated into '$X = F(L,pK/\pi)$, the supply of capital being now represented by its "real value"' (1965a, p. 297). Hicks was interested in historical comparison and wanted a production function which accounted for an increase in production derived from change in technology. He began by assuming conditions of no change in the supply or the value of capital in terms of consumption (hence 'no change in the consumption price-level') or in the supply of labour. He thought that this would allow him to compare within one economy at two different dates two stationary equilibria 'tied together by the condition that there has been no net saving in the interim', as was the case with 'the new equilibrium (1909) and the old (1899)' (p. 297). He felt that a production function constructed with real capital 'measured by its value in terms of consumption goods', pK/π, where p is the price of capital and π the price of consumption goods, could be used for the sole purpose of comparing equilibrium positions (p. 298). The marginal product of capital in this function is the rate of profit, r.

With this sophisticated production function, Hicks considered the impact over time of changes in technology. He contemplated a period of technological adjustment in which the gradual change in technology would cause production to shift continuously. While the emphasis continues to be on technology as the source of the increase in production, Hicks also considered the implications of that increase on the factors of production. 'Production is rising; so capital must be rising' (1965a, p. 299). To speak of capital rising does not, however, paint the full picture, for Hicks continued to speak of both labour and capital as constant. Capital 'is to be the same in 1909 as was in 1899; if it is rising from 1900 to 1909, it must have dropped between 1899 and 1900'. He maintained that the assumed 'fall in the capital stock' can be subsumed under the elasticity of substitution in the production function as designed (p. 299). Loss of capital can appropriately be measured '*in terms of the consumption that has to be forgone in order that the productive power that is embodied in the physical instrument should be replaced*' (p. 300). Thus change in the relative shares distributed to labour and capital can within the production function account for a rise or fall in either labour or capital. For example, 'as capital increases, relatively to labour, the marginal product of capital (the rate of profit) with fall, and the real wage of labour (the co-operating factor) will rise' (p. 301).

Hicks extended his sophisticated production function with three distinguishing features. He allowed for the consideration of change between two points of equilibrium. He granted change in the labour supply provided that capital and production change in the same ratio, that is, that there would be 'no change in output per unit of labour' and that 'positive saving would only have enabled capital . . . to keep step with the supply of labour – so that the K/L ratio, or the $pK/\pi L$ ratio, would remain unchanged' (1965, p. 302). Lastly, recognizing the implications of considering changing technology, Hicks had come to consider conditions of growth and modelling growth. He thought it possible to construct a sophisticated production function emphasizing these features, but called it an artificial production function. Since, as he said, 'the only production function that can be used in a growth model is one which shows the product to be a function of capital that is measured (or valued)', he thought it might be better to consider the sophisticated production function outright 'as a capital function, showing the value of capital that is needed to produce, with given labour supply, a given output' (p. 304). Expressed in this way, Hicks thought his function would 'come into line' with the Keynesian capital–output ratio theory.

As Hicks was only concerned with comparing equilibria, he felt that his sophisticated production function was 'defensible as an instrument of static analysis' (1965, p. 294). He did, however, conclude that 'once it is admitted that basic improvements are made continuously (or even frequently), the repeated attainment of an equilibrium (of some sort) which has been our analytic life-line, will have to be discarded' (p. 303).

Three-factor production function

It seems that the capital concept continued to raise difficulties which Hicks, even much later was not able to resolve. He had, however, realized over time that capital 'must be neither forward- nor backward-looking; it must live in the present and belong to the present' (1973d, p. 177). In constrast to his reduced and sophisticated production functions, the only measurement of capital which Hicks now deemed meaningful in that context would be that of fixed physical capital or 'machines'. He chose in fact to call it 'equipment'. (As will be seen, it was a measurement of which he would later be quite scathing.) For purposes of substitution, output and labour in the function are 'homogeneous', that is, sharing a uniform measurement with capital.

Hicks assumed that the capital or equipment was given. He considered first the relation between equipment and labour. The given equipment either would or would not require 'a particular complement of labour to work it'. Even if it did not need a specific complement, changes in the supply of labour would still affect the intensity of its use. In the first case the marginal product of labour 'lies between the whole product and zero'. Only in the second case 'does labour have a definite marginal product' (1973d, p. 178). If production is to continue, shares of the total output must be divided between labour and equipment and neither wages nor machines can consume all. Equipment and labour in this production function act according to the standard two-factor production function (under constant returns to scale). 'The share of Equipment in the total product will then be determined as a rent – "quasi-rent" as Marshall would have called it' (p. 178). This version of the production function is called a short-period production function. Hicks thought it could only be used for short-period analysis, for 'we get into endless trouble if we try to repeat the construction for anything analogous to the "long-period" of Marshall' (p. 179).

Hicks wanted increasingly to treat change: change in capital, change in labour and change in output. There could, for example, easily be, in a time sequence, change in capital or equipment due to change in technology. The problem he encountered with production function analysis was, however, that 'the increment in Equipment [New Equipment] is a different factor from the initial stock [Old Equipment]', and had therefore, he decided, to be treated as an independent variable. In order to capture the increase in equipment in a production function, a three-factor function would be needed. 'Product must now be a function of Labour, Old Equipment, and New Equipment' (1973d, p. 179). Old Equipment and New Equipment are different entities: Old Equipment represents old machines, or that portion of capital which is not adjusted to the most recent technological change, while New Equipment is the portion which is already adjusted. Even without a further influx of new technology, from one period to the next the proportion of Old to New Equipment will have changed as new machines are integrated and old ones abandoned; hence the need for a three-factor function.

To work with a three-factor production function Hicks employed 'the reciprocal of my old elasticity of substitution, which I have elsewhere suggested might be called the elasticity of complementarity' (1973d, p. 180). The case of the introduction of New Equipment was a good illustration of Hicks's elasticity of complementarity:

> It is possible (1) that the new equipment may be strongly complementary with labour, so that its appearance raises labour's relative share, or (2) that it may be weakly complementary, so that the earnings of labour increase, though the relative share of labour declines, or (3) that it may substitute [for] labour, in such a way that its appearance causes the earnings of labour to decline. (1973d, p. 181)

Hicks conceived of his three-factor production function in parallel to his model of the production process in the context of his neo-Austrian inspired traverse model of *Capital and Time*. When he described the circumstances for applying both approaches, he wrote, 'Suppose that we were analysing an economy which was in the middle of a Traverse from one technology to another ... the economy is not yet fully adjusted to it' (1973d, pp. 181–2). (See chapters 2 and 4 where production process analysis has already been described in the context of the Traverse II growth model.) In contradistinguishing the production process from the production function, Hicks especially emphasized the concepts of forward- and backward bias, according to which the initial impact of the integration of New Equipment would cause a forward bias and a resulting decrease in real wages, while the extended impact would reverse that trend.

Although Hicks felt that the conclusions he could derive from use of the production process analysis were consistent with those of the production function, he felt that 'it may reasonably be claimed that the neo-Austrian approach is richer; it gives us a deeper understanding' (1973d, p. 182). According to Hicks, it had three major advantages. First, it offered 'some comprehension of the whole of a process of adaptation – not just shapshots of stages'. Second, it related the process of growth to saving and investment, which the production function could not; 'it does not work in terms of saving and investment; for it works with Equipment, not with capital; it is negligent of capital in any accounting sense'. Third, it did not have to treat New Equipment as an independent variable. The last drawback, he asserted, was 'really what is wrong with the Production Function' (p. 182).

Over time, Hicks had become extremely conscious of the inherent weaknesses of the production function. By 1979 he avowed that he was not an adherent of it in any of its forms. Inherent in each of them was the fact that the production function could not be conceived except as a state of affairs at a particular point in time. As Hicks said, 'I insisted ...

that this whole function approach belonged to the Static method. That continues to hold, on every interpretation of the production function – however sophisticated is the form into which it is put' (1965a, p. 305). In sum, the production function could serve him no purpose in his dynamic analysis. At most it could be found in 'the field of the "Static Method in Dynamic Theory"'. (p. 293). Although Hicks remained willing to use the production function, 'for some particular purpose, if a purpose is found for which its weaknesses do not matter too much" [1979g, p. 60), the result of his awareness was his ultimate abandonment of the production function for the production process, its dynamic recasting.

Substitution and the distribution of income

In his studies of the labour market and of production, Hicks was mostly interested in the impact of technological improvement on factor shares and later, on employment. He discussed the issues of substitution and distribution of income in the context of both his production functions and his production process. Through the production function he produced a static determination of factor prices and described distribution of income under a circumstance of substitution of factors where a choice is made between alternative combinations with given conditions. Through the production process Hicks addressed change over time in the distribution of income when conditions are changing, and he also considered the substitution effect. Each of these approaches will now be examined.

Hicks's ultimate assessment of the production function was based on the technical difficulties in expressing the factor of capital according to its use and measurement. These difficulties aside, his approach to the discussion of substitution and income distribution was constant, although the meanings of the various factor prices and factor shares were subject to different interpretations.

According to the production function, Hicks concluded that technical change has an impact on the absolute and relative shares paid to each factor. At the scale of a national economy, technical progress has its effect on the national income or dividend. He believed that adoption of a technological change could only be considered profitable 'if its ultimate effect is to increase the National Dividend' ([1932b] 1963b, p. 121). Just as in his discussion of capital, in the context of labour Hicks also concerned himself with the impact of technical progress on labour. He posed the questions 'whether anything which is to the advantage of the National Dividend as a whole is likely at the same time to be to the disadvantage of the poorer members of society' (p. 112) and 'is economic progress likely to raise or lower the proportion of the National Dividend which goes to labour?' (p. 113). Hicks was persuaded that a complete theory encompassing the labour market ought to be able to answer these questions.

In the context of the production function, optimality was a goal, defined as the situation in which 'it is impossible to increase the output of any product on the list, from given resources and with given technical knowledge, without diminishing the output of some other product, or products' (1981, p. 270). The principle of comparative cost was the basis of Hicks's theory of optimization. To achieve optimality he recognized the need for the possible substitution among workers of different efficiencies within a single trade as well as between the factors of capital and labour. Hicks assumed that when factors are paid according to their corresponding marginal product, 'an increase in the quantity applied of one Factor (that of the other remaining unchanged) would increase the absolute share [or total] of the Product going to the other Factor' ([1973b] 1977a, p. 2). His approach 'treated the Social Product [National Dividend] as being made by two Factors of Production, Labour and Capital' (p. 1). This meant that, for him, the national dividend could be derived, 'other things being equal', through the production function (p. 2).

> Since the absolute share of the increasing Factor might be either increased or diminished (according as its Marginal Productivity curve was elastic or inelastic) the distribution of the Product between the Factors (relative shares) might be shifted either way. Which way it went would depend upon the 'shape' which could be represented, as I showed, by what I called the 'elasticity of substitution'. ([1973b] 1977a, p. 2)

Equally important for Hicks's use of the production function was his observation that the absolute and relative factor shares change when technology is changing. In 1932 he had already defined improvement due to invention as being capital-saving, labour-saving, or neutral, according to whether the ratio of the marginal product of labour over the marginal product of capital was decreasing, increasing or constant. Using his later production functions, Hicks continued to assume that when the function is changing, it is being 'shifted by the discovery of new techniques of producing' ([1973b] 1977a, p. 2). He identified such shifts, those due to invention, either as neutral, 'as far as distribution between the factors was concerned' or as biased toward labour or capital. Inventions which economize in labour are biased toward capital and against labour. Hicks thought that when wages rise, their increase might be an incentive for labour-saving inventions to be adopted.

One element in Hicks's analysis in *The Theory of Wages* was that there is an inverse relation between real wages and real rate of profit. One implication of a rise in real wages with its inverse, a drop in the real rate of profit, would be that increase in real wages would take place at the expense of saving. Further, lower saving would lead to lower investment, lower output, and yet lower profit. A lowering of saving would thus foster the substitution of the factors of labour and capital; it would 'encourage the substitution of what are usually more capital-intensive methods' for labour-intensive ones ([1973b] 1977a, p. 7).

The reaction of firms to a falling rate of profit is to seek out new techniques which could raise that rate and ensure thereby that saving will increase and that capital accumulation can occur. In *The Theory of Wages*, Hicks assumed a saving–investment equilibrium, which implied full employment of labour and 'the traditional view that more saving meant more capital accumulation, and that capital accumulation was favourable to rising wages' ([1973b] 1977a, p. 9). According to *The Theory of Wages*, while a shift to capital intensive methods occurs, full-employment is maintained. Hicks realized in retrospect that this would not be the case. Later, when reinterpreting the relationship of the saving–investment equilibrium and full employment assumption, he concluded that the saving–investment equilibrium path is different from the full-employment path. Hicks had already begun in *A Contribution to the Theory of the Trade Cycle* to consider the two paths distinct and constituting his double equilibrium. By 1973, he assumed 'there is saving–investment equilibrium, maintained continuously; and yet there can be unemployment, if the ratio of prices to wages is inappropriate. That is what I ought to have said in *Theory of Wages*' (p. 10).

With his consideration of equilibrium paths Hicks had redirected his attention from the rate of profit on capital to the expected rate of profit on new investment and to ensuing growth. On the one hand, the determination of the rate of profit through the production function had proved to be troublesome because of the problems associated with the valuation of physical capital. On the other hand, he had also come to realize that the production function and its static substitution were not appropriate for investigating the impact of capital accumulation and technological change. It was thus in the context of the double equilibrium path that Hicks came to explain the substitution effect and the saving effect, saying he had found help in Mill's wage fund theory.

The wage bill (or the real wage bill), that is, the difference between final output and what is used for producing that output, included for Hicks 'not only "consumption out of profits" but also the consumption of public bodies'. It is thus easy to see how the substitution effect and saving effect fit together in the context of an increase in the wage bill when final output increases and 'the increment in this take-out is less than the increment in final product. It must do so, along the double equilibrium path.' Hicks described the chain of effects going from 'investment to final output, from final output to wages, from wages to the rate of profit on new investment' and finally from rate of profit on new investment to investment itself ([1973b] 1977a, p. 12).

Hicks came to put much emphasis on the role of new investment in his explanation of the inverse wage–profit relationship and the substitution effect. 'The mainspring of economic progress, it suggests, is invention; invention that works through the rate of profit. Each invention is marked by falling profit; but the cause of the exhaustion (on the FE, or double equilibrium path) is scarcity of labour' ([1973b] 1977a, p. 15).

Hicks concluded that the effect of a substitution brought about by new investment often leads to both the adoption of more capital-intensive techniques and higher wages. He was unsure as to whether the category of 'induced inventions' ought to be regarded strictly speaking as 'shifts in the Production Function' ([1973b] 1977a, p. 2). In fact, he became less concerned with the production function and stressed that

> It is of little importance, from this point of view, whether the substitutions are supposed to take place along an unchanged technology frontier, or whether they themselves partake of the nature of invention. The technology frontier, useful as it has been in the formation of the theory, and still (perhaps) indispensable in the first stages of presentation, is in the end a piece of scaffolding, that we can take down. The puzzles about 'induced invention' then give no trouble. ([1973b] 1977a, p. 16)

Hicks affirmed that in steady state analysis the size of profits can be unambiguously determined. He noted that once the steady state condition is relaxed, however, the ambiguity of expectations would begin to play a role. 'Out of the steady state the profit that is allocated to a particular period depends on expectations, such as are in practice expressed by conventions about depreciation; there is no such convention that is unambiguously right.' When expectations enter into the equation, distribution across factors, or relative shares, are no longer determined by 'the real characteristics of processes' (1973d, p. 184).

As in *The Theory of Wages*, in *Capital and Time* Hicks continued to tackle the question of the impact of technological change on the distribution of income and on employment. Besides its formal theory and technical analysis, *Capital and Time*, was centred on one principle proposition, which Hicks called 'the most important in all this book': that 'the function of substitution, in an expanding economy, is to slow up the rises in wages that come from technical improvement'. He went on to explain that 'the effect of the retardation is to stretch out the rise, making it a longer rise, so that a larger rise, than would otherwise have occurred, is ultimately achieved' (1973d, p. 115). Although a new technique would be brought in whenever wages rise, the eventual effect of every new technique, he concluded, would be the substitution of lower real profit for higher wages.

When the theory of substitution is re-thought in Ricardo–Mill terms, and when wages are read as their rents, he said that what 'we shall learn then from our Principal Proposition is that induced invention, though it may very probably cause a fall in rents in the short run, must in the longer run raise them' (1973d, p. 123). Ricardo had not considered wages to be at issue in his discussion of rents and profits in his chapter on machinery, because of his assumption of an elastic supply of labour. Hicks, for his part, tried to analyse the impact of an improvement in technology on two different aspects of the labour market: (1) on employment, in a fixwage model where the supply of labour is elastic and (2) on wages, in a full-employment model where the supply of labour is inelastic. He thus transformed Ricardo's discussion of rents–profits into his own wages–profits analysis. Although their approaches were different, Hicks confessed that 'all that, in this place, is relevant, is that we are all of us – Ricardo, Mill and I – saying what in terms of economic principle is the same thing' (1973d, p. 124).

In sum, Hicks designed numerous theories and made frequent changes to models to analyse the substitution effect and the impact of technological change on both wages and employment. In three distinct ways he improved his theories and models to his greater satisfaction. His concept of the substitution of factors within the production function changed first from positing the possibility of static substitution to addressing substitution over time. Second, he reformulated his production function into a production process. Third, in his analysis of technological change he shifted his focus from the rate of profit on physical capital to the rate of profit on new investment, revealing his interest and insight into the motivations and causes behind substitution with and within labour. These later concerns were very pertinent to him for throughout his work contemplation of the actual causes of changes and their effects in the real world were of great importance. His interest in the 'real' labour market was no exception.

'Equilibrium' wage level versus 'social' wage structure and wage inflation

In the last section it was established that under competitive conditions Hicks assumed the labour market to be in full employment equilibrium. Even in *The Theory of Wages* he did not, however, lead the reader to believe that the actual labour market works as described in his competitive model. In practice, on-going wages are not equal to the equilibrium wage nor are they equal to the marginal productivity of the employee. Also, unemployment occurs, precisely owing to the fact, Hicks claimed, that actual wages are at times higher than the equilibrium wage, a discrepancy imposed either by the pressures of trade unions or government regulations. As will be discussed in the next chapter, the relation he posited between wages and unemployment was the classical one.

Right after the publication of *The Theory of Wages* Hicks felt embarrassed by its theory and conclusions, especially given the depressed circumstances of the labour market in the early 1930s but also given the harsh criticism the book immediately received. He came back to the theme of labour on many occasions, either to fine-tune his theory or to assert its relevance for inflationary economic circumstances quite different from those of the severe recession in the 1930s. He also presented his analysis of the labour market in a new historical light.

For Hicks the labour market was composed of two components: established labour or solid employment and non-established labour or fluid employment. He claimed that the working of the labour market of the period before the 1930s was very different from that which followed, for three main reasons. First, 'the world we now live in is one in which the monetary system has become relatively elastic, so that it can accommodate itself to changes in wages, rather than the other way about.' Second, since the end of the Second World War, trade unions had grown in size and strength and had changed thereby the previous relation between unemployment and the 'equilibrium' wage-level, 'a wage that was in line with the monetary conditions that were laid down from outside' ([1955b] 1982a, p. 196). Third, monetary policy since the 1930s focused much more on the labour market than in the past.

Few could deny the newly significant presence of trade unions in the labour market since the 1930s; Hicks considered that trade unions and their economic and social influence had become prominent features of the established sector of labour. Collective bargaining, he observed, 'is subject, up to a point, to scale economies, so the trade union is made more effective by increasing its membership' (1989a, p. 31). At the same time he noted that it was none the less misleading to assume that the increase in the size of trade unions had allowed them to behave in a monopolistic manner, for example in threatening to or actually using the strike weapon to force an employer to pay higher wages. However tempting, he felt one could not use the monopoly theory to analyse the impact of trade union manoeuvering. 'We are now learning that pure theory of monopoly has a very limited application to the behaviour of business-men on the markets on which they sell their products; it is even less likely that it has much application to the labour market – on either side' ([1955b] 1982a, p. 199).

Hicks characterized trade unions as, unlike monopolies, 'better at defense than at attack', for two reasons. First, they show 'general resistance to any cuts in previously agreed wage-rates' ([1955b] 1982a, p. 200), and find formal reductions, for the most part, easy to resist. Second, trade unions press for an increase in wages only when they see the wages of their members lower relative to wages among similar workers; 'when wages of one sort of labour rose, the wages of similar sorts would be drawn up with it' (1989a, p. 31). Depending on the economic climate, Hicks felt these two defensive pressures could have two different effects. In the absence of a rise in productivity they could be responsible for the wage inflation which leads to price inflation. In circumstances where, however, there was no disenchantment by workers with the cost of living, they could lead to wage stability, as was the case after 1945.

The role of monetary policy in the workings of the labour market was equally important to Hicks. The stability of the monetary framework itself could have a significant effect on the determination of wages.

> So long as wages were being determined within a *given* monetary framework, there was some sense in saying that there was an 'equilibrium wage' ... Instead of actual wages having to adjust themselves to an equilibrium level, monetary policy adjusts the equilibrium level of money wages so as to make it conform to the actual level. ([1955b] 1982a, p. 196)

Hicks saw this response of monetary policy to labour wages as analogous to the link between the money supply and a nation's gold holdings. 'It is hardly an exaggeration to say that instead of being on a Gold Standard, we are on a Labour Standard' ([1955b] 1982a, p. 196). When wage stability could be maintained, Hicks regarded 'the Labour Standard as an unquestionable benefit'. He said, 'So long as we retain it, we are protected against the unemployment that arises from a discrepancy between the actual wage-level and the "equilibrium wage-level"' ([1955b] 1982a, p. 196). Assuming the condition of Labour Standard as reigning, Hicks enquired after 'any general principles about the ways in which wages are likely to be determined' (p. 198). His major concern was the implication of the Labour Standard for wage inflation; a very rapid 'rate of wage-inflation which, if it can be prevented from accelerating, is by no means intolerable; the question is [given the Labour Standard] what means exist for keeping it within tolerable limits'. For Hicks this question required that a much broader one be answered: 'What are the factors making for inflation, and what (if any) are those by which the inflation may be held in check?' (p. 198).

Hicks asserted that one cannot get a sensible answer to such questions if one persists 'in treating them as pure problems of economics, in a narrow sense' (1955b, 1982a, p. 199). He believed that it was not purely economic causes, such as full employment, which led to changes in wages, for example, to the continual rise in money wages since 1945. He noted that a more revealing analysis of fluctuations in wage rate can be undertaken, if wages are thought of both as 'determined by an interplay between social and economic factors, instead of being based on economic factors – and crude economic factors at that – alone' (pp. 199–200), and as a historical product 'peculiar to the time through which we have been passing' (p. 209). Wage disputes, for example, Hicks believed, were focused not on money wages, but on 'the relations of money wages to money values of other things' (p. 200). Among these 'other things' he lists the three which, for both social and economic reasons, are in general the ones 'with which comparison is most naturally made': '(1) the prices of the things labour buys – the cost of living; (2) the wages of other workers – differentials; (3) the profits earned by the employer' (p. 200). In the context of explaining why wages increased dramatically in Britain in the early 1950s Hicks itemized the importance of two historical factors: '(1) the dismantling of the [wage] control, with its somewhat 'phoney' effect on the cost of living, and (2) the difficulty that has been experienced in the establishment of a new pattern of relative rates after the war-time disturbance' (p. 209).

6

Capital and Accumulation

When Shove harshly reviewed *The Theory of Wages* in 1933 he criticized Hicks's lack of a theory of capital. Shove pointed out that Hicks did not define capital and raised questions: How is capital to be measured? Should 'capital' mean 'concrete capital goods'? Should it correspond to 'waiting or is it to be identified with 'roundabout methods of production'? How are different interpretations of capital related to the interest rate, to wages and to production? Hicks recognized that Shove's concerns were legitimate, and on many occasions thereafter tried to treat these questions. He immediately revised chapter 6 of *The Theory of Wages* and published it as 'Distribution and Economic Progress: a Revised Version' (1936c). Later, however, he considered it to have been 'no more than an apology for not dealing with the subject' (1963b, p. 342). Given the difficult concept of capital, it is understandable that it took Hicks many attempts to arrive at a satisfactory approach. Looking back in 1962 he found his theory of capital in *Value and Capital* acceptable, but limited. Over the course of his life he produced numerous articles on capital and three books which contained the word 'capital' in the title: *Value and Capital* (1939a), *Capital and Growth* (1965a), and *Capital and Time* (1973d).

Hicks was a visible participant in the debate on capital in the 1930s and 1940s, but continued working outside the next major controversial discussions of capital theory in the 1960s and early 1970s. He considered the issue of capital to have been a continuing preoccupation in his profession in the intervening thirty years and thought that the resurging debate was 'just the old controversy in a new guise' (1973a, p. 190). Understanding the criticism about capital and yet wanting to provide a constructive theory, he intended to play a reconciling role between rival factions at the two Cambridges. Since he saw a 'family' relationship between their rival concepts of capital and valued the contributions of each as 'respectable and useful', he did not see the role itself as absurd.

He pinpointed the major problem in all previous theories as incompleteness; 'they rarely reveal more than a part of the issue' (1973d, p. 151). As will be shown in this chapter, it was a delicate position Hicks assumed, provoking for his own capital theory, perhaps, more suspicion than attention.

Hicks's contribution, which ran parallel to the latest capital debate, in addition to his invention of an extensive terminology, was his constructive devising of a manageable concept of capital. While realizing the extreme difficulty of the task and accepting the critics' arguments, his part was to warn of the pitfalls for those who took any concept of capital lightly or who too easily made use of the production function.

A great deal of this chapter will be devoted to explaining Hicks's many attempts at grasping and elucidating the concept of capital, at making the distinction between fixed and circulating capital and at clarifying the related problem of capital measurement. His two ways of measuring capital (the backward-volume and the forward-value measures) will be set out in the context of his efforts to integrate both forms of capital into a dynamic framework. He tried to conjecture from his capital theory at least one major practical implication; he asked the question whether there is a positive effect of capital accumulation. The direct measure by capital of the effect of capital accumulation on capital leads to a trap: the results of measuring by capital value can be deceptive, while measuring by capital volume is inadequate. The effects of capital accumulation can only be measured indirectly. Hicks's conjectures on evidence for its indirect impact on output, income, prices and employment will be discussed.

The concept of capital

The difficulty that the concept of capital entails is not limited to Hicks's work, but extends to economic theory in general. Thus it is imperative that an attempt should be made to clarify its meaning in the context of Hicks's work, even before beginning an analysis of his discussion of its measurement and how he handled it theoretically. Most of the concepts he employed in his writing, including that of capital, were either inspired by or extended from concepts already in use in economics. His discussion of the concept of capital began with the classical notion of the three factors of production where capital is not a stock, as is land; nor is it a flow, as is labour. 'It is a Fund. Each of the three factors has its own attribute, applicable to itself but to neither of the others. Labour works *on* land *through* capital, not on capital nor with capital' (1977a, pp. 155–6).

The place of capital as a factor of production was recognized by all earlier economists; they did not, however, agree on how to characterize that factor. While they all agreed that it was that to which an increase in production must be attributed when there had been no increase in labour or land, they gave it many different names. 'Senior called it Abstinence; Marshall and Cassel called it Waiting; Böhm-Bawerk Roundaboutness; Barone and Wicksell just Time' ([1979c] 1983a, p. 123). Although Keynes did not himself suggest that liquidity was a factor of production, Hicks hypothesized that he might have, since under the condition of 'involuntary unemployment', liquidity passes the test, that is, its increase causes an increase in production. For his own part, Hicks was tempted to call it saving, since he had identified capital as a Fund. Noting, however, that an increase in saving did not necessarily lead to a subsequent increase in output, he decided that saving did not really qualify as capital. None the less, trying to break away from the 'loaded' terms of others, Hicks suggested yet another: 'ITSO, for Intertemporal Switch in Output', of which he actually made very little use (p. 125).

Although when Hicks defined capital as a factor of production in relation to labour and land, he called it a Fund, when turning to define capital on its own ground, he used the concept of Fund slightly differently. He saw that there were basically two ways in which economists had regarded capital: as a factor of production and as a fund. 'According to the one, capital consists of real goods – 'machines' [or] . . . Physical Things . . . There is an alternative concept in which capital appears as a Fund – Wages Fund, Subsistence Fund, or whatever it may be called.' For Hicks, both concepts referred to real things: 'the Physical concept treats capital as consisting of actual capital goods [fixed capital], the Fund concept reduces it to equivalent consumption goods [circulating capital]' ([1932b] 1963b, p. 343).

Those economists for whom capital was actual physical goods were called by Hicks 'materialists'; those who thought of capital as a fund he called 'fundists'. As materialists Hicks identified Cannan, Marshall, Pigou, Walras and J. B. Clark, and anyone 'who uses a Production Function, in which Product is shown as a function of labour, capital and technology, supposed separable'. Among fundists, Hicks included Smith, the British classical economists, Marx, Jevons, Böhm-Bawerk, and Harrod. 'The capital–output ratio is a hallmark of modern Fundism' (1977a, p. 153). According to his own classification, Hicks himself began as a materialist in *The Theory of Wages* and *Value and Capital*; in these works he used explicitly a static production function, was concerned with physical capital and allowed for substitution between factors. He became a fundist, however, in his *Trade Cycle*, which was definitely based on the capital–output ratio. In his traverse analysis Hicks was concerned with production processes where fixed capital was reduced to time and circulating capital is a fund. In his later work he remained a fundist.

Just as Hicks used the concept of Fund in two different ways in his capital terminology, the issue of capital as stock is also somewhat confusing. Hicks affirmed that in relation to land and labour, capital is not to be conceived as stock. On the other hand, on its own ground he frequently referred to capital as stock, owing to its 'real' nature. In fact, he found the most simplistic way of introducing the concept of capital to be to conceive of it, as he did in *Capital and Time*, as 'the stock of real goods' at any given point in time. He did not, however, stop with this concept but proceeded immediately to split his understanding of capital into two. Either capital is the stock of real goods or it stands in relation to the stock of real goods. In both cases, one is faced with the problematic fact that the stock of real goods is equivalent to a list of heterogeneous physical items. Economics, which deals with more than one economic situation in place and time, needs a single conventional measure, an aggregation, 'by which the stock can be represented' and by which real goods within one or more lists can be related. As Hicks noted, 'the obvious aggregate is an aggregate in value terms' (1973d, p. 151).

As if the issue of defining capital was not complex enough, Hicks added a further nuance to his definitions. In his discussion of the price of capital, the rate of interest and the rate of profit, he attempted to identify in a list of 'candidates' the ones which would play the role of capital as a factor of production:

> Capital I is the original meaning, the business sense of the principal of a loan . . . Capital I is not a macroeconomic concept, so it cannot be a factor of production . . . .
>
> Capital II which surely is a factor of production . . . is the initial stock of goods having value, which is inherited by the current period from the past.
>
> Capital III is still the initial stock, but it is to be taken, now, in value terms . . . Capital III . . . cannot be treated as an independent variable, and hence as a factor of production . . . [valued] in terms of its future productivity.

> Capital IV [is] the value that 'stands in the books' of the proprietors, at the opening date . . . Capital IV cannot be a factor of production of *the period*, if it is valued at historical cost. ([1979c] 1983a, pp. 123–4)

Hicks addressed the valuation of these different concepts of capital in one of two ways, according to volume or value. In one, the volume of capital is aggregated 'by adding money values' and deflated 'by an index of the prices of the capital goods themselves' (1977a, p. 151). This was called the volume value and was determined by calculating the replacement cost of existing physical capital or the accumulated past net input. Hicks called this a backward-looking measure. In the other way, the value of capital was to be determined by capitalizing future values of net product, then by deflating those values by product prices to obtain a measure of real capital. Capital III is an example of this type of forward-looking valuation.

Hicks's awareness of the complexity of the possible meanings of capital led him, on various occasions in his six decades of writing on capital, to use parts of the two sets of descriptive terms (stock-fixed-volume-backward and fund-circulating-value-forward). For him all the terms were interrelated, and those of each set were paired to the other. For his theoretical work Hicks's concept of capital can be reduced to capital conceived either by backward-looking at a fixed stock measured in terms of volume or by forward-looking at a circulating fund (flow) measured in terms of consumer goods value.

Fixed and circulating capital

Although Hicks ultimately established clear terminological distinctions between capital as a physical stock and capital as a fund, it cannot be said that he had the full implication of these distinctions in mind before he produced his traverse analysis. References to fixed capital, working or circulating capital, and depreciation are found in his work as early as in *The Theory of Wages*. None the less, these concepts were not integrated in a cohesive manner into his early models.

An explicit and representative example of Hicks's early attempts to include both fixed capital and working capital is his models is found in *A Contribution to the Theory of the Trade Cycle*. He used the distinction between net investment and gross investment and took depreciation of machines and equipment into account. In his trade cycle model, he made a distinction between capital as equipment and capital as working and liquid capital. While the former meant for him simply a stock of machinery, the latter comprised

> *working capital*, which is to include goods in process as well as such minimum stocks of materials and half finished goods as are technically necessary in the productive process, and *liquid capital*, in the sense of reserve stocks not technically necessary. Liquid capital will include finished goods as well as liquid unfinished. (1950a, p. 47)

These distinctions helped him to discuss the phases of the trade cycle in which each type of capital was seen to behave differently. At first glance it might appear that in his model Hicks dealt with fixed capital (physical equipment and goods) and ignored circulating capital (fund); in fact, the reverse is true. Apart from a definition of both fixed and working capital, in the formulation of his model the issue of fixed capital was avoided entirely. Despite his reference to equipment and physical goods accumulated from past and present production, all Hicks's capital is expressed in terms of investment in value terms. What he called working capital was actually his forward-looking circulating capital, even if not explicitly correlated to capital as fund. In his trade cycle model, fixed and working capital are formulated indistinguishably in terms of investment, and induced to respond to demand. So the main distinction between fixed and working capital became, for Hicks, actual investment in one or the other. With regard to induced investment in fixed capital, depreciation was introduced as the difference between gross and net investment.

Hicks assumed a model of the economy in equilibrium in which net investment is equal to zero, and gross investment is equal to depreciation. He posited the case in which for some reason there was an once-and-for-all increase in income. At that time additional equipment is required, entailing in time its ensuing depreciation. Stocks adjust to the new conditions. Net investment increases by the value of induced investment. Gross investment increases by the same amount, while depreciation remains temporarily at its previous level. Hicks envisaged a following period when all the new equipment is in use. The new net investment will decrease to its previous level, but the depreciation of the new equipment will be added to the previous level of depreciation costs, reducing that new net investment. In yet a following period, when it is time for the equipment to be replaced, net investment will increase in order to compensate for the extra depreciation, 'and so on as far as one can see indefinitely' (1950a, p. 41).

After analysing the fixed capital case, Hicks turned next to the analysis of changes in investment on working capital and liquid capital. He observed that working capital and liquid capital behave differently: usually when one is increasing the other is decreasing. This is explained by the fact that when demand increases, it usually takes time for output to increase. In the meantime, stocks decrease. Liquid capital is thus reduced, while working capital is increased in response to the increase in demand. What then is the impact of the investment response to demand? 'The process of the replacement does not have any very definite time-shape' (1950a, p. 49). It can be fast or slow; it depends on the state of the economy and the business people's reaction. The same can be said about the effects of a decrease in demand. Overall, the theory of induced investment in working capital and in liquid capital 'is basically similar to that for fixed capital' (p. 47).

Looking at the effect of a change in income on induced investment as a whole, Hicks retained three phases. In the first, the impact of change in demand is withdrawn from the stock. Next follows a period in which investment in fixed capital and replacement of stock take place. Finally, there is the period of the replacement of the equipment. These phases are distinct in his one-sector model when the change in demand is once and for all. Any complication allowed in the model, such as an increase in demand followed by another increase in demand produces different results.

Despite all the discussion about the behaviour of fixed capital, working capital, depreciation and deterioration of capital during the phases of the cycle, Hicks did not in the formulation of his model deal either with physical capital, a physical stock of equipment, or with working and liquid capital, a stock of material goods, as determinant variables. Instead he dealt with their value and their expression as investment in the production process. The fact that he assumed in his model that prices are constant, or that if they change, they all change in the same proportion, meant that it did not really matter whether the capital values were deflated by an index of prices to obtain real values; value measures and real measures in this case are the same. Given that, in Hicks's model, investment responded to demand, the impact of changing investment was on future output, and the production function was not used, his analysis was forward-looking. Nothing was said about the heterogeneity of capital or about how physical capital was to be measured. His concept of capital in the trade cycle model was circulating capital, in part, but not completely, a fund.

In contrast to the trade cycle where fixed capital was identified but not subsequently used in the formulation of the model, in Hicks's earlier model in *The Theory of Wages* it is circulating capital which is ignored, even though it is mentioned in passing that the circulating capital required for a given employment of labour must be 'equal to the wage paid' (1932b, p. 17n.). To apply the principle of marginal productivity to the labour market, Hicks introduced a production function which depended on labour and capital. In such a context, capital had to be defined unambiguously. If an increase in production was to be identified with a change in capital, then capital had to be expressed in value terms, provided prices remain constant or in physical terms. To identify such a change using the production function, 'it is only if one is using the Physical concept of capital that it is possible to have a Production Function which represents the state of technology in at all a straightforward manner' ([1932b] 1963b, p. 345).

Also, Hicks recognized that if marginal analysis is to be applied to production, capital had to be divisible. The use of physical capital may solve the requirement for the production function, but it raises the question of divisibility, a necessary condition for both marginal productivity analysis and use of the principle of substitution of factors. Hicks thus turned to the concept of free capital: 'free capital, at any rate, is almost indefinitely divisible' ([1932b] 1963b, p. 25).

Depending on convenience Hicks seemed to use one definition or other of capital, a vacillation that caused him problems. On the one hand, if he chose the production function with its component of capital as free capital, he was able to use marginal equilibrium analysis. 'As we have seen, it is free capital, not capital which has been locked up in fixed plant, which matters when we are examining the conditions of equilibrium' ([1932b] 1963b, p. 25). On the other hand, if he chose capital as physical capital, he could employ the production function. As he noted, however, in his Commentary to the new edition of *The Theory of Wages* (1963b), to compare two equilibria, it can make sense to use physical capital. Later he would add that this was only possible if two conditions were met: (1) that 'all components change proportionally' and (2) that 'the price-ratios between the goods, or their marginal rates of substitution, remain constant' (1977a, p. 3). It was, however, also clear to him that these two conditions were untenable, since 'it is clearly impossible, in the case of capital stock, to claim that the first of these conditions, in the practical application, can be even approximately satisfied' (p. 3) and 'the constant-price condition cannot be maintained; it involves a contradiction' (p. 4). Incidentally, the hypothesis of the constancy of price ratio, posing the same contradiction, is also found in Hicks's trade cycle model.

The capital concept as used in *The Theory of Wages* and implicitly in

Value and Capital thus raised difficult, insurmountable problems for capital in the production function, to which Hicks at the time did not give much thought. It was not until 1958, when he was asked to participate at a conference with his paper, 'Measurement of capital in relation to the measurement of other economic aggregates' (1961c) that he began to discuss and conceive of capital both in relation to valuation and to dynamic production. First of all, he began to think of capital both as an input and an output, not just as an input in static production. He would also recognize later that when the same fixed capital produces a stream of outputs at different dates, 'it is impossible to deal with fixed capital, *and also to deal with working capital*, unless one faces up to the joint-supply complication' ([1973a] 1983a, pp. 98–9). The implication for Hicks of these realizations was that he would spend a great deal of time in discussing the measurement of capital and would eventually give up the concept of the production function altogether in favour of a production process of the Austrian type.

Capital measurement

The concepts of value and volume, forward- and backward-looking have already been mentioned in the previous section. They were crucial to the theory of capital which Hicks was to develop in *Capital and Time.* After 1958 Hicks became aware of the formidable difficulty involved in handling and measuring capital. To appreciate how he addressed this difficulty, it is essential to make the distinction between his discussion of the meaning of a measure of capital in pure theory and his contemplation, from a statistical point of view, of the difficulties of actually measuring capital in applied economics.

As for the theoretical approach, Hicks believed that help could be received from his neo-Austrian method. It is with some adjustment of it that he associated his backward-looking concept with volume measure and his forward-looking notion with value measure. The volume measure, or, as he preferred to call it, capital at cost, is derived by summing all past net input valued at a constant market price, assuming a constant rate of interest. The value measure is roughly equivalent to a capitalization of future net output for a given rate of return.

Volume

The backward-looking measure of capital according to volume registers capital invested in the past. There is, Hicks maintained for theoretical purposes, no need to look back indefinitely into the past, since 'the total capital invested in all live processes is clearly finite' (1973d, p. 159). A base date sets the finite beginning and becomes the point from which the volume of capital accumulates into 'subsequent net inputs, valued at base prices and accumulated at the base rate of interest' (p. 160). The volume measure in real terms is thus not a measure in actual 'physical units, tons or cubic feet, but solely by reference to what it was at a base date'. Volume measure of capital is thus 'an index-number measure' (p. 159). The volume measure of capital is itself obtained by dividing the total value of the physical goods by an index-number of capital goods prices at market value, if available; otherwise, these values are imputed.

Value

The forward-looking measure of capital according to value registers the results of capital invested in the future. Although it allows for changes in technology which will occur in the future, it too cannot take an indefinite horizon of the future into account. The capitalization of the time-definite projected future net outputs is registered in terms of the value of the capital stock. 'Value', Hicks reminded his readers, 'must always be reckoned in terms of something – money, a particular good chosen as standard, or a bundle of such goods (money value deflated by a price-index number)' (1973d, p. 152). The value measure of capital is measured by a 'bundle' of consumer or consumption goods; 'we can deflate by an index-number of consumption good prices, such as is very readily available' ([1932b] 1963b, p. 344).

Indexing

Capital found a critical place in one of Hicks's theoretical exercises. The purpose of his exercise was to compare the different growth situations either of two different economies at a particular date, or of one economy at different points in time. In both cases, some measure had to be devised by which one situation could be compared to another. Hicks asserted that capital stocks, if aggregated, might be used. Further, if one should wish to compare capital and output to obtain a capital–output ratio, as was the case in the fundist approach, then 'capital and output must both be measured in the same terms' (1973d, p. 152). It is in this context of aiming for comparison of production aggregates that Hicks discussed the two types of capital measures: the volume measure, according to which the nominal value of the aggregate capital is deflated by an index price of capital and the value measure, according to which real capital is obtained by deflating the value of the aggregate capital by a price index of final output.

Hicks recognized that the choice of measurement is not arbitrary. An arbitrary choice of measure could be very misleading. Take, for example, use of the value measure of capital to compare an economy at two points in time. It would be possible for the value measures of the capital at two time points to be different, since their corresponding prices have changed, and yet for the same capital measured in volume terms to have remained constant. Were one to take a volume measurement for comparison, it would also be possible for physical capital and its corresponding prices to be changing, while the value measure of the same capital remains unchanged. Hence, it would not be sufficient to compare the value of capital stock alone to determine whether there has been an improvement in one situation relative to another. In this case, one would have to compare physical capital.

It was more than simply a matter of making careful choices as to which measurement of capital to apply when; Hicks was well aware that there are difficulties inherent from the start in the indexing of each. On the one hand there are the problems with indexing when a volume concept is considered; 'a suitable index for that purpose will be very hard to construct indeed' ([1932b] 1963b, p. 344). Some items in the capital stock are not for sale, hence there are no market prices for them; some subjective estimation must be used to value them. Hicks noted that severe implications of estimation: 'an "error" in the estimation of the initial capital will greatly affect the increments' (1973d, p. 160). As well, depreciation and appreciation are very difficult to evaluate or are simply unavailable, so these items are expressed in gross terms. On the scale of the firm, Hicks found that 'the crude volume index is not an index of capital *at work*; it is an index of the value of the bits and pieces sold at a junk-shop!' (p. 161n.). Owing to the designed complementarity of the firm's equipment when working together, 'the value of the whole plant in working order may well be greater than the sum of the values *new*' (p. 160). That complementarity alone, Hicks wrote, 'is a chief reason why an "index of capital good prices" is so unsuitable a deflator' (p. 161n.). Such pitfalls of indexing capital volume also pose problems for the assessment of capital on the national scale. To Hicks's mind, the measurement of national capital volume can not really be said to reflect the state of the true physical capital of a nation.

On the other hand, additional and different problems also arise with the indexing of capital to yield the value concept. For example, the structure of goods differs from one period to another. At the end of one period, the stock of goods may contain goods which were not there at the beginning; some goods may have disappeared in the meantime, others may have changed character, or new goods may have been added. Even to start with, information about the true value of the capitalization of future net outputs is virtually unavailable. Then, to turn to the indexed method of estimating it, the index number itself will have a different structure at the beginning of the period, at the middle of the period and at the end of the period. With such changes the comparison is in effect made between two different stocks of goods. In so doing, Hicks admitted, 'in strictness, we do not just lose one of the Laspeyre–Paasche indexes; we lose both. The index-number comparison breaks down altogether' (1973d, p. 154).

When reflecting on these problems, Hicks spoke of the inadequacy of the definition of volume and value measures. 'Something is wrong with both *value* and *volume* measures of capital, as we have so far been taking them in this chapter: neither, in strictness, has been adequately defined.' He recommended 're-formulation', so that what each measurement entailed might be understood, so that each might be applied properly and so that both types of measurement 'can live more quietly together' (1973d, p. 156). He felt that this required a re-evaluation of both the theoretical approach to capital manipulation and the statistical approach to its measurement.

Measurement

Hicks had begun his theoretical contemplation of capital from a neo-Austrian approach, whose roots lie in a suspicion of treating capital at the level of macro-magnitudes. While many neo-Austrians accused Hicks of ignoring the roles of individual plans and individual expectations, they were not about even to tackle, as he did, the recognizably difficult task of handling and measuring the size of individual capital. Any aggregation at all, the neo-Austrians argue, is impossible and irrelevant; the workings of the market process discover its inconsistencies and provide ways of eliminating it. Indeed, in a market economy, every entrepreneur looks at individual capital differently. Investment decisions are not made once and for all but depend on the opportunity cost as well as on the risk and uncertainty. Representing the position of the Austrian economists and their meagre sympathy with Hicks's approach, Kirzner wrote, 'we may dismiss backward-looking measures as having failed, even at the individual level. Forward-looking measures of an individual's capital stock are impossible to achieve in an objective way' (Kirzner, 1976, p. 1940).

When dealing with the workings of a market economy, Hicks did not think he had shirked from micro-considerations at the individual level, but neither did he intend to neglect macro-models where he found the same difficulties further complicated. Considering physical capital at a macro-level is virtually impossible; to handle it some form of aggregation is needed. To add different heterogeneous capital requires some standard measure, common to every individual capital considered. The route to capital aggregation in economics has customarily been to express capital in value terms (avoiding for now the question of what determines these values).

Hicks's independent work on capital seems to have been limited to theoretical analysis, aside from his critique of statistical methods to be noted below. He first formulated a simple profile traverse model for the case of the fixwage assumption. In it he applied the concept of value measurement; in that context it is the more simple of the two measurements because wages are fixed. The interest rate r changes once and for all and then remains constant, and capitalization is easily calculated. In his second assumption, full employment, however, w and r are changing, and thus to measure value poses problems. Hicks adhered, none the less, to the value measure and addressed the difficulties by beginning his analysis from a steady state path and assuming the equilibrium r^* to be constant. Since, in the course of substitution, when the effective r is greater than r^*, r would tend to move back to its equilibrium value, Hicks could thus use r^* as his rate of discount.

Under the conditions of steady state, in Hicks's simple profile traverse model, both the value and volume concepts could be integrated. Steady-state conditions are necessary for the volume (and value) measures to be computed, but they limit greatly the dynamics of the model. Thus, for Hicks, traverse analysis had to evolve to become an analysis of disequilibrium in the comparison of equilibrium paths, and the technical measurement of capital would be a casualty of the theory. As Solow suggested, however, when the world consists of a dynamic, unsynchronized 'bunch of machinery and building, some of which can be worked more or less labour intensively, some of which can be shifted to other lines of production, and some of which can lie idle or go slow without deterioration and some of which can not' (1974, p. 191), ultimately neither value nor volume concepts can be adequate measures of capital.

As for statistical capital measurement, Hicks was fully aware of its many pitfalls. He felt that the information which could be statistically derived through either the volume or value approach to capital measurement was limited to time-consuming complications, and he personally avoided the issue. Physical capital which took the theoretical form in his model of an intermediary in the process of production did not even appear in his equations. This explaining away of physical capital, and consequent neglect of it, was, it seems, justifiable given the role of capital in the Hicksian economy. Hicks's model was fully integrated, that is, his was a one-commodity world comparable to a one-unit micro-analysis.

In Hicks's model, for a given and constant rate of return, there is one present value of the future stream of net output, and one present value of accumulated past inputs. The situations these values represent are hypothetical, knowable only in a very special world. (They have nothing to do with what the neo-Austrians have in mind.) Technically, Hicks did not address himself to the possibility of capital having alternative uses in the present or future, or to the consequences of accumulated capital's having resulted from heterogeneous past sacrifices. These constraints of his model are sufficient conditions for its maintenance in a steady state.

Analogously to the theoretical approach, Hicks considered capital to be hypothetically statistically measurable in one of two ways, either as input, by looking backward, or as output, by looking forward. To measure capital as input, Hicks suggested starting from a 'beginning-stock' and comparing it to an 'end-stock/beginning-stock'. As for the measure of output capital, Hicks recommended taking the 'end-stock' as the output of a process and comparing it to the 'beginning-stock' of that same process. In the case of input measurement, both 'beginning-stock' and 'end-stock' are treated as input capital; analogously, in the case of output measurement, both are treated as output capital. This is a legitimate comparison, Hicks explained, since 'both input and output have stock and flow components; capital appears both as input and output' (1981, p. 194). He saw each stock as involved in a process at the beginning of which it could either be viewed from the angle of 'beginning-stock' of that process or 'end-stock' of the process preceding and at the end of which it could be perceived as either the 'end-stock' of that process or the 'beginning-stock' of the next. 'Each stock must always have the same relation to its own process, if comparability is to be maintained', Hicks wrote, well realizing that with his perspective, the statistician would be able to compare the necessary like with like (1981, p. 195).

He also envisaged the possibility of a statistical cross-comparison of two stocks A and B: either a 'before and after' comparison or a cross-comparison of two 'after' results. The 'before–after' comparison would entail comparing the A-stock before it was 'transferred, by some process of saving (or dissaving) and replacement, into the B-stock' with the B-stock it became (1981, p. 199). Cross-comparisons of two 'after' results involve comparing stocks A and B as two different 'end-stocks' resulting either from two different transformation processes given an identical initial stock or from one process identical for two different given initial stocks. Hicks thought the second of the two types of comparisons might be the easier type to measure. Its measurement could be undertaken in one of two ways: either backward-looking or forward-looking.

The backward-looking cross-comparison measurement would determine, for example, 'whether B-capital [or the value equivalent of "B-(end-)stock"] could have been produced from an A-process' (1981, p. 201), that is, whether the same A-process could have produced two sets of goods with B-end-stock of value equal or greater than A-end-stock. It would assess the possibility for a value of capital (called B-capital or B-end-stock), that is, 'a flow of consumption goods "at least as good as" as that which was [already] turned out in the A-process', to be produced with the same equipment and same labour as were used to produce A-end-stock. The forward-looking measure, on the other hand, would determine, for example, whether 'a stream of consumption goods which is "at least as good" as the stream of consumption goods similarly producable from the A-capital' could be produced from B-capital (p. 201), that is, whether A- and B-capital could each through a similar process produce two sets of goods with B-end-stock of value equal to or greater than A-end-stock. It would assess this possibility in terms of A-process and A-labour.

A major complication to any statistical measurement is the source of data. In the case of Hicks's need to establish the present value of the future stream of net output, the choice of the source of data was not at all simple.

> Whose are the expectations, of future net outputs, from which the forward-looking value is to be derived? . . . the expectations of different individuals are not harmonious, and the statements which they record in their balance-sheets of magnitudes which depend on these expectations are not harmonious. (1973d, p. 161)

The statistician is left with having arbitrarily to select a valuation as his standard and to adjust the rest of his initial values to it. His two main choices of valuations are those of the firm or the shareholder. The firm sets its own backward-looking value upon its assets. The shareholder, however, places a forward-looking value derived 'from the prices of the firm's shares on the stock exchange' (1973d, p. 162). Although Hicks realized that 'the ideal valuation may be thought to be that [backward-looking one] which the firm itself sets upon its own assets' (p. 161), he rejected it: calculation based on 'the "original cost" of the balance-sheets of business . . . is too much oriented towards the past' ([1969g 1981, p. 216). On the other hand, Hicks also rejected the stock exchange market valuation 'because it is too future-oriented; it is too much affected by hopes and fears for the future, by guesses which are not fact but at the best probability' (p. 216). He was inclined to agree with statisticians who shied away from the forward-looking valuation because of the volatility of equity prices.

All in all, Hicks did not hold much hope for useful statistical measurement. He felt that the information that could be derived from either type of measure was really nothing more than time-consuming compilations. What exasperated him most was the impossibility of reducing forward- and backward-looking valuations 'into even a formal consistency' ([1969g] 1981, p. 216). With resignation he concluded that 'the place of the value measure is in theoretical analysis' and that since 'the volume measure . . . does not wholly escape the same weaknesses' (1973d, p. 163), it too is really only useful in theory. One should bear in mind that even though the reference here is to the statistical measurement, in Hicks's view it is with regard to theory. He had in mind his frustrated desire for a theory and its statistics to be able to establish 'a consistent "national balance-sheet"' ([1969g] 1981, p. 216). Of course, he realized that business decisions are based upon compiled data, but their experience and inclination continuously to revise such data over time renders it useful.

Capital theory

Given the various complications inherent in the notions of capital, as described in the previous sections, it will now perhaps be understandable why comprehensive theories of capital have been considered hard to conceive and continuously have raised, and will raised, controversies. Hicks felt that although it was explicable because of the variety of understandings of capital, his predecessors' theories were narrow. They had only integrated, either theoretically or practically, one or another concept of capital, predominantly those defined as the material (fixed) or fund (working or circulating) capital.

> There are some theories that start at the fixed-capital end, and are very weak when they come to working capital (circulating capital). There are others that start from working, on which they are strong, but when they come to fixed capital they tend to lose grip . . . The purest of the *fixed-capital* theory, in Bohm's generation, were Clark and Walras. (1973a, p. 191)

Hicks set out to do one better than his predecessors and contemporaries: to combine these two kinds of capital into one comprehensive theory. He argued that in their treatment of capital his predecessors had assumed that 'there is just one capital good in the economy; that capital has been made, by some device, *homogeneous*' (1965a, p. 34). Despite the different approaches of different schools, he noted that most classical economists assumed that a 'single capital good is a circulating capital good', while for many neoclassical economists a 'single capital good is a fixed capital good (a "machine")', and different machines are 'reduced to definite quantities of the same "capital substance"' (p. 34). Hicks did not condemn either approach: 'neither the classical (circulating capital) nor the neo-classical (fixed capital) version is wrong if it is regarded as no more than a device . . . which has positive achievements to its credit' (p. 35). He did, however, feel that it was 'a disaster' for economists to have been stuck for so long in this phase of capital theory development, which he deemed to have been only 'for preliminary exploration' (1965, p. 35).

The Austrian school of economists believed that it had dealt with both fixed and circulating capital, and thought 'that there was some way in which fixed capital could be "reduced" to working capital' (1973a, p. 192). Hicks felt, however, that this had been demonstrated to be no longer a valid approach and that to deal with both forms of capital together, one must address 'the joint-supply complication'.

To tackle a theory of capital himself Hicks confined his scope to a particular growth model in which he believed the concept of capital plays a dominant dynamic role. He accepted as fact that many growth models failed to meet their dynamic objective because of their lack of an adequate theory of capital. In dynamic analysis an understanding of how the stock of physical capital is handed from one period into another is of crucial importance. Representation of the physical capital handling process poses enormous technical difficulties. To surmount these difficulties, Hicks claimed as usual that simplification was necessary, as a preliminary device.

Aware of the considerable theoretical advances made by von Neumann, Leontief and Sraffa and of the development of linear programming,

Hicks believed that a fully integrated method could be developed. As an alternative to the model of von Neumann and also to that of sectorial disintegration, he proposed a simple profile of a traverse analysis. It could, he felt, deal with both fixed and working capital. Although critical of the Austrian 'period of production', Hicks thought the Böhm–Bawerk approach to capital provided him with some insight. In that approach 'Production was a combination of Labour and Time. The Time that was taken in production was an identifiable figure – the degree of Roundaboutness ... Roundaboutness was a measure of capital intensity' (1973a, p. 8).

Much of the simple profile or traverse model itself has already been explained in the context of dynamics in chapter 4; the concern here is solely in the model's connection with Hicks's treatment of capital. Physical capital stock in his vertically integrated model of *Capital and Time* consists entirely of machines produced and absorbed within the production process. This physical capital stock is measured in his model in a forward manner, as an intermediary factor in a process where, as time flows, a stream of inputs is transformed into a stream of outputs. There, the forward-looking physical capital stock is the translated value of future investment available for physical capital stock. Physical capital stock, measured backward, is, however, also reflected in the model, in the construction of his restricted efficiency curve, as the number of processes started in the past. In fact, however, physical capital stock as fixed capital does not explicitly appear at all in the formulation of his simple profile model.

In Hicks's model, profit or take out (made of net investment and net output) was expressed in social accounts as the difference between the values of production output and input. The only input considered in this profit equation was homogeneous labour. So the value of input consisted entirely of circulating capital (or the wage bill). Although some part of the total profit or income is reinvested to produce more machines, the cost of the material required for these machines must be assumed to be zero. Thus the only feature of interest in expansion through increased profits is that the new machines will require additional labour both to build them and then to operate them when they become available. In this respect, changes in investment are manifest only in terms of circulating capital. 'Capital is an expression of sequential production' (1973a, p. 194).

Under three conditions, initial capital value of each process of production set at zero, (k_0), the output good used as the standard, and the rate of interest equivalent to the price of the exchange of that good now for that good later, Hicks was able to derive a functional relationship between the rates of wage and profit. That relationship described what he called the efficiency curve, with a downward slope. He used b_t 'either to represent the quantity of the goods that are produced in week t of a unit process, or the value of those goods; for these come to the same thing.' His a_t denoted 'the *quantity* of the labour input,' 'the value of that input, in terms of goods, is wa_t' (1973a, p. 38). Net output, q_t, thus, whether positive or not, is equal to $b_t - wa_t$. As already presented in chapter 4, Equation 7,

$$k_0 = \sum_{0}^{n} q_t R^{-t} = \sum_{0}^{n} (b_t - wa_t) R^{-t}.$$

The right-hand side of the equation, once equated to zero, is an expression of w in terms of r.

As for r, Hicks took it to be a *goods* rate of interest, a *real* rate of interest. 'If (as before) $R = 1 + r$, then R is the value of goods, to be delivered at the beginning of the week, in terms of goods to be delivered at the end of the week' (1973a, p. 38). It is also the internal rate of return.

Hicks thus derived a wage–interest relationship, or an efficiency curve ($w(r)$), in terms of output and labour (or input). The effect of his having translated all capital into circulating capital was to allow him to focus his attention on the distribution of total (circulating) capital between wages and interest. He made this distribution dependent on the impact of new techniques on the production process. In fact, Hicks saw his efficiency curve as 'the economic expression of the technique' (1973d, p. 39). In his model, every efficiency curve describes one technique and for each technique there is a corresponding set of input coefficients (a_0 and a_1) which are the quantities of labour input in the construction and in the utilization sectors respectively. Different techniques have distinct sets of input coefficients and distinct efficiency curves. Any two techniques can be classified according to the ratios of $I(r)$, h and H, already explained in chapter 4, as the index measures of improvement in terms of savings in labour, respectively, in the production process as a whole, in the construction sector and in the utilization sector.

It might be noticed that Hicks's new classification of techniques has little to do with his 1932 classification in *The Theory of Wages*. There, the impact of inventions on the relative prices of the production function factors, labour and capital, was contemplated. Hicks examined whether for a given production function (in which a level of output is associated with a particular combination of capital and labour), invention would produce a change in the use of one factor relative to another. He classified all changes as either neutral, labour-saving, or capital saving, depending on whether the ratio of the marginal product of labour to the marginal product of capital was constant, increasing, or decreasing, respectively. While his old classification was closer to the Harrod classification in terms of its focus on new inventions, his new classification resembled Harrod's in its reference to profit, not to marginal productivity. In *Capital and Time* Hicks was clearly no longer primarily concerned with the impact of invention, but rather with the impact of changes in techniques for a given invention. His new efficiency curves were explicitly between 'two techniques (not two technologies)' (1973d, p. 74).

Reswitching (and capital reversal) is another issue related to Hicks theory of capital, which has become so important as to dominate current discussions on capital theory and to render it impossible not to mention. Much was written about reswitching in the 1960s and early 1970s, generating a bitter controversy (see Harcourt, 1972). The issue of reswitching in the capital debate had mainly to do with the existence of a well-behaved production function and the concern with the conditions for the optimal use of factors. To obtain the well-behaved production function, it is necessary to rank the use of available techniques in which the price of one factor is higher than the other, so that more of the less expensive factor will be used. The anti-production function advocates argued that such ranking was not possible. Both the supporters and opponents in the debate were engaged in a purely logical, atemporal exercise. This is not the place to discuss in any detail the complexities the debate raised, but instead to examine the specific relation of reswitching to Hicks's capital theory.

In relation to the standard case of the simple profile model of *Capital and Time*, reswitching does not seem to have been an issue for Hicks, even in the possible instances where technique switches might occur. The reasons for this unimportance of reswitching are many. First, even though Hicks showed within his model 'that in the Standard Case there can be no re-switching; but that outside the Standard Case re-switching can theoretically occur' (1975f, p. 367), he was really not concerned with obtaining a well-behaved (or any other) production function, conditions of optimality, or the particular shape of the frontier of his efficiency curves. Just after the publication of *Capital and Time*, he stated categorically,

> I have become very suspicious, not only of the 'production function' but also of the technology frontier ... The distinction between substitutions along the frontier and change in technology, which shift the frontier, I would now abandon. It is useful as a piece of scaffolding, but when we come to application, it must go. (1975f, p. 367)

To Hicks the frontier shape of the efficiency curves is not really crucial, but rather the fact that whatever the technique chosen, every curve slopes downward and must not bend backward. Whenever the rate of profit (r) is higher than the equilibrium rate (r^*), given the assumptions of his model, there will be a tendency for r to move back to its equilibrium level (r^*). Although a firm will continue to introduce new techniques to forestall the downward slide, no matter what the time frame or whether the curve of each technique is a straight line as in Figure 6.1 or whether switches occur as in Figure 6.2, r will slide downward shifting from one technique to another, until eventually it becomes equal to r^*.

A second reason for the unimportance Hicks attributed to reswitching was that, in contrast to the debate on capital where the concern was over the possibility of logical substitution between various alternative techniques, Hicks was preoccupied mainly with the matter of substitution between techniques over time. When time is taken into account, it is unlikely that a technique (with its coefficients) if used at two different points in time would be considered to be the same technique. As a final reason, Hicks's idea of the substitution of techniques is very special. Assume there are x processes actually in operation and that a new invention which can improve productivity (by saving in labour) is now available. While the newly invented machines are in construction, the economy will continue operating with old processes (Preparatory Phase). Then, when some of the new machines are ready, they will gradually be

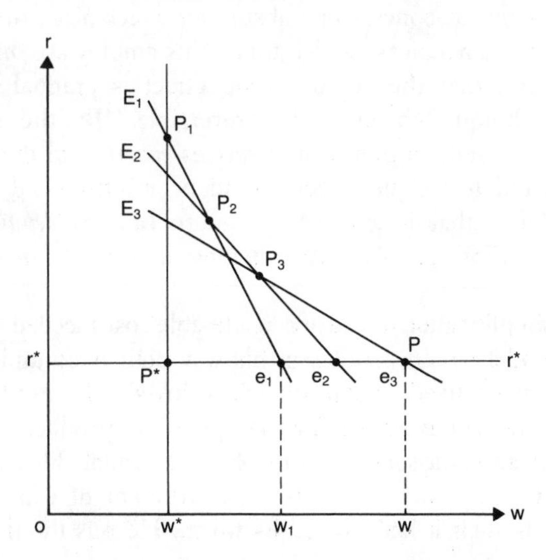

Figure 6.1 Impulses with linear techniques

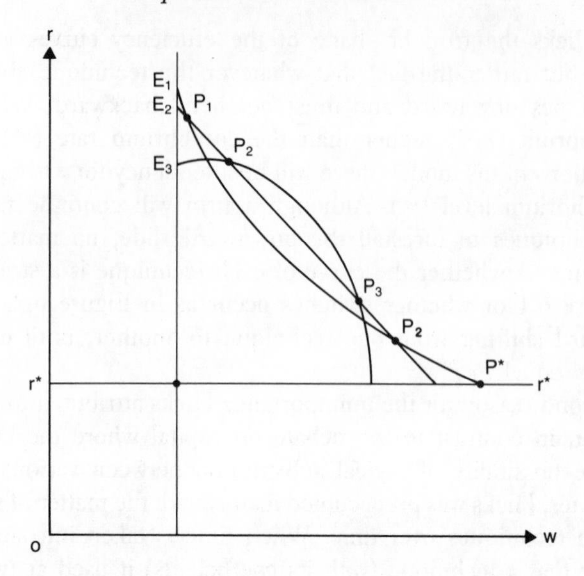

Figure 6.2 Impulses with non-linear techniques

substituted for some of the old ones (Early Phase). Finally, when all the old machines are replaced by the new ones, the economy will settle into a new equilibrium path (Late Phase). In this context, the newer technique means the replacement of old machines by newer (labour-saving) ones, yielding a different labour coefficient. In the Hicksian substitution of techniques, it does not make sense to revert to an old technique. Owing to the fact that in his conception substitution takes place over time and thus that the circumstances at each time of its employ are different and, more important, that the labour-saving effect is gradual and always beneficial, technique changes are irreversible. 'By the substitution something is learned; so that if input-prices reverted to their old ratio, it is not the old technique which would be reintroduced, but something new. Once that is granted ... there can, by *definition*, be no reswitching' (1975f, p. 367). Reswitching in Hicks's model is thus unimportant.

Through simplification he did at considerable cost succeed in building a theoretical model which handles in his way both fixed and circulating capital. By making fixed capital implicit in his simple profile model he showed how one can avoid the Austrian period of production and many of the complications associated with physical capital. Hicks was aware that his model was no more than 'an instrument of exploration' and thought that as such it had proved its worth. He was the first to guard against claiming too much for it. One is conscious, he wrote, 'while one is using it, of the thinness of the plank on which one is walking. We have been piling simplification upon simplification, specialisation upon specialisation' (1973d, p. 125).

From the time Traverse II appeared, Hicks observed that generally economists (from different schools) 'have not known quite what to make of it' (1976f, p. 144). His method raised a whole range of questions: some disputed the use of his fundamental theorem in the problem of truncation (Eatwell, 1975); some tried to show that his model was nothing but a special case of Von Neumann's (Burmeister, 1974); many wondered whether the model could support anything other than the simple profile (Steedman, 1973). Many of these questions were legitimate in the context of the capital debate in which they were raised. It seems, however, that it was the mechanical aspect of the model which retained most of the critics' attention, and thus most of their comments did not really touch on Hicks's own objective. He argued, in fact, that to attack his use of unrealistic assumptions was beside the point:

> I have deliberately removed a number of obvious obstacles to the smooth working of an economy, in order to see if these are the only obstacles. I have cut out money; I have cut out monopolies (of capital and labour); I have cut out government; I have even, excepting in a concluding passage (in Chapter XII) cut out natural scarcities. (1975f, pp. 365–6)

Hicks had aimed, through simplifying his vision of the world, to construct a simple model as a platform from which he could proceed to extrapolate and explain, without having to rely too much on the rigid and constraining mechanics from which he started. One very interesting implication of his simple profile model was the phenomenon of the technological impulse. As Hicks saw it, 'the mainspring of economic progress . . . is invention; invention that works through the rate of profit. Each invention gives an *Impulse*, as we may call it' (1977a, p. 15). According to his model, the impulse takes the form of thrusting r upward out of its equilibrium position, when a new invention or technology is introduced, as can be seen in both Figures 6.1 and 6.2. Since, however, 'the Impulse of any single invention is not inexhaustible' and 'the exhaustion is marked by falling profit' (1977a, p. 15), with time, r slides back to its equilibrium rate, albeit at a different level of w.

Hicks believed that this scenario of the economy's response to technological change would occur at every instance of a new technology's entering the market-place. He also assumed that although there is 'no reason to suppose that the rate of innovation is very regular', the mere sequence of technological impulses would be 'sufficient reason for a [economic] cycle – even a fairly regular cycle – to develop' (1939a, pp. 299–300). Should new technologies follow closely on one another, their impulses could affect r even before it has returned to its equilibrium path. In this case, the whole efficiency curve $w(r)$ would be sustained above the equilibrium r^*r^* path. In a world of rapid technological change, Hicks concluded, 'convergence [to equilibrium] may not be smooth at all . . . it will take a long time; and in most applications before that time has elapsed something else (some new exogeneous shock) will surely have occurred'. Rather than finding such a conclusion dismaying, Hicks was inclined to read from it something more positive: 'convergence to equilibrium has been shown to be dubious; but it has also been shown to be unimportant' (1975f, pp. 365–6).

Capital accumulation

In the last chapters of both *Value and Capital* and *Capital and Time*, Hicks was no longer dealing with the nature of capital, its determination or its transformations in the production process. His concern had become the effects of capital accumulation (or decumulation). In *Value and Capital* he studied particularly the effect of capital accumulation on prices by observing different situations: (1) the case where additional equipment is expected to be ready at the beginning of the second week, (2) the case where additional equipment is already ready by the beginning of the second week and (3) the case where it is not yet ready by the beginning of the second week. Hicks looked at the effect of each case on output, the interest rate, and prices. In this context he defined a boom, or period of economic prosperity, as 'nothing else but a period of intense accumulation'. By the same token, 'the leading feature of a slump is not the decumulation of physical capital; it is the mere cessation of accumulation' (1939a, pp. 295–7).

When discussing capital accumulation, Hicks said nothing about capital *per se*, about how it is measured or, more important, about how it is transmitted from one period into another. Owing to the conditions of the temporary equilibrium model, that the week period is self-contained and that capital is taken simply as given, and also because Hicks did not explain the connection of one week to the next, nothing much could be said directly about accumulation. He none the less felt that the effect of capital accumulation could be identified indirectly. Capital accumulation, according to Hicks, manifests itself first in changes in output, for example in case (1), where the capital inputs cause a large increase in output starting at the beginning of the week. A relatively small rise in the entrepreneurs' income would accompany the increse in output. More important, however, a subsequent manifestation of such capital accumulation would be the downward changes in some prices.

Hicks examined as well case (2) in which the accumulation of capital in one 'week' was applied immediately to a permanent improvement expected to increase output constantly. 'Some of the inputs of the first week have been used . . . in order to make it possible to produce larger outputs (or employ smaller inputs) in later weeks than in the first week' (1939a, p. 284). If the entrepreneurs in this case immediately spend all the return from the increase in output (and they would do so, Hicks assumed, if they anticipated unchanging prices and interest rates), then some prices would rise and some would fall. The general price level would, however, 'be said to be unaffected' (p. 285).

As for case (3), which 'involves the construction of new capital goods which take a large number of weeks to produce, and only come into action as productive instruments after that period is completed' (1939a, p. 286), the indirect influence of capital accumulation would be most noticeable on prices. Given that the new capital in the form of machines would not be ready for production by the second week, the entrepreneurs' incomes would have to rise at least enough to cover the interest on their investment under construction. Yet with no increase in output underway to compensate for the expenditure, prices would have to be raised. 'A period of active investment will witness an increase in expenditure while the capital goods are being constructed, so that little is left to offset the depressing effect of the increased output when it materializes' (p. 287).

In addition to the effects of capital accumulation on output, income and prices, Hicks also considered its impact on employment. The transmitted effect of changes in prices might not, he argued in *Value and Capital*, have a beneficial effect on labour. Given the relative inflexibility of money wages and an elasticity of price expectations, even an apparently welcome drop in prices might have serious consequences for employment, if it cannot be offset. Hicks traced three phases in the course of capital accumulation for its effect on labour, under the assumption of 'a sufficient degree of rigidity in expectations' (1939a, p. 288). In a first phase, accumulated capital is used to introduce new machines into consumer goods production. While the machines are under construction there is an increased demand, for labour to build them. That demand can be financed either through the reorientation of a larger portion of income to labour expenses by a Wicksellian 'contraction of expenditure upon consumption goods (saving)' or through securities. Contraction of expenditure would raise 'real wages, the price of labour in terms of consumption goods' (p. 289). If, on the other hand, the new demand for labour is financed through securities, the price of labour would increase less, but it would still increase to some degree, relative to the price of consumption goods, and thus real wages should rise. If money wages are rigid, real wages could decrease as employment increases.

In a middle phase, the impact of the capital accumulation is only partially felt; only some of the new machines are operational. Some are still under construction and the expansion of employment persists, especially if money wages are rigid. With the new production partially activated, the demand for consumption goods begins to increase. Its sales cannot, however, yet compensate for the capital investment; prices tend still to rise and real wages thus to fall. In a final phase, all the new machines are producing, hence for the first time the output of consumption goods exceeds their capital cost. In this stage prices are falling and wages increase favourably relative to goods. on the other hand, the demand for labour drops and employment may well be decreased.

While in his simple profile model, which occupied a large part of *Capital and Time*, Hicks discussed and refined through his traverse analysis the scenario of the integration of a new production technology or technique, he made little reference and no use of capital accumulation, directly or indirectly, in the model. Along the lines of steady-state analysis, where there is no difference between the forward- and backward-looking measurement of capital and where a Take-Out (*Q*) 'is given exogeneously', Hicks chose predominantly to 'calculate the path of the economy without any reference to a capital aggregate'. At the end of the book, however, Hicks asked his readers to consider both the fixwage and full-employment systems and 'how the story would have run if it had been told in terms of capital aggregates' (1973d, p. 167).

In a fixwage system it was given that capital accumulation would permit the introduction of one invention and one technique for its use, which technique would remain the dominant one 'for as far ahead as we shall go'. This meant that within the model the ratio of r to w was fixed. Account is taken of the course of integrating the new technology and technique by discounting future net outputs as long as the old processes carry on. Hicks used the standard two ways of measuring capital accumulation: capital at cost and capital value.

In his fixwage version of the model, the two measurements are distinct in two ways: in their account of technical change and in their registering of the rate of profit on capital. First, the measurement of accumulated capital according to volume or as capital at cost offers a measurement unaffected by any invention or technical changes 'that occur after its base date'. Since it is backward-looking, it is 'invariant to [postdated] technical change' (1973d, p. 170). In the same model, the measurement of accumulated capital according to value has great difficulty operationally accounting for technical change. Second, capital measurement according to cost attributes a meaning to the rate of profit on capital different from that understood with capital measurement according to value. In cost or volume measurement, the rate of profit on capital 'is greatly dependent on *T*', the allowed time of adjustment to a new technique (p. 172). Since the initial effect of a technique change might be quite small, the initial rate of profit is slow. Since, however, the ultimate effect of the change may be significant, the longer-range rate might be quite accelerated. As for the rate of profit in terms of capital value, it can be understood simply as 'the rate of interest, or rate of return on modern processes' which 'changes when technology [or technique] changes, but not otherwise' (p. 170).

In Hicks's full employment version of the model, both *w* and *r* are 'changing in the course of the Traverse'. In this version, since the measurement of capital at cost starts none the less from an unchanging valuation 'at base prices (now including wages as well as interest)', he envisaged 'a sequence (C_T) that is self-consistent' and that even without 'optimology' can be yielding of useful information. The effect of the changes in *w* and *r* on capital value measurement is far more unsettling. Since re-evaluations are going on all the time and the premises of static expectations is hard to incorporate, not very much about the effect of capital accumulation is revealed through capital value measurement (1973d, p. 172).

The purpose of this section is to bring to light Hicks's own extension of the discussion on capital accumulation. He did not think the economist should become bogged down with the difficulties of capital measurement. Once those difficulties have been recognized, he thought, one ought to proceed to what he saw as one of the ultimate purposes of capital theory, its potential for evaluating the impact of capital accumulation, as a manifestation of progress, on the labour sector. From Hicks's theoretical perspective in *Value and Capital*, 'even in the long run, the accumulation of capital is thus not necessarily favourable to the interests of labour' (1939a, p. 291). He offered, however, two reasons for the expectation that accumulation might be 'favourable in practice'. One reason stemmed from the viewpoint of production function analysis in which complementarity is 'the dominant relation among factors employed in the same enterprise' (p. 291). While new capital which is not yet fully integrated would not yet be labour-saving (to save labour is one measure assumed of benefit to labour), once its impact on production is realized the two factors of capital and labour would be complementarily advantaged.

The second reason, and main reason according to Hicks, why capital accumulation seems to be favourable to labour in practical terms is that it has an impact on the standard of living of labour. The labour-saving use of specific capital will probably reduce the cost of those goods in its production and raise labour's real wages in their terms. If capital is accumulated in many different areas of production, the effect can be quite considerable. The facilitating of production for many different consumption goods will increase on a significant scale the number of goods in whose terms real wages will rise. Hicks observed that this effect on the standard of living of labour had been markedly noticeable during the nineteenth century.

In *Capital and Time* Hicks carried the correlation between the accumulation of capital and a benefit to labour one step further. Even if in many 'happily progressive economies', those employed are enjoying a rise in real wages due to technical progress, Hicks stressed that something meaningful is left out of such an observation: knowledge of what percentage of the potential labour force is actually earning a wage. Technical progress alone will not guarantee that the fund of real wages will expand (or its value continue to rise); that depends on the volume of capital. Should the volume of an economy's capital actually decrease with technical progress, so too will the number of labourers enjoying the rise in real wages (and eventually the economy's potential for further technical progress). 'A great deal of saving is needed to prevent the volume of capital from declining . . . [saving] would be necessary, to keep the "real" wage fund rising, so that full employment could be maintained with the rising real wages' (1973d, p. 176). More will be said on the impact of progress and changes in real wages in the next chapter.

What was ingenious in Hicks's method was his ability to construct very simple models to encapsulate a complex of ideas. He managed to extrapolate powerful corollaries from them and conjectured on their implications for the world he observed. In the case of capital theory, in a few pages at the end of *Value and Capital*, after having studied in its every detail the temporary equilibrium model and having so confined most of the book to investigating equilibrium during the 'week', he attempted in conclusion to extend the model well beyond those initial bounds. Similarly he proceeded in almost the same way in *Capital and Time*, where the bulk of the book is dedicated to the simple profile model and yet in his chapter on the accumulation of capital he lifted himself away from that model to address a factual question. In both instances, Hicks attempted to answer a question which had preoccupied him since the early 1930s (and which has already been discussed in the last chapter): Is progress beneficial to labour?

7

Money, Finance and Liquidity

Hick's contributions to monetary theory spread over a span of almost six decades. They began with his 'Gleichgewicht und Konjunktur' (1933b), which was followed by what is considered, because of its tremendous impact, his major work in the field of money, 'A suggestion for simplifying the Theory of Money' (1935b). After the latter publication, Hicks's attention was diverted to other areas in economics, and monetary theory stayed fairly much in the background until the 1960s, at which time the publication of *Critical Essays in Monetary Theory* (1967) showed that it had once again become one of his major interests. He thereafter produced several volumes and articles on monetary economics, The very last book he completed was a comprehensive treatment of money, *A Market Theory of Money* (1989a).

The hiatus between Hicks's earlier and later work definitely marked a change in his conception of the demand for money. His early work was based on the straight application of the principle of value. Even though his ideas were novel, they were none the less simple and consistent with the growing development, in the 1930s, of marginal theory and general equilibrium. His appealing suggestions for simplifying the theory of money quickly gained the approval of a large portion of the profession and have been extended further ever since. The same, however, cannot be said of his later work. The later contributions were an outcome of much broader thinking and greater historical awareness; Hicks attempted to mould new ideas from his early liquidity theory, and also deliberately distanced himself from the neo-quantitative conception of the demand for money. His reconsidered monetary theory and his overt partisanship in the banking and currency controversy created some confusion for many monetary economists and drew criticism from all sides. His later work was thus not as well received as the earlier and remains yet to be explored in detail.

The object in this chapter is to set out Hicks's monetary theory and to explain the transition between his two major contributions, his earlier portfolio approach to demand for money, and his later liquidity theory and concept of the credit economy. It will be argued that his later rejection of certain elements of his portfolio approach should not be exaggerated. Although his interpretation of the demand for money was different in each of the separate areas he developed, much of his early discussion about liquidity survived in his later work. Hicks remained, throughout, a firm believer that acceptance of money as the medium of exchange and store of value depends greatly on the confidence individuals have in it and that the need for money and the formation of any economic monetary system is generated by a market mechanism and is not imposed by institutional decree. He believed in a strong role for a monetary authority, not so much to engineer economic activity as to respond to public demand for a guarantor and facilitator and to ensure checks and balances so that banking and financial institutions would be responsible. Monetary policy should not be dictated but formulated by the authority's listening to public demands through its 'ears', the banking and financial institutions. In this sense, in contrast to Keynes, Hicks was a very mild interventionist in the monetary sphere.

Portfolio approach

The essence of Hicks's portfolio method consisted in enquiring what, at one point in time, determines the quantity of money an individual would desire to hold. Its novelty was that, unlike his predecessors Wicksell and Marshall, Hicks assumed that money as such has marginal utility and is 'capable of quantitative expression' (1935b, pp. 62–3). (Hicks's marginal utility of money is not be confused with Marshall's utility of income. See Marshall, 1923, pp. 38–9 and Wicksell, 1934, p. 20.) To determine the demand for money, Hicks suggested the use of marginalist value theory in the same manner in which it is used in determining the ordinary demand for goods and services.

In the portfolio method each individual was regarded 'as being, on a small scale, a bank'. Hicks's monetary theory thus became a 'generalization of banking theory . . . a sort of generalized balance-sheet, suitable for all individuals and institutions' (1935b, p. 74). The balance sheet of each individual includes consumption goods, equipment and goods in process, short- and long-term debts, bank deposits and cash. The amount of money an individual is willing to hold is affected by changes in his or her desire to acquire more or fewer assets. An individual can change the amount of money he or she is willing to hold by spending or selling, lending or borrowing, or by paying off debts or claiming repayment.

While Hicks's primary question was what determines the amount of money each individual is willing to hold, in assuming that money is non-interest-bearing he raised another issue: why do people hold money, which does not bear any interest, when they can hold other capital assets which yield profit?

As illustrated in Table 7.1, the demand for money as such depends on three factors: wealth, the cost of transferring assets from one form into another, and risk. An individual has a choice to hold wealth in (non-interest-bearing) money or in interest-yielding capital assets, or both. Hicks argued that the demand for money increases with wealth but less than proportionately because wealth will increase the demand both for (non-interest-bearing) money and for capital investment assets. The demand for money will also depend on the cost of transferring assets from one form into another. Elements entering into calculating the cost of transfer may include the date at which the investing individual expects to have need of the invested sum in the future, the expected rate of return on the investment, and the cost of investing or the brokerage fee. The last of these elements is objective, the other two subjective.

Table 7.1 Hicks's demand for money, M^d (1935b)

M^d depends on	Wealth	An increase in wealth always raises the demand for money but less than proportionately.
	Cost of transferring assets from one form into another	Date at which the investing individual expects to have need of the invested sum in the future
		Expected rate of return on investment
		Cost of investment or brokerage fee which increases at a decreasing rate with M^d
	Risk	Preference for little risk
		Facts on which risk is estimated

Calculations of risk also have an effect on the demand for money. To the same extent they include elements to be weighed, one subjective and one objective. Individual preference for more or less risk is the subjective element; the facts on which risk is estimated are objective. Taking these two risk elements and the law of large numbers into consideration, Hicks asserted that a representative individual will distribute assets among relatively safe and relatively risky investments in such a manner as to optimize the return on investment. He suggested the use of probabilities, represented 'by a mean value, and some appropriate measure of dispersion' (1935b, p. 69), as a convenient form to express particular expectations of a riskless choice.

In 1935 Hicks had, like Keynes, all the ingredients for perceiving the portfolio theory as a composite of a theory of transactional demand for money and a theory of speculative demand for money. Independently these theories were subsequently fully developed mathematically by Baumol (1952) and Tobin (1958) respectively. Hicks himself did not focus on distinctions between the two theories that were embedded in his portfolio theory but rather on their common difficulty of handling subjective factors, such as expectations and deficient foresight. His perception of this difficulty was at the root of his reluctance to express his portfolio theory in any concise mathematical formulation, even though during the same period he was using very precise marginal analysis in a parallel development of value theory. He was of the opinion that the study of money cannot yield tangible and precise results: 'it is not one which can be performed in a mechanical fashion. It needs judgement and knowledge of business psychology much more than sustained logical reasoning' (1935b, p. 76). Hicks's assertion in 'A suggestion for simplifying the Theory of Money' was consistent with his earlier remarks that monetary theory can be operative only under conditions of imperfect foresight and that it 'in the strict sense, falls outside equilibrium theory' ([1933b] 1982a, p. 35).

Hicks's developments in the portfolio theory already discussed were mainly concerned with the general factors determining the demand for money. During the same period (see 1935f and 1939a), he was also attempting to tackle the issue of the demand for money in specific theories, one of which, equilibrium theory, involved a new step, the determination of the interest rate.

His concept of money in his temporary equilibrium model was specific; he considered it to be 'a particular sort of durable consumers' good'. One condition in the equilibrium model was that 'the marginal rate of substitution between the acquisition of money now and of money at a later date would equal the discount ratio over the period of deferment (1939a, p. 237). Hicks equated the discount ratio with the interest rate. Thus the interest rate in the temporary equilibrium model measures the sacrifice in delaying the acquisition of money, or the sacrifice in delaying the purchase of any durable good. 'In other words, the rate of interest would measure the impatience [of the individual] to possess money now instead of money in the future' (p. 238).

In Hicks's general equilibrium model, the demand for money becomes emotionally sterile. As in the temporary equilibrium model, money plays the role of another good; however, since expectations are taken as given and perfect competition is assumed, the difference of money from other goods is restricted merely to its function as the standard of value. So, the interest rate in the general equilibrium model can be defined simply as the price of money. It is determined either by the supply and demand for capital (the Loanable Funds Theory) or by the supply and demand for money (the Liquidity Preference Theory). Hicks did not place particular importance on one theory over the other. He did, however, use his preference for the latter to introduce money into the set of general equilibrium equations.

His attempts at integrating money into an equilibrium model, whether temporal or general, seem at odds with some of his other reflections on the demand for money. Only slightly earlier Hicks had written, 'Since the use of money is closely connected with imperfect foresight, it needs to be analysed in association with the theory of Risk' ([1933b] 1982a, p. 35). Not only did his equilibrium theory eliminate the notion of risk, it seemed to remove any monetary function for money: money as standard of value 'says nothing about the demand for money in its use as money; the tacit assumption of perfect foresight deprives the *numéraire* of any monetary function' (p. 33). While building the temporary equilibrium model of *Value and Capital* Hicks was so preoccupied with the technical aspects of value theory in a general equilibrium framework that his earlier concept of money was a casualty.

Despite this, overall Hicks did provide a new approach to monetary economics. Although he did not devise a utility function which incorporated money, the hint was clear. His suggestion to apply marginal analysis to monetary theory together with his attempt to integrate money in a general equilibrium framework proved to be very fertile ground for further developments by later economists (initially Patinkin, *Money, Interest and Prices* [1955] 1965). From Hicks's early work the following is noteworthy. He assumed that money is a non-interest-bearing asset while other capital assets are interest-bearing; he made distinctions between assets in terms of their degree of liquidity. In his analysis of the motives determining the demand for money he did not make the same distinctions that Keynes did, that is, transaction, precaution and speculation. Instead he distinguished the motives of wealth, cost of transfer and risk. He initially emphasized the importance of expectations in monetary theory, but by 1939 he had already simplified their role considerably by assuming that they were constant. He said very little about the institutional aspects of monetary systems or about monetary history.

Hicks's own theoretical emphases in the late 1930s, the manner in which monetary theory subsequently evolved within his general equilibrium framework, and the revival, in the 1950s, of the quantity theory of money, all left him, by the early 1960s, generally unsatisfied with the state of monetary theory. He then began to reconsider many aspects of his earliest treatments of money and shaped a comprehensive liquidity theory. He already had the embryo of his liquidity theory in his 1935 paper. Keynes too had produced a liquidity theory, in 1936. Hicks claimed that Keynes', was quite another version from his own, but since the two theories share some common ground, clarification of Keynes, and Hicks's historical positions in the monetary debate will shed some light on Hicks's own contributions. His liquidity theory will then be presented.

Hicks and the currency and banking schools

Economists have never been in agreement on the neutrality of money nor on the impact of its transmission mechanism (that is to say, on the impact of changes in the quantity of money on other economic variables). They have not even been able to find a definition of money acceptable to all. Keynes, for example, rejected the neutrality of money and maintained that his understanding of the function of money within an economy was different from that of his predecessors, all of whose works he referred to as 'classics'. Except for *Value and Capital*, Hicks also adhered to the concept of the non-neutrality of money, rejecting, however, Keynes's demarcation line between the 'classics' and himself and arguing that Keynes exaggerated his claim to novelty. Different ways of categorizing scholars according to their interpretation of the role of money, Hicks insisted, were already in existence in the late eighteenth and early nineteenth century, at least since the Ricardo–Thornton controversy.

The two sides in the Ricardo–Thornton controversy, to pursue an example he used (in 'an attempt at perspective', 1967), continued into the twentieth century to have their advocates on the issue of money neutrality. There were, on the one hand, as Hicks showed, the followers of Ricardo, who were convinced that the level of economic activity is determined by real factors alone and that the quantity of money acts only on the level of prices. On the other hand, there were the followers of Thornton who believed that there is a causal relation between economic activity, determined by real factors, and monetary changes. (Hicks recognized, however, that Thornton himself believed the relation to hold only in the short period.) Hicks included Lord Overstone, Pigou, Mises, Hayek, Friedman and all the neo-quantity theorists in the Ricardian group, which he referred to as the Currency School. Hicks numbered among the followers of Thornton, whom he called adherents of a Banking or Credit School, Mill, Bagehot, Tooke, Hawtrey, Robertson, Keynes and himself.

His categorization of economists raised some issues. The distinctions, in some cases, were as great among members of one school as they were between the two schools. Hicks was well aware of each school's internal differences (see, for example, 1989a, pp. 72–9) but seemed more concerned with the common aspects of their theories. Since, however, he was labelled Keynesian, Hicks also felt the need to diminish Keynes's importance in this manner. He wanted to make it clear that both, he and Keynes, belonged to the same tradition and that while he was aware of the work of Keynes whom he admired, he was not to be considered his follower.

The differences in the contributions to monetary theory by many economists within any one school can be due to the changes in the setting in which money and monetary institutions exist. Each analyst is faced with the monetary problems of the moment. Hicks's conception of money was also a product of his time, 'consistent with the broad facts of monetary evolution' (1967, p. 59), for while he felt the functions of money had remained the same, he observed that the form and the nature of money as well as its institutional setting had evolved. Over time, money had changed from a commodity, to metallic currency, to paper, to money deposits; now it was close to becoming pure credit. Transformations in the form and nature of money had brought about the creation and growth of financial institutions which were themselves changing and adapting to new needs. To Hicks, changes in money had also meant 'fundamental change in the financial activities of governments. In the course of [all] these changes there has been a change in the whole character of the monetary system' (1967, p. 158). All these changes had fostered the creation of the nature of money as credit and had facilitated its use as such. Abuses by governments or financial institutions in expanding or restraining credit had, however at times been noted to have been responsible for precipitating crises or depressions, which in turn, in the process of adjustment, had produced more institutional changes.

Hicks recognized that monetary issues are crucial, since they have direct implications on policies which often, when applied, have direct impact on the working of an economy. For him 'money is not a mechanism' but 'a human institution' (1967, p. 59), appropriate to a particular epoch and specific to the degree of development of an economy. Economists, such as Ricardo, Wicksell and Keynes, left their mark on monetary theory, Hicks claimed, because of the timing of their work. All three dealt with practical and urgent problems in the economies of their time. They confronted different situations. Ricardo, he said, was concerned 'with monetary reconstruction after the War with Napoleon' (1977a, p. 45). His was essentially a problem about the convertibility of the national currency, an issue discussed in the context of the classical quantity theory of money. Wicksell provided his monetary ideas on money and banking at the instance of a slowdown in the activity of many industrialized economies during the last twenty years of the nineteenth century which produced a gradual decrease in prices. Keynes was affected by the unexpected and unprecedented Depression, which had a devastating effect on the working of the economies world-wide. Although the monetary ideas of Ricardo, Wicksell and Keynes were theoretical, they were also topical, and the debates they generated carried beyond the academic circle into the political arena.

Hicks felt that the inability of the old monetary policy prescriptions to contain the disturbing economic events of the 1970s and 1980s (unprecedented high levels of inflation and interest rates, and persisting high unemployment) meant that their underlying monetary theory had to be rethought. After the collapse of the gold standard in 1933, the Bretton Wood system was devised in 1944. It too was abandoned when it collapsed with the dollar crisis of 1971. Indeed no international monetary system has yet been found as a replacement. In the meantime violent fluctuations have occurred in price levels, interest rates, and on stock exchanges, all of which have had an impact on the employment and stability of nations. Tremendous changes have happened around the world in financial institutions and their practices, in the structure of economies, in international relations, in government functions and in the political environment. In his last decades, Hicks was very much concerned with rapid institutional changes and believed that, as it had been for Ricardo, Wicksell and Keynes, the time was right for adopting a new theory for pressing new problems. He attempted to provide what he called a monetary theory with a new foundation appropriate to the post second World War circumstances.

From this brief historical perspective on economists' contributions and economic issues, it can be seen why Hicks believed he was part of the core of theorists who would shape the theoretical foundation of monetary theory and that he would not just extend the ideas of those who influenced him. Even though he considered his position to have been between those of Keynes and Robertson, he was indeed innovative. In his reconsideration of the theory of money Hicks placed new emphasis on certain elements of his earlier theory: time and disequilibrium. He also added the distinction between transactionary, precautionary and speculative motives for holding money and designated the precautionary as the active motivator of the demand for money.

Liquidity theory

Hicks rejected his early portfolio approach because it was not sufficiently 'in time'. In his liquidity theory he would insist that an individual's decision to hold money was not a matter of a single choice at one point in time, but rather a sequence of choices. Hicks also came to accept Keynes' M1 and M2 distinction, that is to say, the distinction between money which is needed for transaction requirements and money held for both precautionary and speculative motives. His fundamental innovation was to associate the voluntary demand for money with the precautionary and speculative motives for holding money, not with the transactional motives as was widely the practice. Hicks emphasized the fact that 'it is through the voluntary part that monetary disturbances operate, and it is on the voluntary part that monetary policy must have its effect' (1967, p. 15), and more important, he detected that the transactional demand for money is not voluntary 'save in a very indirect manner'. Furthermore, he abandoned the view that money is inherently non-interest-bearing, saying that it may or may not be (p. 19). Finally, reiterating his early claim that the existing outstanding volume of money is a result of a disequilibrium situation due to risk, uncertainty and lack of foresight, he determined that the demand for money in a liquidity theory could be analysed in conjunction with phases of the business cycle.

Voluntary demand for money

In constructing a model of financial markets, Hicks separated the voluntary from the involuntary demand for money. He laid greater emphasis in his analysis of liquidity on non-financial firms and households (investors) than on the intermediaries or financial firms, because he thought 'it is outside the financial sphere that liquidity is potentially of the greater importance' (1979g, p. 95). These premises allowed him to relate money to both investment decisions and the real components of an economy. The key feature of money in his model was its liquidity. It was considered extremely important in investment decisions since it meant 'freedom'; a lack of liquidity could slow one's 'ability to respond to future opportunities' (p. 94).

Hicks attempted to fit the three traditional functions of money (unit of account, means of payment and store of value) to Keynes's three motives for holding money (transaction, precautionary and speculative), though he did admit that an exact one-to-one correspondence between these two triads could not be established (Table 7.2). Although the three functions of money are indissoluble, he tried, in theory at least, to correlate 'store of value' to both the precautionary and speculative motives and in so doing to isolate them from the transaction motive. He then proceeded to define the demand for liquidity predominantly in terms of the precautionary demand for money.

Hicks made a distinction between Keynes's version of liquidity preference theory and his own. In Keynes's *General Theory* (1936), individuals have a choice between holding money (currency, notes in circulation

Table 7.2 The two triads and the classification of assets (1967)

Functions of money	↗ → ↘	unit of account means of payment store of value	
Keynes's three motives	↗ → ↘	transaction precaution speculation	
Hicks' classification	↗ → ↘	Running assets Reserve assets Investment assets	(These are either financial assets or real assets)

and demand deposits) or 'bonds' (a bundle of securities). For Keynes any change in the liquidity preference implied a change in the demand for money. This is not necessarily the case in Hicks's theory. Hicks distinguished between 'bonds' or assets as fully liquid, more or less liquid and non-liquid; this is a distinction he had already made in 1935. For him, given the spectrum of assets, a change in liquidity preference could create a substitution between the various assets without necessarily changing the demand for money.

Hicks correlated Keynes's motive triad (transaction, precaution and speculation) to his own classification of assets, in terms of running assets, reserve assets and investment assets. These three assets could be either real or financial. Running assets are defined as assets held for payment of everyday transactions. Reserve assets are those assets which, easily marketable and profit yielding, are kept for precautionary measures. Investment assets are assets which are held for the sake of their yield and may serve either precautionary or speculative purposes.

What then determined for Hicks the demand for liquidity? The financial intermediary (called Financier) and the investor (referred to as Fund) both deal with the same triad of assets but each has a different set of liabilities. To the Financier the liabilities are contractual; to the Fund they are non-contractual. Thus Hicks classified assets differently depending on whether they were in the hands of a Financier or a Fund. For instance, the spectrum of more or less marketable securities (bonds, bills, equities, mortgages, etc.) comprises running and reserve assets when they are held by the Financier and for the Financier they are active liabilities. These same assets are considered investment assets and are passive liabilities if they are held by the Fund.

Hicks's classification of assets and his distinction between the Financier and the Fund enabled him astutely to preserve all three functions of money and yet to de-emphasize the transaction motive of the demand for money. For the Fund (that is to say, the investor of non-financial firms, funds and households), investment assets are crucial to the demand for liquidity. These same assets are regarded, by the Financier, as financial reserve and running assets, liable to liquidity shifts, and thus they are held for emergencies or opportunities of doing financial business. For the Financier (financial firm), dealing with financial markets, having assets permits taking advantage of any occasion for gain, thus Financier assets are constantly being substituted in marginal adjustments; for the Fund (investor) holding investment assets is more a question of having liquidity at his or her disposal for precaution. Thus, for the Fund to acquire or dispose of assets is a matter of having a liquidity safeguard to respond to eventual or sudden needs for financial resources. It is not a matter of speculation for the sake of marginal financial gains. Investors' needs mean changes in the demand for liquidity, which require of the Financier in response substitution among the Financier's various financial assets. In Hicks's theory, the precautionary demand for money thus determined 'the demand for liquidity'; the speculative demand for money, on which Keynes placed such emphasis, was for Hicks 'a special not a general phenomenon' (1967, pp. 48, 49).

By 1982 Hicks (in essay 19 of *Money, Interest and Wages*), was observing that the Fund was responding to a new influence, high interest rates, which also determined the desire to hold money. He thus added a nuance to Keynes's three motives (transactionary, precautionary and speculative) by examining both the precautionary and the speculative motives as exercised in either a 'fluid' or a 'solid' manner. The fact that short-term interest rates were high in the 1980s relative to what they were in Keynes's time, led Hicks to make the fluid – solid distinction. Regardless of motive, a solid investor was, for Hicks one who was prepared and able to tie money up in relatively illiquid, but very secure assets. A fluid investor was one who was ready to hold assets in a relatively liquid (interest-bearing) form, either waiting for the right opportunity to invest or as security against unforeseen costs.

Keynes's speculative motive was distinct from Hicks's precautionary motive carried out in a fluid manner, his 'investment' motive. Keynes's speculative motive meant holding non-interest-bearing money only in order to wait for the right investment opportunity to present itself. Hicks' 'investment' motive, while it also meant biding time for the right investment, emphasized as more important that assets in an interest-bearing liquid state would be available in case of an emergency. It should be stressed that to act out of a 'fluid' precautionary motive became advantageous only once the return from interest was high (and the risk involved remained relatively low), despite the fact that it entailed weighing the advantages of liquidity. Given high interest rates, it did not make business sense to hold money that would not bear interest, even for emergencies.

The working of the financial system

Now that the functions of money and the motives of holding it have been elucidated, the relation of liquidity and monetary policy can be discussed. Hicks analysed three aspects of the simple financial system: (1) the short-run effects of changes in security markets in terms of financial running and reserve assets; (2) the impact of monetary policies on short- and long-term interest and the impact of long-term interest on industrial investments; and (3) the effectiveness of monetary policies in a depressed economy and the issue of the liquidity trap.

First, buying and selling in the security markets have three effects: creating substitution between various assets, influencing differently prices of individual securities, and creating excess or shortage of liquidity. Hicks observed the consistent result of the substitution effect (his 'Hawtrey effect) to be an excess or shortage of liquidity. This he labelled the 'liquidity pressure' or 'liquidity effect' or 'wealth effect'. The liquidity effect occurs regardless of whether the economy is in a recession or a boom. Furthermore, every time a monetary authority intervenes in the open market operation, it creates its own liquidity pressures, which have different effects depending on whether the economy is in a boom or a slump situation. There is, according to Hicks, an asymmetrical effect of a monetary authority's liquidity pressure. While a monetary authority's tightening liquidity will most likely bring an economic boom down, its relaxing liquidity will not necessarily guarantee that recovery will take place.

Second, as for the effect of monetary policies on long-term (and therefore short-term) interest, Hicks rejected Keynes's claim that the 'long-term rate of interest could be induced by monetary policy' (1967, p. 54). He said that experience showed the long-run rate of interest to be too volatile to be controlled. While a monetary authority can manipulate the relative supplies of various maturities, speculation, whose effects can be amplified by expectations of future movements in the interest rate, can go either way and can distort the intent of the policy. So it is difficult, over the course of a business cycle, to control financial investment, which in turn renders it difficult for any authority to have an effect on any type of industrial investment.

Hicks considered specifically the possibility of determining the impact of long-term interest on industrial investments in real assets, in the light of two types of industrial investments: net investments and new investments. Net investments he considered to be defensive investments, which consist in building up product stocks or replacing equipment in order to be better prepared for eventualities. Net investment decisions by design reduce uncertainty of the future. New investments, on the other hand, which introduce new techniques or new products, increase uncertainty because of the not-yet-known reaction of the market. Hicks felt that the impact of long-term interest rates was unlikely to be considerable on net or defensive investment. 'Quite severe liquidity pressure will have to be applied in order to stop' defensive investment

(1967, p. 56; see also 1989a, p. 117). New investment would be effected by interest rates, he believed, only at the start of its application: 'A project cannot be started in the middle; and it would rarely be advantageous to stop it in the middle, however high the rate of interest rises. So it is the effect of interest rate on the starting projects about which we have mainly to think' (1989a, p. 119).

One type of investment is more likely in the boom phase of the business cycle and the other more likely in the slump phase. In the former phase, most investment seems to be of a defensive or net nature, whereas in the latter new investment is more likely. Hicks suggested that net investment will be undertaken on almost any terms, provided the necessary finance is available. There are constraints on net investment due to a lack of liquidity, however, rather than the deterrence of the rate of interest. In a boom situation even if a firm is in need of liquidity, there is shortage of it from the financial side and thus not all desired net investment can be realized. In a slump situation the financial terms which would otherwise be sufficient, owing to available liquidity, to stimulate new investment are hard to offer because of the high risk to those offering them. Hicks felt that, save in severe circumstances, the impact of changes in the long-term interest rate in both phases of the business cycle was inconsiderable. For this reason he further asserted that the impact of the manipulation by a monetary authority of long-term interest rates would in turn also be inconsiderable. He concluded that 'it is hard to control investment in a boom' because 'in the boom (so long as it is expected to continue) most investment has become defensive investment; and the reason why it is hard to start up investment in a slump is that it cannot be done without stimulating new investment (1967, p. 57).

Third, as for the effectiveness of monetary policies in a depressed economy and the issue of the liquidity trap, Hicks addressed the question of an economy's recovery from a slump. It seemed to him to be a matter of a long-term mechanism. On the short-term impact of a monetary policy of increasing liquidity in a slump, Hicks agreed with Keynes: any increase in the amount of the supply of money by the monetary authority will end up idle. The only sure hope of recovery from a slump is that money cannot remain indefinitely idle. Hicks, however, felt that if it were possible for the financial system to improve its organization and lower the cost of financial transfers, it could despite the risk increase the desire for active liquidity at reduced rates of interest (1967, p. 58). This reduction may be sufficient to encourage investment to resume and thus to start the recovery.

Hicks's analysis of the impact of monetary policy is somewhat different from that of Keynes. Unlike Keynes, Hicks did not seem very keen on government intervention to bring an economy out of a slump, but preferred the system to rely on liquidity shifts. For him, monetary changes affect the prices of various financial assets, which changes are in turn 'transmitted to commodity markets' (1967, p. 50). The prices of financial assets reflect expectations which in turn can have a positive or negative volatile effect on the interest rate. Even when monetary policies can manipulate the interest rate in a counterbalancing right direction, their impact cannot be fully symmetrical. Such policies can be effective in slowing a booming economy, but cannot guarantee an economy's recovery.

The transmission mechanism

With the following very simple, consolidated balance sheet (Table 7.3) Hicks illustrated how changes in liquidity take place. He assumed the economy to consist of three sectors, modelled as if arranged in rings. His monetary authority, or 'core', issues money which, through the financial intermediaries, or 'mantle', is transmitted to the rest of the economy, 'industry' (the Fund or non-financial firms including households). In Hicks's balance sheet, to every liability there is a corresponding asset, save for the real assets of industry, which appear as 'pure residual' (R) (1977a, p. 76). He analysed the transmission of liquidity from core, to mantle, to industry from different perspectives. Depending on whether one is considering a closed or open economy, the transmission of liquidity from one sector to another occurs differently.

Table 7.3 National balance sheet

	Liabilities		*Assets*
Core	Money	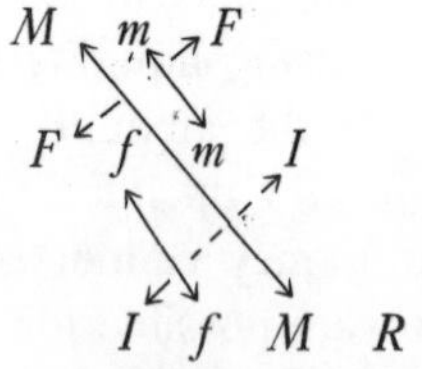 M m F	Financial securities
Mantle	Financial securities	F f m I	Industrial securities and money
Industry	Industrial securities	I f M R	Financial securities, money and real assets

Source: 1977a, p. 76.

In a closed economy, Hicks did not see any insurmountable problems of liquidity presented to the core, since he believed that the core has the means and power to increase liquidity when needed. In a closed economy, when industry is in need of expansion, there are many ways of securing financing. The core can increase the quantity of money (M) and advance the new liquidity to industry (M). That liquidity is matched by debts from industry to the core, which debts, however, may well be 'in such a form as not to diminish the liquidity of industry (1979g, p. 98). Alternatively, industry can borrow money from the mantle. In that case the liquidity of the mantle will diminish, while the liquidity of industry increases. Alternatively again, if industry is self-sufficient in liquidity, it can finance its expansion with its own resources, without having to depend or bargain for funds from the financiers of the mantle. Industry would thus, however, have to exchange its less liquid reserve assets for money such that a decrease in liquidity reserves would occur in both the mantle and industry sectors.

In an open economy, however, the inflow and outflow of international capital make the domestic transmission of liquidity more unwieldy for the core, as well as for the mantle and industry. A monetary authority can have difficulty controlling the liquidity within its economy even with flexible exchanges. The difficulty can be greater the weaker the economy. In an open economy, simple extension or contraction of the money supply as standard responses to liquidity problems may well not be appropriate. Hicks affirmed, for example, that domestic constraints in industry's liquidity in a context of successful growth are of little consequence since they are compensated for by liquidity sources outside the economy. He also asserted that in a weak economic context constraints can have a highly consequent effect. In an open economy the reliance on self-financing is highly desirable, since it is difficult for the core to channel liquidity, a problem which it does not have in a closed economy. In addition, 'the possession of liquid funds by industry will make it easier for opportunities to be taken quickly than if such reserves were absent or scarce . . . We know that successful development makes for a strong economy, in which "stop-go" pressures on liquidity are infrequent' (1979g, p. 99).

Hicks managed with his description of a fairly simple financial system to show how transmission occurs between the economy's monetary authority, the financial sector and the rest of the economy. He also illustrated how changes in the demand for liquidity through the alternate means of financing an expansion of industry create different liquidity pressures. These various pressures affect the prices of securities and interest rates differently, which in turn have their impact on investment decisions. As in Hawtrey, for Hicks it 'is through its effects on speculative markets in commodities' (1989a, p. 113) that interest affects trade activity. He argued, however, that liquidity is crucial to the business operation of a firm which often holds more liquid assets as a precaution to ensure financial freedom at the expense of foregoing extra earning by engaging in speculation.

For example, when new investments are undertaken, some time elapses between the beginning of the construction period and the start of the utilization or running period. During that time, firms are exposed to risk and cannot afford to stop their projects in the middle of the process. Even if the rate of interest is higher than anticipated, often a firm would have no choice but to accept it and to come up with reserve money to finance the additional cost (1989a, p. 118). With this scenario in mind, Hicks distanced himself from Keynes's idea that the interest rate is the crucial variable in investment decision. 'It was very wrong to think that investment is governed by the rate of interest, as if any concern that wanted to invest could always raise as much capital as it required at a ruling interest rate' (1979g, p. 96).

The fact that short-term interest rates are high relative to what they used to be in Keynes's time has made firms more aware of the high financial cost if interest rates increase further. In the face of uncertainty firms are more cautious and hold reserves of greater liquidity even if it means the loss of the tempting financial gain from having less liquid rather than more liquid assets. At the same time, it has come to not make business sense to hold money that does not bear interest. As a consequence, it is becoming common that non-financial firms let financial institutions manage all their financial responsibilities. The experience in the 1970s and 1980s of high interest rates have caused a drastic change in the form in which firms hold their financial assets. 'A gulf has opened between that circulating money and the most liquid of his [any rational operator's] reserves' (1989a, p. 103). Money is becoming more and more a matter of a book-keeping account in financial institutions without actually much cash changing hands. Such recent changes in financial practices led Hicks to believe that 'one is driven back, in the end from Keynes to Wicksell' (1982a, p. 237). Hicks saw Wicksell's pure credit theory becoming more relevant to the actual working of the financial economy.

The credit economy

Hicks observed that in a credit economy with complex multi-exchange trade, information is an essential element in learning about liquidity needs. The gathering of information is timely and costly, which encourages some firms to make information their business. By dealing with specific types of investments financial intermediaries take advantage of specialization to lower the cost of acquiring information and reducing uncertainty. The reason for the existence of financial institutions besides ordinary banks is that they are more efficient in assembling particular financial information. The role of information was crucial in Hicks's credit economy.

A credit economy is, according to Hicks, an economy which has 'no money that does not bear interest' (1982a, p. 266). 'Money as means of payment is just a debt' (1989a, p. 104), and the interest rate becomes 'the key instrument of monetary control' (1982a, p. 266). (It should be noted that he made a distinction between the role of the interest rate in investment decisions at the level of industry or at the micro-level, as in the previous section, and the manipulation of the interest rate and the money market at the macro-level.) In expressing money as a debt, Hicks had in his later work moved away from his early concept of money as 'a particular sort of durable consumers' good' (1939a, p. 237), as presented above in the earlier section on the portfolio approach. At the same time he was also moving away from the concept of money in the Walrasian equilibrium approach used in *Value and Capital*, to debt–credit in a dynamic framework. Since money had become for Hicks simply a debt signal embedding the uncertainty of potential default, its discussion reinforced once again the issue of confidence and expectations as economic concerns.

> In the standard economist's model of multilateral trading (the *n*-good *m*-person market of Walras) it [the issue of confidence] is avoided; for there all transactions are spot transactions, taking place – somehow! – simultaneously. But if payments are made by offsetting of debts, and the debts are owing from different people, it cannot be taken for granted that all will be paid, or will be paid when promised; so the debts may well be of different *quality*. (1989a, pp. 47–8)

Models of the closed and open credit economy

Hicks constructed two models of the credit economy: the monocentric model appropriate to a closed economy in which there is only one monetary authority, and the polycentric model, an economic system relevant to an open economy in which there are many monetary centres. In his basic monocentric model, he expanded the Wicksell one-bank model by letting other financial institutions than the bank borrow and lend, by allowing the bank to offer a deposit rate lower than its lending rate, and by introducing the financial intermediary to 'make use of specialized knowledge about the prospects of particular kinds of real investments, so that it can make advances to firms, or investments in the securities of the firms' (1989a, p. 108). The bank, or the centre, in his simple model refers both to the central bank and to the commercial banks.

In contrast to Wicksell's monocentric model where there was only one monetary rate of interest, in Hicks's theory there was a series of rates. Savers receive an interest rate r^0 for their deposits in the bank. The bank charges r^1 for its money, some of which is borrowed by the intermediaries. The intermediaries receive r^2 for their loans. Firms which deal with these intermediaries pay *r2* for that money and expect to receive a rate of return *R* on their marginal investment. One can imagine a more complex model in which there are many levels of financial institutions with each level borrowing from the one next closest to the centre and lending to the one next removed. In each level farther from the centre the difference in respective lending rates would reflect both a higher loan risk and a higher cost of gathering information of concern in the increasingly higher-risk investment. In the basic chain of lending 'rate *r1* must exceed *r0* to cover the administrative costs of the bank; *r2* must exceed *r1* not only because of administrative costs, but also to provide a liquidity premium. So *r2* exceeds *r0* by two margins, those of the bank and of intermediaries.' Ultimately *R* also has to 'exceed r^2 by another liquidity premium' (1989a, p. 110).

As in Wicksell's theory the economy is in equilibrium when *R* is in equilibrium, that is, when *R* covers at least *r2*. That equilibrium, however, is fragile. In addition to the economic fluctuations generated by changes in technology and productivity, given its uncertain future, imperfect information and risk-taking in multi-exchange trade, an economy driven by credit is prone to further fluctuations. As in Wicksell's model, in Hicks's model the bank can through interest rate policy reduce the discrepancy between the money rate and the yield *R*, provided that gap is narrow, and thus contain the economic fluctuation.

Hicks used the Wicksell model and analogous reasoning for an open economy. In a polycentric model there are many monetary authority centres. In the case of each country within the polycentric model, to its basic monocentricity in which there are many interest rates relating to the financial borrowing and lending of savers, banks, intermediaries and firms, there now are added many foreign currencies and an individual foreign exchange market, which precludes any one bank within the country having a monopoly in dealing with foreign exchange.

In a polycentric credit economy, in a multi-exchange trade, whether within a country or between countries, the medium of exchange used for transactions is an exchange of debts. Domestically or internationally the function of a medium of exchange is the same, even though, for many countries, one currency is used for domestic transactions and another for external transactions. Hicks believed that in a market economy the choice of an international standard is left to the trading parties which often opt for a currency which they trust.

Monetary stability and policy

To understand how Hicks evisaged monetary policy evolving within a single country it would be useful first to consider his conception of how the international monetary system works. Of especial interest to him was the role of the international currency and who would determine and control it. Historically, at least in the last two hundred years, groups of countries accepted a currency of one of their members as their international standard. The leadership of that currency was earned through the confidence expressed by trading parties in it as a sound and strong currency. Leadership 'is not acquired by a decision of the "central" government, or of its banking system; it comes from decisions by others, who choose to make the currency of that country their chief "international"' (1989a, p. 130), and this occurs 'through "market forces", without any treaty having been needed to establish it' (p. 127). Hicks believed that the financial trading arrangements which arise for necessity and convenience are mostly based on confidence and cannot be imposed by governments' policies. Since it will always be the case that some countries will have deficits while others have surpluses, he believed the conventional self-adjusting trade flow mechanism could be effective as long as countries engaged in trade behave responsibly in stabilizing their currency and as long as there is enough internal price and wage flexibility in each country.

In a polycentric model there is a central country whose currency plays the role of international currency and other countries who use their own national currency for their domestic transactions and the central country's currency for their external transactions. The non-central countries' convertible currencies are pegged to the international standard. In such an international monetary system, if the international currency itself is pegged to some other invariant value, say for example gold, then the responsibility of the central country is greatly restrained. In the absence of such an arrangement, as is the case with the present international monetary system, the central country plays an important and unique role, that of being responsible for controlling the supply of the international currency. Any change in its monetary policy will affect other trading partners. It is its monetary policy behaviour which can provide for international financial and economic stability. The problem arises when the central country experiences economic difficulties, such as persistent balance of payment deficits and the accompanying clash between internal and external monetary policies. Unlike the non-central countries, the central country cannot base its policy on internal considerations alone and ignore its international commitments, when it is in a weak position. When it does so it reneges on its responsibilities and undermines international confidence in its currency.

What happens when the international currency begins to lose its strength and the trading partners loose confidence in it? 'Is there any device by which the central country could be taken down from its privileged position . . .?' (1989a, p. 127). Hicks thought there was, the same international market mechanism based on confidence which had earlier elevated it to that privileged position. For instance, in the gold standard era it was the British government's imposition of exchange controls which destroyed the reigning confidence in the centrality of sterling. The Bretton Wood system collapsed when confidence in the dollar was lost and American authorities abdicated their central responsibility. In both cases, it was owing to weakness of the currency and to the fact that the central country had become concerned with internal policy that the non-central countries lost confidence in the international standard and started looking for another standard. Out of such situations of loss of confidence, it was not, however, strictly speaking, the governments who through policy arrived at a new recognized standard. To Hicks's mind, it was and ought to continue to be the market itself that makes its choice of a new standard, which the countries subsequently institutionalize.

Monetary stability was as crucial to Hicks's analysis of the credit economy as it was to his conception of earlier traditional monetary systems. He was persuaded that on the international scale the market signals of demand, supply and currency confidence were highly effective in maintaining a form of stability. Even at times when confidence in a particular standard had eroded, market forces eventually selected another currency to take its place. For Hicks the very fact at the international level that more than one currency and national monetary authority presented themselves for choice as the standard medium of exchange and monetary authority distinguished the stabilizing mechanism of the polycentric model significantly from that of the monocentric model. Although analogous components could be found in the two models in periods of stability (international traders and investors analogous to national producers and investors, the financial market of currencies analogous to the interest rate market, and a single monetary authority the centre in each case), in periods of instability the analogy could not hold.

In periods of instability, at the international level more than one country would vie for the role of authority, while at the national level, each country was left with its one and only monetary authority. Hicks saw two options available at the national level for the restoration of confidence in a country's monetary system: a political response, to replace the standing political authority (and its economic policies) with a new political authority, a response most frequently, and often violently, assumed in countries of great monetary distress, and an institutional or organizational response. In countries governed by constitutional law, the institutional option was the one Hicks advocated.

Confidence in a national monetary system on the part of individuals engaged in market activity at the national level derived, Hicks felt, from a sense similar to that at work in the international market: that money, that is, credit, ought be available as it is required in the production sector. Adequate response to the credit needs of that sector would thus be the key to the maintenance of confidence in a nation's monetary strength and lead to its monetary stability. Since the desired response on a national scale must stem from the nation's central monetary authority, Hicks affirmed that authority must be aware of the needs of the real production sector at all times. Information would be the instrument to guarantee this awareness, since in a complex credit economy all kinds of general as well as of specialized information are required to signal the state of an economy's production and multi-exchange trade. Hicks attempted, therefore, to devise a national hierarchical organization of the Wicksellian rings of financial activity which would provide at all levels for the most direct access to information and the most efficient transmission of that information to the monetary authority.

To this end, Hicks asked, what kind of viable market structure can be devised to gather information in the most efficient way? The centre, or the bank, cannot do without the assistance of specialized institutions, which he called 'listening points', to gather information about specific investments in response to liquidity pressures. In the monocentric financial sector, he argued, the functioning of financial institutions according to the market price mechanism would not necessarily be the most efficient way to see that information is collected and that the interests of the production sector are well understood. Instead, some concentration of institutions and information in the financial sector was, he believed, desirable (1989a, pp. 110–11). More important, close collaboration between the specialized intermediaries and the centre (which plays the role of 'lender of last resort') could better provide the desired stability in economic activity. Through the form of monopolistic control Hicks contemplated, the centre aided by close consultation with the intermediaries orchestrates monetary policy with a primary goal: to narrow the gap between the monetary interest rate and the rate of return on marginal investment in the effort to maintain the economy in a state of monetary equilibrium.

It might seem that in advocating this goal Hicks was countenancing government monetary intervention. His scheme should, however, be interpreted not in the context of unilateral policy decisions dictated by a government or a central monetary authority. In a monocentric economy a Hicksian policy decision in the monetary sphere derives from the collaboration of all parties within the broad monetary authority, consisting of the many financial intermediaries ('listening points') and the centre ('the lender of last resort'). A final policy decision should therefore reflect the public need for credit. Hicks simply felt that the process by which a policy decision might be reached would be more effective the more information was made available to all concerned, and would be less unwieldy the fewer the representative bodies involved. In the monetary sphere concentration of the institutions for collecting and sorting information concerning the need for credit takes advantage of the economy of scale and its diminishing cost. Hicks's scheme implied, however, that if policy making for the general good were to depend on information from institutions with individual vested interests it would only function well if these institutions were widely representative. They should provide information for the good of society, rather than withholding it for their own advantage – should that be perceived as different in the short run.

Recognizing that in the discussions of monetary theory economists most frequently note inflation as a subject of great concern, Hicks was certainly willing to acknowledge that even the best of financial institutional organizations could not protect an economy from being subject to shocks and liable to fluctuation. This was, however, quite different from his accepting inflation as a monetary phenomenon. For Hicks, not only was inflation not a phenomenon to be controlled or corrected by monetary policy, it was not a phenomenon fundamentally caused by monetary circumstances at all. It was instead the reflection of an economy's production sector as weak for non-monetary, and to his mind probably rectifiable, reasons.

For Hicks, the most essential aspect of such assertions was that monetary policy, national or international, should not, and could not, assume the role of after-the-fact therapy to cure the ill health of an economy. At best it might act as a form of preventative in fostering the strength (or even renewing the strength) of a nation's economy with its modest goal of maintaining a narrow gap between the monetary interest rate and the rate of return on marginal investment. Hicks disapproved of using interest rates to control an economy for political ends. He was aware that the use of changes in interest rates, without reference to the real rate of return on investment (R), to exercise central control could be far more detrimental than effective to the course of an economy. The results desired from the changes might be very long in materializing, or, as in a recessionary economy, not forthcoming at all.

Hicks also objected to reliance on any other (non-interest-rate-based) monetary policies to foster specific ends, such as inflation fighting or unemployment, especially when their advocates saw these ends foremost as political objectives. He noted, along with Marshall, that central monetary authorities in the guise of governments can act as part of the cause of economic problems, such as fostering inflation and a rise in interest rates owing to their unfunded expenditures and their unwillingness to raise taxes (1989a, p. 79). Unlike some of his contemporaries, Hicks did not perceive any economic advantage in turning a blind eye to inflation even at a rate so slow and continuous, 'that people have had time to adjust themselves to it' (1989a, p. 132). Inflation, Hicks was strongly persuaded, ought to be arrested, not, however, because of its direct impact, whose hardship he admitted could be argued away, but rather because it is a symptom of a much greater economic malaise.

> Perhaps what is bad about inflation is principally not its effects – the losses of 'convenience and security' to which older economists gave so much attention – but the weakening of the economy, which is the cause of the evil. If that is cured, inflation, with only a little help from monetary policy, will cure itself. (1989a, p. 135)

To integrate the concept of money as debt into a dynamic framework, as described above, is a formidable task. In contrast to his models of temporary equilibrium, trade cycle and growth, where he used both static tools and equilibrium devices to analyse economic dynamics, Hicks did not pursue that route in his later analysis of money and monetary dynamics. Furthermore, with regard to the working of a monetary economy, he was all along very concerned with economic fluctuations and identified their primary causes in the non-monetary sphere. Hicks thus chose deliberately to emphasize 'the real (non-monetary) character of the cyclical process' (1950a, p. 136). Since for him money was only 'a complication' to fluctuations, not their cause (1973, p. 55), it is not surprising that a foremost objective in most of his work was 'to show that the main features of the cycle can be adequately explained in real terms' (1950, p. 136). In his traverse model, Hicks re-emphasized that 'monetary disorders may indeed be superimposed upon other disorders; but the other disorders are more fundamental' (1973d, p. 134).

These seem to be the reasons why Hicks attempted in many of his models to underemphasize their monetary aspect and to concentrate his theoretical analysis overwhelmingly on the non-monetary angle. This emphasis has yielded the unfortunate appearance of a dichotomy between most of his models, which were restricted to the real or non-monetary sphere of the economy, and his various theories of money. Hicks himself saw them as part of the same overall perception and did provide a small bridge between his approaches to the real and the monetary sectors in *A Market Theory of Money* (1989a). Much bridging of the gap is, however, still left to his readers to do.

8

Keynes and Keynesian Economics

In the early 1930s, while Hicks was a lecturer at the London School of Economics, Keynes was already a powerful scholar with a fledgling school of his own in Cambridge. Even though Hicks showed a keen interest in and made an effort to understand the Cambridge economics of Marshall and Pigou, which was quite different from the Continental-influenced economics of the LSE, his economic philosophy and theory were far removed from those of Keynes. However Keynes, as editor of the *Economic Journal*, in 1936 asked Hicks to be the first non-Cambridge-trained reviewer of *The General Theory*. Hicks's initial interpretation of the book gave the impression, at least outside Cambridge, that he was sympathetic to Keynes's theory. These two facts have misled many generations of economists into believing that Hicks was a 'whole-hearted Keynesian'. He has often been represented as a follower and as an expositor of Keynes when in fact his interest in Keynes was always expressed in light of his own theory. Being paired with Keynes prompted Hicks more than ever to clarify his work as being distinct from that of Keynes.

From the appearance of Keynes's *General Theory* in 1936, Hicks commented on, or related and compared Keynes's ideas to his own in almost all his writings. Specifically he produced two reviews of *The General Theory*, 'Mr Keynes's Theory of Employment' (1936b), and 'Mr Keynes and the "Classics"' (1937a), which he called his 'most convenient summary of the Keynesian theory' (1950a, p. 137), in which he suggested the IS–LM device as a simplification of Keynes's general theory. In *A Contribution to the Theory of the Trade Cycle* (1950a) he borrowed and adapted Keynes's notion of the multiplier and the saving–investment relation. In his article, 'Two-Triads' (1967) he related and drew parallels between his liquidity theory and that of Keynes. In 1974 he wrote *The Crisis of Keynesian Economics* (1974b) as an assessment of the situation at the time. He also devoted several essays to Keynes, most important of which was 'A note on the Treatise' (1967) on Keynes's *Treatise on Money*; 'Probability and judgement' (1979g) on Keynes's *Treatise on Probability*; and 'IS–LM – an explanation' (1980a).

While Hicks admired Keynes and was influenced by him, in his own mind he never thought of himself as Keynes's disciple. By the same token, he did not deny that he shared some ideas with him and even at moments counted himself as a Keynesian in relation to some specifics: 'I counted myself a Keynesian, it was an *IS–LM* Keynesian that I meant. I was contending that Keynes's model, though an extreme case of the *general IL–LM* model, is an extreme case that is outstandingly important' (1979f, p. 210).

Despite the many overlapping themes in their work, Hicks, as an independent thinker, disassociated himself from Keynes. The general relationship of the two as distinct thinkers will be discussed immediately below. This discussion will be followed by the analysis of four different themes as illustration of the specifics of Hicks's general perspective on Keynes: money wages; real wages and the labour market; the liquidity theory and the interest rate; the multiplier and the saving–investment equilibrium and the IS–LM device. In the context of each theme it will be shown how Hicks perceived his own ideas as, for example, more general than those of Keynes. The starting point will be the Hicksian interpretation of Keynes, not in light of Keynesians' interpretation of Keynes himself, but rather according to Hicks's use of the ideas of Keynes for his own ends.

Hicks and Keynes

Hicks never denied the influence on him of other economists, including Keynes. For example, in the preface to *Value and Capital* he wrote, 'the latter half of this book would have been different if I had not had the *General Theory* at my disposal' (1939a, p. 4). That Keynes had an impact on Hicks's ideas should not, however, be viewed as exceptional. To Hicks's mind, Keynes was indeed a major figure in economics, but one like all others who should be viewed in the whole context of the evolution of economic thought. Although Keynes was already attracting tremendous attention in the early 1930s, Hick's strong interest in him began only when *The General Theory* appeared. Hicks liked to remind the economics profession that his liquidity theory, for example, was conceived before he knew much about Keynes. Hicks may well have discussed some of the Cambridge ideas with Robertson, who was very familiar with Keynes's work, but Hicks claimed that he had not studied Keynes's *Treatise on Money* before writing the first draft of 'A suggestion for simplifying the Theory of Money' (1935b), which was dated 30 November 1932. Only when his LSE colleague Barrett Whale noted that the draft paper reminded him of Keynes's *Treatise* did Hicks turn to examine that work: 'at that point (but not earlier), I did go to the *Treatise*' (1977a, p. 141). After revising the paper, Hicks sent it to Keynes, who liked it. It was subsequently published in *Economica* (1935b).

Perhaps the fact that there were aspects of Hicks's monetary approach in 1932 with which Keynes agreed led Keynes shortly thereafter to invite Hicks to review his *General Theory*. As Hicks remembered it, 'I knew no more of the details [of Keynes' ideas] until I was asked, very much to my surprise, to review the *General Theory* for the *Economic Journal* (on its publication in January 1936)' (1977, p. 142). By that time, Hicks had already worked out not only the ingredients of *Value and Capital* (1939a), but had also devised his IS–LM framework in his 'Wages and interest' article (1935f). To distinguish the ideas of *Value and Capital* from those of Keynes, he emphasized in its preface that most of the book had taken shape between 1930 and 1935, implying that most of its ideas were already conceived before *The General Theory* appeared.

Hicks's initial treatment of Keynes's ideas (mainly those in *The General Theory*) was to weigh them in relation to past and contemporary contributions to economic theory and to recognize their original elements. Evaluating Keynes's theory in the context of the existing economic literature, he detected limits in it and thus attempted to show that Keynes's was simply a special case theory, not a general one as Keynes had claimed for himself. Later, even though Hicks considered inappropriate some of the devices he had earlier used in assessing Keynes's work, he continued to identify which of his own ideas, while close to Keynes, had developed independently and which were decidedly different in conception and purpose.

From his first impressions of Keynes, Hicks felt that while he himself had begun as a Walrasian, Keynes was more a part of the Marshallian tradition. Hicks's work *vis-à-vis* Keynes can be placed in context by beginning with Hicks's paper on Walras, in which he noted the striking affinity of the ideas of Walras and Marshall: 'Walras and Marshall go together; and when they separate, it is a difference of interests, rather than of technique, that divides them . . . They each tell us that Cournot showed them how to use the differential calculus in economics' (1934d, p. 338). To Hicks's mind Walras and Marshall used the same methods to tackle economic problems. In his 1934 paper, Hicks explained that

Walras's method was the more general, however, since Marshall had confined himself to a partial analysis. In an analogous way, as Hicks saw it, Keynes used the Marshallian method; 'I felt, from the start, that Keynes's was not a *general* theory' ([1979f] Wood and Woods, 1989, vol. 3, p. 210). It has already been explained in chapter 2 that Hicks saw Keynes as having divided the economy into two industries (capital goods and consumer goods). By making the capital industry dependent on given long-term expectations, Keynes could focus his attention on one industry and thus apply Marshallian analysis to the consumer goods industry. This is one of the ways in which Hicks thought that Keynes's theory of Marshallian orientation was less general than his own Walrasian one.

As already briefly discussed in chapter 2, Hicks was favourably disposed to Keynes's method in *The General Theory*. The method consisted in analysing a process of change using an equilibrium analysis into which expectations have been introduced. Hicks found Keynes's clear integration of expectations very attractive. He saw chapter 12, on long-term expectations, as 'one of his most brilliant chapters' ([1936b] 1982a, p. 89). It was Keynes's method and the model that Keynes used of which he 'so warmly approved' ([1979f] Wood and Woods, 1989, vol. 3, p. 210). None the less, even in Keynes's handling of expectations, Hicks found his uniqueness and generality limited, on the one hand because others, most notably the Swedish economists, had already led the way to the use of expectations, and on the other hand because Keynes had introduced long-term expectations as an independent variable.

At first Hicks thought he could reduce *The General Theory* to a special case model of what he believed to be his own general theory, which encompassed all other theories including the classical one. It was for this reason that Hicks encapsulated Keynes's theory in his initial IS–LL framework (1937a). Later, however, on rereading Keynes while rethinking his own IS–LL framework, Hicks found that Keynes's theory had specific limitations, which he had not seen in the mid-1930s. On the one hand, he came to the realization that Keynes's theory had characteristics which precluded its being embraced by his IS–LL framework which, since it was static, could not handle such Keynesian elements as time, expectations and uncertainty. For example, Hicks went so far in 1969 as to find Keynes's treatment of long-term expectations, which he had earlier described as brilliant (see above, 1936b, p. 89), now 'the root of the [theory's] trouble' (1969b, p. 113). On the other hand, and more important, Hicks detected flaws in the integrity of Keynes's theory, for example, Keynes's mixing up of stock and flow relationships, which led Hicks to 'have ventured doubts, not just about the details of Keynes's construction, but about its basis, the stock–flow method of analysis, itself' ([1979f] Wood and Woods, 1989, vol. 3, p. 213).

It is thus clear that Hicks did not accept Keynes's theory without reservation. For some time he continued to eye it with a Walrasian monocle and attempted to graft on to Keynes his own 'general' theory of expectations and stock–flow analysis. 'I find that there are some things to be said about that, which are rather interesting. And they may perhaps point to ways by which one could possibly push on further' ([1979f] Wood and Woods, 1989, vol. 3, p. 213). Indeed Hicks did push some of Keynes's ideas further, but this does not mean that he adopted the empirical premisses and policy implications of Keynes's theory. 'On some, at least, of his empirical assumptions, and on the policy prescriptions that he held to follow from them, I already had some reservation' (p. 210).

Money wages and real wages

Since Hicks's first theoretical work was in labour theory and much of Keynes's *General Theory* was about employment, it is appropriate to begin a discussion of the connections between the two economists' thought by analysing the importance that Hicks and 'Keynes' (that is, what Hicks interpreted to be Keynes) attached to real wages, money wages and the effect of changes in these wages on employment. At the start Hicks and Keynes held theories that were far apart from each other. Hicks had adopted the labour theory of the classical tradition; for Keynes it was the very target to attack. Hicks's initial simplistic classical treatment of wages in *The Theory of Wages* appalled Keynes, and also Hicks's close friend, Robertson, although he lent a somewhat sympathetic ear at Cambridge to elements of the classical theory. For reasons which will be explained, Hicks seems subsequently, on many occasions, to have changed his mind as to whether it is the real wage or the money wage that is important in the determination of employment and output. At times he appeared to come quite close to Keynes's ideas; at others he was still very distant. The initial similarities and differences in Keynes's and Hicks's theories are revealed in the context of Hicks's sketches of the classical theory and the theory of Keynes.

Hicks's classical theory

Hicks devised his own version of the classical theory, but it contained many elements which made it unquestionably part of the classical tradition. Its most classical feature was Hicks's insistence on a dichotomy between the real and the monetary economic sectors and hence on a distinction between real and monetary wages. At issue in classical theory was the real wage, not the money wage, for it was asserted that it is the real wage that is affected by changes in the real economy. Hicks thus turned his attention to real wages and to a theory for describing them. He began with the assumption that while trade unions and government policy makers can push for increases in real wages, such wages 'only change as a result of changes in the real elements of the system, changes in productivity and the like' ([1932b] 1963b, p. 359; pages numbered beyond 305 are additions made for the 1963 edition of *The Theory of Wages*). Without an increase in productivity, a rise in real wages could be obtained, but, it was argued, never without cost. Most frequently, it would be 'at the expense of a certain amount of unemployment' (p. 357).

As a classical theorist Hicks boldly maintained that 'in "real" analysis' money wages can simply be ignored ([1932b] 1963b, p. 356). 'Changes in money wages are not real changes'; nor can they 'affect real wages (or employment) at all' (p. 359). He presented as illustration the situation in which should money wages rise 'in a closed system' with an elastic money supply, their increase would 'simply result in a rise in prices in the same proportion, thus leaving real wages where they were' (1977, p. 6). An increased money income cannot continue to buy an unchanged quantity of goods at an unchanged price; demand will increase. Further, as Hicks noted in 1937, 'unless the price-level rises, the prices of goods will not cover their marginal costs' ([1937a] 1967, p. 130).

Shortly after the publication of *The Theory of Wages* Hicks was to conclude, apparently contradictorily, that 'a rise in the rate of money wage' would have an impact; it 'will *necessarily* diminish employment and raise real wages', (emphasis added). He explained that unless prices rise, and consumers continue to buy in unchanged amounts at the higher price, there will be a necessary drop in employment. At the same time, 'as employment falls, marginal costs in terms of labour will diminish and therefore real wages rise' ([1937a] 1967, p. 130). Hicks's conclusion was, however, still consistent with his claim that one could simply 'neglect' money wages:

> Since a change in money wages is always accompanied by a change in real wages in the same direction, if not in the same proportion, no harm will be done, and some advantage will be secured if one prefers to work in terms of real wages. Naturally most classical economists have taken this line. ([1937a] 1967, p. 130)

There was, however, one respect in which money wages could not be ignored. Although limited to this effect, Hicks did note that money wage increases can have inflationary consequences and saw it as 'the practical problem of the ability of monetary policy to cope with wage inflation' ([1932b] 1963b, pp. 359–60). He relegated their consideration to 'the Quantity [Theory] of Money (*M*) and the income-velocity (*V*)', both '*entirely* determined by monetary causes, which are quite separate from the real causes which determine relative prices' (p. 356). In addition to the real wage as against money wage dichotomy of his classical theory, Hicks also included 'the traditional view that more saving meant more capital accumulation, and that capital accumulation was favourable to rising wages', a 'natural' position to take, he asserted, for the time of *The Theory of Wages* (1977a, p. 9). This was the essence of his monetary theory, derived, such as it was, he supposed, 'from Hayek or (more justly) from the Hayekian atmosphere in which I was working' ([1932b] 1963b, p. 355).

Not only were the tenets of Hicks's classical theory at odds with Keynes's ideas, but Keynes found annoying Hicks's understanding of the tradition of classical theory itself. Hicks noted that his own classical theory 'descends from Ricardo, though it is not actually Ricardian; it is probably, more or less the theory that was held by Marshall' (1937a, rpt. 1967, p. 130). Keynes's understanding of classical theory was also 'that of Marshall' as well as 'of that of Pigou' ([1932b] 1963b, p. 356). From Keynes's point of view, however, Hicks 'had got the "classics" all wrong'. Indeed Hicks realized that his classical theory, which he called the much more primitive one, was different from Keynes's conception of it (1989a, p. 72). Hicks contrasted the two in 1964, saying,

> Keynes' *classical* theory is . . . a much more sophisticated affair than the crude things which I was summarizing. My 'classical' theory is a caricature of that which was really held by the deeper Quantity theorists; but it is pretty much what I had myself held when I wrote the *Theory of Wages*. ([1932b] 1963b, p. 356)

Hicks did not maintain a static relationship even with his own version of the classical theory. To form it he analysed and re-analysed the classical tradition at arm's length, picking and choosing which of its attributes to adopt and emphasize. At one point he wrote about his own earlier perspective, 'I wrote it out quite explicitly. It appears as the *classical* theory in my article "Mr Keynes and the 'Classics'"' ([1932b] 1963b, p. 355). Hicks also periodically reflected with regret that he had not included certain strong points of classical theory. In the case of *The Theory of Wages*, for example, 'the neglect of it [the distinction between money wages and real wages] in chapter 1 of the first edition is (to my present mind) a more important defect than the neglect of Imperfect Competition' (p. 328). Despite Hicks's changes of focus, there was no doubt in Keynes's mind that Hicks was on the wrong track.

Hicks on Keynes's theory

With the classical theory as his target, Keynes had set about establishing a new would-be general theory. It contained a decidedly different initial assumption from the classical theory. It maintained that wage earners and those representing them, such as trade unions, were 'concerned with money wages, not real wages' (1977a, p. 6). Keynes 'resolutely denied' that trade unions and government policy could increase real wages (p. 9).

Keynes's general theory was worked in terms of the wage unit as the measurement of everything from investment and income to money supply. The universality of the unit depended 'upon a principle, very important to Keynes' and one which he thought was 'usually true', the wage theorem, as Hicks called it. 'When there is a general (proportional) rise in money wages, says the theorem, the *normal* effect is that all prices rise in the same proportion – provided that the money supply is increased in the same proportion (whence the rate of interest will be unchanged)' (1974b, pp. 59–60).

As far as Hicks was concerned, the mechanism of Keynes's wage theorem was 'no more than a piece of comparative statics' whereby one '"equilibrium" at a particular level of money wages' is compared to another 'at a higher level of money wages'. The new equilibrium is attained through 'prices adjusted in the same proportion as the wage-level has risen, and a money supply adjusted to the extent that is needed to finance the high *value* of output'. Although the new equilibrium would be established at a higher wage level, 'real wages, and indeed all *real* price-ratios, would be unchanged' (1974b, p. 72). The only increase to speak of would be in output and then only in terms of its money value. To Hicks's mind, Keynes's concept of the wage theorem implied a fixprice setting in which a new equilibrium could be established after the former equilibrium had been disrupted by 'a change in the level of money wages'. He reasoned that in a fixprice context, 'prices are likely to be fixed, in the short run, so as to cover normal costs; so when wages are raised, prices are likely to be raised correspondingly' (1974b, pp. 72–3) and equilibrium re-attained.

Their differences on wages

The differences between the initial basic wage theories of Hicks and Keynes were not particularly subtle. The emphasis each placed on money wages and real wages was quite opposite and had important bearing on the effect each attributed to a change in one type of wage or the other. The points on which Hicks and Keynes appear to converge perhaps reveal their differences most strongly.

A first area in which Hicks and Keynes differed was in their perspective on the period of disequilibrium, for Hicks, the traverse. Hicks sensed that he and Keynes did not agree 'about the route which the system is supposed to take from one equilibrium to the other'. Hicks came to this conclusion, having realized that 'so long as we [Keynes and himself] stick to comparative statics, to the comparison of equilibria, there is no essential difference; so the difference must lie in a view about the traverse' (1974b, p. 72). Indeed, they were able to agree that a change in wages, money or real, could be the catalyst for disequilibrium, although Keynes was not willing also to entertain change in the money supply as a possible initial cause of wage change, whereas Hicks was. The major difference between them would, however, become evident in their models for a return to equilibrium, when they asked the question, 'By what means are we to suppose that the new equilibrium is established?' On the one side, 'Keynes, was it seems to me ... in this context, thinking in a fixprice manner' (p. 73), whereas Hicks, on the other side, was ultimately attempting to address the issue of wage instability with both a flexprice and a fixprice hypothesis. In effect, Hicks concluded, Keynes's approach 'does not throw any light upon the *path* by which the system moves from one *equilibrium* to another' (1950a, p. 17).

Secondly, together they agreed that the labour force can in part enjoy an increase in money wages with only a negligible effect on prices. Hence 'a rise in the money wages of a particular group will raise their real wages relatively to those of others' (1977a, p. 6), and for that portion of the labour force, real wages can rise 'in practically the same proportion as their money wages rise'. While Keynes theorized that this would be possible for the whole of the labour force, Hicks maintained that if the portion of the labour force in question is significant, 'the rise in prices may cancel out a substantial part' of the wage increase and 'the real wages of other labour will perceptibly fall' ([1932b] 1963b, p. 328). Even if one takes account of the possible substitution of one labour pool into another, competition in the depleted labour pool will drive its wages up. Also, 'substitution effects are liable to be damped down by transmission of the wage-rise (by one means or another) to other sectors' (pp. 329–30). Hicks believed that 'ultimately there will be a general rise in prices, which will offset the rise in money wages (of each section)' (pp. 328–9), but that 'a widespread rise in money wages will not raise real wages to anything like the same extent' (pp. 329). As he saw it, 'Money wages will thus have risen, but real wages will not have risen; employment (of each sector) will be much the same as before, the whole system merely reproducing itself at a higher level of money wages' (p. 329).

As a third example, one might consider Hicks and Keynes on the factor of unemployment in the context of wage changes. To start with, Hicks agreed with Keynes's proposition, 'that a uniform rise in money wages will leave real wages unaffected, and employment unaffected', if it is applied strictly and exclusively 'to a closed system' ([1932b], 1963b, p. 330). As for an open economy, it also seemed to Hicks that both the Keynesian and the classical economist would be in agreement that while an increase in money wage level would lead to 'a rise in real wages', it would also mean 'a fall in employment'. Just as he exclaimed, 'we seem to be in sight of some degree of reconciliation', he turned to the 'essential difference' between the two sides. According to classical theory, unemployment is due to the direct effect of the demand on the employer to pay higher wages: the employer must lay off those workers he or she cannot afford to pay when gross output fetches the same prices as before or even somewhat higher ones. On the Keynesian side, however, 'the fall in employment comes about through a *rise* in the rate of interest', thus indirectly (p. 361).

Hicks said, 'Keynesian unemployment is unemployment which can be reduced by an increase in Liquidity' ([1979c] 1983a, p. 127). For Keynes, an unemployment equilibrium occurs with a rise in money wages 'because the shortage of money pushes up the rate of interest' ([1932b] 1963b, p. 361).

> If the money supply is not increased proportionately, the rate of interest will rise; as a result of the rise in interest there will be a fall in the demand for labour. The cause of the unemployment is then identified as the inelasticity of the money supply. (1977a, p. 6)

Lastly, in Hicks's initial interpretation of classical theory, 'there should not be a rise in the rate of interest. There should be a fall in interest . . . the high level of real wages [which accompanies the rise in money wages] pushes the rate of interest down' ([1932b] 1963b, p. 361). With *The Theory of Wages* under severe attack, Hicks came, in 1935, with his 'bread' model very close to Keynes's way of seeing the relation of wages, the interest rate, and unemployment: 'In the [*Theory of Wages*] book I had made interest fall when wages rose, but in "Bread" I made interest rise. I was convinced when writing "Bread" that what I was saying there must be correct; so I accepted that what I had said in the book (chapters 9–10) must be wrong' ([1935f] 1982a, p. 65). In his 'bread' model Hicks 'examined the effect of such a rise [in real wages], and the effect on interest which I seemed to get was the same as Keynes's. The rise in real wages would raise the rate of interest' ([1932b] 1963b, p. 361).

In the instance of a relatively elastic supply of money, Hicks found his classical theory unquestionably in harmony with the Keynesian theory. 'For if money wages rise *and* the supply of money is increased, "classical" theory would agree that the Keynesian effects would follow; real wages would not rise, employment would not fall, and (incidentally) the rate of interest would remain unchanged' ([1932b] 1963b, p. 360). Changes in the money supply, though not the catalyst to the events in question, evoked for Hicks the quantity theory of money. In the quantity theory, change in the money supply 'affects no *real* price ratios'; hence wages and prices, as well as the interest rate would all be 'adjusted in the same proportion' (1974b, p. 72). As for the situation of tight money, 'that in which the supply of money is not increased, and the state of Liquidity Preference is not such that the additional money is made available' by other means, it also appeared to reinforce Hicks's Keynesian alliance. If 'there is not enough money to finance the money value of total income . . . if there is not enough money to support full employment at the enhanced level of money wages, the rate of interest will rise, employment will *therefore* fall, and (probably) real wages will rise, since a smaller volume of labour is being applied to an unchanged capital stock' ([1932b] 1963b, p. 360).

Ultimately, however, Hicks would return to his earlier non-Keynesian assertion, that a rise in real wages should push the interest rate down. However, it had become for him no longer a question of which theory was absolutely right, but rather which theory was right for which period.

> The way out, I said in the commentary, was to insist that 'what was being discussed in the "Bread" paper (and also what was being discussed by

> Keynes) was a short-period, or impact effect. But that, quite certainly, was not was I was discussing in *TW*. All I was doing there . . . was to examine how things would work out in the "long run". ([1936b] 1982a, p. 65)

The interest rate and liquidity

Hicks and Keynes also each developed an individual perspective on interest rate and liquidity theory. Much of the discussion turned on what determines the interest rate, the relation of saving and interest, and the static or stock view of borrowing and lending as opposed to the dynamic or flow of such exchanges over time. Again their separate postures will be sketched briefly and then their more striking differences presented.

Hicks's approach

Hicks felt that there were two conditions which governed a theoretical discussion of the interest rate. First, he saw the rate of interest as an issue fully integrated with many others on the working of the economy. One 'cannot possibly regard the rate of interest in isolation'. For him it was 'part of a mutually interdependent system.' Second, he wrote, 'we cannot determine *the* rate of interest excepting in an economic system where there is only *one* rate of interest'. To this second end, Hicks devised 'two different simplified models in which there is only one rate of interest'. Each represented 'the spot economy'; one with 'short lending', the other with 'long lending' (1939a, p. 154). The short rate of interest was the *one* rate of both models because Hicks's long interest rate was simply an arithmetic average of the short rate (see p. 145). In his own general theory Hicks made money, investment and saving functions of both income and interest rate. From his classical point of view an interest mechanism was at work in the economy, such that an 'increase in saving would *directly* reduce the rate of interest' ([1957a] 1967, p. 144).

On the one hand Hicks referred to the interest rate as 'a price, like other prices' which 'must be determined with them' (1939a, p. 154). According to his classical price theory, 'the rate of interest will be determined at that level which makes the demand for money equal to the supply' ([1936b] 1982a, p. 92). On the other hand, Hicks devised one definition of interest rate in terms of liquidity. For Hicks, if money were conceived as 'as a sort of durable consumer good', the amount of interest charged over a certain amount of time would be the measure of the 'sacrifice' involved in the loaner's postponing the holding of the money loaned until the end of the period. In other words, 'the marginal rate of substitution between acquisition of money now and the acquisition of money at a later date would equal the discount ratio over the period of deferment' (1939a, p. 237).

Just as he made a distinction between real and monetary phenomena in his theory of wages, in modelling the interest rate Hicks recognized a distinction between the natural or real rate of interest and the monetary rate. He believed that he had integrated into his interest rate model both the real as well as the monetary sector. This was facilitated greatly, for instance in *The Theory of Wages*, by the fact that he dealt only with an equilibrium situation. No matter which way the price determination was to be carried out, within the model's perfect competition, perfect foresight and absence of risk, the natural rate of interest equalled the monetary rate of interest. In his equilibrium theory Hicks made no distinction between the internal rate of return and the interest rate.

The interest rate in Hicks's theory is determined by solving simultaneous equations of supply and demand. His model consisted of $n - 1$ equations of supplies and demands for commodities, one equation of supply and demand for loan(s) (only one type of lending is assumed in the model), and one equation of supply and demand for money. His model had $n + 1$ equations with n unknown prices to be determined, while one price is taken to be *numéraire*. Hicks's system thus had one equation too many. To discard one equation Hicks turned to Walras's law for equilibrium conditions retaining n equations to determine $n - 1$ prices and one interest rate. Hicks felt that 'it does not matter in the least which equation we choose to eliminate' (1939a, p. 158).

Keynes on interest and liquidity

According to Hicks, Keynes's general theory posited the rate of interest as 'the link between money and investment'. On the one hand then, Keynes discussed the relation of the money supply and interest, 'the liquidity preference theory of money'; on the other, he considered quite separately 'the effect of interest on investment, the marginal efficiency of capital' (1974b, p. 32). Keynes laid most of his emphasis on the long-term rate of interest and paid most attention to the speculative market; Hicks said, 'Mr Keynes seems to mean by "the" rate of interest, the long-term rate on gilt edge' ([1936b] 1982a, p. 94). Keynes conceived interest as 'the reward for parting with liquidity'. It was not, however, 'the "price" which brings into equilibrium the demand for resources to invest with the readiness to abstain from present consumption. It is the "price" which equilibrates the desire to hold wealth in the form of cash with the available quantity of cash' (Keynes, 1936, p. 167).

The demand for money seemed for Keynes to function either as a cause or as an effect in its relation to the rate of interest. For example, 'an indefinite rise in the prices of consumption goods . . . would lead to a more or less corresponding rise in the demand for money', which might in turn provoke a potentially indefinitely expanding supply of money. An increased demand for money and no expansion in the money supply would cause a rise in the rate of interest. Hicks pointed out that according to Keynes the demand for money could also depend 'upon the rate of interest and the state of confidence (the desire for liquidity)'. This demand was determined by many things, 'in particular by the level of money income' ([1936b] 1982a, p. 93). The view advanced by Keynes in his *General Theory* was that the rate of interest is determined by supply and demand in the money market. (1939) For example, 'diminished demand for transactions balances would lower the rate of interest (if interest is flexible)' ([1957a] 1967, p. 144). Its price, at least in the short term, is 'the sum of marginal factor cost and marginal user cost' (1939a, p. 198).

Their differences on interest and liquidity

Hicks's approach to the differences between himself and Keynes regarding the interest rate and liquidity was fundamentally to minimize them either by demonstrating that the distinctions which Keynes made were unnecessary, minor or at least not novel, or by encompassing Keynes's theory within his own more general one. Examples of both of these postures are numerous; some will be presented here.

On the topic of the determination of the rate of interest, Hicks noted two different views. By some, the rate of interest is thought to be 'determined by the supply and demand for loanable funds (that is to say, by borrowing and lending)'; by others, it is considered to be 'determined by the supply and demand for money itself'. Hicks reduced the importance of these two views to insignificance: 'I shall hope to show that it makes no difference whether we follow his [Keynes's] way of putting it, or whether we follow those writers who adopt what appears at present to be a rival view. Properly followed up, the two approaches lead to exactly the same results' (1939a, p. 153).

This choice would present an apparent dilemma in the context of the above mentioned model of $n - 1$ equations of supplies and demands for commodities. To Hicks's mind, however, to determine the interest rate one can use either the loanable funds equation or the equation of the demand and supply of money. 'It does not matter in the least which equation we choose to eliminate' (1939a, p. 158). The loanable funds advocates might eliminate the money equation, while Keynes might prefer to do without the 'equation of borrowing and lending' (p. 162). Hicks's posture was one of superior indifference: 'it seems to me that either of these methods is perfectly legitimate; the choice between them is purely a matter of convenience' (p. 161). He saw this as tenable for one of two alternative reasons: either 'if the equations of supply and demand hold for commodities, factors and loans, it will follow automatically that the demand for money equals the supply of money' or 'the equation for loans becomes otiose, automatically following from the rest' ([1936b] 1982a, p. 92).

Hicks also noted another case, the effect of an increase in saving on employment in which Keynes's theory and the classical one 'lead to the same result'. Hicks compared the different paths of analysis of the two theories undertaken under the same initial conditions. Modelled is an economy in which money wages are fixed, the money supply is inelastic, and 'where the interest-mechanism can always operate – where the rate of interest is flexible, and sufficiently flexible, in either direction, for its movements to have a significant effect on (saving or) investment' ([1957a] 1967, p. 144). In 1957 Hicks described the path of analysis in Keynes's theory as follows: a rise in the propensity to save will have the direct effect of lowering employment; increased saving, which means a reduction in the demand for money held for transactions, will cause a drop in the rate of interest; the reduced demand for transaction balances will have the subsequent impact of increasing investment and in turn, employment, although not quite to their earlier levels. The classical theorist 'properly equipped' would lay the argument out as follows: an increase in saving will lower the rate of interest directly; with the lower rate of interest, employment levels will shift to rise in the investment sector, while declining in the consumption goods sector; along with the increase in saving, there will be a slowing of the velocity of circulation, since not all the saving will immediately be released to investment; this slowing will cause a decline in the net level of employment.

Hicks described both theories as 'true'; 'though the paths of analysis are different, the end-results, achieved when all the same things have been taken into account, are the same'. He further diminished the achievement of Keynes by noting that both analyses could be presented in 'a general-equilibrium form in which it is directly apparent that they come to the same thing' ([1957a] 1967, p. 144). Furthermore, 'a general-equilibrium theorist would show the saving operating on interest and employment simultaneously' (p. 145). Of course, Keynes's theory was reflecting something real, no less that any other of the three methods, but there was nothing, in this instance, to recommend particularly his theory either. 'One can put the systems through their paces in many ways, and – so long as the interest mechanism functions – one must come in the end to the same result by each method' (p. 145).

Hicks thought that Keynes's approach in *The General Theory* was from the start too narrow and unworthy of the title 'general'. The fact that Keynes had put such strong emphasis on the long-term rate of interest and on the speculative market for Hicks spelled restriction. 'The market he so largely considers . . . is not a general description of a financial market; it is an isolation of a particular aspect' (1974b, p. 35). For Hicks, the particular purpose or interest of Keynes could not justify such a restriction in a 'general' theory. To make something significant of Keynes's theory Hicks felt he had to establish 'a theory of the distribution of assets in a portfolio, in which the speculation considered by Keynes appears as a special case' (p. 37).

Generalization of aspects of Keynes's theory, Hicks asserted, eliminated its originality. For example, when Hicks made money, investment and saving functions of both income and interest rate and allowed for the money wage to vary, he 'discovered' that 'Mr Keynes's theory begins to look very like Wicksell's. Hicks did not find this surprising, however, for in fact Keynes's own presentation of the theory contained already 'one special case where it fits Wicksell's construction absolutely, the case of full employment ([1937a] 1967, p. 140).

The narrowness of Keynes's approach to the rate of interest was mentioned frequently by Hicks. He wrote, for example, that he thought Keynes was 'precluded by his method from illuminating the relation between this [long-term] rate and other rates as much as he could do, and has indeed done by other methods' ([1936b] 1982a, p. 94). This method of determining the rate of interest gave Hicks a specific area in which to find Keynes limited. First of all, the fact that Keynes's rate of interest was determined in the money market was not new to Hicks. 'This monetary character of interest is, of course, no novelty; it has been generally recognized at least since the time of Wicksell' (p. 92). Hicks had himself proposed a similar theory. Keynes, Hicks maintained, could not pursue this line of thinking, however; 'the way of expressing it used by Wicksell and his followers has, of course, to be abandoned by Mr Keynes's – since a "natural rate" of interest would be a concept foreign to the whole present trend of his ideas' (p. 92). Since Hicks believed that he had integrated into his model both the natural as well as the monetary rate of interest, he came to think that both Wicksell's and Keynes's stipulating rules about interest rates were simply special cases of his own general model: 'Wicksell's rule that the rate of interest equals the *relative* marginal productivity of waiting appears as a special case of our first condition' (1939a, p. 197), and 'Mr Keynes' rule that "short-period supply price is the sum of marginal factor cost and marginal user cost" is a combination of our first and third condition' (p. 198). Thus in his model Hicks integrated both Wicksell's and Keynes's theories of interest.

When considering the relationship of the rate of interest to the demand for money, Hicks also found Keynes restricted and less than original. 'The more important is the level of money incomes relatively to the rate of interest in determining the demand for money, the less does the comparative advantage of Mr Keynes's method become' ([1936b] 1982a, p. 93). Hicks felt Keynes's theory could be partially rehabilitated by pursuing its course along the same lines, surprisingly, as those of Hayek. 'When the supply of consumption goods does not prove to be very elastic Mr Keynes's analysis of this case . . . would be an indefinite rise in the prices of consumption goods – producing a state of "true inflation"'. 'Unless the supply of money was indefinitely expanded, the rate of interest must rise, and the boom be checked. I do not think that this differs at all essentially from what has been said by earlier writers.' (p. 93) (Among those writers Hicks cited Hayek.)

On the subject of expectations Hicks also found Keynes's ideas derivative and limited. Although the 'famous proposition . . . about the "cumulative process"' was, Hicks wrote, at the time 'naturally' associated 'with the name of Mr Keynes', it was based on Wicksell. Further, said Hicks, although Keynes used the proposition correctly in his *General Theory*, he gave only limited proof of it, since he assumed 'a unity elasticity of expectations only for prices expected to rule in the near future; for prices expected in the further future he assumes that they move with money wages' (1939a, p. 256). Hicks felt Keynes's limitations were of some consequence, for he had done relatively little to reduce the instability of the system which takes expectations into consideration, a system which is subject to dangerously large fluctuations. 'As soon as we take expectations into account (or rather, as soon as we take the elasticity of expectation into account), the stability of the system is seriously weakened.' In Keynes's method, the system is frequently vulnerable to being weakened, since it is 'when money wages move that instability (or imperfect stability) declares itself' (p. 256). Hicks thought he was proposing an extension of Wicksell's proposition with a far more general proof.

In at least two instances concerning issues related to the interest rate and liquidity theory, Hicks labelled Keynes's approach completely wrong. For example,

> When the argument is stated as Mr Keynes states it, it looks possible to maintain that the instability (alleged to occur when money wages are flexible) is due simply to the special assumption about the nature of expectations which he has made. My proof shows this to be wrong. (1939a, p. 257)

Hicks corrected the 'error' by explaining that 'in itself, the instability has nothing to do with wages ... it is a property of money and of securities' (1939a, p. 257). 'The instability of the system may be expected to reveal itself only slowly, expectations becoming more elastic as more time is allowed' (p. 280).

In a second example, Hicks described Keynes's misinterpretation of the impact of two conditions he placed upon his own system: '(1) that the supply of consumption goods, in terms of wage-units, is inelastic; (2) that the level of money wages does not depend only on employment, but also on the prices of consumption goods'. Hicks noted that while both assumptions seem 'to be appropriate to post-war conditions', their impact has not been clearly understood ([1947a] 1982a, p. 153n.). In a footnote he implied that the conditions Keynes placed on his theory would lead him to a conclusion opposed to his assertion that a rise in saving yields an decrease in employment. Owing to the assumption of fixed consumption-good spending, a larger proportion of income will be saved. As far as Hicks could see, this would lead to the contrary conclusion: 'the larger the proportion of income which is saved ... the larger in consequence will be the maximum level of employment' (p. 154n.).

The multiplier and the saving–investment equilibrium

Hicks's use of the multiplier and the S–I equilibrium

Hicks's use of the multiplier and the saving–investment equilibrium is derivative of not only Keynes but several others. He openly acknowledged that he was inspired by them, especially in the context of the theory of the business cycle. *A Contribution to the Theory of the Trade Cycle* is one of Hicks's works in which Keynes's influence is perhaps most obvious. Goodwin, for example, believed that Hicks's theory of the economic cycle was 'an elegant restatement of the *General Theory* on dynamic lines' (Goodwin, 1951, p. 316). Such statements, of course, overemphasize Hicks's dependence on Keynes; in the *Trade Cycle* as in several other works in which Hicks made use of Keynes's concepts, his ideas remained fundamentally un-Keynesian.

Hicks felt the abundance of ideas from Keynes and others about the business cycle had actually given him a duty. As it stood, he thought the ideas were fragments, disconnected and cognizant of only one aspect of the total picture. He hoped that by integrating various elements of the theories suggested by Clark, Harrod, Robertson, Keynes, Samuelson and many others, he could claim to produce 'something which may have a better claim to be regarded as *the* theory of the cycle than any that have preceded it' (1950a, p. 2).

It was from Keynes that Hicks took the multiplier theory and the saving–investment mechanism. In the context of the business cycle very little else of Keynes is retained. He did not give much importance to Keynes's interest theory, liquidity preference or marginal efficiency of capital, relegating them to the level of 'secondary' causes (1950a, p. 3). Hicks employed a consumption function, measured in real terms, 'such that it can reasonably be expected to remain stable over time' (1974b, p. 9). To study 'fluctuation about a rising trend', he proceeded with a theory of output, rather than a theory of employment (1950a, p. 8). Investment was considered by Hicks to be composed only partly of autonomous investment, whose volume is given exogenously; the balance of investment was induced investment. In Hicks's model, induced investment increases output beyond the level needed to replace stocks; this relationship between investment and output produces his 'super-multiplier' effect (1974b, p. 16; see also 1950a).

In 1939, in *Value and Capital*, Hicks was not involved in the dynamics of saving–investment any more than Keynes had been in *The General Theory*. By 1950, however, he showed preference for the multiplier theory of Kahn as 'a piece of dynamic analysis in the way that the Keynes multiplier theory is not' (1965a, p. 65). Change and movement can be described by using Kahn's convergent series to obtain a dynamic multiplier. Hicks showed that this would be the case no matter what the complexity of the lags or the assumptions made about them.

Keynes's concepts

Hicks recognized that Keynes's was an integrated monetary theory, a general Marshallian theory of output; he summarized Keynes's ideas on the multiplier and the saving–investment equilibrium, according to him 'most conveniently', in his article 'Mr Keynes and the "Classics"' (1937a). It gives an account of Keynes's lagless multiplier process, as well as the importance Keynes gave to interest theory, liquidity preference and the marginal efficiency of capital in the context of his trade theory. Keynes did not introduce lags nor distinguish between *ex ante* and *ex post* investment, and his period is identifiable with the Marshallian short period. 'In Keynes, the volume of investment depends upon the rate of interest; it is read off from the "marginal efficiency of capital" schedule' (1965a, p. 104). If Keynes's theory is interpreted 'in a Fixprice sense ... the rate of interest becomes an exogenous variable (like other prices), so that the *given* marginal efficiency of capital schedule becomes a *given* volume of investment' (1965a, p. 104). According to Hicks, Keynes's theory 'proclaims the necessary equality of Savings and Investment' ([1936b] 1982a, p. 231).

Hicks described the correlations in Keynes's 'simplest – and crudest – version of the multiplier theory': income is mechanically 'determined from investment'. Defined as 'the difference between income and consumption', saving is hence 'a function of income'. This function is, however, also one 'which is capable of being inverted'; hence income can also be taken as 'a function of saving' (1974b, p. 9). With investment given and thereby saving, income can be determined. Since income governs employment, the level of employment is in turn determined by the level of income. In Keynes's simple model, there is no induced investment, and the output of materials and consumption goods rises no higher than 'necessary to stop the fall in stocks' (p. 15). The system is in equilibrium.

According to Hicks, Keynes's theory neglected the acceleration principle and emphasized employment. His theory of employment was built around the underemployment percentage and buttressed by the concept of wage-unit.

Their differences on saving and investment

One of the main distinctions Hicks saw between his own approach to the multiplier and the saving–investment equilibrium and that of Keynes was that here again he felt his was the more general. There were several ways in which Hicks characterized Keynes's theory as a special case theory.

One way Hicks devised was to identify the common (and uncommon) ground that existed between Keynes and his predecessors and to show that his and other current theories could be integrated into one of broader scope. As Hicks noted in many places, he felt Keynes's ideas were frequently directly inspired by his predecessors, to whom one would do just as well to turn. One could, for example, Hicks maintained, just as well find 'one special form of the monetary explanation of the cycle' in Wicksell and Hawtrey as in the monetary side of Keynes's *General Theory*; 'the differences are secondary' (1950a, p. 136). In other instances Hicks seemed to feel that Keynes differed clearly, though not incompatibly from those who had come before. For example, 'one can suppose that there is saving–investment equilibrium, maintained continuously; and yet there can be unemployment . . . So interpreted, the Keynesian view and the "classical" view fit together' (1977a, p. 10).

The actual integration of Keynes's ideas into a more general theory would require, Hicks realized, a great deal of shifting of his concepts and intent. For example, referring to the lagless multiplier process of *The General Theory*, Hicks said, 'some significant reshaping of the foundations' is necessary 'so as to fit them for a place in a structure which is different from that for which they were originally designed' (1950a, p. 4).

One of Keynes's foundational elements with concerned Hicks most was his notion of period. Although Keynes's theory 'works with a *period* which is taken to be one of equilibrium', that period was in Hicks's interpretation 'identified with the Marshallian "short period"'. Thus, while the theory's equilibrium condition requires that the period used 'not be too short', the Marshallian component 'seems to require that the period should not be too long'. Hicks concluded, 'it is not easy to see that there can be any length of time that will adequately satisfy both of these requirements.' This observation led him to describe the 'period' foundation to Keynes's theory as 'shaky' (1965, pp. 64–5).

As another example, Hicks reflected on the consequences of 'Keynes's neglect of the acceleration principle'. If one takes that principle into consideration, it can still be employed in a theory of employment such as Keynes's, 'but it cannot be built around the underemployment percentage in the way Keynes's was.' Also, Hicks maintained, 'the concept of the "wage-unit" which Keynes introduced to buttress his employment approach, has to be abandoned.' Further, 'the concept of "Full Employment" has to be looked at in a new way'. According to Hicks, all these changes to Keynes were necessary, since 'we have throughout to go back to the pre-Keynesian (or rather, pre-*General Theory*) practice of thinking in real terms, in terms (that is) of money values corrected by the price-level of final output'. Of Keynes's contribution in the *General Theory* he noted, 'the Keynesian emphasis on employment, and all that went with it, turns out after all to have been a red herring' (1950a, pp. 8–9).

In order to render Keynes's theory adequately dynamic Hicks also saw a number of alterations as necessary. He noted that the strict Keynesian assumption of a fixprice system, in which the rate of interest is an 'exogenous variable' and 'the *given* marginal efficiency of capital schedule becomes a *given* volume of investment', should be relaxed in some way or other (1965a, p. 104). According to Hicks there are at least two ways in which this could be done. Either one could introduce lags or distinguish between *ex ante* and *ex post* investment, or one could suppose that only part and not the whole of the volume of investment is given exogenously. Hicks favoured making the latter change to Keynes's approach.

The second way Hicks envisaged for relaxing the fixprice system would be to step beyond the limitations of Keynes's theory. One might, he noted, for example, posit the situation of induced investment, as well as the situation of no induced investment, which was Keynes's exclusive position. In that case, as he had said in his book on the trade cycle, 'output will expand beyond the point that is shown in the simple Keynes model', beyond the point at which the drop in stocks has been stopped. Just as Keynes had described a system without induced investment, this one would not come into equilibrium, but would be under the effect of a 'super-multiplier' (1974b, p. 16).

The IS–LM device

Of all Hicks's reflections on Keynes's *General Theory* it is those on the IS–LM apparatus which have retained most of the economics profession's attention. The device became the standard tool for introducing Keynes to students but also provided, for a long time, a piece of theoretical artifice around which Keynesians and anti-Keynesians debated their differences.

As Hicks recalled, 'the idea of the IS–LM diagram' occurred to him during his work on 'three-way exchange, conceived in a Walrasian manner' (1980a, p. 142). It found its origin in his 'bread' paper (1935f). Later Hicks applied it in his book on the trade cycle, in chapters 11 and

12 (1950a), as well as in a paper called 'The classics again' ([1957a] 1967, pp. 143–54). By 1980, however, Hicks was expressing dissatisfaction with it.

In 1935 Hicks used the IS–LM device in a full-employment model of perfect competition with all prices completely flexible. For a time frame, he used what he called an 'ultra-short-period, a week' (1980a, p. 141). His model had four markets: labour, goods, loan and money. For Hicks, any one of the four markets could serve as a *numéraire*, whereby its price is taken to be unity. The model then is composed of three equations of supply and demand for determining the remaining corresponding three prices.

To Hicks the IS–LM device was simply a convenient way to represent a three-way model, 'in which there is just one price (P_b which becomes the rate of interest) that is determined on a flexprice market, and one quantity (y) which plays the part of D_a [demand for labour]' (1980a, p. 144). In his first use of the IS–LM, the *LM* curve was modelled 'on the assumption of a given stock of money'. By 1936, however, Hicks had already relaxed that stipulation to mean 'on the assumption of a given monetary system'. The elasticity of the curve will then depend 'on the elasticity of the monetary system (in the ordinary monetary sense)'. The LM curve must refer 'to a point in time, not to a period' (1980a, pp. 150–1), and the point at which the IS and the LM curves intersect is an equilibrium position.

Hicks had found it a very natural step to move from applications of the IS–LM device as a way of representing three-way exchange two-dimensionally in his own work to using it in illustrating Keynes's theory. The diagram of the IS–LM, initially referred to as SI–LL, was suggested in 'Mr Keynes and the "Classics"' (1937a). Though not universally accepted as 'a convenient synopsis of Keynesian theory', when Hicks first began to use it, the IS–LM device became widely used to represent Keynes's ideas (1980a, p. 139). Hicks himself ceased to use it, even as an explanatory aid, in his last reconstructions of Keynesian theory.

Using the Marshallian short period, Keynes, according to Hicks, employed in *The General Theory* three basic elements: 'the marginal efficiency of capital, the consumption function, and the liquidity preference', which represented 'the market for goods, the market for bonds, and the market for money' (1980a, p. 142). Keynes also included a market for labour. To Hicks's mind, Keynes had proceeded to establish the market prices in the same way he himself had, with the exception that in Keynes one of the market prices, that of labour, was fixed from the start. As already noted, in Keynes's model the level of money wages was determined exogenously, making the model 'consistent with unemployment' (p. 141). With supply in excess in the labour market, it is demand which is observed, the actual demand to which the existing actual supply corresponds.

> The actual amount sold will be equal to the demand or to the supply, whichever is the lower . . . if it turns out that at these prices $S_a > D_a$, it is only D_a that can actually be traded. When calculating S_x and D_x, we must use this *actual* D_a for both D_a and S_a. With that substitution, we have $S_x = D_x$ as before. (1980a, p. 143)

With one commodity price as *numéraire* and the price of labour exogenously given, the remaining two commodity prices will be determined by their corresponding equations of supply and demand. Thus a supply and demand equality still holds in all three commodity markets, and it automatically follows that the *numéraire* market is in equilibrium. In Keynes's theory the four markets thus determine two prices and one quantity.

Hicks observed that of Keynes's general theory, which was skilfully divided into two parts, there was only one part which was 'in time'. The part 'concerned with the Marginal Efficiency of Capital and with Liquidity Preference', was 'unquestionably in time'. As he put it, 'it is basically forward-looking; time and uncertainty are written all over it.' The other part, 'the multiplier theory (and indeed the whole theory of production and price which is – somehow – wrapped up in the multiplier theory)', did not take time into consideration ([1976f] 1982a, pp. 288–9).

Hicks's application of the IS–LM device

In developing the IS–LM device as a graphic convenience Hicks found it applicable to Keynes's at first because of the similarities he assumed existed between his theory and that of Keynes: he recognized immediately, 'as soon as I saw *The General Theory*', that 'my model and Keynes's had some things in common' (1980a, p. 140). Among their shared features, Hicks noted was the fact that they both had period and exogenous expectations. Neither theory made assumptions about rational expectations. From Hicks's point of view he and Keynes were considering the same markets. With his interpretation of Keynes's theory as being similar to his own, he tried to apply to it some of the same techniques he had himself used: the preserving of Walras's law and the treating of the labour market just like almost any other commodity market.

After his initial satisfaction with the application of the IS–LM device to Keynes's *General Theory*, Hicks grew to feel that its use was becoming rapidly out of proportion and far too widely employed in the economic literature. He became less and less satisfied with it in two respects: in terms of its depiction of the market as not a truly mixed (fixprice–flexprice) one, and its dependence on equilibrium.

He reflected on the three types of market models: the fixprice market, in which prices are changed 'by acts of policy'; the flexprice market in which 'prices are more directly determined by supply and demand'; and 'a *mixed* model, with some markets working one way and some the other' (1979f, p. 211). He ruled out the application of the IS–LM to 'an all-round flexprice system'; in at least one market, 'the exogenously fixed prices of products must still be retained' (1980a, p. 148). Hicks felt the mixed model 'looked better than either extreme' model, but recognized that Keynes did not offer quite such a convenient mixed model with which to work (1979f, p. 211). Keynes had asserted that his model had only one fixprice market, labour. If, however, 'Y is taken to be an index not only of employment, but also of output', the prices of products will also be fixed 'in terms of the standard'. Hicks found it hard to equate Y 'unless the prices of products are derived from the wage of labor by some markup rule'. The consequence of such an equation was, however, clearly that there would be 'not one but two, fixprice markets' (1980a, p. 145).

To Hicks's mind, 'if one is to make sense of the IS–LM model, while paying proper attention to time, one must, I think, insist . . . [that the economy] must be assumed to be, in an appropriate sense, in equilibrium' (1980a, p. 148). This equilibrium condition implied a 'formal concept of full equilibrium over time' (p. 152), that is, 'it is not only the market for funds, but also the product market which must be assumed to be in equilibrium' (p. 148). The existence of such equilibria as components of the theory to which the IS–LM could be applied came to disturb Hicks greatly. 'I must say that the diagram is now much less popular with me than I think it still is with many other people' ([1976f] 1982a, p. 290). In the context of its application Hicks had come to ask himself numerous questions, for example: how is the long-term rate of interest to be considered in the static strait-jacket of the IS–LM? How is it that liquidity and money which do not belong to equilibrium theory form part of the equilibrium IS–LM device? How can a flow be reconciled in its stock analysis?

Although Hicks had initially been pleased to discover in *The General Theory* that Keynes was using an equilibrium technique to explain a disequilibrium situation where expectations have a role to play, a method that he himself had started to construct, he reached the conclusion after many years that the two could not be reconciled and certainly not through the use of the IS–LM diagram. The IS–LM is an equilibrium analysis which is conceived in a Walrasian manner and does not pay any attention to time. As Hicks noted, 'it reduced the *General Theory* to equilibrium economics; it is not really *in* time' ([1976f] 1982a, p. 290).

According to Keynes and Hicks, expectations and hence time both had a role to play in liquidity preference. For Hicks, there was no sense in even bringing liquidity preference into the analysis, unless expectations were uncertain and time was a factor. The IS–LM model depended, however, on the virtual neglect of uncertain expectations and time, achieved through the use of 'a relatively long period, a "year" rather than a "week"' and the premiss that 'the behaviour of the economy over that "year" is to be *determined* by propensities, and such-like data' (1980a, p. 152). Neither feature was thus truly present in the equilibrium of the IS–LM device, a crucial point when the very 'purpose of generating an LM curve' was to 'represent liquidity preference'.

To Hicks's mind both the LM and the IS curves posed further problems, related now to stock and flow analysis. As noted above, the LM curve was to have been generated 'on the assumption of a given stock of money'. Hicks was disturbed very early by the need to assume a given stock of money and by 1937 had relaxed the stipulation to mean 'a given monetary system of given elasticity'. Hicks continued to maintain that 'the relation expressed in the LM curve is, or should be, a stock relation (as Keynes so rightly insisted)' (1980a, pp. 150–1). As for the IS curve, the relation it expresses is a flow relation over a period. Under the equilibrium interpretation, however, since 'the economy must be treated *as if* it were in equilibrium', the flow relation and period of the IS curve must be reconciled with the stock relation and point in time representation of the LM curve (p. 151). For the device to function, it would only be logical to treat them both similarly, Hicks observed, and under equilibrium the stock or static relation must dominate.

Without the existence of the IS–LM device and its application to Keynes in the 1937 paper, Hicks's work would probably have evolved completely differently. As a consequence of the actual course of events, economists' perception of Keynes's method have been greatly affected by several aspects of Hicks's interpretation of *The General Theory*: his assimilation of Keynes's theory of expectation to that of the Swedish economists and his own; his attempt to establish that the interest rate is determined in a Walrasian general equilibrium fashion; his presentation of Keynes's work in the Walrasian fashion, yet his association of Keynes with Marshall; his assumption that Marshall's approach is less general than that of Walras, and his analysis making Keynes's theory look like a special case of his own general equilibrium theory. Despite the fact that Hicks later came to realize that parts of his early assessment of Keynes had to be reconsidered, he none the less continued to maintain that Keynes's theory was limited and not as original or general as Keynes claimed it was.

Followers of Keynes may find much of Hicks's interpretation of Keynes's ideas, not to mention his manipulation of them, objectionable. Hicks asserted clearly that what he provided his readers by way of a presentation of Keynes's theory itself was at best 'a terribly rough and ready sort of affair', 'a skeleton apparatus', which was probably already 'a slight extension of Mr Keynes's theory ([1937a] 1967, p. 141). To study further the degree to which Hicks's interpretation might have distorted Keynes's ideas might be engaging to Keynes's followers and others. The essential argument here is that Hicks gave sufficient indications to show that he himself was not, strictly speaking, a follower of Keynes even though he commented extensively on and made use of Keynes's ideas.

Undoubtedly Hicks respected Keynes's ideas. While he felt that *The General Theory* had really only been appropriately designed for the circumstances of the 1930s, he counted himself among those who wanted to keep Keynes's contribution alive. Perhaps as a tribute to him, Hicks was ready to accept the Keynesian label for himself in the sense 'of trying to do what I think he would have tried to do, if confronted with different real problems from those with which we are now confronted' (1979f, p. 992). The difference in the problems to be faced, however, meant that Hicks could not simply 'go on applying his theory, without drastic amendment' (1976e, p. 217). He had to step in, to revise, alter and at times extend the very foundations of Keynes's theory.

9

Economic Causality: Circumstance and Explanation

Although Hicks was early on aware of the complexity of economic issues and concepts, he was then more preoccupied with the technical aspects of his theories and with consolidating the marginalist revolution. He contemplated the idea that economics is a branch of science and that, as all sciences, the study and its tools are neutral, conceived for 'purely intellectual interest' (1979g, p. viii). He gradually realized, however, that his abstract models, although useful and helpful for understanding the world, were partisan. Having changed from his position of the 1930s, he was by the 1970s asserting that most economic theory is ideology and was beginning to discuss such fundamental questions as 'What is the purpose of economics?' and 'Is economics a science?' Hicks's interest in methodology was expressed in numerous works written since the mid-1950s, the central piece being his *Causality in Economics* (1979g). Most of his ideas are found, scattered, in 'Methods of dynamic analysis' (1956c), his review (1965c) of R. G. Lipsey's *An Introduction to Positive Economics*, 'The scope and status of welfare economics' ([1975c] 1981), '"Revolutions" in economics' (1976e), 'Some questions of time in economics' (1976f), 'A discipline not a science' (1983a), 'Is economics a science?' (1984b), 'New causality: an explanation' (1984a), and *Methods of Dynamic Economics* (originally published as *Capital and Growth* ([1965a] 1985a).

Hicks tackled the question of the role and the purpose of economics from a broad, philosophical perspective. Since the economics discipline was becoming increasingly more preoccupied with its mathematization and technicality, the contemporaneous philosophical concerns of Hicks were viewed as unconventional. Some, for example H. Johnson, thought that in raising philosophical questions, Hicks was sailing against the wind (Johnson, 1975). Economists generally feel uncomfortable with methodological questions about the foundations of their discipline and often choose deliberately to avoid rather than to address them. It is not surprising that Hicks's work in this area has been neglected or ignored, for fear that it might prove destructive.

Indeed, on the surface many of Hicks's ideas on methodology might be judged as crude, simplistic or even counterproductive. He asserted that 'economics is more like art or philosophy than science' (1976e, p. 207). He also emphasized the limits of economics: 'there is, there can be, no economic theory which will do for us everything we want all the time' (p. 208). As will be discussed in this chapter, a thorough reading of Hicks shows that his philosophical questioning made his economics in the end much stronger. After a few decades of applying, mastering and demystifying the tools of mathematics in economics, he had come to find it important to consider the limitations of such tools and to embark on a post-scientific phase. (See Hamouda and Price, 1991, pp. 41–42.)

The nature of economics

Hicks became increasingly reluctant to claim much scope or strength for his theories as his conviction grew that all economic assertions should be scrutinized. The 'besetting vice of economists', Hicks once reflected, was 'to over-play their hands, to claim more for their subject than they should' (1983a, p. 365). He noted that he himself had not always resisted that vice. Undeniably, however, over time Hicks not only withdrew from its temptation, but identified the seductive aspects of economics by which one might be easily misled.

The very nature of the study of economics ought, Hicks believed, render the economist wary of what he or she can claim. The story begins with the very 'facts' with which economists must deal. The practical concern of the economist is with 'the facts of the present world' and of the 'past world'; all these facts are in their time fleeting, constantly changing and do not repeat. They do not lend themselves to the detection of 'general patterns among the mass of absorbing detail; shapes that repeat among the details which do not repeat' ([1975c] 1981, p. 232). Yet this is the calling of the economist.

Hicks well knew that the economist might find individual events enticingly interesting. 'Every business has a history of its own, every consumer a history of his own; any of these histories may have its own drama when we come close to it.' He warned, however, that it is not the job of economists to 'come close'. It is the pattern or shape of human economic activity, not the every detail, which is the object of the economist's study. None the less, pattern does not emerge easily for examination. To reveal it the economist must selectively extract 'something less than the detail that is presented' ([1975c] 1981, p. 232).

Simplification is the price of even beginning to identify the pattern or shape created by the multitude of individual events. 'In order to analyse, we must simplify and cut down' ([1975c] 1981, p. 232). Hicks might have initially emphasized that the process of simplification entails loss of scope and breadth as well as the depth of detail. Although aware of the cost, instead of regretting it, Hicks insisted on its necessity. 'In practice, we must simplify quickly . . . we must select, even select quite violently.' Hicks felt that haste and ruthlessness in simplifying the many details of the world are essential for the economist.

A quick and 'violent' selection and interpretation of economic facts was, for Hicks, a necessity in order 'to say useful things about what is happening, before it is too late'. Since a prominent characteristic of economic facts is that they are fleeting, in practice the economist is always doomed to the study of a 'present' which is already 'past', either recently or long since. To be able to produce a useful analysis rapidly, especially of recent events, requires a disciplined concentration of the investigator's attention: 'we must work, if we are to work effectively, in some sort of blinkers . . . Or it may be politer to say that they are rays of light, which illuminate a part of the target, leaving the rest in darkness' ([1975c] 1981, p. 232). Hicks's metaphorical blinkers or rays of light are his conscious constraints on observation. Restriction of the view to a specific 'target' was to Hicks's mind crucial. Although it might well mean economists averting their eyes 'from things which may be relevant', relying on the hope that their focus has been on the 'right place' (p. 233), and 'continually butting their heads against its boundaries' (1979g, p. 22), only such selectivity can assure the clearest recording of what is chosen for scrutiny. As Hicks saw it, it is 'entirely proper' that economists should be selective, 'since otherwise we should see very little' ([1975c] 1981, p. 233).

Theory and economic laws

According to Hicks, theory plays the most significant role in the process of selection and interpretation. In observation, theories are the blinkers in a sense which guide the economist in fixing his or her eyes on specific events. In interpretation, they are the 'tools of analysis' ([1975c] 1981, p. 232). Theory, in Hicks's work, was the abstract construct of particular real situations about which it is proper to hold a certain kind of belief. For him, the necessity for selectivity ruled out, from the start, the possibility of a theory's completeness, even in its representation of the specific economic activity observed. For this reason especially, he emphasized that in order for a theory to perform its function satisfactorily, it must be 'well chosen' (p. 233). At the same time, the exercise of selection must be undertaken for the very purpose of identifying a pattern in economic activity, a pattern for which the economist could assume some regularity over time.

Economists form economic 'laws' based upon their theories. These laws entail the selection embedded in the theories from which they stem. In their formulation, that selection is identified by the noted *ceteris paribus* clause. The value of all economic laws in the context of the real world is thus highly dependent upon the pertinence of the choice of variables to the events analysed. As Hicks stated it,

> All economic laws depend for their validity – their applicability to particular real situations, which I take to be the same thing – on the correctness of the supposition that the variables of which they have taken account are the only ones which matter. (1983a, p. 367)

No group of variables or function can ever, Hicks realized, be comprehensive enough to rule out the appearance of an 'invalidating' element, but this should not deter economists either from continuing to be selective or from formulating laws.

The issue for Hicks was never really one of the appropriateness of the formulation of economic laws, but rather of their significance. The concept of law implies, in some theoretical constructs, the inevitability of recurrence of the phenomenon in question under the conditions stated. Economic laws fall thus under judgement about their reliability as tools of predicting recurrence. For Hicks, this judgement was twofold. It involved the definition of prediction and the method of assessing reliability.

Hicks identified two kinds of predictions which tend to 'slide into each other': 'predictions of what will happen' or strong, though 'not perfectly strong', predictions, and 'predictions of what will probably happen' or weak predictions (1983a, p. 369). Economic theories and their laws offer the possibility of only weak prediction. Since they are always subject to a *ceteris paribus* clause, their explanations of events are incomplete or partial, and their predictions likewise. Thus, although plans for economic activity must be based on expectations rationally formed in order for processes which have been started to continue, these expectations can only be determined by weak predictions. Hicks saw room for improvement in the construction of the theories on which predictions would be made; but even if they are as good as they might ever be, they can only predict the possible.

The implication of this realization for assessing the reliability of economic laws is profound. 'Once it is accepted that economic theories (those which are not mere tautologies) can offer no more than weak explanations', in addition to the fact that they cannot be used to predict absolutely, 'it becomes clear that they cannot be verified (or "falsified") by confrontation with fact'. The verification process Hicks referred to was, of course, commonplace in the experimental sciences where 'when theories and fact come into conflict it is theory, not fact, that must give way' (1983a, pp. 371–2). About the appropriateness of its application to economics, however, Hicks could not help but have grave doubts: 'the issue is whether that reliability is suitably assessed by the method that is appropriate in experimental sciences, by a statistical standard error' (p. 369). Hicks seemed to approach the issue differently for special case and more general economic theories. While a special case theory might be seen to be describing or analysing particular real situations, a general theory, such as that of *Value and Capital*, would make 'no claim to be realistic'. While a special case theory might be referred back to the real world, the general theory would have created its own world, including a laboratory 'in which ideas can be tested' (1983, p. 374). The defence for the reliability of each type of theory would be distinct, with the general theory in avoidance of any *post hoc* deference to the initial events from which it stemmed. (See Hamouda and Price, 1991, ch. 3.)

Is economics a science?

With the application of such concepts as law, prediction and verification to economics, the question easily arises whether economics is a science. Hicks took this very question quite seriously and addressed it in several of his writings. To start with he turned to the etymological roots of the word science, meaning knowledge. (This can be a quite revealing path especially when the classical philosophical use of the term is considered; see Hamouda and Price, 1991.) Using this etymology, Hicks defined a science most generally as 'a body of knowledge' (1984b, p. 213). He continued to refine his definition:

> A science, I would say, consists of a body of propositions, which have three distinguishing characters. (1) They are about real things, things we observe, about phenomena. (2) They are general propositions, about classes of phenomena, about relations between the properties of classes

of phenomena. (3) They are propositions on which it is possible to base predictions, predictions which command some degree of belief. (1984b, p. 213)

Hicks was convinced that all three 'characters' were necessary conditions for a body of propositions to form a science. According to the criteria, both narrative history and mathematics fall outside the bounds of science. Narrative history does not qualify because it gives no role to general propositions (2) or to predictions (3). Neither is mathematics a science, for it fails to meet the first condition: its propositions bear no relation to observables. They are not about observables; nor is observation needed to confirm them. Mathematical propositions are logically true.

Is then economics a science? Hicks reflected on the question in two ways: in relation to his definition of a science and in relation to changes in economic thought over time.

As noted above, Hicks's definition of a science had three components. As for (1), although 'the range of phenomena with which economics deals is so narrow' (1979g, p. 22), economics is indeed 'about real things'; it is based on evidence collected inductively from observation. As for (3), the predictions made from economic data and theory do 'command some degree of belief'; 'if a relation has held, with no more than intelligible exceptions, over (say) the last fifty years, we may reasonably guess that it will continue to hold this year, and perhaps next year, and perhaps for the year after that' (p. 38). When, however, the second condition (2) is added to the third (3), the ability of economics to meet (3) seems to break down. Economics fails to have the essential characteristic of having general predictive propositions, that is, propositions which represent relations over a longer period of time than about fifty years. Its relations are limited by being restricted to the very historical context in which they initially exist: 'all economic data are dated'; they 'can never do more than establish a relation which appears to hold within the period to which the data refer . . . we cannot even reasonably guess that it will continue to hold for the next fifty years' (p. 38).

To Hicks's mind, economics did not therefore meet the definition's conditions sufficiently for its body of propositions to qualify as scientific. It certainly did not measure up to scientific status in the way the natural sciences would. He noted numerous deviations. For example, 'economics is in time, in a way that the natural sciences are not' (1979g, p. 38). And, in the sciences, the assumption that a relation will continue to hold is 'reasonable'; in economics it is not. Also, 'the sciences are full of measurements which, over a wide field of application, can be regarded as constants'; 'there are no such constants in economics' (p. 39). Finally, 'it must indeed be conceded that the abundance of exogenous elements in economics is no cause for congratulation; it is an indication of the modesty of the scientific status, if indeed it is a scientific status, which is all that economics can hope to achieve' (p. 22).

Economists have none the less attempted to acquire a scientific status for economics by imitating some of the methodology of the sciences. (See Hamouda and Price, 1991.) Economists construct their theories like scientific theories, bodies of reasoning 'with an empirical basis'. They devise their laws on the model of the inductive laws of the sciences, as generalizations based on observations (1984b, p. 216). In doing so, Hicks observed, economists 'are inevitably drawn to a study of the nearest approximations to constancy which their subject permits, to a study of those relations which appear to be fairly persistent, so they can be taken, over long periods, to remain more or less unchanged'. A striving for constancy in data and relations has led and continues to lead many economists to develop static theories. Static economic theories can claim the 'nearest parallels, in economics, to physical theories' (1979g, pp. 40–41). While they depend directly on facts, they can do so without having to acknowledge any change in those facts.

Revolutions in economics

The other respect in which Hicks contemplated the scientific nature of economics was in relation to the evolution of economic thought. 'Do shifts in economic thought resemble shifts in the ideas of the natural sciences?', he asked. Even if economics might be seen to present a body of knowledge in the 'scientific' form of generalized propositions about observables from which a certain kind of prediction might be made, the reasons for shifts in the content of that body of knowledge might be, Hicks realized, further revealing of its scientific nature. Hicks chose to compare so-called revolutions in economics with decisive changes in scientific thought, or scientific revolutions, defined in a quasi-Kuhnian, quasi-Popperian way, as paradigm shifts which represent 'clear *advances* in the scientific sense'. 'In the history of science there are "revolutions", when one hypothesis, or a system of hypotheses, which has had a long run, extending over many years, has nevertheless in the end been rejected in favour of another' ([1975c] 1981, pp. 231–2). In science the shifts occur on the grounds that 'a more powerful theory' has been set forth. The new theory may simply do a 'better' job of explaining phenomena already under scrutiny, or it may fill the need to account for facts newly discovered through experiment or observation. The new explanation for facts which have, in a sense, always been there often yields 'pure permanent gain' in knowledge (p. 233).

Hicks argued that the shifts which occur in economic thought are primarily the result of 'changes of attention'. They occur when the reigning theories in economics are rejected or neglected (though not destroyed), 'because in the course of time, they have become inappropriate' ([1975c] 1981, p. 233). Earlier theories of economic activity survive, for new ones do not present any intellectual superiority, strictly speaking. They none the less fade, owing to their inappropriateness, because, as has already been noted, the world which economists study is changing. Either new facts come into existence from new events in the course of history and require new explanations (1976e, p. 211), or 'things neglected may have gained in importance relatively to the things considered' more significant in earlier theories ([1975c], 1981, p. 233).

For either of these two reasons or for different reasons entirely, the focus of the interest of economists also changes. The old theories' inappropriateness is not due to their being 'superseded by a more powerful theory', a reason which would draw economics closer to fitting the scientific pattern. It is instead primarily a function of the economists' change of focus within a changing world ([1975c] 1981, pp. 231–3). When 'things which were formerly left unnoticed', in the economists' new frame of mind, 'rise up and become essential', theories which previously did not consider them will be abandoned, and a shift in economic thought will be effected (p. 233). Hicks found the shift in interest more inevitable than surprising. He noted at least three strong catalysts: criticism of other theories, the filling-in of other theories' gaps, and the building of 'some sort of bridge between one selective theory and another' (1976e, p. 218). The initial intellectual stimuli to the refocusing of attention in economics might resemble those at work in the sciences, and hence revolutions in economics might sometimes appear similar to those of science. Most of them are, however, 'of another character' ([1975c] 1981, p. 233).

Undoubtedly, as Hicks noted, analysis of the history of economic thought can shed light on the philosophy of economics. It is, however, also worth noting that Hicks's perspective on economic revolutions is equally revealing of his sense of the psychology of the study of economics. Instances of economic revolutions are not hard to spot. The major figures to have contributed to economic thought are universally recognized within the discipline, and, as can be extrapolated from Hicks's account, they appear with striking regularity every forty to fifty years. For example, the ideas of Smith (*c.*1776) were replaced by those of Ricardo (*c.*1824), signalling a minor revolution, at the very least. Subsequently two simultaneous revolutions occurred with the appearance of the work of Marx (1867, 1885, 1894) and of Jevons, Walras and Menger (all *c.*1870). In Hicks's lifetime, Keynes (1936) and the impact of his ideas had caused the most recent revolution.

The shift from Smith's ideas to those of Ricardo, while perhaps less dramatic than subsequent shifts, was no less a product of a change of attention. Ricardo, like economists to follow, was stimulated by contemporary problems. The difficulty of the land's meeting the food demands of an expanding population had been brought to his attention by the Napoleonic blockade and the issues of post-war reconstruction. History had produced *new* facts from *new* events which Ricardo addressed through his rent theory and ensuing growth theory. To Hicks's mind, 'Ricardian economics is a remarkable intellectual achievement; but it could not have taken the form it did, except under the pressure of particular events' (1976e, p. 211).

After a time (the theoretical requisite of a half century, to be exact), Ricardo's theory lost its relevance, in that the issue of land had become less acute. 'So', as Hicks put it, 'the time came when economics was ready for another "revolution"' (1976e, p. 211). There then occurred two different shifts of economic interest, one toward production and distribution introduced by Marx, and the other toward exchange by Jevons, Walras and Menger. In the case of the marginalist side of the revolution Hicks argued on the one hand it had nothing fundamentally to do with political notions of socialism or individualism. On the other hand, he also affirmed that the catallactics, or marginalists, Jevons, Walras and Menger, were not concerned 'with the changes that were occurring at that time in the "real world"' (p. 214). Somewhat unusually, their theory was instead the product of the realized 'construction' of a powerful economic theory from its already-proposed possibility. While the earlier Ricardian theory, like all economic theories, survived, relatively unnoticed, through this double revolution, economists meanwhile divided, siding either with Marx or with Jevons, Walras and Menger.

The ideas which constituted the Keynesian revolution represent, again after a fifty-year interval, a marked change of attention for the economics profession to the phenomena of economic fluctuations and monetary crisis. Keynes himself was no doubt stimulated to contemplate such topics as a result of their prominence from 1920 to 1935, that is, 'because of the times in which he was living'. His *General Theory of*

Employment was truly a product of its time. Its revolutionary contribution was not to the body of general economics, since little of which Keynes made selective use had not been around for exploitation long before. It did, however, define a conscious change of focus, even if not a definitive one: 'there were things, of some of which some of Keynes's predecessors had been well aware, which Keynes left out – for his purpose rightly left out; but in later work we have seen them creeping back' ([1975c] 1981, pp. 233–4).

Theory, deduction and induction

Knowledge, time and decision

Three specific characteristics of economics led Hicks to assert that the form of causality at work in economics is 'a particularly interesting, and particularly revealing, case' (1979g, p. 1): (1) the imprecision and uncertainty connected with economic facts and knowledge; (2) the function of time in the study of economic activity; and (3) the concern of economics with 'the making of decisions and with the consequences that follow from the decisions' (p. 5). These three features of economics would, he argued, restrict his very general definition of causality, 'the relation between cause and effect' (p. 1), to one much more narrow and tailored to the discipline.

Concerning the first characteristic, Hicks's persuasion as to the quality of economic 'facts' has already been discussed. The gist of the phrase from his *Causality in Economics*, 'there are very few economic facts which we know with precision' (1979g, p. 1), reappeared in many different ways and places throughout his work. As for the cumulative body of knowledge such facts yield, Hicks never belittled its quantity. None the less, he was ever ready to emphasize that the knowledge economic facts afforded was incomplete, 'so extremely imperfect', not knowable 'with precision', and very 'uncertain' by its very nature (pp. 1, 2). All we can know derives from 'what has been remembered, or recorded; or perhaps it has left some mark upon the present world from which we can deduce what happened, probably what happened' (1976f, pp. 135–6). These characteristics of economic 'facts' would have major implications for the concept of causality in economics.

The role of time in economics is also an important characteristic, since, it concerns causality; it is one that has been of particular fascination to a number of economists of the twentieth century, including Hicks.

Of wonder to economists such as Hicks is that any economist could relegate no role at all to time. Models, 'often of great intellectual complexity', are built, he noted, which are virtually 'out of time, and out of history'. Without hesitation he labelled such an effort 'a waste of time', 'practically futile and indeed misleading', with 'many bad marks to be set against it' (1976f, p. 143).

When time is given a role in economics, it is transformed into space (just as economic activity is transformed into 'facts'). Whether in simple or in highly complex models the never-ending uni-directional forward flow of minutes, hours and days finds its representation in the bi-directional spatial coordinate convention of economic diagrams. To Hicks's mind, the use of this convention is flawed for two reasons. First, 'that representation is never a complete representation; it always leaves something out', and second, 'it is quite hard to get away, in any part of our thinking, from the spatial representation' (1976f, p. 135).

As consequences of this convention and its inherent incompleteness and spatiality, two aspects of time are misrepresented in economics: its irreversibility and the distinctiveness of the past from the future. Economics must, Hicks felt, take account of the sequence aspect of time. It must acknowledge both that some things have already taken place, while others have not yet and that the relationship of cause and effect is in the sequence of time. In respect of the first, knowledge is the factor: the past is knowable, albeit incompletely, through the extant collection of facts about it, while knowledge of the future, however charted, is 'no more than knowledge of probabilities' (1976f, pp. 135–6). In respect of the second, Hicks harked back to philosophical preoccupations: 'A property which was stated by David Hume to be "essential to causes and effects" is that of "priority in time in the cause before the effect"' (1979g, pp. 2–3).

The concern of economics with the making of decisions and their consequences, the third related aspect of economics, reflects directly the importance of causal connections. 'The immediate cause of an economic effect is, nearly always, a decision by someone; or it may be the combination of decisions that were made by different people' (1979g, p. 88). Thus the causal chain, or process of causal connection, in economics has the special character of acknowledging intermediate stages between each event in the chain and its effect. While this causal chain will appear as an economic time series, or 'sequence of observations of a historical process, each item having its own distinct individuality' (1983a, p. 372), akin to the sequentially ordered steps of political or diplomatic narrative history, it will have embedded in it consideration of an unobservable series of mediating direct causes, or decisions. Between event A, which causes A1 which in turn causes A2 and so on until An is the cause of B, are recognized to be decision (or decisions) A! which directly causes A1, and decision A1! which in turn causes A2 until decision An! causes B. It is obvious that the consideration of the element of decisions and decision-making can have a profound effect on the understanding of causality in economics. (See Hamouda and Price, 1991, ch. 4.)

Logical classifications of causality

Hicks was well aware that in many respects causality can be contemplated, at least initially, according to its logical classifications. His version of these classifications are scattered throughout his work. They will be individually introduced here briefly, both to present a kind of Hicksian catalogue of logical causal relations and to allow for a later comparison of them with Hicks's far more distinctive classifications of causation in its temporal senses. As mentioned above, he defined causality most generally as 'the relation between cause and effect' (1979g, p. 1). A cause and its effect can be classified, according to Hicks, as 'the members of two different classes of events'. 'It is', he wrote, 'the characteristics which they have, as members of those classes, which we claim to be causally connected' (1984a, p. 13).

For Hicks, any study of causality should reap specific fruit. If successfully conducted, it should establish that a recorded event (or events) A was the cause of event (or events) B. It should also lead to the identification of the immediate decision which would have been the direct cause of B, and of 'who it was that made the decision – who it was that was responsible' (1979g, p. 5). Hicks cautioned that it might be tempting to treat the results of the study as offering a complete description of the phenomenon, one which can effectively replace the phenomenon, 'in our minds' (1984a, p. 13). The findings, however, while essential to understanding causality, need not, and normally do not capture the whole of the phenomenon under investigation.

Hicks distinguished two systems of logical thought concerning causation: old causality and new causality. The logic of the old causal system focused, according to Hicks, on the agents of the effect and their responsibility as causes. Every event has a cause and causes are 'always an agent, either a human agent or a supernatural agent' (1979g, p. 6). The gods were frequent candidates as agents, even as they adhered to natural laws to bring about an effect. Hicks saw this type of causal explanation as normative, as necessarily praising or condemning.

The logic of Hicks's new causal system is much more akin to Hume's. It is focused not on the agents of an event, but rather on the time context of one event as cause and another as effect. Hicks distinguished three logical types of causation, in relation to time: static, contemporaneous and sequential. Hicks relaxed Hume's understanding that 'effect cannot come before cause' to posit the logical static and contemporaneous relationships of A and B (1979g, pp. 19, 26). Static causality is the case of causality 'in which the period, during which the cause operates and takes effect, has been so stretched out to become indefinite' (p. 25). In static causality both cause and effect are constants in time in relation to one another. Contemporaneous causality is the case where both cause and effect relate to the same specified time-period. Hicks noted that static causality might be regarded 'as a limiting case of contemporaneous causality'. In the case of sequential causality, 'A, we may take it, is some event that occurred at some time in the past, and B is some event which here we will still allow to have occurred at some later time' (p. 7). In other words, in sequential causality, cause precedes effect, effect comes after cause.

Within his Humian system of new causality, Hicks made numerous further logical classifications without reference to time. His distinction between weak causation and strong causation was, for example, to eliminate the ambiguities in the affirmation, 'A caused B'. It might mean that among many causes of B, A was one, in which case one would speak of weak causation. It might, however, mean instead that A alone caused B, in which case it would be labelled an instance of strong causation. 'Strong causation implies weak causation; but it also implies that there is no other potential cause which is admitted to be *a* cause of B' (1979g, p. 13). To Hicks's mind, Hume had not 'paid enough attention to the distinction between strong and weak causation' (1984a, p. 12). This was a slight which he felt no economist could permit, since the majority of statements in economics are ones of weak causation, including those of economic laws because they hold almost always only under a *ceteris paribus* condition.

Hicks further subdivided his crucial classification of weak causation into separable and non-separable causation. Separable causation is found when A quite independently, by itself, is one of the possible causes of B. Hicks described the instance of its separable occurrence with other necessary causes as 'overlapping causality'. Non-separable causation exists when A is affirmed to be no more than 'a part of a separable cause' which might also include A*, A**, etc. (1979g, p. 13).

In describing the non-separable relationship of A and A*, Hicks noted the logical classification of mutual causality, inspired by Kant. 'In the English translation of his *Critique*, the relation [between A and A*] is called *reciprocity*; but his German word was *Wechselwirkung*; the literal translation of that is *mutual causality*' (1979g, p. 19). Hicks also described the state of non-separability as either additive (positive) or negative. In the case of an additive non-separable cause, the effect comes about only when the 'parts' of its cause are added together and collectively produce a separable cause. In the case of a negative cause, if it is not neutralized, the effect of another part of the cause might be prevented from occurring.

These subsequent classifications could pertain to any of the temporal senses of causality. Hicks specifically noted that 'even static causality may be strong or weak; it may be additive or overlapping; negative causes are not ruled out. It may be one-way, or it may be mutual' (1979g, p. 26). In the case of contemporaneous causality, as Hicks well noted, the relation between cause and effect may be either reciprocal or mutual, 'each of the elements being a cause of the other', or non-reciprocal (p. 21).

Induction and deduction

To Hicks the logical classifications of causality were to be pursued according to the methods of induction and deduction. He recognized, however, that these methods were not linked exclusively to logical classification. With their use 'we are asking that two senses of implication, empirical and logical, should be brought together'. In economics, empirical observation is predominantly quantitative, based on measurement. It lacks explanation for its associations. 'When we demand a reason', Hicks observed, 'we are asking that the empirical association should be brought into a logical system' (1979g, p. 29).

The method of induction begins with the empirical exercise of collecting observed facts. While primitive inductions abound in 'the practical arts' (1979g, p. 36), there are, Hicks noted, many examples of empirical relations in economics. 'They have been elaborately studied, on their own account, and ways of dealing with them have continually improved' (p. 28). Their content and method form the foundation of descriptive economics, 'economics which describes, but does not attempt to explain' (p. 37). The demand for reasons or explanation, however, extends the empirical associations of economics beyond their purely descriptive function.

Explanation of the relation between two events depends on the observer's having a theory, or broad picture of interrelations. While pure theory is 'at liberty to choose its own axioms', a theory which is to provide an explanation for economic facts must begin with inductive propositions. Such statements are the observations of associations which appear to hold between recognized characteristics for the period from which the data stem (1979g, p. 28). To Hicks's mind, such initial propositions, though purely empirical, are already logical propositions in that they carry within them their logical implication, which is how there is seen to be a theoretical relation between facts. As if in confirmation of his belief, economists have seen fit to concentrate on the logical proceeding corresponding to observation and thus on 'the refinement of the practical concepts so as to fit them better to be tools of thinking' (p. 37).

Hicks noted that since Hume it has frequently been supposed that theories which provide the basis for asserting causal relations, and thus encompass A and B and imply not-B if not-A, can, if not must, be purely inductive. Indeed, induction, Hicks affirmed, provides the empirical basis of economic theory. To his mind, it can also offer a method of verification. Some logical implications in economics can be tested inductively, that is, identified characteristics can be quantitatively re-correlated to the new empirical data of 'secondary observations'. It is such secondary observations which are seen to *verify* the theory. 'If the test is successful, a bridge, a logical bridge, has been built between two inductions; the coherence, the logical coherence, of the bridge strengthens our confidence in the inductions which are its supports' (1979g, p. 29).

Hicks was himself less sure that induction was the only method economists ought to apply: 'the scientist explains by means of his "ladder"; but where in economics is the "ladder", the regular progression from one established induction to another? We have hardly more than fragments of it' (1979g, p. 37). He harked back to the issue that the facts of economics are grounded 'in time': 'economics is in time, in a way that the natural sciences are not'. Since 'all economic data are dated', the inductively-acquired evidence reflects only the state of relations at the time of the induction (p. 38). Thus on the one hand, from the initial information itself, only a reasonable guess can be made for the future state of relations. On the other hand, further induction can neither affirm nor deny the validity of the implications of the first empirical data. 'No induction can provide a proof, a complete proof' (1984b, p. 216). As an added complication to reliance on induction for verification, Hicks noted that when the pertinent characteristics are remeasured, there is rarely an exact correlation, hence the significance of the data is often rendered questionable. As he said, 'the discovery of a fact (or observation), which is inconsistent with an established theory, does not always cause that theory to be abandoned, or not at least to be abandoned straightway' (1979g, p. 33).

For Hicks, then, deduction is a method complementary to the use of induction in economics. He believed that although neither characteristics nor initial propositions can be deduced, deduction had an important part to play in economic theory. With the purely axiomatic study of mathematics as his model of the application of the deductive method, Hicks however argued that the asserting of causal relations is based on theories which could no more be purely deductive than purely inductive (1979g, p. 28). Deduction serves to create its own bridge between inductions. Rather than the inductive bridge of simple coherence or coincidence, deduction proposes a bridge based on pattern and generalization. Its logical chain of reasoning may take many forms: 'short or long, simple or complex' (p. 32). In all cases, however, its role is to proceed deductively from primary observations, such that the initial set of deductions indicates 'what secondary observation, or experiments, should be made to seek for confirmation' (p. 33).

Economic theory

Both induction and deduction were in Hicks's opinion to play an indispensable role in his method of theory building. According to him, the method of building any causal theory would entail the following four steps:

1. Induction
2. Deduction
3. Introduction of economic principle or justifier
4. Verification (induction)

The methods of steps 1, 2 and 4 have already been briefly introduced in the previous section. In Step 1 observations and empirical facts are ushered in. Step 2 is a bridging step, in which the deduction is constructed which follows from the inductions of Step 1. Step 4 entails a method of verification, or 'the confrontation of the effect, which has been deduced, with experience' (1979g, p. 42).

Step 3 presents the only theoretical element not yet discussed, the economic principle or justifier. The economic principle, a definition or classification, is in effect the most binding theoretical component and the most important premises of the model. It sets the parameters of the model and limits the variables to those according to which it is both feasible and reasonable to seek an explanation of economic causality within the devised theoretical model. The economic principle is especially important in connection with the different logical classifications of causality in relation to time. It is the proposition most responsible for the significance of the role of time within the theory and thereby for the type of theoretical causation to be applied.

Different kinds of theoretical causation

From the logical classifications of causality and the methods, induction and deduction, for investigating causal relations, the discussion now turns to the role of these components in the building of economic theories. According to Hicks, a theory of causality is virtually embedded in the very expression of a causal relation: 'in a statement of causality, theory is being *applied*' (1979g, p. 8); 'it is always true that any statement of causality, of whatever kind, has reference to a theory' (p. 26). This belief is significant when Hicks's definition of theory is kept in mind: 'a theory is the abstract construct of particular real situations about which it is proper to hold a certain kind of belief'. The definition helps explain that although Hicks was able to reflect on numerous logical classifications of causality without reference to theory, the moment 'particular real situations' were under discussion his analysis of causality became imbued by theory.

As already noted, Hicks affirmed his overriding conviction that weak causality dominated economic analysis. Of all the other logical classifications Hicks maintained that the most revealing for economics were those of the new causality which categorize causes and effects in relation to time. While many of the other logical classifications (separable or non-separable, mutual, additive or negative, etc.) were also pertinent in economics, to his mind economic theories distinguish themselves most markedly according to whether static, contemporaneous or sequential causality is being applied to describe the connection between A and B in a particular economic situation. Further, he observed that any statement of static, contemporaneous, or sequential causality in an 'economic' situation refers to the theoretical significance attributed to the time context of the particular real situation in question. Because of their importance to Hicks, these three classifications of causality in relation to time will now be briefly described.

Static causation

In Hicks's classification static causality refers to static theory. As noted above, in static causality both cause and effect are constants in time in relation to one another. Thus if the real economic conditions to which a theory is to be applied are such as appear to be constant, static causal analysis can be used to create a theoretical model. Of course, as Hicks well realized, 'actual conditions, in an actual economy over a particular period, would not correspond exactly with the model, but there would be some configuration of coefficients which would be approximately actual' (1979g, p. 47). Hicks's conditions for the model entailed the modelling of the single period in which 'the cause operates and takes effect', 'so stretched out as to become indefinite' (p. 25) and excluding change as irrelevant except in the case of one factor. 'Only the things which in the actual experience remain, more or less, unchanged over time', he wrote, can play a role in the model (p. 45). They function as a backdrop of constants against which comparisons can be made. Only one factor, which changes over the time within the period modelled, is taken into consideration.

Hicks considered the theoretical construct of economic equilibrium most convenient for modelling static causation. First, in equilibrium, change was precluded. The modelled equilibrium state could thus be used to compare one set of circumstances (what is/was at one time), with another set (what would have been if one factor was altered and all other things remained equal or unchanged (*ceteris paribus*)). Second, in the model of any particular equilibrium, the economic principle functions to define the parameters of the model such that all the conditions whereby equilibrium can be maintained are possible and integrated within the model: 'when the Economic Principle is applied to such a model, it will follow that all opportunities for advantageous change that are presented within the model must within the model be taken' (1979g, pp. 45–6). In equilibrium not only can the inconvenience of considering reaction time be ignored, but so too can the would-be disruptive impact of exogenous variables. It is thus that the equilibrium model can be used to show 'how the system would have been modified if some of these exogenous elements, the technical coefficients, had been different' (p. 47).

To illustrate the use of static causality within static theory, Hicks took a historical example, Adam Smith's theory explaining the improvement of the wealth of a nation. According to Hicks's interpretation, Smith had constructed a theoretical model in which within one and the same period the relative costs of land and water carriage could be altered, while all other things remain unchanged. He analysed Smith's argument according to the four common steps of any causal theory in the Hicksian methodology. First, inductively Smith had both accumulated observations of economic specialization and noted the empirical fact of the relative cheapness of water carriage to other modes of transport. (In his discussion of Smith's method, Hicks identified this inductive step as two steps, 1979g, p. 42.) Second, from the induced data Smith deduced that advantage accrues from geographic location. Third, Smith adopted the economic principle that relative locational advantage implies relative wealth. Fourth, Smith checked his conclusions by confronting the deduced effect 'with experience' (p. 42).

To Hicks's mind, Smith had conceived his model as one governed by static causation, 'since it is only the things which in the actual experience remain, more or less, unchanged over time which are relevant to the comparison' (1979g, p. 45). To Smith, it thus seemed that a model of static causation for the situation in question could be found which could itself be unchanging or static. Indeed, the situation which concerned Smith met the criteria necessary for equilibrium modelling and analysis. As one example, Smith's system of prices and incomes was operative in an equilibrium. He representatively modelled the prices of products such that they were determined 'by the quantities of the factors of production (already identified as labour, capital and land) which are required to make a unit of each finished product'. Smith saw 'these technical coefficients' as determinates of the cost of production of each product (1979g, p. 46). His deduced economic principle had the effect of maintaining the equilibrium of prices equal to production costs, since any increase in the cost of production over price would be rectified 'by the opportunities for movement of capital and of labour from a less to a more advantageous line of production' (pp. 46–7).

In the context of Smith's model, Hicks spoke of the ability of the model to establish static causation, at least for some problems. If the value of the technical coefficients alters, the equilibrium will change, but in such a way as can be deduced. Hicks felt that when the methodological step of verification revealed exceptions to the conclusion of any static causal theory, it did not dismiss the validity of the theory. One might still well assert that one, if not all, of the causes had been found.

Contemporaneous causality

It was into his theories of stock and flow magnitudes, 'what is produced, or consumed, or paid over' (1979g, p. 24), that Hicks introduced contemporaneous causality. As noted above, contemporaneous causality is applicable in cases where both cause and effect are dynamically related 'contemporaneously', that is, within a single specified time-period. Hicks felt he had identified many relations within economic dynamics which are contemporaneous, even to the point of seeing them as 'particularly important' (p. 21). Most specifically, he observed that the conditions of contemporaneous causality made it especially well suited to an application to stock–flow analysis. The economist's concern with stock and flow is focused, for example, on the activity during a specific single period.

The modern economist already thinks in terms of a quasi-theoretical convention, 'accounting periods', that is, in terms of historical periods, each with a definite beginning and end. Each accounting period is treated separately from all others. Each begins with a given stock of equipment, considered to be an inheritance from the past, and closes with an end stock, the result of the production performance within the period. The beginning stock determines the parameters of production possibilities; 'whatever is possible during the period must be consistent with it' (1979g, p. 65). The end stock is determined by changes made to equipment and production performance during the period.

Hicks felt that a causal relation between 'possible contemporaneous events' within a single period of economic dynamics could be constructed (1979g, p. 22). Analysis could reveal whether the observed factors within the period were due to each other or due to other circumstances entirely, that is, whether they had a mutual effect on their contemporaneous occurrence, or whether the cause of their being contemporaneous was exogenous to both. Since the factors in question extend over the length of the period, Hicks thought it natural 'to look for causes which themselves extend over the period' (p. 66).

Hicks thought that the best-suited model for encompassing contemporaneous causality was his temporary equilibrium model of fixed expectations. With fixed expectations in temporary equilibrium, change over the period could be incorporated without the model's having to admit of unexpected events (1979g, p. 83). Expectations appropriate within the period are set at the period's outset. The expectations, which relate to the unfolding of events in the future of the period, over the period smoothly become past experience, realized or unrealized, without having to be revised within the period.

The relationship of stocks and flows was to Hicks's mind rooted in the activity of the consumer. As one example of the temporary equilibrium model of contemporaneous causality, Hicks constructed a model around the consumer. (Another possible example might have focused on the causes of changes in production performance.) First, the activity of the consumer is observed inductively. Second, a generality about it is deduced: 'the consumer chooses his purchases so as to maximise utility' (1979g, p. 68). The ensuing economic principle of the consumer's activity, a principle which must hold for every period, is subsequently formulated, the utility function: 'consumer utility is expressed as a function of quantities purchased'. As the consumer adheres to this economic principle and thus maintains an invariant 'want-system', he or she causally reveals his or her response (or effect) to changes in the environment.

In this example of the model the attempt is to establish causality or the probability of causality for changes in consumer activity. The consumer's expectations must be fixed. Although there is always a response on the part of the consumer to environmental change, the response may or may not have an 'economic' cause or causes. The possible contemporaneous causes of changes in demand were, in Hicks's opinion, divisible into two types: (1) economic (or mutual) causes and (2) not strictly-speaking economic (or exogenous) causes. Changes in demand governed by the economic principle would qualify as mutual 'economic causes'. Hicks warned that it is especially easy to treat such mutual causes mistakenly; 'we often find ourselves treating one as exogenous, others as consequences; the one therefore as cause, the others as effects' (1979g, p. 24). 'Non-economic' circumstances would be, for instance, 'changes in population, in the age-distribution of population, the degree of education and so on'. Hicks did not discount these as possibly important exogenous causal factors in the model. He did, however, caution that, given the construction of the argument, 'we have to use our judgement how far it is worth while to test them for relevance' (1979g, p. 69).

As noted above, Hicks observed that static causality might be regarded 'as a limiting case of contemporaneous causality' (1979g, p. 7), and like the case of the static model, the ability of the temporary equilibrium model to establish actual causal relations is limited. It too is not a model of reality. 'A model of this kind is not realistic; it makes no claim to be realistic. We are just to use it as a standard of comparison with the actual.' As a model, it provides two possibilities, either to reexamine the past or to examine hypothetical alternatives. Hicks believed that 'for the historical application, at least, it is not inappropriate.' The limitations of equilibrium are not constraining to that application, 'since from our point of view nothing in the past can be unexpected'. From that perspective the model can be in equilibrium, while the actual circumstances it has captured were not. In the case of the model's application to hypothetical alternatives, the temporary equilibrium model does not differ from the static model. With the added dimension of change within the period, it too can demonstrate 'what *would have happened* if some cause had been different' (p. 83).

In either application the model functions 'experimentally', with each period under consideration conceived as a separate 'experiment'. The succession of periods has no bearing on the model. If similar time series hold for possible causes, time-series analysis can be used for efficiency, but the statistical methods estimate only the probable effect of each cause on each period.

Sequential causality

Sequential causality provided the causal explanatory structure for Hicks's dynamic theories. As noted earlier, in the case of sequential causality, 'A, we may take it, is some event that occurred at some time in the past, and B is some event which here we will still allow to have occurred at some later time' (1979g, p. 7). Thus sequential causality is the category of causality in which the effect chronologically follows the cause: the time of the occurrence of the effect is later than the time of the occurrence of the cause. For anything that occurs in the realm of economic activity, Hicks noted that one can not simply speak of a cause and a later effect. Although in sequential causality, cause precedes effect and effect comes after cause, between the two always comes a decision. The three components, cause, decision and effect, together form the most basic links in chains of causation.

In economics, sequential causality is analysed as a time-consuming two-step process of which all components, cause, decision and effect, are of concern. In a first or prior step, a root or 'objective' cause effects the formation of a decision 'based on it or influenced by it' (1979g, p. 88). In a second, or posterior step, the decision as mediate cause of the effect executes the ultimate 'objective' effect. 'The economist will often be concerned with chains of causation; but each link in his chain will, in general, consist of these two steps' (p. 89). Further, the steps, prior and posterior, together incorporate the concept of time lapsing, for each step constitutes a lag, prior and posterior.

According to Hicks, to establish a statement of sequential causality well a model would have to be able to answer the following questions: When did B (the possible effect) occur in relation to A (the possible cause)? What is to be supposed to have happened between the two dates? Why did just so much time elapse between them, neither more or less? (1979g, p. 87). Answers to these questions should explain the causal connection between 'objective' cause and 'objective' effect, as well the prior and posterior lags. Hicks attempted in his traverse analysis to address these questions and to model sequential causation.

Two examples illustrate his use of sequential causality: forward-looking process and backward-looking process. In each example the effect has been isolated, in the forward-looking process to the future, and in the backward-looking process to the present. Neither effect is unusual, for as Hicks noted, 'in most economic causations the effect is on one or the other'. In both instances a posterior lag is detectable and its occurrence is described by Hicks as 'fairly straightforward'. The prior lag is, however, less easy to model. In general, 'the objective cause does not necessarily compel a reaction'. Most often it elicits a decision, or reaction, by being perceived as it were as a 'signal'. There is little to determine the length of time or lag between the cause and the decision, which is the response to the signal. Hicks called determination of the prior lag 'tricky', for 'the reaction to the signal may be fast or slow' (1979g, p. 90).

Different kinds of causation

In both his logic classifications and theoretical applications of causes Hicks clearly revealed his conviction that different kinds of causality are at work in economic dynamics. Further, he affirmed that in the case of each kind of actual causation 'there is, or can be, a kind of theory that corresponds' (1979g, p. 101). As has been shown, to his static causality he tied static theory, to contemporaneous causality, the temporary equilibrium theory and to sequential theory, the beginnings of a traverse theory. Hicks was well aware that the fit of a kind of causality to a type of theory would not be the same in each case. He saw the development in economics of the correspondence between causality and explanatory theories as a process of the historical evolution of the discipline.

Hicks clearly recognized that static or equilibrium theory was the oldest and most completely developed part of economic theory. None the less, owing to the narrowness of its field of application, he observed that many economists, including himself, had become dissatisfied with it and with time were turning to other kinds of theories to explain economic phenomena. The temporary equilibrium model of Keynes's and Marshall's theory applied in a micro-context answered the need for an explanatory theory broader than static equilibrium theory, one integrating a different kind of causality, that is, contemporaneous causality. From Hicks's perspective the correspondence between contemporaneous causality and the early economic theories of Marshall and Keynes had become quite well developed. A measure of this development was for Hicks that 'a considerable part of the practical problems of contemporaneous causation that arise in our experience can be dealt with fairly well by this corresponding theory' (1979g, p. 101). He saw the confusion between static and other types of equilibrium theories, which impedes the best understanding of the latter, continually being reduced and was encouraged that contemporary causality, 'the characteristic form of the causal relation in modern economics', had found an appropriately representative corresponding theory.

In Hicks's opinion, however, the development of economic theories to correspond to logical categories of causation had not yet gone far enough. Economists, he noted, rightfully manifest dissatisfaction with a theory of contemporary causation, 'for there are so many questions to which we desire to have answers with which it cannot cope'. Hicks felt that the unanswered questions (some were noted above), suggested the need for an explanation of sequential causality and revealed that no satisfactory economic theory had yet been developed to correspond to sequential causality. Including himself among the searchers for such a theory, he wrote, 'we have so far no more than the beginning of a theory which will help us with such questions' (1979g, pp. 101–102). His idea of the traverse (discussed in chapter 4) had been his modest proposal to answer the need for an economic theory of sequential causality.

Probability, prediction and judgement

Hicks's four-step method of theory building in economics and his analysis of causality reflect the importance he placed on induction in establishing connecting chains of reasoning. He emphasized its role both in drawing connections between different observations and between observation and logic. In addition to selective observation and the wedding of induction and deduction, Hicks was also to affirm the use in economics of another induction-based methodological technique, adopted from the experimental sciences, in which attention is concentrated 'not on the single experiment, but on a sequence of experiments' (1984b, p. 216). In this method, experimental instances are connected in sequence according to how they are considered to be repetitions of one process under the same conditions. The importance of this method lies in the possibility it offers of predicting future results based on the assertion that any future 'experimental' conclusions would continue to average out in a way consistent with the confirmed instances obtained in the past or present.

Prediction based on past induction, however, in economics is not a simple procedure of observation and arithmetic. Hicks referred to prediction as estimation, and addressed the complexities involved by analysing the notion of the probability of an economic phenomenon occurring or recurring. He also discussed the conditions imposed on prediction in economics by the very economic phenomena themselves. Further, he reflected on the implications for prediction of the process of verification or theory testing in economics. Each group of his ideas will be discussed in succession.

Types of probability

Each of Hicks's understandings of prediction entailed a notion of probability. He first identified two levels of probability analysis. The first level is fixed within the process of theory building itself and referred to by Hicks as 'inverse probability'. The probability in question relates to the hypothesis about the representativeness of the sample compared to the larger group of instances. Every prediction, or anticipated result, is at its root perforce based on an observed or contrived sample which is deemed in some respect representative, both in time and space, of a larger group of instances. That prediction derives directly from a hypothesis constructed on the representative sample. Embedded in the hypothesis is the asserted relationship between the larger group of instances and the sample. That assertion is a probabilistic one; that is, it is deemed probable that the sample represents the larger group to the degree and in the way asserted. 'The hypothesis that proportions in the parent population are the same as in the sample is just one hypothesis, to be tested against others. We are concerned with the probability that that hypothesis is correct' (1979g, p. 104).

The second level of probability analysis is located at the limits of the particular probability theory. There are, Hicks noted, two distinct theories governing the use of a notion of probability: a frequency theory, and an axiomatic theory. 'According to the frequency theory, probability is a property of *random experiments*' (1979g, p. 105). The theory posits the repetition of experiments, which while they may appear to be exactly the same, are not so. 'If the repetitions were exact, the outcome of the second trial must be the same as that of the first, and so on', and there would be no role for probability. Instead what is envisaged by the theory is experiments which are so similar as to be recognized as repetitions, and yet different enough not to be exactly alike in every respect. Most important, 'the differences between them must be *random*' (p. 106). Random differences are by definition unpredictable; while they unquestionably affect the individual experiment, they are without detectable effect 'on the average outcome of a long series of experiments (1984b, p. 217). Thus, following frequency theory, one would, in asserting that there is 'the probability of event, E, cast as an experiment, being equal to P', mean that after many repetitions of E, differing only randomly, 'it is practically certain that the frequency of E will be approximately equal to P' (1979g, pp. 105–6).

By 1979 Hicks felt that the frequency theory, while 'thoroughly at home in many of the natural sciences', was not a wide enough theory for economics (1979g, p. 105). Given the subject matter of economics, as Hicks noted, often formally cast, as for example in portfolio theory as 'states of the world', probabilities 'cannot be interpreted in terms of random experiments' (p. 107). Hicks seemed to feel that only a much broader theory would have real application and meaning in the study of economics. He found advocates of this same view in Jeffreys and Keynes, who both advanced an axiomatic theory of probability. Where the two of them differed in their version of the theory, Hicks sided with the more generous theory of Keynes.

Jeffreys's axiomatic theory of probability, as its name indicates, was based on the axioms that play a significant role in economic theory. Jeffreys listed the following axioms, which are important in and to economics:

1. Either one event is more probable than another: 'A and B are exclusive alternatives', so that if A is more probable to happen, B cannot be more probable to happen, or two events are equally probable: A and C are equally probable events;
2. Transitivity is possible: if 'A is more probable than B, and B than C, then A is more probable than C';
3. There is a relation between probability and certainty;
4. If axiom (1) holds for the pairs (A and B) and (C and D), such that if A, not B, and if C, not D, and for the pairs (A and C) and (B and D), such that within the pairs (A and C) and (B and D), each is

equally probable, 'then the occurrence of *either A or B*, and the occurrence of *either C or D*, must be equally probable' (1979g, pp. 108–9).

On the surface it looked as if Jeffreys's axioms led to 'the classical theory of games of chance, in which the occurrence of a head and that of a tail are taken to be "equally probable"' (1979g, pp. 109–10). Hicks tried, however, to find a distinction between the two. First, in examining the strict parallels between frequency theory and Jeffreys's axiomatic theory of probability, and the theory of utility, he noted that the postulates of modern utility theory, although 'precisely similar' to Jeffreys's axioms, 'provide nothing more than an ordinal relation' (p. 108). With his fourth axiom Jeffreys had managed, as in the frequency theory of probability, to make his theory additive, and hence cardinal. While cardinality rendered both theories distinct from utility theory, it was not enough to eliminate any confusion of axiomatic theory with the classical games-of-chance theory.

Second, however, Hicks did observe a crucial distinction between Jeffreys' axiomatic theory and both the classical and the frequency theories of probability, and this was the role of information. The part of Jeffreys's conception of an axiomatic theory of probability which had so favourably impressed Hicks was its emphasis on 'the degree of confidence that we may reasonably have in a proposition, even though we may not be able to give either a deductive proof or a disproof of it' (1979g, pp. 107–8, citing Jeffreys, p. 15). Of utmost importance in acquiring 'confidence' was not the arithmetic weighting of one event over another; as noted above, weighting had been axiomatically reduced to insignificance. 'If two alternatives are equally probable, the *relative probability* is unity; this, in Jeffreys' construction is clearly implied' (1979g, p. 110). Essential, however, was the information available about the situation of the equally probable A and B (and C and D), for that situation is indeed one in which A is in some important way 'intermediate between alternatives which (if they were open) would be more probable than B, and others which would be less probable than B' (p. 110). As Hicks saw it, the information is relevant, for although it balances A and B (C and D), it gives grounds for ranking them equally as alternatives. In Jeffreys's theory information allows judgement to be exercised in the situation of a 'proportion considered' and 'the data in relation to which it is considered' (1979g, p. 108, citing Jeffreys, p. 15).

In identifying the importance of information to axiomatic theory, Hicks felt that Jeffreys had released it from the bounds of strictly mathematical probability theory. Probability had come to mean 'the degree of confidence that may reasonably be expressed in a proportion on the basis of given evidence' (1979g, p. 114). While Jeffreys had initially associated both frequency and axiomatic theory with a cardinal interpretation of utility theory, for Hicks the former theory was consistently measurable, the latter, judgemental. 'One can', Hicks wrote, 'welcome Jeffreys' insistence that probability, in the widest sense, is a matter of judgement ... a matter of rational judgement, based on information, or on evidence' (p. 110). He called this approach subjective, but not irrational.

In emphasizing the subjective nature of axiomatic theory, Hicks noted that it was not an exclusively cardinal, or even mathematical, theory. The probabilities based on interpreted information 'are of various kinds, of which the particular kind which leads to cardinal probabilities, and so to a calculus of probabilities, is no more than one' (1979g, p. 110). He acknowledged one sub-class of assessments, 'in which information is sufficient for a judgement of greater, or less, or equal, to be always possible' and its sub-subclass 'in which exclusive alternatives can be distinguished', noting that it is only 'in this sub-class, out of the wider class of cases to which the general notion of probability can be applied, that we can proceed to the calculus'. The reason for this subcategorization was that, to Hicks's mind, axiomatic probabilities may not always be numerically expressible, since the alternatives may not always be comparable, and hence not orderable. Hicks went so far as to rewrite Jeffreys's first axiom, that 'of two alternatives, on given evidence, either A is more probable than B, or B more probable than A, or they are equally probable, *or that they are not comparable*' (p. 115). Further still, he contemplated the instance when observation does not seem to provide even two alternatives. This is the case when observations along a time-series do not appear independent, or 'cannot by some device be divided into groups that can be treated as independent'. The economist is then logically faced with 'no more than one observation, all of the separate items having to be taken together. For the analysis of that the probability calculus is useless; it does not apply.' Here too Hicks insisted on the role of judgement: economists must make sense of what has happened as best they can (1979g, p. 121).

Hicks illustrated his hierarchy of probability theories with a diagram of concentric rings A, B, and C and a superimposed shaded area.

> A is the field where probabilities are unquestionably numerical – the classical field of games of chance, and of random experiments (or observations of what is accepted to be the same phenomena). The ring B is that in which probabilities are orderable, but not expressible as numbers. The

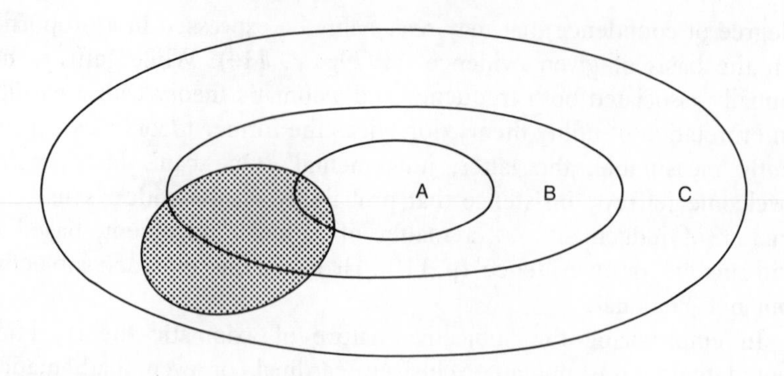

Figure 9.1 Hierarchy of probability Theories

> ring C is that in which they are not even orderable, or not completely orderable.
>
> I am maintaining (1) that even in ring C probability judgements can sometimes be made, and that they can be rational since it is conceivable that they could be improved by additional evidence, (2) that the field of economics has the character of the shaded area, some part of it being in A, some in B, and some in C. (1979g, p. 115)

Probability may pertain to either past or future events. The economist freely speaks of his knowledge of the past as 'largely a matter of probabilities', and the knowledge of the future is definitely 'no more than a matter of probabilities' (1976f, pp. 135–6). The two types of probabilities do, however, differ. Their differences are reflected in two ways: (1) in the level of probability analysis each emphasizes, (2) in the kind of knowledge entailed in each. As for the levels of probability analysis discussed above, in the case of conclusions about the past, the role of probability at the hypothesis level of analysis is extremely important, while in the case of the future, the type of theory chosen for probability study is critical.

As for the kind of knowledge about past or future events, the past obviously is composed of events which definitely have happened, while future events are yet to happen, and this or that may yet transpire. Knowledge about the more recent past is probabilistic in the sense that the events of that past may or may not be able to be predicted from knowledge about a point in the yet more remote past. Knowledge about the future is probabilistic in the sense that it results from the weighing or judging of the past so as to predict the future. Making predictions seems to be within the calling of most economists. It is especially in the context of this part of the economist's vocation that theories of probability come to play an important role.

Predictions

Just as Hicks went about classifying logical and theoretical causality, he also classified predictions, first into conditional and unconditional predictions, then into strong and weak conditional predictions. As the name reflects, the distinction between conditional and unconditional predictions is based on the presence or absence of qualifications or conditions. 'A conditional prediction says that something will happen if some condition is satisfied . . . unconditional prediction makes no such qualifications.' Conditional predictions are far more prevalent than unconditional ones. Economic dynamics are most frequently scrutinized as situations isolated from the whole, as in experiments as it were, whose conditions are those 'from which it is claimed that the result will follow' (1984b, p. 215).

The strong and weak conditional predictions differ on the degree to which the result is an inevitable consequence. If a prediction is strong, it affirms that, 'given the stated conditions, the event will follow'; what is predicted will occur. If a prediction is weak, 'it says no more than that the event will follow, if there is no [sufficient] disturbance'. A weak conditional prediction affirms that 'some of the conditions for the event to follow have been identified' (1984b, p. 215). It also acknowledges, however, that there may well be disturbances or other conditions, which cannot be specified yet or at all.

It is appropriate in this context to reiterate Hicks's opinion that economics is not an experimental science. Although economists must examine the world under specific conditions, as if experimentally, the conclusions they draw from such examination must be understood differently from those of the experimental sciences. The predictions of economic activity 'are in time, in historical time, in a way that most scientific predictions are not'. As a consequence, Hicks asserted, the predictions economists can make based on their experiments are 'essentially weak predictions' (1984b, p. 217). None the less, he added, there was still value in the weak concluding proposition of an economic conditional prediction. Its best results are solid enough to be subject only to exogenous disturbances and therefore of some use.

The dissimilarity of economics and the experimental sciences always raised doubt in Hicks's mind about the usefulness of 'statistical' or 'stochastic' methods in economics. 'I am bold enough to conclude',

Hicks wrote in 1979, that their usefulness 'is a good deal less than is now conventionally supposed. We have no business to turn to them automatically; we should always ask ourselves, before we apply them, whether they are appropriate to the problem in hand. Very often they are not.' Further, Hicks doubted whether the econometrician 'has any right to make predictions in the form of an "expectation", subject to confidence limit "±"', especially given his questioning of Jeffreys's first and fourth axioms (1979g, p. 121).

Testing economic theories

There are numerous ways of testing economic theories. All of them, falsification or refutation, confirmation, testing under precaution, etc., test in some way for conciliance between conclusion or prediction and 'new' facts. The famous Popperian test to establish whether a conclusion, or prediction, is scientific asserts that the prediction is not true if 'it can be falsified by experience'. In the case of economics, only strong predictions would come under Popper's falsification test. Since, in the case of a strong prediction 'that the predicted event will occur', the predicted event either does occur or it does not; the moment of potential falsification comes to pass (1984b, p. 215). At its time, a strong prediction will either be refuted or not. If the predicted event does occur, the prediction is deemed confirmed. Hicks found the whole notion of simple falsification somewhat absurd: 'a well-established theory based on many observations, cannot be falsified by a single experiment' (p. 216).

Weak predictions, Hicks stated, were completely outside being subject to test, by falsification, confirmation, or any other means. The most that can be said after whatever was found to happen is that disturbances sufficient to be disruptive to the predicted outcome either were or were not present. 'In neither case is it shown, at all directly, by the experience that the prediction was right or wrong' (1984b, p. 215). Neither result establishes that the reasons for the prediction were correctly or incorrectly assessed. Whatever the analysis for prediction, the situation remains 'subject to exogenous disturbances' (p. 217).

The assessment of the value of a prediction which is based upon a test, whether falsification, refutation or confirmation, has ramifications for the theory which produced the prediction. Hicks was extremely concerned about the implications of such tests. The first implication at issue was the assumption that a test sets the prediction, and thereby its theory, against fact. This assumption carries with it the separate assumption that the facts are the far more solid point of reference. Hicks could think of many respects in which facts might not be of adequate standard for comparison, and hence he objected strongly to Lipsey's assertion in his *An Introduction to Positive Economics*: 'We are told in the last sentence of the book, that "when theory and fact come into conflict it is theory, and not fact, that must give way". This is a dangerous proposition, particularly in economics' ([1965c] 1983a, p. 384).

'The choice of the right facts is as important a part of the testing process as any other' ([1965c] 1983a, p. 384). Defective or inappropriately chosen facts have no validity in the test of a theory, not to mention its rejection. Equally without bearing is the uninformed use of certain facts. Frequently, Hicks noted, 'the description of the facts should be improved, so that we may think about them more clearly' (1983a, p. 372). He pointed to a specific example: 'when, as occasionally happens, numerical "facts" are presented, no indication is given of the criticism, and elucidation, which needs to be performed on them, before they are used ([1965c] 1983a, p. 384).

Hicks went so far as to assert that not only is a theory 'not to be rejected because it has been tested against the wrong facts', but the test itself should be seen to be setting both theory and fact on an equal footing 'against' each another. When a test reveals a conflict between them, Hicks exclaimed, 'as Hume taught long ago, all that is shown by such a conflict is that *either* the theory *or* the fact is wrong' ([1965c] 1983a, p. 384). Hicks felt that 'a lack of conciliance between theory and fact in economics' was a result not so much of error, but of a lack of compatibility between the theory and the chosen facts. This lack of compatibility was for Hicks manifest in 'a lack of correspondence between the terms in which the theory runs and the terms in which the fact is described' ([1979d] 1983a, p. 372).

Hicks thought that a test could reveal a theory's need for improvement, although not for wholesale rejection. A theory might be able to be improved 'so as to run more closely in the terms in which the relevant facts are commonly described' ([1979d] 1983, p. 372). Or, it might be able to be reformulated and modified in such a way as to identify and integrate disturbances which, according to the low probability of a stochastic prediction, 'are not random, but in some way systematic' (1984b, p. 217).

As this chapter has tried to reveal, on the subject of economic causality Hicks had many ideas. As a historian of ideas, Hicks was never one to deny the ideas of his predecessors, but as an independent thinker, he did not rest with those ideas alone. Not surprisingly, not all of Hicks's ideas on causality have struck other economists and philosophers as immediately acceptable. For example, there were, and no doubt still are, readers who feel that he placed himself too much in league with Hume and too much with determinism.

For some readers, Hicks's 'new causality' was far too Humean. Hicks acknowledged his indebtedness to Hume, but denied that he had restricted himself to Hume's principle that cause necessarily precedes effect. That 'would amount to saying, in my terminology', Hicks noted, 'that sequential causality is the only form of causality' (1984a, p. 12). As described above, however, for Hicks sequential causality was, along with static and contemporaneous causality, but one of three forms of theoretical causality, all three of which, Hicks felt, had found or were finding strong representation in economics. Aside from his own determination to devise an economic theory to apply sequential causality, Hicks had detected the application of static causality in the economics of John Stuart Mill, and contemporaneous causality in the 'kind of reasoning of which Keynesian economics is a major example' (p. 12).

Perhaps because of his statement, 'with respect to the past, one can be fully deterministic', Hicks has been accused of being too deterministic. In his earliest discussions of determinism he had explained, however, the particular meaning he attributed to his statement: 'I put it by saying that "there are no events in the past that one may not *attempt* to explain"' (1984a, p. 12). While willing to count his approach as a kind of determinism, Hicks none the less considered it quite different from what is usually meant by the term, that one can explain the past, present and future, by certain knowable events which are the one and only ones to afford explanation. 'Mine is a *mild* determinism', he wrote 'theirs, by contrast, is *hard*' (p. 12).

Hicks saw a correspondence between his mild determinism and weak causation, and between hard determinism and strong causation. As noted earlier, he found little place for strong causation in economics. Little could be done, he felt, in the study of economics to permit the establishment of a theory of strong causation, 'save by excluding the possibility of anything being important which will not fit into one's model' (1984a, p. 14). As seen above, causal analysis of economics is, however, rarely adequate to establish models of such 'economic determinism', an exclusive connection between the importance of specific causes and specific effects. Economic analysis is, none the less, frequently sufficient in information and modelling to establish weak causation, whereby the situation is described as causally effected, primarily in the absence of serious disturbances. Such weak causal explanations, extrapolated from economic time-series, or records of a historical process (not of laboratory experimentation), can only be partial. Still, believing it better to have a partial explanation rather than none at all, Hicks supported the possibility of weak causation and mild determinism. While he recommended that 'we should be on our guard against claiming too much for them' (1984a, p. 14), to his mind they offered a liberating alternative to the strong causation and hard determinism so often identified with economics.

10

History

John Richard Hicks was fascinated by history. He had developed a passion for it in early childhood and this was fostered by his father's absorption in the subject. History was his favourite subject at school and in his library book reading. Hicks attributed his eventually becoming an economist to the circumstances and professional advice given to him during the difficult time of the 1920s, not to an initial devotion to the subject. If the choice had been entirely his own, Hicks would most likely have become a history scholar. For many of his years in academia, and perhaps for his entire life, he preferred the study of history to economics.

Indeed, Hicks's interest in history remained so strong throughout his life that even during the times when he was engaged in the most technical part of his theoretical work in economics, he kept in mind the historical perspective. His historical outlook was manifest in four principal forms: (1) the history of economic theory, (2) the theory of economic history, (3) economic history, and (4) general history. He emphasized the continuum, both of economic thought and of economic activity. As is already obvious from other chapters in this book, Hicks consistently saw his contribution as part of the historical continuum of economic thought and hence made frequent references to the work of his predecessors. He also gave much importance to the continuum of economic activity, in two ways. First, he believed in the possibility of establishing a theory of economic activity over time; second, he valued the data of economic activity from the past as relevant to model building and to projection for present and future circumstances. Underlying all of Hicks's specific applications of historical thinking to economics was his fundamental interest in the content and philosophy of general history.

History of economic theory

Hicks recognized the intellectual contributions of economists as part of history, as a historical sequence of ideas. In practically every area of economic theory he acknowledged his predecessors as well as his contemporaries. He valued the study of their historical sequence as worthwhile both for acquiring the fullest historical picture of a particular period and for understanding the evolution of the discipline of economics itself. To his mind, each of these two purposes for the study of 'the history of economic theory' derived from a distinct but equally valid objective approach. For the first purpose, the acquiring of the fullest historical picture of a particular period, the history of economic theory can be undertaken as the study of 'one element in the general *Weltanschauung*' of one or more periods 'when economists have played a significant part in the formation of public opinion' ([1943b] 1982a, p. 132). With the second purpose in mind, that of grasping the evolution of the discipline of economics itself, the history of economic theory 'can be studied for its own sake as the evolution of a technique, in the spirit of the historian of Greek mathematics or Renaissance painting' (p. 133).

For the most part Hicks as a historian of thought seemed to have played the role of the general ('normal') or specialized historian, providing the information about each economist's contribution as objectively as possible, without a distortive posture of *parti pris*. As the description of the intellectual relationship of Hicks and Keynes in chapter 8 reveals, however, Hicks seemed to have lost his ability to maintain scholarly distance when it came to the ideas of Keynes. What is more striking is that this occurred even when Hicks was aware of the pitfalls of a partisan history of economic thought, the most blatant offences being committed, he noted, in the history of monetary theory.

> The author, having himself developed strong views on the problem, turns to the work of his predecessors partly to fortify himself in his own views, partly to explain to himself how it has been possible for other people to come to hold views different from his. In this case the past is studied not for its own sake, but directly for the light it may be expected to throw upon present controversy. ([1943b] 1982a, p. 133)

As part of the same notion of a historical connectedness of economic ideas, Hicks observed that the work of the economist is a historical artefact, his or her perspective, a product of the time. He thought that the kind of economics which economists in a community contemplated at any one time was a result of their collective contemporaneous 'stage in the development of economics' (1969a, p. 9). Over time, as experience, observation of others, and purely theoretical advances teach the economists' community about other perspectives, a new stage develops within the discipline. In one example of the collective response, Hicks mentioned the labour theory of 'the "classical economists", Adam Smith and his followers'. Theirs was a long-period theory, a product of the Industrial Revolution. In another instance, Hicks wrote about the economists of the second quarter of the twentieth century: they 'were so wrapped up in market economics that they were unwilling to contemplate anything else – unwilling to grant that there was any other organization which could ever be a serious alternative'. Three factors caused them to learn to take the alternative of the non-market economy quite seriously: 'the experience of war-time', 'observation of what was happening in "centrally planned economics"' and 'some purely theoretical developments (in Welfare Economics and Linear Programming)' (1969a, p. 9).

In an example of the individual as product of his time, Hicks identified Keynes and his ideas about the situation whereby the state can always borrow from its own banking system and the banks can always create money to finance their loans. To Hicks's mind, Keynes was so steeped in his own era that he had sometimes given the impression that this important and fairly new economic power arrangement 'had always existed' (1969a, p. 97). He had spoken of it as if it were 'in the nature of things' or a product of ages past, 'as in his rhetorical passages about pyramids – and medieval cathedrals' (p. 97, n. 1). Hicks felt it necessary to remind his readers that the situation 'had not existed for so very long', but was 'a consequence of the development of modern banking'. By being caught up in his own time, Keynes, Hicks felt, had missed his calling 'to urge that it [the power relation of state and banks] should be taken up' (1969a, pp. 96–7).

The theory of economic history

To Hicks's mind, the treatment of history according to economic theory was a feasible and extremely interesting endeavour. As the title of his 1969 study revealed, he thought of it as providing a theory of economic history. Hicks's comments in the study specifically about the city state could be taken generally to express his understanding of the relationship between history and theory:

> When the city state is considered as a political organization, it has a history ... and it has a theory ... When it is considered as an economic organization, it has a corresponding history; and in that aspect also it is so distinctive a history that we might expect it to deserve something of a theory to correspond. (1969a, p. 42)

In the opening of his book he explained his methodological approach. A theory of economic history derives from taking from economics those general ideas which can be applied to history. Although Hicks was far from specific about what he meant by 'general ideas', his work, *A Theory of Economic History*, reveals that among them he counted the general methodology of economics, as well as some of its specific deductive propositions, some economic principles and whole economic models. The fact that this collection of 'general ideas' about economic activity had been generated within the discipline of economics meant, for Hicks, that economics was able to provide 'extra-historical support' for the observation and explanation of patterns in history (1969a, p. 2).

The general methodology of economics held great sway over Hicks's interpretation of a theory of history. From the perspective of an economist, only phenomena which ultimately conform to a notion of statistical uniformity are of interest; the economic event must be considered in light of the aspects by which it is a member of a group. The economic theorist's attention is thus transfixed on the group. As Hicks put it, what economic theorists try to explain is 'the average, or norm, of the group ... We shall be able to allow that the individual may diverge from the norm without being deterred from the recognition of a statistical uniformity' (1969a, p. 3). As will be discussed below, Hicks thought this aspect of economic methodology quite suitable for history.

Extrapolation from the micro-economic particular to the macro-economic general is a methodological tool Hicks also applied to historical situations. For example, the firm is taken to be analogous to the whole economic system. Offering the instances of the customary economy and the command economy as 'extreme types', Hicks noted, 'it is entirely possible ... to be something in between ... The case is the same as that in the firm, with which we began; some "belowness" as well as some "aboveness" is bound in the end to be a necessary part of its organization' (1969a, p. 15).

In his theoretical analysis of the history of economic activity Hicks sought to apply concepts widely used in economics. They are frequently glossed to make their historical use both clear and more acceptable. For example, the reader is told about 'equilibrium', that it implies 'a regular income' (1969a, p. 16–17), or, that an equilibrium can 'sustain violent shocks' and 'restore itself after the shock to very much what it was before' (p. 20). Another economic concept, income, 'is quite sophisticated', Hicks told his reader of history (p. 83). First, one of its definitions, the one which reflects the ascertaining of 'income' and thus determines how an income tax is levied, changes from time to time. Second, this pragmatic definition has no more 'than a very rough relation to the theoretical ideal' (p. 83n.).

About money, there was much to be explained. Hicks wrote that he did not emphasize that the mercantile economy is money-using in his initial description of it, since 'I wanted to go, in the usual economist's manner, "behind the veil of money"' (1969a, p. 63) – to its tri-partite functions of unit of account or standard of value, store of value, and medium of exchange or means of payment, perhaps. In his discussion of currency reform, for example, Hicks noted that reform itself 'implies a recognition that the money which is unit of account (in which debts are expressed) is sometimes different from the physical coinage' (p. 92). It is clear from his comments, such as 'the needs for a standard of value must often have arisen, even in pure barter transactions' where no money was available or 'bronze coins, unquestionably token coins, pure means of payment . . . must have circulated', that Hicks considered two of the tri-partite functions of money to have been present in the earliest days of its use in the West. He identified the presence of the store-of-value function as the marker for Greek society's having 'a fully monetized economy' (pp. 64, 67). This is in contradistinction to money's functional evolution in the monetary system of China: 'Chinese money passed straight into being a means of payment' (p. 68n.).

Hicks's deductive notion of the meaning of time in the context of economics was also extremely influential in his analysis of history. For him, once time entered the equation, the focus of the study had to be on the absence or presence of change. He frequently asserted its absence or presence intuitively. For example, on the absence of change in the primitive form of market exchanges, he wrote, 'it is entirely possible for trading to continue for long ages in nothing more than this simple manner'. At the same time, for many components of an economic system, Hicks felt change was inevitable and was quite convinced that change would mean growth. For example, an organization 'has to grow, being based at every moment on what has gone before' (1969a, p. 11).

Economic principles also provided a ready source of general ideas about economics which would prove useful to Hicks in their application to history. In his discussion of the mercantile economy, Hicks introduced the idea that 'it is only by constant improvements in organization . . . that the tendency of the profit rate to fall can be offset' (1969a, p. 56).

As shall also be seen in the case of economic theories below, Hicks was alive to the fact that the application of such principles should not be done needlessly. He found, for instance, the well-known economic principle, 'taxes on trade are obstacles to trade', to be highly unenlightening when trying to assess custom duties and taxes as limitations to trade. 'What is historically of greater importance is that duties on trade can only be collected cheaply and efficiently if there is a large volume of trade that passes, and can be relied on to pass, a few specified points at which tax will be paid' (p. 82).

Hicks's discussion of trade expansion and 'imperfect foresight' provides a further example of the need for care in the application of economic principles. Since under the principle of perfect foresight, there are no losses and wastes, it would not at first appear to be unreasonable to state that 'the losses, and wastes, which result from the opening up of sources of supply that in the end are not wanted, are consequences of "imperfect foresight"'. In such a case, however, he noted that while the principle and its corollary are true, they are not helpful, 'for the [trade] expansion itself is a matter of imperfect foresight; it is a process of finding out, and finding out implies mistakes'. A much more helpful economic principle in this case would be the one which asserts that 'in any expansionary endeavour, merely as a matter of distribution on the large scale, gains are dominant over losses'. In contrast to the former economic principle, this is, Hicks argued, a much more appropriate one for the historical situation where 'it is more to the point to emphasize that . . . there are gains as well as losses . . . [which] accrue to different people'. Although advantage inevitably accrues to the group as a whole, 'we cannot easily set one [person] against the other'. According to Hicks, Greek trade expansion is such a case, for in that instance, 'there is a sense, which is recognizable when we look at the matter from a distance . . . in which the gains must be dominant' (1969a, p. 55).

Another important source of 'extra-historical support' for understanding history was economic models. In the context of sketching out a model of the city state, Hicks partially explained the purpose of a model to pure economic theory. According to him, some models are used by economists 'to elucidate the working of economic institutions'. 'We do not suppose, when we use such a model, that it is describing what actually happens, or has happened, in any particular case. It is a "representative" case, from which particular instances must be expected to diverge, for particular reasons, (1969a, p. 42). Many textbook models are obvious examples of this.

Hicks felt it was also important to think of models as representative in a non-theoretical sense, since it is very often the standard aspects of a particular situation which are its essence and can be captured in a model. It strengthens a theory, in its model, if it can be 'used for the interpretation of a particular set of historical data'. It puts the model, he thought, 'into a different class from many of our theoretical models' (1977a, p. 125). Not all textbook models are, however, of that 'different class', applicable to historical situations. One reason may be that they are 'modern models' whose theories arise out of modern experience which may not be appropriately applied.

There were, however, other reasons as well why models might not be applicable to history. Hicks suggested, for example, that the following model might not be suitable:

> If the wants of society formed a single self-consistent system (such as could be expressed in an indifference map or in a 'Social Welfare Function'), and if all the decisions about provisions to meet those wants were taken by a single decider, it would only be necessary that the single decider should take the 'right' decisions, and the Social Optimum would be attained. (1969a, p. 10)

While Hicks considered this model might have a useful place in pure economic theory, its drawback for an application to history is that the concept of social organization embedded in it is 'not really an organization at all' (1969a, p. 10). Another model which Hicks felt could not be adopted lock, stock and barrel for historical purposes was the competitive model of the stationary equilibrium. In the case of the mercantile economy, for example, cessation of expansion does not mean the settling into an equilibrium, the way it would according to the model of equilibrium theory.

Much better examples of applicable models are those of the nineteenth-century Gold Standard, of the supply–demand, investment–demand, and employment–wage relations, of maintenance–investment and profit–saving ratios, and even the model of demand theory. For the model of supply and demand there are many scenarios. One Hicks identified for historical application correlated growth in trade with an increased demand for labour. An increase in the demand for labour beyond that for which the supply can provide will, also according to the standard employment–wage relation model, cause an increase in wages, since competition for labour causes a rise in wages. 'With sufficient expansion labour abundance should give place to labour scarcity' (1969a, p. 137). The employment model reveals that a ban on movement or the imposition of maximum wages, 'though it was tried in the historical case [of mid-fourteenth-century England]', is relatively ineffective, or at least is without much success in increasing labour supply (p. 11). Only an increase in supply, 'from rising population or accelerated influx from [or to] the "country"' will alleviate the demand, and hence wage, pressure (p. 137). When an increasing mobile population is coupled with the integration of labour-saving inventions, a veritable absence of labour shortage can be explained, as can the 'failure of real wages to rise (or to rise at all considerably)' (1969a, p. 153).

Models which focused on investment could also be historically pertinent. One model considered the forces at work to determine 'the effect of the new opportunities for fixed capital investment on the demand for labour' (1969a, p. 149). It went as follows: 'a strong switch to fixed capital' investment may cause a rise in 'the growth rate of the whole capital stock'; meanwhile the growth rate of the circulating capital stock will fall. The investment in fixed capital inventions, which may be labour-saving, 'not only with respect to the labour most immediately affected, but over the economy as a whole', will initially slow expansion in the demand for labour (p. 152). A time will come, however, 'when the adverse effect [on labour] of the swing to fixed capital would be exhausted', and a 'favourable effect of the higher growth rate would alone survive' (p. 153). Hicks felt that, in brief, there were 'outstanding (and very well authenticated)' historical examples of the first phase of the model, among them what happened in England 'during the first quarter or even first third of the nineteenth century' (pp. 152–3).

Another investment model was the maintenance–investment ratio model, according to which the more cheap and easily obtainable the commodities, the more 'it will pay to keep the sums invested in their maintenance to a minimum'. It is thus to the advantage of the self-preservation of the commodity, that the commodity be hard to acquire and that the amount spent on its maintenance 'should be as large as possible' (1969a, p. 127). Hicks found this model at least hypothetically applicable to the instance of both late Roman and seventeenth-century English slaves. The profit-saving model is the following: given that 'profits are the main source of saving', the higher the profits the more the saving. Hicks spoke of the model as an easy fit to much of history; it is an assumption, 'valid enough in many times and places, and surely valid for industrial revolution England' (p. 150).

As for the theory of consumer demand, as Hicks saw it, it is a theoretical construct which implies no determinism or universality. It can be applied to the actual activity of human beings throughout history. Indeed, it is well suited to do so, for it concerns itself with the 'statistical' behaviour of the consumers in question. Hicks stressed, however, that 'we make no question that each of the consumers, as an individual, is perfectly free to choose' (1969a, p. 34).

Each of these models is suitable as it represents a case in which both generalization and deviation have a historical significance. The generalization is not historically misrepresentative, nor the deviation irrelevant. If a deviation from the model is found to exist, the question 'why?' which the model brings forth will be interesting and pertinent to answer.

Hicks made a distinction between two levels of analysis of historical situations. They differed in their degree of abstraction or distance from the time specificity of the event. The least abstract was a generalized illustration of a time-specific instance. Of a ruler's gain at the expense of his subjects, Hicks wrote, 'an even more sinister example . . . is to be found in the way the expansion of a slave trade encourages slave raiding, as we know that it did among the tribal communities of West Africa in the seventeenth and eighteenth centuries' (1969a, p. 44, n. 2). Far more abstract was the construct of 'the simple or simplest case', composed 'in the regular tradition of model-builders', as, for example, 'our simple corn-oil trade (which is no more than an example)' (p. 44). Despite Hicks's commitment to using virtually all aspects of economics to build up economic historical theory, he was well aware that he was not writing solely for an audience of economists. He therefore avoided excessive technical language in descriptions and relegated such sections to footnotes (as on p. 44).

In addition to his inspiration from pure economics, Hicks drew upon the theoretical conclusions or assertions from numerous other disciplines to provide 'extra-historical support'. As he explained in his conclusion to *A Theory of Economic History*, he wanted "to indicate the lines that connect the economic story with the things we ordinarily regard as falling outside it'. He wrote, 'There are threads that run from economics into other social fields, into politics, into religion, into science and into technology; they develop there, and then run back into economics.' He realized that being conscious of such links was not enough, but he also knew the limitations on his time and space for writing about them and made little attempt to follow them out. None the less, he was 'in no way concerned to deny their existence' – quite the opposite (1969a, p. 167). Thus it is that political theory and law, sociology and anthropology all figure prominently in Hicks's theory of economic history.

Political theory infused Hicks's body of extra-historical support. He incorporated such premises as 'it is only in the emergency that a wide range of orders from the [organization's command] centre will be accepted', and made the following 'inductive' extrapolation:

> In the emergency the community has to become, to all intents and purposes, an army; but the time will come when the army has to be transformed into an instrument of civil government. This (many instances confirm) is a very difficult stage; it may happen that the empire fails to pass it, so that the central power, save perhaps in nominal terms, just disappears. (1969a, pp. 15–6)

Hicks did not find in political theory any justification for seeking economic strength in any particular political system. To his mind, it was not necessarily pertinent to economic theory to distinguish between 'the ways in which those who rule are selected, or select themselves' (1969a, p. 99). Economics, theoretical or practical, does 'not have much to do with the generation of the power itself', Hicks felt. Continuity of power, however, is important, 'but if continuity is achieved, it does not matter [to economics] how it is achieved' (pp. 99–100). As far as Hicks was concerned, political systems are of concern only in terms of the power they possess and use. If a government does not possess a power, it goes without saying that it cannot use it. If, however, a government has a power, it may for ideological or other reasons prefer not to use it, which may or may not have an economic impact.

Within the domain of law Hicks also found extra-historical support for his theory of economic history. He referred particularly to Herbert Hart's *Concept of Law* (1961) as a useful guide for clearing the mind. Hicks posited the need for the existence of specific legal structures as prerequisites for other kinds of societal organization. For the lord-and-peasant system to develop, for example, Hicks observed, 'the boundary itself [between the two groups] must first be established; some form of jurisdiction is needed to establish it' (1969a, p. 103). 'I do not think', he wrote in another instance, 'that the legal systems of Eastern Asia, before the Western impact, ever accommodated themselves at all easily to the needs of the merchant' (p. 37). Legal (or at least quasi-legal) institutions, he noted, could provide a means of settling disputes, an essential support before economic contracts could be recognized as reliable (p. 35).

Definitions from the realm of sociology also form part of Hicks's extra-historical support. On the subject of equilibrium he wrote, 'an organization whose rules are not accepted can hardly be in equilibrium' (1969a, p. 12). Or, a system in equilibrium continues 'without the need for new decisions of an organizational character' (p. 13). On the ancient cities he asserted that they must 'be regarded, in the first place, as extended royal households, inhabited by the servants of the King, and the servants of those servants, and the servants of these, to many degrees' (p. 32).

Anthropology also offered Hicks a source of extra-historical support. On the subject of gifts, he wrote,

> There will be occasions, such as weddings, at which it is proper to give presents; and if presents are given one way, it is necessary for the preservation of dignity that they should be given in the other. The presents must be suitable, but there is no need for them to be in any recognizable sense equivalent. The wide dispersion, over areas inhabited by primitive peoples, of certain articles considered suitable for gifts . . . needs no more than this to explain it. (1969a, pp. 25–6)

> Any great King will be receiving embassies from neighbouring chieftains . . . They will bring presents which he will receive as tribute; but it will be beneath his dignity not to give presents in return . . . The steward who is employed upon this task [of bringing presents] is already performing, by order, some of the functions of a merchant. (1969a, pp. 29–30)

Even archaeology receives honorable mention by Hicks. He considered it an indispensable resource in confirming the expansion of trade *c.*750–550 BC: 'from that early period we have little that is relevant in the way of literary sources, though archaeology makes the fact of the expansion incontestable' (1969a, p. 40). In his opinion, archaeology served not only as a source of extra-historical support for his economic history theory but also as a reinforcement of the economic theories of others. On the subject of money, Hicks wrote that the Austrian economist Carl Menger had perceived 'on purely theoretical grounds' that 'in its origin, money was a creation of the Mercantile Economy'. He had assessed it as the first of the states' creations which governments 'learned to take over'. By way of supporting comment he noted, 'what Menger perceived theoretically has been abundantly verified by the archaeologists' (p. 63).

Hicks's predominant source of theoretical support for his analysis was economics. He was, however, well aware that not all aspects of history, or of the past, could be enlightened through economics. In the historical context, he took 'economic' in a narrow sense, so the subject matter in question had to have a relatively close connection to economic activity. A nation, for example, although it is first and foremost a political unit, was deemed a worthy subject since, 'as a consequence of its political unity . . . it becomes an economic unit' (1959a, p. 162).

Hicks considered many subjects, however, excessively tangential to his theory of economic history. The violent end of a city-state system might, for example, be deemed to have occurred 'for external reasons' (1969a, p. 60). Consistently he excluded technology, as being a non-economic subject. While he affirmed that money and the law of the merchant were 'the two great economic legacies of the "ancient world"', he considered technological legacies as beyond economic influence (p. 71). Nor was technology the 'economic answer' Hicks sought when he asked what essential mark distinguished modern industry from the ancient handicraft industry (p. 141).

The type of historical data pertinent to historical economic theory was also of concern. In general, Hicks considered his task, of applying theory to facts of the past, to be that of explaining what has happened (1979g, p. 63). For the purposes of treating history according to economic theory, a distinction must, however, be made between those questions which can usefully be discussed in terms of the notion of statistical uniformity and those which cannot. It is the economist's belief in the existence of evidence for 'statistical' behaviour in the past that led Hicks and others to pursue the application of economic theory to history at all. Hicks believed that pertinent historical data, that is data having a statistical character, can be derived from many historical phenomena, if only 'in the light of our interest in them' (1969a, p. 4). Those which cannot be so derived must be disregarded, as instances 'which from our point of view are mere chance' (p. 60). The ready availability of pertinent data to economic analysis made Hicks assert that there is no distinction in the principles behind economic and any other kind of theory of history. Instead, 'the distinction is between an interest in general phenomena and an interest in particular stories' (p. 4). If he asked, 'every statistical time-series can be analysed, by purely mechanical methods, into trend and cycle', why not the economic history of the world? (p. 7).

A theory of the history of general economic phenomena which Hicks undertook was, as he saw it, a theoretical enquiry, which would 'proceed in general terms' to classify 'economic states of society'. His purpose was to discover intelligible reasons for change, the chain of causation for why one state should give way to another (1969a, p. 6). He endeavoured to ground his reasons for change on suppositions both less deterministic and less evolutionary than those of Marx or the German historical school. While his focus was on 'normal' economic development, Hicks did not excuse himself from trying to explain exceptions to that normalcy. A particular economic developmental process might well be seen to have been cut off from its earlier external causes or to have encountered internal difficulties.

Hicks classified and discussed three different possible economic states of society. One was the market state in which a system of an exchange economy is in evidence. He defined what is meant by 'exchange' and 'market' and endeavoured to see what logically followed from the definitions. Another state was the non-market economy, of which he identified four different types: customary economy, command economy, feudalism (mixed customary and command economy), and classical bureaucracy. The common feature of all types of non-market economies is, Hicks noted, that 'their central economic nexus is revenue: the tax, or tribute, or land rent (for in the absence of a market, these are not distinguished) which is paid by the peasant or cultivator, the producer of food, to some recognized authority' (1969a, p. 22). The third state Hicks identified was the state of industrialism, which he saw as a reaction against the pure exchange economy of the market. In this state, the range and variety of fixed capital goods in which investment is embodied, and most importantly which are used 'in production, otherwise than in trade' is noticeably greater than in any other state (1969a, p. 143).

It is interesting to note that Hicks identified 'feudalism' as a non-market economy. He shied away from extensive use of the term, especially to describe the lord and peasant system of an agricultural economy. 'We need something more general, and more specifically agricultural, than "Feudalism"', he wrote, something that is, however, 'readily extensible, when required'. He rejected 'Seignorial system', a term of Marc Bloch, the famous medieval historian, as being 'too suggestive of the particular form of the system that was prevalent in the Middle Ages in Western Europe' (1969a, p. 101n.). With the emphasis on the 'lord and peasant' relationship, in which the lord as 'protecting power' enforces his decisions, Hicks hoped to distinguish that system from the mercantile system of intertwined rights and responsibilities.

In addition to the descriptive economic states, the actual theoretical structure of Hicks's theory of economic history was composed of four evolutionary phases of progressive economic change. His aim was 'to exhibit economic history, in the way that the great eighteenth-century writers did, as part of a social evolution much more widely considered' (1969a, p. 167). For only the last phase or transformation did Hicks offer any precision of dates. The city-state system, a market exchange economy state, was the first phase. In its context Hicks discussed the historical evolution of specialization, trade and stock-holding, as well as legal steps toward mercantile organization, contracts and protection of property.

The second, or 'middle' phase, as Hicks called it, was that of mercantile development. Hicks described this phase as the situation in which, in addition to the honed market sector, 'the formerly non-mercantile environment is open, in a variety of ways, to penetration by the market' (1969a, p. 62). The mercantile system has been, Hicks noted, 'a standard form of economic organization over a great part of recorded history' in which 'trading centres survive, under the protection – the somewhat fitful protection – of a [king or emperor's] State that is no more than semi-mercantilized' (p. 61). Hicks characterized middle-phase governments as finding it difficult 'to raise the revenue that they required' (p. 85). Their 'tax-base' was usually narrow; however inevitable, their collection was inefficient.

The third phase was the Industrial Revolution. Hicks identified it as the turning point to emphasis on fixed capital investment on an increasingly larger and cheaper scale. There were, however, numerous steps to this phase, and it was only when all the steps had played their part that one could speak of a revolution.

> The impact of science, stimulating the technicians, developing new sources of power, using power to create more than human accuracy, reducing the cost of machines until they were available for a multitude of purposes; this surely is the essential novelty, the essential revolution, working so vast a transformation because it can be repeated, one might almost say it repeats itself over and over again. (1969a, p. 148)

The fourth phase was the administrative revolution in government. Hicks dated the beginning of this phase quite precisely to the First World War.

Hicks was convinced that the history of economics is, in large part, the history of people no less than is general history. One of the historical aspects of the four phases which especially interested him was therefore the human disposition of a whole culture, or part of it, at any particular time to aspects of its economic side. For example, as was noted above, he felt that before western influence in eastern Asia the legal systems had not accommodated themselves easily to merchants' needs. He took as an indication of this 'the drastic reform of their legal system which the Japanese were obliged to undertake, as part of the modernization which followed the Mejii revolution'. By the seventeenth century, however, the merchants of Osaka were able 'to proceed to the most sophisticated mercantile dealings, such as the establishment of futures markets' (1969a, p. 37).

In western culture too, however, Hicks also found instances of non-economic, if not anti-economic, attitudes. The early official theological doctrine of the Christian Church on interest or usury reflected the crystallized perspective of the non-merchant. He found it an attitude 'very understandable in mundane terms' and 'perfectly intelligible' as Church policy, noting it as 'just another example of the clash, which we have so often encountered, between the viewpoints of the merchant and of the non-merchant' (1969a, pp. 72–3). He saw, however, in 'the appearance of banking, as a regular activity . . . an indication that the bar against interest, at least in appropriate fields' had broken down during 'the sixty or seventy years that centre on 1300' (p. 78).

In western attitudes toward money, especially minted coinage, there were also appreciable differences. Most of these were to do with the confidence of one group in the money issued by another. By the second economic phase, not only did the very creation of a minted coinage by a monetary authority have to be acknowledged, but the individual coins had to pass the scrutiny of a new group, 'professional dealers who had a sharp eye for currency manipulation' (1969a, p. 90). Abuses in the issuance of money compounded the wariness in its function. Monarchs became notorious for having currency reforms, admitting debasement, changing 'the debased coins, at a reduced value, into a more full-bodied money' and then insisting 'that it is in terms of this reformed money that the taxes are to be paid' (p. 91). While a monarch might emerge unscathed for a single early currency reform by blaming his or her predecessors for the necessity, so unwelcome would the public find any other reform that he or she would be anxious to avoid one.

The loaning and investing of money was another area of economics in which the receptivity of one group within a single society to a project or to another group was a crucial ingredient. Even with the existence of a legal structure of debt contracts, institutions as large as governments had periodic difficulty assuring their credibility as reputable borrowers. The credibility of a government's repayment of a loan depended in part 'upon the prospect of faith being kept over a long period of time, extending into decades'. Hicks noted that, 'it can be appreciated that there would be governments which had need to borrow, but were unable to offer a high probability of such continuity' (1969a, p. 93). However, laws which required a government to honour the debts of its predecessors, for example those introduced in France, in 1715, and borrowing on 'annuity' were two steps towards increasing lender confidence.

Investment of capital in production also requires a certain degree of confidence. Individuals

> must either themselves be in possession of other resources, which they hold in a more liquid form, so that they can be quickly realized to meet emergencies; or they must be confident of being able to borrow – and that means borrowing from someone else (it may be a bank) who is able to borrow, or who has liquid funds. (1969a, p. 144)

It all comes down to the availability of liquid funds which Hicks felt was a condition not satisfied in England, France and Holland before 'the first half of the eighteenth century' (1969a, p. 145).

It is within the overall fusion of Hicks's choice of economic theoretical support and historical data that both the tension and the brilliance of his theory of economic history lie. Of some of the pitfalls of such a fusion Hicks was well aware. The misapplication of a theory to a particular historical situation was an important one. His sensitivity was well honed through the 'classical misapplication of Ricardian rent theory' in which 'it is by no means the case that in the settlement of a new country the best land will be the first to be occupied' (1969a, p. 47). Hicks detected a very similar point in the situation of trade: it is

> by no means necessary that the first of the opportunities for trading to be opened up should be those which prove to be most profitable; there may be more profitable opportunities from going further afield which will not be discovered until the nearer opportunities have been explored. (1969a, p. 47)

Hicks also recognized that the time-scale of phenomena was critically important to generalizations. He compared, for example, the US dollar with the 'great' currencies of the middle phase,

> that proud sequence which begins with the solidus of Constantine, continues with the nomisma of the Byzantines, the dinar and dirhem of the Arabs, the florin of Florence, the ducat of Venice, leading on to the gulden of Holland and the pound sterling – currencies which maintained their value for centuries, sometimes many centuries, on end. (1969a, p. 89)

He concluded in a note that 'on such a time-scale as this the US dollar hardly counts' (1969a, p. 89n.).

Hicks's most important confession, which is not pronounced until the conclusion of *A Theory of Economic History*, pertains to his predominant emphasis of theory over historical data, the major weakness of the book.

> I am very prepared to believe that many of the examples I have chosen would not stand up to closer examination . . . On that principle, I should not be much disturbed if in a particular instance the reason for a change turned out to be different from that which I alleged. A particular bank, for instance, may have come up in a different way from that which I sketched, but that does not matter; my business has been with the general way in which banks (and all the rest) have come up. So interpreted, I am hopeful that what I have been saying makes some sense. (1969a, p. 167)

Hicks echoed this aloof posture again in 1977 when he reflected on Hawtrey's use of historical data. He felt that Hawtrey's emphasis on the historical 'in the exposition of the theory' was actually unfortunate; 'it distracted attention from its *general* significance' (1977a, p. 125). Hicks own implementation of the fusion of theory and historical data never left him open to criticism of that kind. He never failed to emphasize theory over historical data. For this very reason, however, his approach was faulted in two distinct respects: the exposition of the theory at the expense of a historical perspective, and the construction of grandiose generalizations and characterizations from relatively little concrete documentation.

Historical data frequently appear at the mercy of Hicks's theoretical construct. He seems to have felt comfortable integrating or abandoning historical data 'as needed'. At the opening of chapter 4 of *A Theory of Economic History* for example, Hicks acknowledged that 'the pure theory of commercial development' had in fact been the subject of the preceding chapter. At the same time he reminded the reader of his two 'leading examples, the Greek expansion and the Mediæval Italian expansion'. These introductory comments are all by way of explaining that, while in his discussion of pure theory he was able to 'concentrate upon elements that are common to different expansions' and thus to run the two examples 'in double harness', when it came to his description of the second phase of economic development, further collective study of the two examples would 'hardly work' and would 'not get us very far' (1969a, p. 62). Hicks elaborated further on, that in the case of the two examples in the later phase, history did not simply repeat itself; the experience behind the medieval Italian circumstance, the Roman heritage, gave it an advantage in money-usage and law. 'There was part of the work that was needed that did not have to be done again'; unlike the Greek city-state, the medieval Italian republics 'did not have to start from scratch' (p. 71).

Examples also abound of broad generalizations and characterizations which left Hicks open to criticism for their relatively little concrete documentation. Of note is the extent to which their content is presented quite free of direct 'extra-historical' theoretical support and thus the degree to which they must be evaluated by historical documentation and according to the rigours of purely historical arguments. One example should suffice.

Early on in *A Theory of Economic History* Hicks offers a very concise description of the characteristics of the employment of the earliest civil servants. Their most essential function is the collection of revenue, and to that end they are first 'employed to keep watch, or check, on other servants' through methods which evolved from mere spying, to observation according to rule, to 'the audit system of modern bureaucracies'. Second, there occurs 'a division of function between military and civil officers, so that (in particular) the collection of revenue is taken out of the hands of the military'. A third characteristic of the employment of civil servants is that it becomes regulated through both 'a system of promotion – or just moving-around – which prevents particular individuals from acquiring the independence which almost necessarily follows from long-continued exercise of the same office' and 'a system of recruitment, by which the bureaucracy is continually refreshed by new entrants, deliberately selected for suitable qualities, so that it does not settle down into an inherited caste' (1969a, p. 19).

By way of framework, Hicks offered no particular methodological or theoretical 'extra-historical support' for his general observations about the earliest employment of civil servants. Further, while he cited some interesting sources as documentation, only one is a primary source and none is adequately detailed to allow for scrutiny of the evidence. Hicks cited the biography of Weni of sixth dynasty Egypt (about 2300 BC), identifying it as 'the oldest biography of a civil servant'. He interpreted it to reveal 'that there already existed a system of promotion, and a system of recruitment' (1969a, p. 19). Subsequent supporting historical observations, albeit from Egypt, China, Peru, and Japan, are backed by secondary sources only.

Sometimes the tenuousness Hicks himself recognized between his theoretical constructs and his historical data placed doubt on the link he had made between the two. As a theoretical scenario for the competitive expansion of trade, Hicks wrote about the time when the first impediments to the growth of a trade centre are recognized: 'the competition of the others, which had formerly been tolerated, is now a danger ... it is at this point, when the growth of their trade begins to be constricted, that the formidable struggles between them are likely to break out'. To the reader's surprise, the historical instances Hicks offered of this theory are extremely tentatively presented: 'Such, we may reasonably suppose, was the long war between Venice and Genoa . . . and it is hard to avoid the suspicion that the Peloponnesian War, which began as a struggle between Athens and Corinth, is . . . another example' (1969a, p. 57). Hesitation is also apparent in the way Hicks' gave the Hansa as an example of the long decline of a city-state system (p. 60). Here is yet another example:

> when the time comes for a military monarch, fortified by the reflection of the expansion of the Mercantile Economy, to have overcome his local enemies, the defense of the trading states, which had in the past been sufficient, is likely to fail. That is how it seems to work out in the cases I have taken as my principal examples. The Greeks become subjects (or subject-allies) of Macedonian monarchs; the Italian republics fall a prey to France and Spain. (1969a, p. 61)

To his question, 'should we not expect that merchants, as well as kings, would be stamping their "coins"?', Hicks replied that 'it would not be surprising if some of them sometimes did' (1969a, p. 66). Evidence that they did so is offered only tentatively, in a footnote: 'there may indeed be some evidence that they did . . .' (p. 66n.).

Most often Hicks did offer some form of evidence for his arguments, and his historical sources were extremely eclectic. They run the gamut from city wall plaques of Urbino, Egyptian monuments, the Bible, Greek poetry, law and history, Roman law, and English legal statutes, to portolan maps, perspective painting, monastic transaction records, the poetry of Arnold, Dante's *Divine Comedy*, legends, and the correspondence of Voltaire, Gay and Swift.

In addition, Hicks used modern-day conditions for comparison with the past: the presence side by side of the shops of pure traders and the workshops of artisans seen by him in the market of Isfahan, the phenomenon of the government city exemplified in the Canberra of today, contemporary losses and wastes which result from the opening up of sources of supply, and a modern-day trade advantage. On the subject of labour demand in the pre-industrial conditions of Europe, Hicks noted that the relationship between supply and demand did not follow the standard economic model. He reasoned that 'part of the explanation must be that the expansion that occurred was so limited and so localized. The agricultural sector of the economy was so vast; the opportunities for commercial employment, even when rising, were still so small.' Turning to modern-day conditions, Hicks observed, 'we are acquainted with this kind of situation in the development of "underdeveloped" countries in our own day; there can be little doubt that the analogy holds' (1969a, pp. 137–8). On the financial system of today and earlier, Hicks observed that in our time 'the control of the State over the money supply, which for long ages was so imperfect, has become complete'. This is due to the fact that most recently the banking system provides 'the channel of money creation' (1969a, p. 96).

Hicks used his comparisons of the present to the past frequently to provoke questions about historical evolution. For example, in contemplating the impact of technical changes, Hicks observed that 'the technical innovations of our day have aggravated the problems of depressed groups and depressed areas; but there is no reason why they should not have appeared, long ago, in consequence of a trade expansion which was purely geographical' (1969a, p. 55). Such comparisons could even be telling within the past. Looking back from the time of the Industrial Revolution to the fifteenth century, Hicks wondered, 'would it have been impossible, if capital could have been raised (and it may be that even that would not have been a major difficulty), and if the regular water power of Lancashire had been available, for something very like it [Industrial Revolution] to have occurred (say) in fifteenth-century Florence?' (p. 148).

Periodically Hicks offered justification for the kinds of sources he employed. In the case of his using Homer's *Odyssey* as counter-evidence to the affirmations of ancient historians about the involvement in trade of the ruling classes of the Greek city-states, Hicks wrote,

> Mentes, of course, is a fictitious character, a fiction within a fiction. But this strengthens my contention. The story he tells would be pointless unless it was plausible, unless it was the kind of thing which the poet's hearers would accept without saying to themselves 'how odd'. (1969a, p. 40n.)

As supporting evidence for his assertion that 'the expansion of trade had been an intellectual stimulus', Hicks acknowledged that 'the forms of this stimulus are often quite obscure, but the fact can hardly be doubted'. He conjectured, 'Could Herodotus' have written his history save by drawing on the knowledge of the East that had been accumulated by the traders? (1969a, p. 58).

In the opening chapter of *A Theory of Economic History* on the rise of the market system, Hicks actually provided some general observations about the sources of information available to the historical economic theorist. In three points he gave some of his historiographic justification for the use of certain past and modern-day data. He acknowledged that in many instances the historical transformation of a particular economic activity into a recognizable new form was slow and gradual. First, in such a case, it may be that it is only information from specific stages, perhaps the later ones, when the increments of change were distinct enough to be detectable, which is of solid research value. Second, the transformation in question may not have been one which necessarily occurred once and for all; data and anthropological information is thus frequently provided in the examples of societies which have 'slipped back' from their transformed state. Third, some underdeveloped countries might still be undergoing the transformation of interest and might serve therefore as 'observation laboratories' for the historical question.

Hicks did acknowledge the expertise of historians among the sources he employed. In an almost puckish way he would hark back to his schoolboy history lessons: 'if there is one thing' about kings and emperors 'which we seem to learn from the history books, it is that more often than not they were hard up' (1969a, p. 81). In a more serious manner, to exemplify his assertion that 'local production, in a community that was already oriented towards trade, would easily grow, if the land were suitable, into production for export', Hicks turned to the case of 'the very early (seventh to sixth centuries BC) export of wheat from the Greek colonies in Sicily' (pp. 53–4). Hicks cited T. J. Dunbabin, *The Western Greeks* (1948), especially chapters 1 and 7, which, he acknowledged, 'gives a graphic reconstruction of the stages in the economic evolution of the Greek colonies in Sicily and Italy: a reconstruction which to the economist is very acceptable indeed' (1969a p. 54n.). Hicks also cited the historian Andrewes on ancient Greece to support his own assertions on the subject of the demand for slaves: 'the large landowner, who could rely for service upon 'his' peasants and their children, might have little demand for the imported [slave] article; but if slaves were cheap enough there would be a demand for them much lower down the scale' (p. 125). Among economic historians Hicks especially prized his friend T. S. Ashton, citing him frequently (e.g. p. 91).

By the same token Hicks was equally comfortable at boldly exhorting historical research in new areas or disputing the already advanced assertions of economic and general historians. On connections between the expansion of trade and intellectual stimulation, for example, Hicks wrote that they 'must exist in the Renaissance case, though they have not (to my knowledge) been much explored. One, which does not seem to have been remarked' is the connection between portolan maps and perspective painting (1969a, p. 58, n2). On 'that greatest of historical mysteries, the decline and fall of the original Roman Empire', Hicks ventured that part of the explanation might be the 'parting with State property, and parting with taxing power' (1969a, p. 87).

> The financial history of the Roman Empire is (not surprisingly) one of its darkest aspects. We know that taxes were supposed to be collected, but we do not know what they yielded, nor much about the ways in which 'extraordinary' expenditure was covered. What is known does nevertheless seem to fit without obvious straining into the theoretical pattern. (1969a, p. 87n.)

Occasionally Hicks acknowledged that historians were justifiably baffled, but in far more numerous examples he took the approaches or the conclusions of economists or historians of all kinds to task. While offering his own guess that the English population movement of the late eighteenth century was part of a general contemporaneous social change which included a new form of workers' association, Hicks noted that 'the causes of the upsurge of population in England . . . are still very much of a mystery' (1969a, p. 155n.). Contrast this example, however, with his attitude on the subject of 'the distinction between the pure trader, who buys to re-sell, to re-sell what is physically the same as what he had bought, and the artisan or "producer" who works on the things he has bought, so as to re-sell them in a different form'. This distinction is, Hicks wrote, 'often regarded as fundamental; but economically, and even socially, it is not as fundamental as it looks. It is a technological, not an economic distinction' (p. 28). He returned to this false distinction, noting that economists (and philosophers) find it hard 'to admit the correspondence' between the handicraft industry and trade; 'in practical life', Hicks insisted, 'it is admitted' (p. 141).

Hicks, also in the same vein, thought there were numerous instances where scholars missed the mark. Discussing the phenomenon of the English Industrial Revolution, he commented,

> One has a feeling that our view of what happened is pulled out of shape by that early textile 'machinery': an episode which must be granted to be of major importance in the economic history of England, but which when more widely considered is revealed to be something of a sideline. Or perhaps one should say that it fits better as an appendage to the evolution of the 'old' industry than in the way it is usually presented as the beginning of the new. (1969a, p. 147)

On the issue of the effect of the Industrial Revolution on the real wage of labour, 'which historians have long been discussing – with results that even now give no very decisive answer', Hicks also detected a scholarly distortion. 'They hardly touch on what, from my viewpoint, is the essential issue. There is no doubt at all that industrialism, in the end, has been highly favourable to the real wage of labour . . . The important question is why it [the rise in real wages] was so long delayed' (1969a, p. 148).

In Hicks's day, it was common among economic historians to interpret currency history 'in terms of class interests (*debtors* versus *creditors*)' (1969a, p. 92). Hicks challenged this interpretation by offering a new one in terms of public finance.

> The *direct* pressures which must have been exerted upon those who had to take the relevant decisions were surely those which came from the condition of the State treasury; it is hard to see that it is usually necessary to go any further in order to get a sufficient explanation of what happened. (1969a, p. 93, n. 2)

In another example Hicks targeted ancient historians:

> It is generally held by ancient historians that the ruling classes of the Greek city states at this date were landowners, not merchants; it may, however, be respectfully suggested that when trade is as active as it appears to have been, even a landowning class is likely to have been engaged in trade to an extent which is sufficient for the trade orientation. (1969a, p. 40)

In a historiographic observation Hicks pointed his finger at the 'mercantilist' perspective on the growth of the economy. '"Mercantilism" marks the discovery that economic growth can be used *in the national interest*; as a means to national objectives of all sorts, including the pursuit of influence over other nations, of prestige and power.' For his own part, he noted that he had 'deliberately avoided using the term "mercantilism" when discussing 'the growth of the Mercantile Economy'. Although not often appreciated by its users, the term alone implied a specific historical perspective which Hicks did not wish to pursue: history 'from the standpoint of the State, from the standpoint of the rulers'. 'Mercantilist' history would include an examination of 'the regulation of trade, for *national* purposes' and the realization by rulers and nations that 'the merchants can be used as an instrument'. Hicks had chosen instead not to neglect the economy's relations with the State, but to keep those relations, 'as it were, "outside"' his discussion (1969a, pp. 161–2).

Economic history

Economic history was one among several ways of interpreting the past that interested Hicks. Economists whom he respected, such as Hawtrey in his book *A Century of Bank Rate*, had written as economic historians. Like them, Hicks contrasted his own theoretical approach to economic history with the traditional narrow interpretation of the subject. Economic history, he thought, could best be appreciated as the telling of the historical process of specialization, both among economic activities and within specific economic activities, or what are becoming economic activities. For Hicks, the study of economic history ought to focus on something which has happened in the 'real world' at a time which, when the historian writes, must be 'at least to some extent, in the past' (1977a, p. 125). 'It is the past that provides him with his facts' (1979a, p. 4).

As Hicks saw it, economic history is 'rather barren of events' (1979g, p. 63). The economic historian works therefore with facts, as opposed to events. The facts become his or her observations, each of an item having its 'own distinct individuality' (1983a, p. 372). These observations can either be submitted to historical analysis or to statistical extrapolation. The former can yield an explanation of what has happened, while the latter offers an economic time series.

According to Hicks, economic history is frequently conceived as a 'narrow' subject, in two respects. First, it does not envelop the whole of history. It sticks to economic activity and does not imply that economic motives underlie apparently non-economic behaviour. The restricted boundaries of its subjects and sub-subjects were, however, to Hicks's mind, primarily pragmatic. Contraction makes the chosen subjects more manageable. Second, the economic historian analyses the economic activity or situation which 'he holds to have operated at a particular place and time', nothing more (1977a, p. 125).

Hicks noted that there had been historical development in the study of economic history, just as there had been changes in all other areas of economics. 'There was indeed a stage, at the beginning of modern work on economic history, when it was customary to write it as if it were political history'. In that phase, pieces of legislation were treated as 'events'. When, however, 'questions were asked about the effects of those events, they could not be answered in those terms' (1979g, p. 63). This opened up the way for the shift from the 'record-of-events' style of economic history to the 'statistical' or quantitative style.

While understanding the shift, Hicks lamented the predominant swing to the quantitative side in economic history. It will be remembered that he had little respect for obsession with numbers generally, and in economic history as well, for two reasons. For one reason, he felt that often the data that were available for study, especially those deriving from the distant past, were patchy and could not therefore be relied upon to give an accurate historical picture. For another, what the numbers can capture for the historian is not really a representation of the economic activity of the time. Quantitative economic history cannot significantly measure or even describe, for example, the gain entailed in the extension of trade. Its only semi-appropriate measuring stick, 'index-numbers of real income' is 'ill-fitted', since expansion of trade implies a reshuffling of goods, 'so that they are made more useful', as well as an increase in their variety (1969a, p. 56). The problems of measurement to which Hicks alluded so often in his work on pure economic theory could not, he felt, be avoided, or ignored, by the quantitative economic historian. How can one measure 'the widening of life' that economic changes bring with them, or quantitatively differentiate economic aspects of past lives from their many other aspects?

Hicks felt non-quantitative economic historians had a very important role to play in keeping economics soundly rooted in the past. 'The economist is concerned with the future as well as with the past; but it is from the past that he has to begin' (1979g, p. 4). 'Even if our business is with forecasts, of what is likely to happen, or with the probable results of policies to be adopted now, historical analysis comes first' (p. 63). The past is the economist's source of facts. From those facts is derived economic 'knowledge' in the form of analytic generalizations. It is the work of the economic historian which can, Hicks felt, guide the economist by providing sound bases for his or her predictions for the future or advice on planning in the present.

The base provided by economic history can be sound in two ways: it can be historically analytic, not just a statistical extrapolation, and it can offer a formed view from the past. The importance of each of these components is great. 'Unless we have attempted such [analytic] explanation, our forecasts can be no more than mere extrapolation' (1979g, p. 63). Further, in order to predict or plan, the economist needs 'double vision', the ability to look at the past 'from its point of view and from his own; or, as he has learned to say, *ex ante* and *ex post*' (p. 10). It is the economic historian who can help the economist to appreciate both how important for the sake of the present is the past and how to project from the past to the present. Although 'all the economist is ever able to do, is to speculate about things which, more or less probably, may happen' (1969a, p. 8) that speculation, Hicks believed, can have firm historical roots.

General history

As mentioned at the outset, Hicks's first intellectual passion was for history – general, traditional, narrative history. Throughout his life he seemed to have held a certain envy for the historian who can without compunction 'go to his date in the past – his "period" – and stay there' (1979g, p. f). Hicks's youthful enthusiasm for going into the past pours out from a poem he wrote in his early twenties.

British History

One summer afternoon I sank
Piers Plowman like upon a bank
And there with sleep uncarried I
Beheld in gorgeous pageantry
The whole of British History.

I saw the Pithecanthropus
Who slew with weapon dangerous
The holied hippopotamus
And thence returning to his cave
The skin unto his wife he gave
And with the skull he tipped his slave.

And there a recent savant found
The skull reposing on the ground
And whispered, 'Man has been 'round.'
Thus we detect the mighty plan
To teach the modern Englishman
Something of how his race began.

At length the isle from mammoths freed
Became a paradise indeed
Where Druids exercised their creed,
And at the summer solstices
They raised tremendous effigies
To Isis and to Taranis.

Then first was writ a moral code
Beginning 'Man shall dress in wode;

The Heavens are the gods' abode.'
I saw the patient Druids go
And worship beneath the mistletoe.

This fortunate and happy state
Might have gone on 'till very late
And only ended when James Watt
Found out that steam was boiling hot.
Things didn't work that way at all:
Julius Caesar crossed from Gaul.

[*Section unclear.*]

Religion then became the craze,
And Britain's isles saw hectic days
When reverent monks and curates ran
To captivate the Isle of Man.

Now I maintain these ancient saints
Were not as black as history paints
And some of them were very good;
I wish that other people would.

Time came the Romans had to go;
Honorius cried, 'Oh, come back quick,
Leave battling with the foreign foe;
Rome is besieged by Alaric.'
Their ships the cunning Saxons saw
And marked the end of Roman law.

Hangius noticed the Roman sail
And put on his shirt and woke up Horser.
They dressed in leather, they had no mail;
They spun a coin for their only courser.
They did good work at the breakfast trencher
And then embarked on the great adventure.

Hangius was hearty but getting old,
Horser was young but inclined to be stout,
Yet in counsel wary and battle bold
Their general good sense was not open to doubt.
Is it a wonder such heroes as these
Gave us the Britain that conquered the seas?

[*Section forgotten.*]

Helmets, swords and breast plates rattle;
It is Hastings bloody battle.
Norman William on his charger
Growing every minute larger
Watches Saxon Harold die
With an arrow in his eye.
'That', says William, 'by my troth,
Is the way to keep an oath.'
Turning around he puts a tax on
Each surviving Anglo-Saxon.

(*Transcribed from Hicks's recitation from memory, July 1986*)

Although Hicks did not pursue the study of pure history as a career, its many varieties interested him throughout his life, and despite the waves of fashion he felt no aspect of it should be ignored, especially not political or diplomatic history and the history of famous people. In addition to his interest in the content of general history, he was fascinated by the purpose and scope of the historian's task.

That essential ability to 'stay in the past' entails first the ability to transport oneself in the mind to another time. Further historical imagination is required to preserve the reality of the past, in which all that has happened before the time in question plays a role as its past and what is to come after it functions as its yet-unknown future. The figures of the historian's recreation must share one characteristic of all people: they do not know what is going to happen. 'They must take their decisions in the light of possibilities that look as if they might be realized, but which (as we now know from hindsight) are not going to be realized.' The way such an insight into the past might be developed, Hicks suggested, might be to begin by asking the question, 'What should I do if I were in that position?' (1969a, p. 6).

The historian can only rest content, however, if, in addition to offering a lively imaginative account, 'he can tell an intelligible story' (1979g, p. 88). When the historian tells a story, or a drama, the facts or record of events which have occurred at particular dates are 'strung together' (p. 63). The intelligibility of the story is thus based on the degree of plausibility of the story in connecting the events in question. The general historian tries to construct in a string, a causal chain of stages, 'in a way which is not inconsistent with such evidence as he possesses' (p. 88). Although direct evidence may be lacking, the historian will construct the same logical causal connection between each of the stages of the story, 'as belonging to a process': 'A was a cause of A_1, A_1 of A_2 and so on; then A_n was a cause of B' (p. 88).

Hicks found pure historians to be not quite so distant from economists as they might at first appear. The historical imagination was, to his mind, a no less critical tool for the theoretical study of economics than for that of history. Like the figures in history, the 'actors' of the economic models 'if the models are to be practically useful' should be characteristic of real people in that they too do not know what is going to happen and make decisions based on the unknown, and act on them (1969a, p. 6). Interestingly enough Hicks warned both the economist and the historian from losing a modern-day analytic perspective: 'we should not analyse (say) nineteenth-century history in terms of nineteenth-century theories; for our knowledge of the facts of that time is different from that of contemporaries, and the questions we ask are different from those contemporaries asked' ([1976e] 1983a, p. 16).

Also, while prediction and planning appear to be missing in pure history, Hicks saw them, in many cases, simply as less prominent. 'It is easy to name historians who desire to draw from the past some lessons for the present and future, lessons which may be implied rather than stated, yet do not differ in principle from those which the economist draws.' Philosophers of history such as Spengler and Toynbee came to Hicks's mind, but he thought also 'of the element of concern with the problems of their own time which is traceable in more regular historians, such as Gibbon or Rostovtseff', as well as his own contemporaries. The difference is one of perspective: 'the historian is concerned with the past, in its relation to the present; the economist is concerned with the present, and for the sake of the present with the past' (1979g, p. 4).

Conclusion

This book has been dedicated to showing that although Sir John Hicks has been perceived solely as a theorist, he none the less had endeavoured throughout his life to find practical applications for his theories. He consistently used the techniques of models, model-building, mathematical formulations, and technical devices only for the sake of representing the economic problems which were his concern. When he had completed his abstract analysis by means of such techniques, he would then, as he said, 'throw the ladder away' and attempt to make reasoned sense of the real world and the place of his theoretical conclusions in it. It was this that made him a complete economist, and his view of the role of economics a healthy and balanced one.

A chronological account of Hicks's writings and experiences can do no more than begin to explain the abundance and diversity of his ideas. Hicks's real power lay in his ingenious way of simplifying the complexities of the world into a manageable picture in order to produce a model or theory by which he would then slowly, pushing step by step beyond the technical aspect of his work, attempt to make sense of its complex origins. One of his most elementary and crucial devices was the concept of equilibrium. For Hicks, equilibrium lay at the foundation of all economic theory. At a time when some had reduced the notion of equilibrium to a dull mechanical concept and others had dismissed it as irrelevant, he succeeded in giving it an important place in theory without allowing it to dominate his perception of the world.

On the subject of markets, while the discipline seemed to be locked into developing either a flexprice theory at the micro-level or a fixprice theory at the macro-level, Hicks came to realize the two needed to be integrated, and attempted to devise a theory which could work with both markets, those in which prices adjust while quantities are given (flexprice), and those in which quantities adjust while prices are given (fixprice). His traverse analysis, however, demonstrated the difficulty of such an integration of the two types of markets as interdependent. Hicks struggled hard throughout his life to follow his own guidelines for an economist's task, that is, to describe all economic activity, even its most dynamic aspects. In developing his theories of dynamic economics he acknowledged that not only is there more than one approach to the subject, but also that to understand it requires much more than a mathematical model of, for example, the Harrod or Samuelson type or even his own standard profile model of the traverse.

Hicks's approach to a theory of labour and wages is another example of his ingenuity. With time he turned the initial presentations of his conservative, elaborate free-market theory of perfect competition, in which trade union and government interference were perceived as nefarious, into an enlightened version which tried to make sense of the real world of unions, monopolistic firms, and government. By the 1950s Hicks was re-presenting his theory of the 1930s, which in the interim his critics had persuaded him was inappropriate, as a theory of new and lasting value. It was his intermittent evolving work on the concepts of both capital and money which allowed him over time to rethink his earlier theory of labour and wages. Unlike many others who had either focused on fixed capital to the neglect of circulating capital or vice versa, Hicks came to deal with both, in which attempt he devised his novel traverse analysis.

His early work on the portfolio approach to the demand for money, in the tradition of utility theory, had a tremendous impact and follow-up. It was, however, the later work on liquidity theory, in which Hicks stressed the precautionary motive as the main determinate of the demand for money, that made his ideas different from those of both the traditional economics schools and Keynes. Despite the many overlapping themes, such as money, in the work of Hicks and Keynes, Hicks generally established himself as an independent thinker from Keynes. On the topic of money, like Keynes, Hicks did link liquidity to uncertainty and paid great attention to the role of knowledge and information acquisition. Unlike Keynes, however, because of his emphasis on the precautionary rather than the speculative motive, Hicks saw collaboration between government and market institutions as more desirable than policy dictates. In that sense he was only a mild interventionist in the monetary sphere.

Another area in which he demonstrated independent strength was methodology and the philosophy of economics. Hicks succeeded in making philosophical sense of the shakiest foundations of economics without disguising their weaknesses. He was energetic enough to challenge and question whether the fashionable Popperian approach was appropriate to economics. He admitted that most of economics' conclusions, however conditional, are worthwhile, but that any attempt to reach the absolute truth through them is undertaken in vain.

Hicks was an eclectic thinker, whose work benefited immensely from his wide variety of intellectual interests. More than any other post-war economic theorist, he lay tremendous emphasis on the historical aspects of economics: economic history and the history of economic theory. In his challenging linking up of economics and history, he set out an entire theory of economic history. For him, history and economics went together. But then so too did literature and economics, sciences and economics, technology and economics, in fact, while not obsessed with this realization, Hicks none the less maintained that all aspects of life and economics are in a very practical sense conjoined. They certainly were for him.

A book on Hicks's contributions to economics could not be considered complete without the inclusion of at least a mention of his important, well-known work on welfare economics, which has become a permanent feature in the foundation of teaching economics. Hicks's welfare economics, though referred to in passing throughout the book, is mentioned here only in conclusion because his contribution in this area has already been so extensively discussed, honoured and debated. This aspect of his work for which in part he was given the Nobel Prize, deserves to be considered separately; a distinct volume on his theory of value, welfare economics and general equilibrium should eventually be written. The exposition, impact and evolution of Hicks's welfare theory and application could be analysed in conjunction with the work of many other contributors who also have played a determinant role in welfare economics.

Hicks's ideas on welfare economics were original and stimulating. They stirred up much controversy, generating lively and long debates. Arrow, Bergson, Lange, Little, Kaldor, Kuznets, Machlup, Robertson, Samuelson, Scitovsky, and Schultz, to name just a few, all took part in what Hicks called 'the social process' which has shaped the technical and methodological aspects of welfare economics. As was noted throughout this volume, Hicks's general approach was to raise questions to which he did not always provide direct answers. More often than not, however, he suggested hints as to how to go about resolving his queries. Generally, when Hicks offered theories, he was usually very cautious, initially giving highly nuanced statements, leaving room for reconsiderations and then taking full advantage of his critics' comments. As in other areas, Hicks greatly benefited from his critics in developing his welfare economics. The variety of exchanges helped him not only to clarify his ideas and to make sense of the theoretical side of the subject, which is often seen as an abstract gymnastics, but also to seek useful, practical applications for its conclusions.

There is one particular topic that can hardly be avoided in any treatise on welfare economics, although it does not at first glance appear to fit into its normative ranks: the theory of the macro-economic concepts. By way of persuading his readers of its pertinence, Hicks offered the example of the concept 'the Real Social Income, or Social Product' (1981, p. xiv). Following Pigou, Hicks had become convinced that an understanding of the terminology was an essential starting point for welfare economics.

Hicks recognized that most of his early work on welfare economics was just an application of the demand theory and admitted modestly that it was put in 'crude' form. Nevertheless it attracted considerable attention. Hicks's contribution to welfare theory actually had two origins. One lay within his article with R. D. G. Allen, 'A reconsideration of the Theory of Value' (1934a), in which together they independently rediscovered the income and substitution effects which had already been discovered by Slutsky. His other inspirations, the work of Kaldor and Pigou, led to the devising of his well-known compensation test, which became termed the 'new welfare economics' or the 'Kaldor–Hicks welfare economics'. Both of these developmental streams led to Hicks's analysis of the concept of consumer surplus. The issues of the measurement of a consumer's surplus and the valuation of social income occupied a great deal of his time. His preoccupation with the social income had in fact begun as early as his writing of *The Theory of Wages*.

Hicks recalled that in the beginning he 'was a disbeliever in welfare economics'. He said, 'I was aware of the weakness of Pigou's foundations, but I had nothing to put in their place' (1981, p. xii). Even though his subsequent work on welfare economics was first formulated theoretically, it was not the technical aspects of it that were most crucial to him. In attempting to make practical sense of what welfare economics is, he kept one question in mind: 'Why should we be interested in the Social Product, however measured? It is not enough to say that it is an analytical convenience ... its wider justification, is the responsibility of economists' (p. xv).

Hicks took this responsibility as a economist very seriously. He was convinced that there was 'practical fruitfulness' to be gleaned from the theoretical techniques of welfare economics, such as cost benefit analysis (1981, p. xvii). As he believed in general, theory could play the role of assisting in the formulation of problems, but in welfare economics, as in all other areas, it had to be extended to yield the practical information desired. Practical welfare economists had to be ready to 'push on' beyond the formal theory. The extension would not be in the direction of quantitative experiments, such as the estimation of numerically measurable gains and losses in the market-place, but toward qualitative estimations, such as of fairness, need, desire, etc.

Theoretical information about such institutions as markets, the labour force, the national income, of both the direct and indirect kind, could be very useful when complemented by 'other kinds of information – any kind of relevant information on which they [practical welfare economists] can lay their hands' (1981, p. xvii). With its limited number of information variables, the concluding 'optimum' of formal theory was, however, never the 'top'. The more aspects of a problem which could be taken into account as the embrace of practical welfare economics extends, the closer and closer to a practical optimum the economist can push. 'I have been trying to show that 'Welfare economics' as I would now regard it, is composed of a series of steps . . . None of our 'optima' marks a top of that staircase. We must always be prepared to push on, if we can, a little further' (p. xvii).

Hicks the man, the theorist and the practical thinker pushed on through the whole of his life. The step he found the hardest to mount was the one which demanded of him that he carry on his personal and professional life without his lifelong companion, his wife and co-economist, Ursula Webb Hicks. He never failed to credit her with his learning of the practical side of economics: 'there is no part [of *Value and Capital*] which has not profited from the constant reminder which I have had from her work, that the place of economic theory is to be the servant of applied economics' (1939a, p. vi).

In many respects Hicks saw the specialist in welfare economics as the model economist. Welfare economists more than any other had, to his mind, come to terms with the impact of the endeavour. They had recognized that 'it is impossible to make "economic" proposals that do not have "non-economic aspects"'. Thus while Hicks recommended that an economist 'keep within his "own" frontiers' and advise courses of action 'for economic reasons', he felt that it was a virtual impossibility, and in fact a shirking of one's responsibilities not also to concern oneself with the non-economic aspects of the recommendation. 'When the economist makes a recommendation, he is responsible for it in the round' (1959a, pp. x–xi). Hicks regretted being honoured for the Nobel Prize predominantly for his equilibrium and welfare economics. In light of his own thinking, however, to honour him as a welfare economist was to honour him not only as a brilliant economist, but as a responsible one as well. He was not only an economist's economist, but an economist for 'everyman'.

John Richard Hicks, Published Writings

1928: 'Wage-Fixing in the building industry', *Economics*, June, pp. 159–67.

1930a: 'The early history of industrial conciliation in England', *Economica*, March, pp. 25–39.

1930b: 'Edgeworth, Marshall and the indeterminateness of wages', *Economic Journal*, June, pp. 215–31 (repr. 1983a, pp. 72–84).

1931a: 'A reply' to M. Dobb, 'A note concerning Mr J. R. Hicks on "The indeterminateness of wages"', *Economic Journal*, March, pp. 145–6.

1931b: Review of W. W. M. Amulree: *Industrial Arbitration*, *Economica*, February, pp. 105–6.

1931c: 'The theory of uncertainty and profit', *Economica*, May, pp. 170–89 (repr. 1982a, pp. 11–27).

1931d: Review of W. H. Hatt: *The Theory of Collective Bargaining*, *Economica*, May, pp. 244–7.

1931e: Review of M. T. Rankin: *Arbitration Principles and the Industrial Court (An analysis of decisions 1919–1929)*, *Economica*, November, pp. 480–2.

1931f: With W. Beveridge, 'Quotas and import boards', and 'The possibility of imperial preference', In W. Beveridge, *Tariffs: The Case Examined by a committee of economists under the chairmanship of Sir William Beveridge*, London: Longmans, Green, pp. 210–29.

1932a: 'Marginal productivity and the principle of variation' followed by 'A reply' to Henry Schultz, *Economica*, February, pp. 79–88 and August pp. 297–300.

1932b: *The Theory of Wages*, London: Macmillan (Italian edn 1934).

1932c: Review of D. M. Goodfellow: *A Modern Economic History of South Africa*, *Economic Journal*, March, pp. 109–11.

1932d: Review of D. H. Robertson: *Economic Fragments*, *Economica*, May, pp. 255–6.

1932e: Review of C. Bresciani-Turroni: *La Vicende del Marco Tedesco*, *Economica*, August, pp. 370–2.

1932f: Review of F. Simiand: *Le Salaire, l'évolution et la monnaie, Essai de théorie experimentale du salaire*, *Economic Journal*, September, pp. 451–74.

1932g: Review of L. Mises and A. Spiethoff (eds), *Probleme der Wertlehre*, *Economic Journal*, September, pp. 477–8.

1933a: Review of E. W. Taussig: *Wages and Capital*, *Economica*, February, pp. 101–4.

1933b: 'Gleichgewicht und Konjunktur', *Zeitschrift für Nationalökonomie*, June, pp. 441–55, trans. as 'Equilibrium and the trade cycle', *Economic Inquiry*, October, pp. 523–34 (repr. 1982a, pp. 28–41).

1933c: 'A note on Mr Kahn's paper (on elasticity of substitution)', *Review of Economic Studies*, Vol. 1, no. 1 October, pp. 78–80.
1933d: Review of A. E. Monroe: *Value and Income*, *Zeitschrift für Nationalökonomie*, vol. 4, pp. 663–5.
1933e: Review of Reichenau: *Die Kapitalfunktion der Kredits*, *Zeitschrift für Nationalökonomie*, vol. 4, pp. 668–9.
1934a: 'A reconsideration of the Theory of Value', Part I; Part II by R. G. D. Allen, *Economica*, February and May, pp. 52–76 and 196–219 (repr. 1981, pp. 5–29 and 30–55; and in Helm, 1984a, pp. 25–48).
1934b: Review of K. S. Isles: *Wages Policy and the Price Level*, *Economic Journal*, September, pp. 473–75.
1934c: 'A note on the elasticity of supply', *Review of Economic Studies*, 2(1) October, pp. 31–7 (repr. 1983a, pp. 237–45).
1934d: 'Leon Walras', *Econometrica*, October, pp. 338–48. (repr. 1983a, pp. 86–95).
1934e: Review of G. Myrdal: *Monetary Equilibrium*, in F. A. Hayek (ed.), *Beiträge zur Geldtheorie*, and *Economica*, November (repr. 1982a, pp. 42–5).
1934f: Review of F. A. Hayek (ed.), *Beiträge zur Geldtheorie*, *Economica*, November, pp. 479–86.
1934g: Review of P. H. Wicksteed: *Common sense of Political Economy* (repr.), *Economica*, August, pp. 351–4.
1935a: 'Annual survey of economic theory: the Theory of Monopoly' *Econometrica*, January, pp. 1–20 (repr. 1983a, pp. 132–52).
1935b: 'A suggestion for simplifying the Theory of Money', *Economica*, February, pp. 1–19 (repr. 1967, pp. 61–82; 1982a, pp. 46–63; and in Helm 1984a, pp. 168–85).
1935c: Review of C. E. Ross: *Dynamic Economics*, *Economic Journal*, June, pp. 336–7.
1935d: Review of H. von Stackelberg: *Marktform und Gleichgewicht*, *Economic Journal*, June, pp. 334–6.
1935e: Review of S. M. de Bernardi (ed.), *De l'utilité et de sa mesure par Jules Dupuit: écrits choisis et republiés* (Turin repr.), *Economica*, August, pp. 341–2 (repr. 1983a, pp. 329–30).
1935f: 'Wages and interest: the dynamic problem', *Economic Journal*, September, pp. 456–68 (repr. 1963b, pp. 268–85 and 1982a, pp. 67–79).
1936a: Review of A. C. Pigou: *The Economics of Stationary States*, *Economic Journal*, March, pp. 98–102.
1936b: 'Mr Keynes's Theory of Employment', *Economic Journal*, June, pp. 238–53 (repr. 1982a, pp. 84–99).
1936c: 'Distribution and economic progress: a revised version', *Review of Economic Studies*, 4(1) October, pp. 1–12 (repr. 1963b, pp. 286–303).
1936d: 'Economic theory and the social sciences', contribution to a symposium on the Social Sciences, *Institute of Sociology*.
1937a: 'Mr Keynes and the "classics"', *Econometrica*, April, pp. 147–59 (repr. 1967, pp. 126–42; 1982a, pp. 101–15; and in Helm, 1984a, pp. 186–99).
1937b: *La Théorie mathématique de la valeur en régime de libre concurrence*, trans. G. Lutfalla, Paris: Hermann.
1939a: *Value and Capital*, Oxford: Clarendon Press (other edns: Spanish (Mexican) 1945; Japanese, 1950; French, 1956; Hindi, 1971; Polish, 1975;

Urdu, 1975; Hungarian, 1978).

1939b: (with Ursula Hicks), 'Public finance in the national income', *Review of Economic Studies* 6(2), February, pp. 147–55.

1939c: Review of R. G. D. Allen: *Mathematical Analysis for Economists*, *Economica*, February, pp. 92–4.

1939d: Review of A. G. Pool: *Wage Policy in Relation to Industrial Fluctuation*, *Economica*, May, pp. 233–5.

1939e: 'Mr Hawtrey on bank rate' and 'The long-term rate of interest', followed by 'A reply' to Hawtrey, *Manchester School of Economic and Social Studies*, vol. x, pp. 21–39 and pp. 152–5 (repr. of 'Mr Hawtrey . . .', 1982a, pp. 116–26).

1939f: 'The foundations of welfare economics', *Economic Journal*, December, pp. 696–712 (repr. 1981, pp. 59–77, and in Helm, 1984a, pp. 126–43).

1940a: 'The valuation of the social income', *Economica*, May, pp. 105–24 (repr. 1981).

1940b: 'A comment' on O. Lange's 'Complementarity and interrelations of shifts in demand', *Review of Economic Studies*, 8(1), pp. 64–5 (repr. in Wood and Woods, 1989, vol. I, pp. 42–4).

1941a: (with Ursula Hicks and L. Rostas) *Taxation of War Wealth*, Oxford: Clarendon Press (2nd edn, 1942).

1941b: 'Rehabilitation of consumer's surplus', *Review of Economic Studies*, 8(2) February, pp. 108–16 (repr. 1981, pp. 101–13).

1941c: 'Saving and the rate of interest in war time', *Manchester School of Economics and Social Studies*, April, pp. 21–7.

1941d: 'Education in economics', *Manchester Statistical Society*.

1942a: *The Social Framework: An Introduction to Economics*, Oxford: Clarendon Press (other edns: Swedish, 1945; Spanish (Mexican), 1950; Greek (pirated), 1955; Portuguese, 1956; German, 1962; Sinhalese/Tamil, 1964).

1942b: 'The monetary theory of D. H. Roberston', *Economica*, February, pp. 53–7 (extracts repr. 1982a, cf. pp. 127–31).

1942c: 'Maintaining capital intact: a further suggestion', *Economica*, May, pp. 174–9.

1942d: 'Consumers' surplus and index numbers', *Review of Economic Studies*, 9(2) Summer, pp. 126–37 (cf. 1981, pp. 114–32).

1942e: Review of Davis: *The Theory of Econometrics*, *Economic Journal*, December, pp. 350–2.

1942f: 'The budget White Paper of 1942', *Journal of the Institute of Bankers*.

1943a: (with Ursula Hicks) *Standards of Local Expenditure*, Cambridge: Cambridge University Press (National Institute of Economic and Social Research, Occasional Papers)

1943b: 'History of economic doctrine', Review of C. Rist: *History of Monetary and Credit Theory*, *Economic History Review*, 13, pp. 111–15 (repr. 1982a, pp. 132–9).

1943c: (with Ursula Hicks) 'The Beveridge Plan and local government finance', *Review of Economic Studies*, 11(1) Winter, pp. 1–19.

1943d: 'The four consumer's surpluses', *Review of Economic Studies*, 11(1) Winter, pp. 31–40 (repr. 1981, pp. 114–32).

1944a: 'The inter-relations of shifts in demand: comment', a discussion with

D. H. Robertson and O. Lange, *Review of Economic Studies*, 12(1)(31), pp. 71–8 (repr. in Wood and Woods, vol. I, pp. 97–101).

1944b: (with Ursula Hicks and C. E. V. Leser) *Valuation for Rating*, Cambridge: Cambridge University Press (National Institute of Economic and Social Research Occasional Papers).

1945a: (with Ursula Hicks) *The Incidence of Local Rates in Great Britain*, Cambridge: Cambridge University Press (National Institute of Economic and Social Research Occasional Papers).

1945b: 'Recent contributions to general equilibrium economics', *Economica*, November, pp. 235–42.

1945c: 'La théorie de Keynes après neuf ans', *Revue d'économie politique*, 55, pp. 1–11.

1945d: Review of A. C. Pigou: *Lapses from Full Employment*, *Economic Journal*, December, pp. 398–401 (repr. 1982a, pp. 140–3).

1945e: *The Social Framework of the American Economy* (adapted by A. G. Hart) New York: Oxford University Press.

1946a: 'The generalized theory of consumer's surplus', *Review of Economic Studies*, 13(2)(34), pp. 68–74 (cf. 1981, pp. 114–32).

1946b: *Value and Capital*, 2nd edn, Oxford: Clarendon Press.

1947a: 'World recovery after war: a theoretical analysis', *Economic Journal*, June, pp. 151–64 (repr. 1959a, pp. 3–19 and 1982a, pp. 148–61).

1947b: 'Full employment in a period of reconstruction', *Nationalokonomisk Tidsskrift*, 85, pp. 165ff. (repr. 1982a, pp. 162–72).

1947c: 'The empty economy', *Lloyds Bank Review*, July, pp. 1–13.

1948a: 'The valuation of the social income: a comment on Professor Kuznets' *Reflections*', *Economica*, August, pp. 163–72 (extracts repr. 1981, pp. 98–9).

1948b: Review of F. Sewell Bray: *Precision and Design in Accountancy*, *Economic Journal*, December, pp. 562–4.

1948c: 'L'économie de bien-être et la théorie des surplus du consommateur' and 'Quelques applications de la théorie des surplus du consommateur', *Economie appliquée*, January–March, pp. 432–46 and 447–57.

1948d: *The Problem of Budgetary Reform*, Oxford: Oxford University Press (Spanish edn, 1957).

1949a: 'Devaluation and world trade', *Three Banks Review*, December, pp. 3–23 (repr. 1959a, pp. 20–39).

1949b: 'Les courbes d'indifférence collective', *Revue d'économie politique*, 59, pp. 578–84.

1949c: 'Mr Harrod's dynamic theory', *Economica*, May, pp. 106–21 (repr. 1982a, pp. 174–92).

1950a: *A Contribution to the Theory of the Trade Cycle*, Oxford: Clarendon Press (other edns: Italian, 1951; Spanish, 1954; Japanese, 1954).

1950b: Articles on 'Value', 'Demand', 'Interest', 'Wages' and 'Rent', *Chamber's Encyclopaedia*.

1950c: Part II of *Report of Commission on Revenue Allocation*, Nigeria, pp. 45–56 (repr. 1959a, pp. 216–36).

1951a: 'A critical note on the definition of related goods: a comment on Mr Ichimura's definition' *Review of Economic Studies*, 18(3)(47), pp. 184–7.

1951b: 'Free trade and modern economics', *Manchester Statistical Society*, March

(repr. 1959a, pp. 40–65).
1951c: Review of C. Menger: *Principles of Economics* (trans. J. Dingwall and B. Hoselitz), *Economic Journal*, December, pp. 852–3 (repr. 1983a, pp. 333–4).
1952a: *Social Framework*, 2nd edn, Oxford: Clarendon Press.
1952b: Review of T. Scitovsky: *Welfare and Competition*, *American Economic Review*, September, pp. 609–14 (repr. 1982a, pp. 155–62).
1952c: 'Contribution to a symposium on monetary policy and the crisis: comments', *Bulletin of Oxford University Institute of Statistics*, April–May, pp. 157–9 and August, pp. 268–72.
1953a: Inaugural lecture: 'Long-run dollar problem', *Oxford Economic Papers*, June, pp. 117–35 (extract repr. 1959a, pp. 66–84; revd version 1983a, pp. 207–16).
1953b: 'A note on a point in *Value and Capital* (a reply to M. Morishima)', *Review of Economic Studies*, 21(3)(56), pp. 218–21 (repr. in Wood and Woods, 1989, vol. I, pp. 164–8).
1954a: 'The process of imperfect competition', *Oxford Economics Papers*, February, pp. 41–54 (repr. 1983a, pp. 163–78).
1954b: 'Robbins on Robertson on utility', *Economica*, May, pp. 154–7.
1954c: Review of Myrdal: *The Political Element in the Development of Economic History* (trans. P. Streeten), *Economic Journal*, December, pp. 793–6 (repr. 1983a, pp. 343–6).
1955a: (with Ursula Hicks) *Report on Finance and Taxation in Jamaica*, Kingston, Jamaica, Government Printer.
1955b: 'Economic foundations of wage policy', *Economic Journal*, September, pp. 389–404 (repr. 1959a, pp. 85–104 and 1982a, pp. 194–209, 210–13).
1955c: *The Social Framework of the American Economy*, 2nd edn, (adapted by A. G. Hart and J. W. Ford), New York: Oxford University Press.
1956a: *A Revision of Demand Theory*, Oxford: Clarendon Press (other edns: Spanish (Mexican), 1958; Japanese, 1958).
1956b: 'The instability of wages', *Three Banks Review*, September, pp. 3–19 (repr. 1959a).
1956c: 'Methods of dynamic analysis' in *Twenty-five Economic Essays in English, German and Scandinavian languages in honor of Erik Lindahl*, Stockholm: Ekonomisk Tidschrift, (repr. with addendum 1982a, pp. 219–35 and in Helm, 1984a, pp. 200–15).
1957a: 'A rehabilitation of "classical" economics?', Review of D. Patinkin: *Money, Interest and Prices: an Integration of Monetary and Value Theory, Economic Journal*, 67, pp. 278–89 (repr. 1967, pp. 143–54 as 'The classics again').
1957b: 'National economic development in the international setting', and 'Development under population pressure', in *Bulletin*, the Central Bank of Ceylon (repr. 1959a, pp. 161–95 (revd version) and pp. 196–215).
1958a: 'The measurement of real income', *Oxford Economic Papers*, June, pp. 125–62 (repr. 1981, pp. 142–88 and in Helm, 1984a, pp. 57–95).
1958b: 'Future of the rate of interest', *Manchester Statistical Society*, March (revd version, 1967, pp. 83–102).
1958c: 'A world inflation', *The Irish Banks Review*, September (repr. 1959a, pp. 121–51).
1959a: *Essays in World Economics* (including 'A Manifesto [on welfarism]' (repr. 1981, pp. 135–41); 'Unimproved value rating (the case of East Africa)'; 'A

further note on import bias' (extract repr. 1983a, pp. 217–23); 'The factor-price equalization theorem'), Oxford: Clarendon Press (other edns: Japanese, 1965; Spanish, 1967).

1959b: Review of H. Leibenstein: *Economic Backwardness and Economic Growth*, *Economic Journal*, June, pp. 344–7.

1959c: 'A "Value and Capital" growth model', *Review of Economic Studies*, June vol. 26, pp. 159–73.

1960a: *Social Framework*, 3rd edn, Oxford: Clarendon Press.

1960b: 'Linear theory', *Economic Journal*, 280(70) December, pp. 671–709 (repr. 1966 in *Surveys of Economic Theory*, vol. III, American Economic Association, London: Macmillan and in 1983a, pp. 246–91).

1960c: 'Thought on the Theory of Capital: the Corfu Conference', *Oxford Economic Papers*, June, pp. 123–32.

1961a: 'Prices and the turnpike: the story of a mare's nest', *Review of Economic Studies*, 28 February, pp. 77–88 (repr. 1983a, pp. 292–307).

1961b: 'The Nature and Basis of Economic Growth' in J. R. Hicks et al. (eds) *Federalism and Economic Growth in Underdeveloped Countries*, London: Allen & Unwin, pp. 70–80.

1961c: 'The measurement of capital in relation to the measurement of other economic agregates', in F. A. Lutz and D. C. Hague (eds), *The Theory of Capital*, Institute of Economic Affairs, London: Macmillan, pp. 18–31 (repr. 1981, pp. 189–203).

1961d: 'Pareto revealed', Review of V. Pareto: *Pareto's Letters to Pantaleoni*, *Economica*, August, pp. 318–22 (repr. 1983a, pp. 338–42).

1961e: 'Marshall's third rule: a further comment', *Oxford Economic Papers*, October, pp. 262–5, (extract repr. 1963b, pp. 376–8).

1962a: 'Liquidity', *Economic Journal*, December, pp. 787–802 (repr. 1982a, pp. 238–47).

1962b: 'Economic theory and the evaluation of consumer's wants', *Journal of Business*, University of Chicago, July, pp. 256–63.

1962c: Review of J. E. Meade: *A Neo-Classical Theory of Economic Growth*, *Economic Journal*, 286(72) pp. 371–4.

1962d: Review of A. K. Sen: *Choice of Techniques: an Aspect of the Theory of Planned Economic Development*, *Economic Journal*, June, pp. 379–81.

1963a: 'International trade: the long view', Cairo: Central Bank of Egypt.

1963b: *The Theory of Wages*, 2nd edn (with reprint and commentary) London: Macmillan (Spanish edn, 1973).

1963c: (with Ursula Hicks) 'The reform of budget accounts; *Bulletin of Oxford University Institute of Statistics*, May, pp. 119–26.

1963d: Review of M. Friedman: *Capitalism and Freedom*, *Economica*, August, pp. 319–20.

1963e: Review of F. Modigliani and K. J. Cohen: *The Role of Anticipations and Plans in Economic Behaviour and Their Use in Economic Analysis and Forecasting*, *Economic Journal*, March, pp. 99–101.

1965a: *Capital and Growth*, Oxford: Clarendon Press (other edns: Spanish, 1967; Italian, 1971; Polish, 1982).

1965b: Review of T. Scitovsky: *Papers on Welfare and Growth*, *American Economic Review*, September, pp. 882–3.

1965c: Review of R. G. Lipsey: *An Introduction to Positive Economics*, *Economica*,

May, pp. 229–31 (repr. 1983a, pp. 347–8).

1966a: Dennis Robertson: 'A Memoir' in D. H. Robertson, *Essays in Money and Interest*, London: Collins, pp. 9–22.

1966b: 'After the Boom', *Institute of Economic Affairs*, Occasional Papers, II.

1966c: 'Growth and Anti-Growth', *Oxford Economic Papers*, November, pp. 257–69.

1966d: Review of J. E. Meade: *The Stationary Economy, Economic Journal*, June, pp. 370–1.

1966e: 'Essays on balanced economic growth', *The Oriental Economist*, Tokyo.

1967: *Critical Essays in Monetary Theory*, Oxford: Clarendon Press (other edns: Spanish, 1971; Italian, 1971; Japanese, 1972).

1968: 'Saving, investment and taxation: an international comparison', *Three Banks Review*, June, pp. 3–21.

1969a: *A Theory of Economic History*, London: Clarendon Press, Oxford University Press (other edns: Swedish, 1970; Japanese, 1971; Portuguese (Brazilian), 1971; French, 1973; Norwegian, 1974; Spanish, 1974).

1969b: 'Autonomists, Hawtreyans and Keynesians', *Journal of Money, Credit and Banking*, 1(3), pp. 307–17 (revd version 1977a, pp. 118–33).

1969c: 'Direct and indirect additivity', *Econometrica*, April, pp, 353–4 (repr. 1983a, pp. 308–11).

1969d: 'Maintaining capital intact: a further suggestion', in R. H. Parker and G. C. Harcourt (eds) *Readings in the Concept and Measurement of Income*, pp. 132–8.

1969e: 'The rehabilitation of consumer's surplus', in K. J. Arrow and T. Scitovsky (eds) *Readings in Welfare Economics*, pp. 325–35.

1969f: 'Value and volume of capital', *Indian Economic Journal*, October–December, pp. 161–71.

1969g: 'The measurement of capital – in practice', *Bulletin of the International Statistical Institute*, 43 (repr. 1981, pp. 204–17).

1969h: Review of B. P. Pesek and T. R. Saving: *Money, Wealth and Economic Theory, Economic Journal*, March, pp. 129–31.

1970a: 'Expected Inflation', *Three Banks Review*, 87, pp. 3–34 (extract repr. 1977a, pp. 108–17).

1970b: Review of M. Friedman: *The Optimum Quantity of Money, Economic Journal*, December, pp. 669–72 (revd version 1982, pp. 276–81).

1970c: 'Inflazione e interesse', *Bancaria*, June, pp. 675–82.

1970d: 'Capitalism and industrialism', *Tahqiqat Eqtesadi* (*Quarterly Journal of Economic Research*) Teheran, Spring, pp. 1–13.

1970e: 'Elasticity of substitution again: substitutes and complements' *Oxford Economic Papers*, November, pp. 289–96 (revd version 1983a, 'Elasticity of substitution reconsidered', pp. 312–26).

1970f: 'A neo-Austrian growth theory', *Economic Journal*, June, pp. 257–81.

1971a: *The Social Framework*, 4th edn, Oxford: Clarendon Press (other edns Japanese, 1972; Portuguese (Brazilian), 1972).

1971b: 'A reply to Professor Beach "Hicks on Ricardo on machinery"' *Economic Journal*, December, pp. 922–5 (repr. in Wood and Woods, 1989, vol. II, pp. 170–3).

1972a: 'Ricardo's theory of distribution', in M. Preston and B. Corry

(eds) *Essays in Honour of Lord Robbins*, London: Weidenfeld & Nicolson, pp. 160–7 (repr. 1983a, pp. 32–8).
1972b: (with Ursula Hicks) 'British fiscal policy', in H. Giersch (ed.) *Fiscal Policy and Demand Management*, Tubingen: Mohr.
1973a: 'The Austrian Theory of Capital and its rebirth in modern economics', in J. R. Hicks and W. Weber (eds) *Carl Menger and the Austrian School of Economics*, Oxford: Clarendon Press, pp. 190–206 (repr. 1983a, pp. 96–112).
1973b: 'The mainspring of economic growth', *Swedish Journal of Economics*, December, pp. 336–48 (repr. 1977a pp. 1–19).
1973c: 'Recollections and documents', *Economica*, February, pp. 2–11. (repr. 1977a, pp. 134–48).
1973d: *Capital and Time, a Neo-Austrian Theory*, Oxford: Clarendon Press (other edns: Italian, 1973; Japanese, 1973; French, 1975; Spanish (Mexican), 1976).
1973e: (with H.-C. Recktenwald) 'Walras' economic system', in H.-C. Recktenwald (ed.) *Political Economy: An Historical Perspective*, pp. 261–5.
1973f: 'On the measurement of capital', *The Economic Science*, Nagoya University, Japan.
1974a: 'Capital controversies: ancient and modern', *American Economic Review*, May, pp. 307–16 (repr. 1977a, pp. 49–65).
1974b: *The Crisis in Keynesian Economics*, Oxford: Basil Blackwell (other edns: Italian, 1974; Spanish, 1976; Japanese, 1977; Hungarian, 1978).
1974c: 'Preferences and welfare', in A. Mitra (ed.) *Economic Theory and Planning: Essays in Honour of A. K. Das Gupta*, Calcutta: Oxford University Press, pp. 3–16.
1974d: 'Real and monetary factors in economic fluctuations', *Scottish Journal of Political Economy*, 21(3), pp. 205–14 (extract repr. 1977a, pp. 171–81 and in M. Monti (ed.) 1976, *The 'New Inflation' and Monetary Policy*, New York: Holmes & Meier Pub., pp. 3–13).
1974e; 'Future and industrialism', *International Affairs*, April, pp. 211–28 (repr. 1977a, pp. 20–44).
1974f: (with N. Nosse) *The Social Framework of the Japanese Economy*, Oxford; Oxford University Press.
1975a: 'The permissive economy', in 'Crisis '75 ... ?' *Institute of Economic Affairs*, Occasional Papers, 43.
1975b: 'Pareto and the economic optimum', Rome: Accademia nazionale dei lincei.
1975c: 'The scope and status of welfare economics', *Oxford Economic Papers*, 27(3), pp. 307–26 (repr. 1981, pp. 218–39).
1975d: Annual survey of economic theory: 'The Theory of Monopoly' in E. Mansfield (ed.) *Macroeconomics: Selected Readings*, pp. 188–205.
1975e: 'The quest for monetary stability', *South African Journal of Economics*, December, pp. 405–20.
1975f: 'Revival of political economy: the old and the new' (a reply to Harcourt), *Economic Record*, September, pp. 365–7.
1975g: 'What is wrong with monetarism?', *Lloyds Bank Review*, 118, pp. 1–13.

1976a: Review of J. R. Whittaker (ed.), *The Early Economic Writings of Alfred Marshall (1867–1890)*, *Economic Journal*, January, pp. 367–9 (repr. 1983a, pp. 335–7).
1976b: 'Forward trading as a means of overcoming disequilibrium', in B. A. Goss and B. S. Yamey (eds) *The Economics of Futures Trading: Readings*, New York: Wiley, pp. 63–7.
1976c: 'The little that is right with monetarism', *Lloyds Bank Review*, 121, pp. 16–18.
1976d: 'Must stimulating demand stimulate inflation?', *Economic Record*, December, pp. 409–22 (repr. 1982a, pp. 301–17).
1976e: '"Revolutions" in Economics', in S. J. Latsis (ed.) *Method and Appraisal in Economics*, Cambridge: Cambridge University Press, pp. 207–18 (repr. 1983a, pp. 3–16 and in Helm, 1984a, pp. 244–56).
1976f: 'Some questions of time in economics', in A. Tang, F. M. Westfield and J. S. Worley (eds) *Evolution, Welfare and Time in Economics: Essays in Honour of Nicholas Georgescu-Roegen*, Lexington, Mass.: Heath Lexington Books, pp. 135–51 (repr. 1982a, pp. 282–300 and in Helm 1984a, pp. 263–80).
1977a: *Economic Perspectives: Further Essays on Money and Growth*, Oxford: Clarendon Press (other edns: Portuguese (Brazilian), 1978; Italian, 1980).
1977b: (with S. Hollander) 'Mr Ricardo and the moderns', *Quarterly Journal of Economics*, August, pp. 351–69 (repr. 1983a, pp. 41–59).
1978a: Review of V. Lachmann: *Capital Expectations and the Market Process*, *South African Journal of Economics*, December, pp. 400–502.
1978b: 'La funzioni della moneta internazionale', *Bancaria*, July, pp. 661–7.
1978c: Review of R. D. Collison Black (ed.), *Papers and Correspondence of W. S. Jevons*, vols. III–V, *Economic Journal*, June, pp. 347–8 (extract repr. 1983a, pp. 331–2).
1979a: 'The Ricardian system: a comment', *Oxford Economic Papers*, March, pp. 133–4.
1979b: 'The formation of an economist', *Banca Nazionale del Lavaro Quarterly Review*, September, pp. 195–204 (repr. 1983a, pp. 355–64 and in Helm 1984a, pp. 281–90).
1979c: 'Is interest the price of a factor of production?', in M. J. Rizzo (ed.) *Time, Uncertainty and Disequilibrium* Lexington, Mass.: Lexington Books (repr. 1983a, pp. 114–28).
1979d: Review of E. R. Weintraub: *Microfoundations: the Compatibility of Microeconomics and Macroeconomics*, *Journal of Economic Literature*, December, pp. 1451–4 (repr. 1983a, pp. 349–52).
1979e: 'The concept of income in relation to taxation and business management', *Greek Economic Review*, December, pp. 1–14 (repr. 1983, pp. 189–203).
1979f: 'On Coddington's interpretation: a reply', *Journal of Economic Literature*, 17, pp. 989–95 (repr. in Wood and Woods, 1989, vol. III, pp. 209–16).
1979g: *Causality in Economics*, Oxford: Basil Blackwell and New York: Basic Books (other edns: Italian 1981; Spanish (Argentinian), 1982).
1980a: 'IS–LM: An explanation', *Journal of Post Keynesian Economics*, Winter, pp. 139–54 (repr. 1982a, pp. 318–31 and in Helm, 1984a, pp. 216–29).
1980b: 'Equilibrium and the trade cycle' (translation of 1933b 'Gleichgewicht

und Konjunktur'), *Economic Inquiry*, October, pp. 523–34 (repr. 1982a, pp. 28–41).
1980c: Review of J. Presley: *Robertsonian Economics, Canadian Journal of Economics*, August, pp. 517–20.
1981: *Wealth and Welfare, Collected Essays on Economic Theory*, vol. I, Oxford: Basil Blackwell (including 'Valuation of the Social Income III: the cost approach', (repr. in Helm, 1984a, pp. 96–121)).
1982a: *Money, Interest and Wages, Collected Essays on Economic Theory*, vol. II, Oxford: Basil Blackwell (including 'The foundation of monetary theory, part IV, The credit economy', repr. in Helm, 1984a, pp. 230–9).
1982b: 'Limited liability: the pros and cons', in T. Orhnial (ed.) *Limited Liability and the Corporation*, London: Croom Helm (repr. 1983a, pp. 178–88).
1982c: Forward to Andrew Shonfield, *The Use of Public Power*, Oxford: Oxford University Press.
1982d: 'Planning in the world depression', *Man and Development*, India.
1983a: *Classics and Moderns, Collected Essays on Economic Theory*, vol. III, Oxford: Basil Blackwell.
1983b: 'Culture as capital, supply and demand', Rome: Accademia nazionale dei lincei.
1983c: 'Edgeworth', in Murphy (ed.) *Studies of Irish Economists*.
1983d: 'A sceptical follower', *The Economist*, June, pp. 21–4.
1984a: 'The "new causality": an explanation', *Oxford Economic Papers*, 36, pp. 12–15.
1984b: 'Is economics a science?', *Interdisciplinary Science Reviews*, 9(3), pp. 213–19.
1984c: (with S. K. Ghosh and M. Mukherjee), *The Social Framework of the Indian Economy, an Introduction to Economics*, India and New York: Oxford University Press.
1985a: *Methods of Dynamic Economics*, new edn of the first part of *Capital and Growth*, Oxford: Clarendon Press.
1985b: 'Sraffa and Ricardo – a critical view', in G. A. Caravale (ed.) *The legacy of Ricardo*, Oxford: Basil Blackwell, pp. 305–19.
1986a: 'Toward a more General Theory', *Symposium on Monetary Theory*, Taipei, Taiwan: The Institute of Economics, Academia Sinica, January, pp. 5–19.
1986b: 'Loanable funds and liquidity preference', *Greek Economic Review*, December, pp. 125–31.
1986c: *A Revision of Demand Theory*, Oxford: Oxford University Press. (Published posthumously).
1989a: *A Market Theory of Money*, Oxford: Clarendon Press.
1989b: 'The assumption of constant return to scale', *Cambridge Journal of Economics*, March, pp. 9–17.
1990: 'The unification of macro-economics', *Economic Journal*, June, pp. 528–38.
1991: *The Status of Economics*, Oxford: Basil Blackwell.

References

Addison, J. T., Burton, J. and Torrance, T. S. 1984: 'Causation, social science and Sir John Hicks', *Oxford Economic Papers*, 36, pp. 1–11.

Alexander, S. 1951: 'Issue of business cycle theory raised by Mr Hicks', *American Economic Review*, 41(5), pp. 861–78.

Asimakopulos, A. 1978: 'Keynesian economics, equilibrium and time', *Canadian Journal of Economics*, 11(4) Supplement, pp. 3–10.

Bauer, P. T. 1971: 'Economic history as theory', *Economica*, 38, pp. 163–79.

Baumol, W. J. 1952: 'The transaction demand for cash: an inventory theoretic approach', *Quarterly Economic of Economics*, 66(4), pp. 545–56.

—— 1972: 'J. R. Hicks' contribution to economics', *Swedish Journal of Economics*, 74, pp. 503–27.

Beach, E. F. 1971: 'Hicks on Ricardo on Machinery', *Economic Journal*, 81(4), pp. 916–22.

Blaug, M. 1988: 'John Hicks and the methodology of economics', in N. DeMarchi (ed.) *The Popperian Legacy in Economics*, Cambridge: Cambridge University Press.

Bliss, C. 1987: 'Hicks, John Richard', in J. Eatwell et al. (eds) *New Palgrave Dictionary*, London: Macmillan.

Brunner, K. 1981: Review of J. R. Hicks: *The Crisis in Keynesian Economics*, *Journal of Political Economy*, 89, pp. 1052–4.

—— and A. H. Meltzer 1973: 'Mr Hicks and the "Monetarists"', *Economica*, 157, pp. 44–59.

Burmeister, E. 1974: 'Synthesizing the neo-Austrian and alternative approaches to capital theory: a survey', *Journal of Economic Literature*, 12(2), pp. 413–56.

Burns, A. F. 1952: 'Hicks and the real cycle', *Journal of Political Economy*, 60(1), pp. 1–24.

Chick, V. 1982: 'A comment on IS–LM: an explanation', *Journal of Post Keynesian Economics*, pp. 439–44.

Clay, H. 1929: 'The public regulation of wages in Great Britain', *Economic Journal*, 39, pp. 323–343.

Clower, R. W. 1984: *Money and Market*, ed. D. Walker, Cambridge: Cambridge University Press.

—— 1988: 'Keynes and the classics revisited', in O. F. Hamouda and J. N. Smithin (eds) *Keynes and Public Policy after Fifty Years*, London: Gower and New York: New York University Press.

Coddington, A. 1979: 'Hicks' contribution to Keynesian economics', *Journal of Economic Literature*, 17(3), pp. 970–88.

—— 1980: Review of J. R. Hicks: *Causality in Economics, Economic Journal*, pp. 395–7.
Collard, D. A., Helen, D. R., Scott, M. F. G. and Sen, A. K. (eds) 1984: *Economic Theory and Hicksian Themes*, Oxford: Clarendon Press.
Dalton, E. H. 1920: *Inequality of Income in Modern Communities*, 1920.
Davidson, P. 1980: 'Causality in economics: a review', *Journal of Post Keynesian Economics* 2, pp. 576–84.
Dobb, M. 1929: 'A sceptical view of the Theory of Wages', *Economic Journal*, 39(4), pp. 506–19.
—— 1931: 'A note concerning Mr J. R. Hicks on "The Indeterminateness of Wages"', *Economic Journal*, 41(1), pp. 142–5.
Duesenberry, J. 1950: 'Hicks on the trade cycle', *Quarterly Journal of Economics*, 64(3), pp. 464–76.
Dunbabin, T. J. 1948: *The Western Greeks*, Oxford Clarendon Press.
Dye, H. S. 1952: 'Certain questions raised by Hicks' theory of the trade cycle', *Southern Economic Journal*, 19(2), pp. 200–10.
Eatwell, J. 1975: 'A note on the truncation theorem', *Kyklos*, 28(4), pp. 870–5.
Edgeworth, F. Y. 1961: *Mathematical Psychics*, New York: Kelley.
Ford, J. L. 1991: 'Uncertainty, liquidity preference and portfolio choice: aspects of the Hicksian approach', *Review of Political Economy*, 3(3), pp. 321–48.
Fisher, I. 1963: *The Purchasing Power of Money*, 2nd edn, New York: Kelley.
Fraasen, Bas C. Van. 1970: *An Introduction to the Philosophy of Time and Space*, New York: Random House.
Frazer, J. G. 1911: *The Golden Bough*, London: Macmillan.
Frisch, R. 1935: 'On the notion of equilibrium and disequilibrium', *Review of Economic Studies*, 3, pp. 100–5.
—— 1967: 'Propagation problems and impulse problems in dynamic economics', in *Economic Essays in Honour of Gustav Cassel (1933)*, New York: Kelley, pp. 171–205.
Gerschenkron, A. 1971: 'Mercator gloriosus', *Economic History Review*, 24, pp, 653–66.
Goodwin, R. M. 1951: 'A non-linear theory of the cycle', *Review of Economic Statistics*, 32, pp. 316–20.
Hagemann, H. and Hamouda, O. F. forthcoming: *The Legacy of Hicks*, London: Routledge.
—— and —— 1991: 'Hicks on European monetary system' *Kyklos*, vol. 44, fasc. 3, pp. 411–23.
Halevy, E. 1926–32: *L' histoire du peuple anglais*, 2nd vols, Paris: Hachette.
Haley, B. F. 1939: 'Review of *Value and Capital*', *American Economic Review*, 29(3), pp. 557–60.
Hamouda, O. F. 1983: 'The analysis of economic dynamics – treatment of time – an illustration: the work of Hicks', Ph.D. thesis, McGill University.
—— 1984: 'On the Notion of Short-Run and Long-Run', *British Review of Economic Issues*, 6(14), pp. 55–82.
—— 1985: 'The Evolution of Hicks' Theory of Money', *Bulletin of Economic*

Research, 37(2), pp. 131–51 (repr. in J. C. Wood and R. N. Woods (eds) *Sir John R. Hicks: Critical Assessments*, London: Routledge, 1989, vol. IV, pp. 159–77).

—— 1986: 'Beyond the IS–LM Device: Was Keynes a Hicksian?', *Eastern Economic Journal*, 12(4), pp. 370–82.

—— 1988: 'Hypothèses et réalisme', in *Philosophy of the Social Sciences*, December 18(4), pp. 519–21.

—— 1990a: 'Hicks Changing Views on Economic Dynamics', in D. E. Moggridge (ed.) *Perspectives on the History of Economic Thought*, Aldershot: Edward Elgar, pp. 162–76.

—— 1990b: 'Time, choice and dynamics in economics', in S. F. Frowen (ed.) *Unknowledge and Choice in Economics*, London: Macmillan, pp. 129–55.

—— forthcoming: 'Hicks' Trade Cycle', in D. Glasner (ed.) *Encyclopedia of Business Cycles, Panics, Crises and Depressions*, New York: Garland Publishing.

—— and Price, B. B. 1991: *The Notion of Verification in Economics and History*, London: Routledge.

—— and Rowley, J. C. R. 1987: 'Troublesome probability and economics', *Journal of Post Keynesian Economics*, 10(1), pp. 44–64.

—— and 1988: *Expectations, Equilibrium and Dynamics in Economics: a History of Recent Economic Ideas and Practices*, Brighton: Wheatsheaf.

—— and Smithin, J. N. 1987: *Keynes and Public Policy after Fifty Years*, vol. I: *Economics and Policy*, vol. II: *Theories and Method*, London: Gower.

—— and —— 1988a: 'Rationality, Expectations and deficient foresight', *Eastern Economic Journal*, 16(3), pp. 277–85.

—— and —— 1988b: 'Some remarks on uncertainty and economic analysis', *Economic Journal*, 98(389), pp. 159–64.

Hahn, F. 1966: Review of J. R. Hicks: *Capital and Growth*, *Economic Journal*, March, pp. 84–7.

—— 1990: 'John Hicks the theorist', *Economic Journal*, 100, pp. 539–49.

Hansen, A. H. 1941: *Fiscal Policy and Business Cycles*, New York: Norton.

—— and Tout, H. 1933: 'Annual survey of business cycle theory: investment and savings in business cycle theory', *Econometrica*, 1, pp. 119–47.

Harcourt, G. C. 1972: *Some Cambridge Controversies in the Theory of Capital*, Cambridge: Cambridge University Press.

—— 1975: 'Decline and Rise: the revival of (classical) political economy', *The Economic Record*, 51(135), pp. 339–56.

—— 1979: Review of J. R. Hicks: *Economic Perspectives*, *Economic Journal*, 89, pp. 144–6.

Hardy, C. O. 1923: *Risk and Risk Bearing*, Chicago: University of Chicago Press.

Harrod, R. F. 1939a: 'An Essay in dynamic theory', *Economic Journal*, 49(1), pp. 14–33.

—— 1939b: 'Review of Hicks' *Value and Capital*', *Economic Journal*, 49(2), pp. 294–300.

—— 1948: *Toward a Dynamic Economics*, London: Macmillan.
Harrod, R. F. 1973: *Economic Dynamics*, London: Macmillan.
Hart, H. L. A. 1961: *Concept of Law*, Oxford Clarendon Press.
Hayek, F. von 1928: 'Das intertemporale Gleichgewichtssystem der Preise und die Bewegungen des "Geldwertes"', *Weltwirtschaftliches Archiv*, 28 (II), pp. 33–76.
—— 1931: *Prices and Production*, London: Routledge.
Helm, D. R. (ed.) 1984a: *The Economics of John Hicks*, Oxford: Blackwell.
—— 1984b: 'Prediction and causes: a comparison of Friedman and Hicks on method', in D. A. Collard, D. R. Helm, M. F. G. Scott and A. K. Sen (eds) 1984: *Economic Theory and Hicksian Themes*, Oxford: Clarendon Press, pp. 118–34.
Hicks, E. Sir 1928: *Thomas Malory: His Turbulent Career*, Cambridge: Harvard University Press.
Hicks, P. 1952: *A Quest of Ladies: the story of a Warwickshire School*, Birmingham: F. Juckes.
Hicks, U. *Finance of British Government 1920–1936*, London: Oxford University Press.
—— 1951: *Public Finance*, London: Nisbet.
—— 1954: *British Public Finances, Their Structure and Development 1880–1952*, Oxford: Oxford University Press.
Hume, D. [1896] 1978: *A Treatise of Human Nature*, ed. L. A. Selby-Bigge. Oxford: Clarendon Press.
Jeffreys, H. 1939: *Theory of Probability*, Oxford: Clarendon Press.
—— 1975: Review of J. R. Hicks: *The Crisis in Keynesian Economics, Journal of Political Economy*, 83, pp. 671–3.
Johnson, H. 1976: 'What is right with monetarism', *Lloyds Bank Review*, 120, pp. 13–17.
Kaldor, N. 1939: 'Welfare propositions and interpersonal comparisons of utility', *Economic Journal*, 49, pp. 549–52.
—— 1951: 'Mr Hicks and the trade cycle', *Economic Journal*, 61(4), pp. 833–47.
—— 1972: 'The irrelevance of equilibrium economics', *Economic Journal*, December, pp. 1237–55.
—— 1984: *Economics without Equilibrium*, New York: M. E. Sharpe.
Keynes, J. M. 1921: *A Treatise on Probability*, London: Macmillan.
—— 1930: *A Treatise on Money*, 2 vols, London: Macmillan.
—— 1936: *The General Theory of Employment, Interest and Money*, London: Macmillan.
Kirzner, I. M. 1976: 'The Theory of Capital', in E. G. Dolan (ed.) *The Foundations of Modern Austrian Economics*, Mission, Kan.: Sheed & Ward.
Knight, F. 1921: *Risk and Uncertainty*, Boston, Mass.: Houghton Mifflin.
Lachmann, L. M. 1973: 'Sir John Hicks as a neo-Austrian', *South African Journal of Economics*, 41(3), pp. 195–207.

Latsis, S. J. 1976: *Method and Appraisal in Economics*, Cambridge: Cambridge University Press.

Leijonhufvud, A. 1979: 'Review of Economic Perspectives by Sir John Hicks', *Journal of Economic Literature*, June, pp. 525–7.

—— 1981: *Information and Coordination: Essays in Macroeconomic Theory*, New York: Oxford University Press.

—— 1983: 'What was the matter with IS–LM?', in J. P. Fitoussi (ed.) *Modern Macroeconomic Theory: an Overview*, Oxford: Blackwell.

—— 1984: 'Hicks on time and money', in D. A. Collard, D. R. Helm, M. F. G. Scott and A. K. Sen (eds) 1984: *Economic Theory and Hicksian Themes*, Oxford: Clarendon Press, pp. 26–46.

Lerner, A. P. 1940: 'Professor Hicks' Dynamics', *Quarterly Journal of Economics*, 54, pp. 298–306.

—— 1951: Review of J. R. Hicks: *A Contribution to the Theory of the Trade Cycle*, *Econometrica*, 19, pp. 472–4.

Lindahl, E. 1939: *Studies in the Theory of Money and Capital*, New York: Kelley.

Lipsey, R. C. 1963: *An Introduction to Positive Economics*, London: Macmillan.

Lutz, F. A. and Hague, D. C. (eds) 1961: *The Theory of Capital*, London: Macmillan.

Machlup, F. 1940: 'Professor Hicks' Statics', *Quarterly Journal of Economics*, 54, pp. 277–97.

—— 1967: *Essays on Economic Semantics*, New York: Norton.

Marshall, A. 1920: *Principles of Economics*, 8th edn, London: Macmillan.

—— 1923: *Money, Credit and Commerce*, London: Macmillan.

Maes, I. 1984: 'The contribution of J. R. Hicks to macroeconomics and monetary theory', Ph.D. thesis, Catholic University of Leuven.

Maling, C. 1980: 'Hicks' neo-Austrian Capital Theory', *Atlantic Economic Journal*, 7, pp. 20–32.

Matthews, R. C. O. 1989: 'Memorial address for John Hicks', delivered in the University Church of St Mary the Virgin, Oxford, 28 October.

Metzler, L. A. 1945: 'Stability of multiple markets: the Hicks conditions', *Econometrica*, 13, pp. 277–92.

Morgan, B. 1981: 'Sir John Hicks's contributions to economic theory' in J. R. Shackleton and G. Locksley (eds) *Twelve Contemporary Economists*, London: Macmillan.

Morgenstern, O. 1941: 'Professor Hicks on value and capital', *Journal of Political Economy*, 49(3), pp. 361–93.

Morishima, M. 1960: 'On the three Hicksian laws of comparative statics', *Review of Economic Studies*, 27, pp. 195–201.

—— 1961: 'Proof of a turnpike theorem: the "no joint production" cases, *Review of Economic Studies*, pp. 89–97.

Morrison, L. A. 1933: Review of J. R. Hicks: *The Theory of Wages*, *American Economic Review*, December, pp. 686–7.

Myrdal, G. 1962: *Monetary Equilibrium*, New York: A. M. Kelley.

Opie, R. 1931: 'Marshall's time analysis', *Economic Journal*, 41(2), pp. 199–215.
Pareto, V. 1927: *Manuel d'économie politique*, 2nd edn, Paris: M. Giard.
Patinkin, D. 1959: 'Keynesian economics rehabilitated: a rejoinder to Professor Hicks', *Economic Journal*, 69(3), pp. 582–7.
—— [1955] 1965: *Money Interest and Prices*, 2nd edn, New York. Harper & Row.
Pigou, A. C. 1952: *The Economics of Welfare*, 4th edn, London: Macmillan.
—— (ed.) 1956: *Memorials of A. Marshall*, New York: Kelley & Millman.
Reder, M. W. 1965: Review of J. R. Hicks: *The Theory of Wages*, 2nd edn, *Economica*, February, pp. 88–90.
Robertson, D. 1915: *A Study of Industrial Fluctuation*, London: P. S. King & Sons.
—— 1940: *Essays in Monetary Theory*, London: King & Sons.
Robinson, J. 1971: *Economic Heresies*, New York: Basic Books.
Rosenstein-Rodan, P. N. 1934: 'The rôle of time in economic theory', *Economica*, 1(1), pp. 77–97.
Rizzo, M. J. 1979: *Time, Uncertainty and Disequilibrium*, Lexington, Mass.: Lexington Books.
Samuelson, P. 1941, 1942: 'The stability of equilibrium', *Econometrica*, 9, pp. 97–120; *Econometrica* 10, p. 125.
—— 1944: 'The relation between Hicksian stability and true dynamic stability', *Econometrica*, 12, pp. 256–7.
—— 1947: *Foundations of Economic Analysis*, Cambridge: Harvard University Press.
—— 1948: 'Dynamic process analysis', in H. S. Ellis (ed.) *Survey of Contemporary Economics*, vol. I, pp. 352–87.
—— 1974: 'Complementarity – an essay on the 40th anniversary of the Hicks–Allen revolution in Demand Theory', *Journal of Economic Literature*, 12, pp. 1255–89.
Schultz, H. 1932: 'Marginal productivity and the Lausanne School', *Economica*, (3), pp. 285–96.
Schumpeter, J. A. 1939: *Business Cycles*, 2 vols, New York: McGraw Hill.
Scitovsky, T. 1942: 'A note on welfare propositions in economics', *Review of Economic Studies*, 9, pp. 89–110.
Shackle, G. L. S. 1958: *Time in Economics*, Amsterdam: North Holland Publishing Co.
—— 1967: *The Years of High Theory*, Cambridge: Cambridge University Press.
—— 1972: *Epistemics and Economics*, Cambridge: Cambridge University Press.
—— 1979: 'On Hicks's causality in economics', *Greek Economic Review*, 1, pp. 43–55.
—— 1982: 'Sir John Hicks' "IS–LM: an explanation": a comment', *Journal of Post Keynesian Economics*, Spring, pp. 435–8.
Shove, G. F. 1928: 'Varying costs and marginal new products', *Economic*

Journal, 38(2), pp. 258–66.

—— 1933: 'Review of Hicks' *The Theory of Wages*', *Economic Journal*, 43(3), pp. 460–72.

Sims, C. A. 1981: 'What kind of a science is economics?', *Journal of Political Economics*, 89, pp. 578–83.

Smithin, J. N. 1989: 'Hicksian monetary economics and contemporary financial innovation', *Review of Political Economy*, 1, pp. 192–207.

Solow, R. 1966: Review of J. R. Hicks: *Capital and Growth, American Economic Review*, 56(5), pp. 1257–60.

—— 1974: Review of J. R. Hicks: *Capital and Time, Economic Journal*, 84(1), pp. 189–92.

—— 1984: 'Mr Hicks and the classics', first annual Hicks Lecture, delivered in Oxford on 3 May 1984, in D. A. Collard, D. R. Helm, M. F. G. Scott and A. K. Sen (eds) 1984: *Economic Theory and Hicksian Themes* Oxford: Clarendon Press, pp. 13–25.

Steedman, I. 1983: 'Review of Hicks' *Capital and Time*', *The Manchester School of Social Science*, 41, pp. 469–70.

Stephens, W. 1915: *The Book of France*, London: Macmillan, and Paris: E. Champion.

—— 1916: *The Soul and Russia*, London: Macmillan.

Symposium on increasing returns and the representative firm, 1930: *Economic Journal*, 40(1), pp. 79–116.

Termini, V. 1981: 'Logical, mechanical and historical time in economics', *Economic Notes*, 10, pp. 58–102.

Tinbergen, J. 1938: 'Statistical evidence on the accelerator principle', *Economica*, 5(2), pp. 164–76.

Tobin, J. 1958: 'Liquidity preference as behaviour towards risk', *Review of Economic Studies*, 25, pp. 65–86.

Walras, L. [1874] 1952: *Eléments d'économie politique pure*, édn définitive, Paris: Librairie générale de Droit et de Jurisprudence.

Wicksell, K. 1934–5: *Lectures on Political Economy*, vol. I (1934), vol. II (1935), London: Routledge & Kegan Paul.

Withers, H. 1921: *The Meaning of Money*, New York: E. P. Dutton.

Wolfe, J. N. (ed.) 1968: *Value, Capital and Growth: Papers in Honour of Sir John Hicks*, Edinburgh: Edinburgh University Press.

Wood, J. C. and Woods, R. N. (eds) 1989: *Sir John Hicks: Critical Assessments*, 4 vols, London: Routledge.

Young, A. 1928: 'Increasing returns and economic progress', *Economic Journal*, 38(4), 1982, pp. 527–42.

Young, W. L. 1982: 'Time and concept formation in economics', *Journal of Economic Issues*, 16, pp. 161–80.

—— 1987: *Interpreting Mr Keynes: the IS–LM Enigma*, Oxford: Pilty Press.

Index